I0078733

CHRISTIAN THEOLOGY

BY

MILTON VALENTINE, D. D., LL. D.
Late Professor of Systematic Theology in the Lutheran
Theological Seminary, Gettysburg, Pa.

www.JustandSinner.com

CHRISTIAN THEOLOGY BY MILTON VALENTINE

Permission inquiries may be sent to
JustandSinner@yahoo.com

Just & Sinner
1467 Walnut Ave.
Brighton, IA 52540

www.JustandSinner.com

ISBN 10:0692248250

ISBN 13:9780692248256

Original publishing info:
COPYRIGHT, 1906,
BY THE LUTHERAN PUBLICATION SOCIETY
Rev. Milton Valentine, D.D. LL.D.

PREFACE

IT has fallen to the lot of a son to see these volumes through the press. On February 7th of the present year the hand and brain so long active were suddenly stilled in death, and the author passed from his labors in the Church on earth to the rest and joy of the Church above. It so happened that he was engaged with the subject of Eschatology when the summons came, and that while his mind was thus intent on the things that lie behind the veil, he fell asleep to awaken into the personal experiences of the everlasting life. The point he had reached in the discussion is indicated in the text. It will be found under the topic, "The Resurrection of the Dead."

It is the natural desire of an author not only to complete his work, but to issue it under his personal direction and supervision. He covets the opportunity of giving the text a final revision, of further elaborating it at various points, and, perhaps, of introducing additional matter where he may feel that a fuller discussion would be helpful. The manuscript of this work bears evidence, in the form of many marginal notes, that such was the desire of the author. This privilege, however, was denied him. Nor was it deemed advisable that another hand should undertake to carry out the suggestions of these marginal insertions. They looked to no change or modification of the teachings herein set forth, but only to amplifications. The work is issued, therefore, as it came from the author's pen, with only such minor changes and corrections as are incidental in all proof reading.

These volumes are the outgrowth and expansion of the author's "Outlines of Theology," which formed the basis of his lectures to successive classes during his incumbency, for nineteen years, of the chair of Systematic Theology in the Seminary of the General Synod of the Lutheran Church, at Gettysburg, Pa. His plan of the Introduction included a chapter on the Authority of the Scriptures, involving the discussion of Inspiration, but its preparation was deferred to the latest moment that he might have the benefit of the most recent literature of this burning question. But death intervened before the chapter could be written.

He is no longer here to voice any general acknowledgments of help and suggestion he might have wished to make, but the notes and references scattered through the pages indicate at least some of the sources upon which he has drawn. Grateful appreciation is due Dr. Charles E. Hay, of Baltimore, for the Index.

If these volumes shall magnify the glorious Gospel of the Son of God, and serve the cause of truth and righteousness, and the Church in which he labored for so many busy years and which he loved so deeply, they will realize the author's desire and purpose in their preparation.

M. H. VALENTINE.
PHILADELPHIA, November 10, 1906.

CONTENTS

Milton Valentine

INTRODUCTION

NEVER, perhaps, has there been more need than at present of settling carefully the great presuppositions to a correct formulation of Christian theology. The need has come from the special direction and activity of modern inquiry and speculative criticism. New conditions have arisen. Theology must face them.

These presuppositions concern the fundamental basis and scope of theology, its subject-matter, its rightful sources, and true method. A safe and justly articulated system of its essential, constitutive doctrines is necessarily conditioned in correct views on these subjects. They, therefore, stand as preliminary and introductory. The whole theological system, as well as many of its particular doctrines, must of necessity vary according as different conceptions are held on these premier subjects; for these conceptions take the place of first principles in determining dogmatic conclusions. This fact shows the fundamental and vital importance of the questions which thus meet us on the threshold of theology.

As a result of ever-increasing knowledge from continued examination and re-discussion, each new generation attains some additional light for correct and certified view of these questions. Account must always be taken of whatever helpful information has been attained. This rule is justly applicable at all times. But it is specially enforced in our day; for the latter half of the nineteenth century and the opening years of this new century have given these questions an unparalleled attention and investigation. To a most extraordinary extent recent scholarship, in comparative religion, in archeological exploration, in historical research, in science, in philosophy, and in criticism, carried forward with untiring industry, and, sometimes, with hostile or revolutionary spirit, has concentrated itself upon studies along the lines touching these presuppositions of theological introduction. The settlement and statement of them now must be made under all the light which this scrutinizing scholarship has supplied. Different thinkers may, as they do, disagree as to the value of the results of this recent study and discussion, and the degree in which they are entitled to modify hitherto accepted views. But whether they be accorded a greater or a less weight of influence, theological fidelity requires their frank and discriminating consideration, accepting what is true and resisting unsustained claims. In this way theology remains loyal to its fullest light, while conserving its firmly established truths. It is assuring to Christian faith in our much agitated age, that, while the modern progress in knowledge calls for some modification in the formal setting of some of these presuppositions or introductory truths, it has in fact verified and strengthened the essential foundations and principles of the Church's theology.

CHAPTER I
THE SUBJECT-MATTER OF THEOLOGY

1. Christian Theology is based on the great fact of Christianity in the world. Its specific materials are found in the whole history of God's redemptive and light-giving self-manifestation, and the truths involved and established in that divine movement. The scope of its inquiries and formulations, therefore, embraces the essential facts and meaning of the most unique and wonderful phenomenon that the records of time present, the mightiest and most beneficent power that proves itself to be not only the spiritual salvation of men, but social regeneration and advancing civilization to the nations.

This scope is only partially indicated in the etymology of the term, as derived from Θέος and λόγος, meaning, literally, discourse concerning God, or the knowledge of God. Though sometimes used in this restricted sense of designating simply the particular discussion "concerning God," it is usually employed to denote the whole science which treats of the doctrines of religion. Theology may, therefore, be defined as the doctrine concerning God and the relations between God and the universe. Some specific things should be noted:

(a) The term comes over from pagan into Christian use. It was employed by various heathen writers to denote the views entertained with respect to the Greek gods and their doings in the world. Writers who gave accounts of the gods and taught concerning their nature were called "theologians" (θεολόγοι). Aristotle termed the highest branch of philosophy "theological" (θεολογική).

(b) The earliest Christian use seems to have been the very peculiar and narrow one of denoting the Deity of Christ, according to John 1:1, "And the Word (ὁ Λόγος) was God" (Θέος), and also the doctrine of the Trinity. It was from his assertion of this doctrine that St. John was called "the theologian," and Gregory Nazianzen was afterward honored with the same title. This special sense passed away after the Nicene period.

(c) From the fourth century Christian writers appropriated the word, according to its etymological sense, to denote the discussion of the nature, attributes, and works of God; but it was not until the twelfth century that it assumed the comprehensiveness of its modern meaning, as including the entire circle and sum of Christian doctrine or religious truth as completed in the redemptory revelation. But from the time of Abelard's *Christiana Theologia* this has been the scope of its signification.

(d) Among Protestants generally the sense of the term has been deepened in import, so as to mean more than a cold speculative view of God and the truths of the sacred Scriptures. It implies, and carries in its method and content, the living insight of the regenerate mind, the clarified vision and appreciation of the Christian consciousness, in accordance with the word of St. Paul concerning Christian verities: "They are spiritually discerned." This conception correctly assumes the principle that it is only through the experiences of a living, obedient faith in Jesus Christ that the realities of redeeming grace and the truths of the Christian life can be rightly and profoundly understood. The true theologian, therefore, must be a genuine Christian, into whose innermost life the subject-matter of theology has entered with its self-explaining and guaranteeing power.

The practical aim of theology, as well as the clear, deep insight into its spiritual verities, implies this same qualification. Its end is not realized in the mere production of a theoretical system. Though no range of thought is in itself more replete with mental interest, it, nevertheless, properly looks beyond itself to the religious and moral service for which the knowledge with which it deals has been given. It stands for the efficient exhibition and vindication of the truth designed for the life of the world and the holiest interests of humanity. Its value is not in its speculative import, but in its relation to the divine utilities of the kingdom of God. It is unvitalized and dwarfed if attempted apart from its Christian spirit and as a mere intellectual dialectic. It attains its proper relations and dignity only when it keeps loyally and steadily in view the great practical service for which Christianity itself exists in the world. Were it not so often divorced from this practical mission and held as having its end in simple theoretic interest and the exploitation of fresh system-building, it would not so frequently appear in speculative misconstructions or modifications which obscure and confuse the divine adaptations. The sacred truths of religion are for more serious use than display of ever-changing theological pyrotechnics; and nothing short of a genuine experience of their living power and object will suffice to mold and hold all the theological explanations and systemization in true focus of power for the accomplishment of the great purposes which form the reasons of the existence of Christianity.

Combining in a single statement the ideas thus suggested, theology, in the fullest sense now used, denotes the entire body of truth ascertainable concerning God, and especially the doctrine embraced in Christianity, as taught in the Holy Scriptures and apprehended and developed into accepted view by the sanctified mind and heart of the Church under the training of the Holy Spirit

2. The subject-matter is scientific, and theology is a science. The method of theology is the scientific method of thorough investigation, exact definition, and logical conclusion. "Wherever observation establishes a group of facts, visible or invisible, linked together by internal relations, forming a distinct class in the midst of others, there is room for a special science." This is the case here. The disclaimers on this point by a few Christian writers and the denials often made by scientists are alike based on misconception either of the necessary constituents to science or of the actual data of theology. Phenomena become subjects for science, not by reason of their source, but by reason of their existence—not by virtue of their class, but by virtue of their occurrence. The phenomena of religion, especially those of Christianity, are among the most outstanding, indubitable, and operative in the history and experience of the world, and as truly open for investigation, elucidation, and theoretic view as any facts that form the subjects of the most fully recognized sciences. The distinction between material and spiritual phenomena, or between natural and supernatural, cannot legitimately be pleaded against a possible science of theology. For the plea is but an assumption, prejudging the very

question involved, when it assumes that the universe, of which this world is a part, includes and manifests no spiritual or supernatural reality, purpose, and movement. The notion could be of force only after its advocates had shown the falsity of the whole teleological conception of the world, which holds to the existence of God as Creator and Moral Governor, who seeks moral ends through an historical movement of creation, providence, revelation, and redemption—ends which form the divine reason for the existence and order of the physical cosmos. There is no reason why God may not be a God of order in the sphere of spiritual and supernatural activity as well as in the sphere of material movements—especially if the order be the higher and supremely authoritative one of moral relations, necessities, causation, and manifestation. As long, therefore, as it is recognized that there are spiritual realities embraced in human life and well-being, and that there is a God over and in the world, whose absolute supernatural reason, love, will, and power hold and subordinate to their divine aims the whole system of nature and the course of history, so long the phenomena and teachings of Christianity must be entitled to the careful and comprehensive consideration and formulation which mark the genuine scientific spirit and method in its loving search after the truth. And when this method is justly applied, the result reached, and logically validated by the actual facts, forms an organized knowledge which has a distinct and authentic place in the circle of known truth. Moreover, as the subjects of which theology treats are of the highest order, the culminating realities and truths in the realm of being and interests, such as God, His purposes and plans in nature and history, the moral capacities, obligations, responsibilities, and destinies of men, its position among the sciences or groups of organized knowledge must be highest of all. Not without propriety, therefore, has it often claimed to be the "queen of the sciences." Even Aristotle, with his limited pagan material for scientific theology, gave it rank as the "first philosophy."

Not only is its material capable of scientific formulation, but the supreme interest which thus attaches to its high rank specially impels to such treatment; for it means verification and assurance. The subject-matter attracts the strongest affinities of the scientific faculties of the human mind. There was, therefore, a deeper reason than the mere necessity of safeguarding Christianity from the attacks of disbelief and the perversion of heresies, that led Christian scholars in the early centuries of the Church to begin to formulate, define, and systematize its facts and doctrines. Back of such practical necessity, and even deeper than that, was the scientific instinct toward exact theoretic explanation, attracted by the grandeur of the verities and doctrines brought to view. These doctrines rose to the loftiest problems of thought and possibilities of life and destiny. Pagan philosophers, when converted to Christ, could not fail to bring these problems under the defining and constructive action of their trained faculties. At the root of the theological movement lay the scientific aptitude and propensity of the human mind. This incentive to theology is an abiding one. It operates in all ages, and, concurring with the practical aim, evermore insures the turning of this peculiar and supremely important material into systematized view.

The very purpose and mission of Christianity requires this process. The proper preservation of it in its purity and power demands it. The self-revelation of God, through His Son Jesus Christ, as recorded in the sacred Scriptures, having advanced from the beginning to the completion of redemptory provision and of needful teaching, furnished, indeed, at once the essential saving facts and truths of Christianity, the standard of all doctrine and the living fountain of all practical instruction and life in the Church. But there is evermore needed a distinct and consolidated view of all these facts and truths of the original deposit, in order to the proper conservation of Christianity in its integrity. It must have the strength and security which stand in exact statement of its essential parts and a clear integration of all in a consistent unity of the full truth. Except by St. Paul, it does not appear to have been made an object of scientific reflection in the New Testament writings. The time of completing the data had not yet closed. But when the apostles were gone, came the need of gathering the manifold facts and teachings into such orderly view as would insure them against being lost or corrupted. We have the first step towards this arranging and systematizing labor in the earlier forms of the Apostles' Creed, though this is rather a simple aggregation of items of truth or historic facts, without theoretic elucidation—a mere enumeration of the cardinal points in the Christian faith. But the work could not stop with this. Differing interpretations of the items in that creed called for settlement, and enforced a process of development of the great essentials of doctrine. Creed after creed from the Councils of the Church formulated one truth after another, as the urgencies of the times required. These formulations by the regenerate mind of the Church, as its general consensus of doctrinal understanding, have been a strong factor in exhibiting Christian truth to the world and fortifying its position. A similar service has been done by the great Church Confessions in the beginning of the modern centuries. By their combinations of terse statements of the fundamental doctrines they have become anchorage amid the shifting tendencies of individual opinion to the saving content of Christian teaching. They protect it against changeful, erratic speculation tending to varied reshapings inconsistent with the abiding permanence and self-identity of truth. The elaborate monumental works of Biblical and churchly dogmatics have had a like fortifying and strengthening force. And though both confessions and dogmatic theologies may sometimes incorporate some incorrect, defective, or onesided views, and carry them along, perhaps through centuries, yet the boldness and vigor with which the great determinative fundamentals are set forth and accentuated, tend to maintain the central and essential current of doctrinal view aright, and thus prove corrective also of partial errors or faults.

3. Theology in this comprehensive sense is naturally divided into various branches according to the particular subject-matter and its peculiar place in the whole investigation.

The first underlying division is that into Natural and Revealed Theology. This division rests upon a difference in the sources.

(a) NATURAL THEOLOGY denotes the knowledge of God as it may be derived by reason from the works of nature. These works, rationally interpreted, become a natural revelation of His existence, will, essential attributes, and relation to the world. The primary idea upon which this theology proceeds is that if there be a God as the Creator and First Cause of the universe, His being and character must be found impressed upon it and discoverable from it. The author of a work is revealed in the work he does. The world is viewed as an understandable expression of the existence and the thought of its Source. One of the fundamental conceptions of science is that nature holds and presents in its constitution and order some record, legible to the reason of those who honestly study it. Natural Theology, therefore, examines this record, takes its testimony, and thus ascends through nature up to nature's God.

But while it thus certifies some great and momentous truths, it falls sadly short of affording the degree of knowledge for which the condition and needs of humanity imperatively call. It is voiceless as to the supply of man's most deeply-felt necessity of redemption, deliverance from conscious guilt and the sore bondage of human life to moral evil. Though Natural Theology is able to discern, and, in fact, recognizes the great reality of moral law, and hears the ceaseless cry which the sense of guilt and helpless weakness is ever forcing from the heart of the race, it is able to give to this cry no satisfying response from God.

(b) REVEALED, OR CHRISTIAN, THEOLOGY is that which grounds itself upon the data of the special revelation given in the Christian Scriptures. While it recognizes and incorporates whatever pertinent truth is furnished by Natural Theology, it constructs its system out of the material furnished in God's supernatural self-disclosure and teaching, as recorded in the Old and New Testaments. It assumes—what will be vindicated in another section—both the possibility and reality of a supernatural divine manifestation in the world, and the validity of the distinction between this and the simply natural revelation which God makes of Himself in His creative activity and its products in the universe. Revealed Theology is rightly divided into four leading departments, namely: Exegetical, Historical, Systematic, and Practical.

Exegetical Theology is concerned with the interpretation of the Holy Scriptures, and investigates all questions as to their origin, authorship, character, history, and teachings. It is a field of wide and varied inquiry. It includes Archeology, Criticism, Hermeneutics, Introduction, and Interpretation—all the different studies by which the teachings of the Scriptures are understood and exhibited. The other branches of theology depend on this and use the material which it furnishes. It has, therefore, the first place in the logical order of theological work.

Historical Theology traces the historical development of Christianity in the thought and life of the Church. It is theology as embodied in Ecclesiastical History, especially in the History of Doctrines. It studies Creeds, ecclesiastical writers, controversies, decisions of Councils, and Church Confessions, noting from the first onward through the Christian centuries, the rise and settlement of doctrinal questions, the elimination of heresies, the agreements and differences of view and types of belief within the Church, and withal the characteristic ethical and spiritual life which the different types produce. In its result it exhibits Christian theology in its historical setting and reality.

Systematic Theology, termed also Didactic, Dogmatic, or Thetical, arranges the material thus available in the order and form required by the real relations, dependencies, and bearings of the essential truths of Christianity, exhibiting each in its separate integrity, and all together in their logical and consistent unity. Its work is exact definition and just systemization. It presents Christianity in its total doctrinal view, which becomes at once a vindication of it and an enlargement of its practical power. For these clear statements of the divine truth, all throwing their light in impressive unity on the one great design of redemptive love, cannot but tend to strengthen the intellectual conviction and quicken the religious affections. This branch has its proper place after the two already named, because it uses both the results of Biblical study and those presented by the history of discussion and doctrinal development. In every age systematic theology is helped by the preceding ages.

Practical Theology directs the use of all theological truth for the conversion of men and their present and eternal salvation. It, therefore, passes beyond the determination of the true theoretical view and doctrinal content of Christianity, and seeks their right and best application to all the ends for which Christianity has been divinely established in the world. It is concerned especially with the place and function of the Church and the duties of the ministry, both in preaching and pastoral care, and in all the branches of service these functions imply. It includes as its subdivisions such topics as Homiletics, Liturgies, Catechetics, Church Polity, Missions, Education, and Charities.

These divisions of theology are closely allied. They move on co-operative lines of mutually helpful study and aim, converging to the great ends for which the Gospel has been given. And it is plain that Systematic Theology, which is here to engage us, has its position in the centre of general theology, employing the material furnished by the Exegetical and Historical branches, and looking, all the time, forward to Practical Theology.

4. RELIGION must be included in the subject-matter of theology. It presents the phenomena out of which theology arises, and which underlie all its investigations. The Christian religion existed before the scientific examination and formulation of its realities and doctrines.

What is religion? The term needs distinct definition. Though applied to almost endlessly diverse and changeable manifestations, it nevertheless designates essentially the same fundamental fact. And the fact, wherever found in the human race, is worship and service of deity, This is the most generic and universally applicable sense of the term. The word is differently derived. According to Cicero, it is from *re* and *legere*, to read again or to reflect, because of the thoughtfulness and meditation involved. He says: "*Qui omnia quœ ad cultum deorum pertinent diligenter tractarent, et tanquam relegerent sunt dicti religiosi, ex relegendo*" (De Natura Deorum, ii. 28). But Lactantius derives it from *re* and *ligare*, to bind back or again, because it results in fixing obligation in the conscience toward some supreme power. He writes "*Hoc vinculo pietatis obstricti deo et religati sumus; unde ipsa religio nomen recipit; non ut Cicero interpretatus est, relegendo*" (Institutiones, iv. 28). With this Augustine agrees (City of God, x. 3).

Religion is rooted in man's nature and relations. It is a necessary product of forces that act in him and upon him. It springs out of his essential constitution and environment. The world in which he lives and moves becomes to his intelligence and conscience a constant revelation of some power above him, awing into reverence and fear. Not only is he evermore touched by mysterious powers, but compelled to see in many of them the reality of evident purpose and will. Spontaneously and necessarily, to greater or less degree, he recognizes Mind acting in and through the energies and movements of nature, impressing him with the conviction of a sovereignty which he must respect and obey. This presence of an intelligent Power in the order and adaptations of the world is one of the mighty fundamental facts of human experience, forcing an unavoidable impression, however faint or confused it may often be, of some divine Will, fixing law and penalty in the world, to which deference must be paid and homage must be rendered. It cannot but be true that man meets God walking among the trees of every garden of nature's order, life, adaptations, and beauty. The existence of religion becomes an inevitable consequence of what man is and what the world is, establishing an omnipresent living relation between man and the Author of nature. Nature is vocal with divinity. "From the things which are made," the invisible reality, even "the eternal power and Godhead are understood," necessarily evoking some recognition, however low and confused, in the human reason and consciousness. This furnishes adequate explanation of the origin and universality of religion. It is the human effort, impelled by the deepest realities in the soul and its environment, to adjust itself to the mysterious divinity that moves and speaks through, and out of, the great universe of nature. Religion, therefore, is normal to man's faculties and relations, the tendency toward it manifesting itself spontaneously and by a certain necessity the world over and in all ages, even where no positive institutes of religion are supernaturally given.

The immense diversity in the types and forms of religion in the various parts of the race and in different times becomes fully explicable in this understanding of its natural basis and genesis. When it appears altogether apart from supernatural revelation, its forms and manifestations depend, of course, upon the degree of the intellectual and moral development of the people. If the race or tribe is low and undeveloped, or brutalized, the religious discernments are crude and indistinct. In the worst ignorance and barbarisms, it is not wonderful that the coarse and untrained thinking fails to distinguish the Divine Mind which is working in and through nature from nature itself, and the religious manifestation appears largely as only a fetishistic worship or reverence of natural objects. This has been, to a great degree, characteristic of pagan religionism. In higher intellectual conditions, the discernments distinguish the Mind, whose presence is recognized, from the physical forms and movements which exhibit it, and a higher conception of God as an intelligent Spirit who is the former of the world, is reached. In the best of these discernments the divine Intelligence is apprehended as One, a unity, both above and in nature, as in the case of henotheistic and monotheistic religions, according to the discovered unity and harmony of the system of nature itself. Sometimes, instead of this high and philosophic theism of monotheistic belief, gross polytheism prevails, crude thought peopling all parts of nature with special and local divinities, an idolatry of imaginary gods. Sometimes the fetichistic confounding of the mind in nature with nature itself assumes pantheistic form. This reappears again and again, even in cosmic philosophies. But while the interpretation of the divine Intelligence and moral Authority which nature and life reveal, thus presents a bewildering and endless confusion of form, the one great fact of recognition of a Divinity that shapes the ends of nature and claims the reverence and homage of men persists, through all time and in all the world. It is, however, only when and where God has added to this self-disclosure in nature a supernatural revelation of Himself and His relations to the world, of His will and human duty and destiny, that the great truths of religion are adequately and reliably known and defined.

The comparative study of religions, which in recent years has been pursued in widest range and with able scholarship, has greatly enlarged our information of the subject. It has made clear both the truth embodied in the ethnic or non-Christian religions and their defects, insufficiencies, and errors. Even the greatest and best of them, however ancient or prevalent, clearly appear as simply natural products of human thought, seeking to interpret the world and human life. They exhibit the fruits of effort, in different degrees of success, to read the revelation which nature gives of the existence, power, character, and will of its Author, and to learn therefrom how men should conduct themselves in order to escape evils and attain happiness. The study of this prolonged and manifold effort is full of deep interest and varied instruction. It shows us both how much and how little human reason alone, interpreting nature, can furnish for the moral and spiritual need of mankind.

The amount of its showing can easily be summed up. It appears in two general results: (a) A greatly varied and confused rational theism, and (b) a large body of ethical truth and precepts for the right order and conduct of life. From the two sources of the world of external nature and the action of conscience within men, the world-wide effort of reason has established many of the great natural truths concerning God and the life of duty. Culled out of the immense and often inane or misleading material thus accumulated, appear some precious findings of theistic truth and many gems of moral conception and teaching. These precious, though broken, insights into the truths of the being and character of God and into the principles of ethical obligation, have captivated many minds and led to much overestimation of some of these religions. In the most ancient religions of Egypt and China, in Buddhism and Confucianism, and in Zoroastrian teaching, some imagine they discover close approaches to the excellence of Christianity—so close as to require us either to assume for them a divine inspiration or to abandon such claim for Christianity. But such views and claims are hasty and superficial. For the truths in question are, after all, plainly within the reach of purely rational finding. Moreover, the conceptions which these religions give of the nature, character, and will of God, and of His relations to the world, as well as many of their moral directions, are radically defective and misleading. While among the immense rubbish of their moral counsels many single, isolated rules of conduct are found, here and there, which stand parallel with and rival in excellence and beauty the highest and noblest Christian precepts, yet their ethical systems, taken as systems, are greatly inferior and fail either to disclose the full foundations of virtue or to supply an adequate dynamic for the realization of the ethical task. Their isolated moral rules are not integrated in the living principle or force of any adequate religious provision or power. This ethical defect brings to view the fatal lack in the ethnic faiths as religions. This needs to be distinctly noted. To the question of deliverance from the guilt and thraldom of sin, the great reality which forms the deepest and most persistent fact in human life, these religions are either voiceless or mutter only incoherent and misguiding suggestions. In most of them God is either reduced to identity with the merciless forces of wasting and pitiless nature, in fatalistic pantheisms, or He is enthroned in such absolute transcendence above the world as to take no concern or interest in human affairs. Though the wail of the race's misery has piteously cried to the heavens for deliverance from the bondage and consequences of sin and vanity, yet through these ethnic religions no effective answer of salvation has come. Not one of them is redemptory. In not one is God conceived of as a Being of redeeming love and redemptive administration. Not a single one of them exhibits God as lovingly and actively a Saviour from the consequences and power of sin or moral evil. In Christianity alone He is presented as historically carrying forward for man a course of redemptory activity, whose manifestation and record form revelation, and whose effects become a gracious forgiveness of sin and recovery of the sinful to an obedient, holy, happy, eternal life. This is the great, unique fact in Christianity, setting it apart from all the ethnic religions, and still justifying the distinction which theology has been wont to make between it and all the rest when it classes the rest as "false religions." They do not truly unfold God's gracious way of love and salvation. In Christianity alone there has been adequately furnished a true knowledge of God, of His character, relations, will, and government, the way of deliverance from the guilt and evil of sin, right and holy worship, duty and destiny.

These brief statements concerning the fact of religion as a reality, normal in some form or other to the relations and life of man, everywhere and always, and the explanation thus given of its universal appearance in various manifestations in all the world, together with the unique position of Christianity, will suffice to indicate how Christian Theology stands related to the whole subject of religion. It is secondary to the great fact of religion, and must treat of the materials which religion pre-supposes and furnishes, and develop its systematic view out of the essential realities and implications thus presented. Underneath Natural Theology lies the whole realm of natural religion, and under Christian Theology are all the divine activities, facts, and truths embodied in the Christian religion.

CHAPTER II
THE SOURCES OF THEOLOGY

The sources of theology must be adequate at once to account for the origin and to exhibit the content of the faith. They must be authoritatively legitimate for both the substance and the form of the theological teaching. Nothing short of such sources, as the basis of its determinations, can give to theology its right character and standing as a scientific exhibition of the truth which belongs to its sphere of investigation.

For merely natural theology the sources are justly found in the data of the human consciousness and reason in connection with the natural self-revelation of God in creation and history. These supply it with abundant evidence of the existence of God and certify some of His essential attributes, making clear, at the same time, a large realm of moral and religious obligation for man. For Christian theology the chief source is found in the Old and New Testament records of the supernatural self-manifestation of God in His redemptive love, work, and teaching. The possession of this additional and unique revelation, of course, does not annul or displace the data from which natural theology derives its invaluable theistic and religious truth. These continue in their own rightful force and validity, for full consideration in theological grounds and verifications. The disposition, sometimes shown, to contemn and exclude from Christian theology the data that have illuminated the way of natural theology into the great fundamental realities of the divine existence and many of the divine prerogatives and attributes and of the religious nature and responsibility of man, is manifestly unjustifiable. These have lost none of their intrinsic legitimacy by reason of the added light, and rightly form auxiliary sources in theological determinations. This is fully endorsed by the Scriptures themselves in the recognition they give of the revelatory function of nature as the divine handiwork in showing the divine glory, and of the office of reason for discerning the eternal power and Godhead from the things which are made. (Ps. 19:1; Rom. 1:20.) But as the supernatural revelation in redemptory providence and communication, meeting and providing for the distinctively spiritual and moral need of mankind, has flooded the whole religious view with the fullest and completest light, the Scripture records of this legitimately become the principal and decisive source for the verities and formulations of theology. They are the standard of faith and the Christian life. This, at least theoretically, though not always practically followed, was the conception of the leading writers of the early centuries of the Church, maintained essentially down into the Middle Ages. As the great "formal principle," reasserted in the reformation of the sixteenth century against practical encroachments upon it by exaggerated claims for tradition and ecclesiastical authority, it has ever since been justly accredited as a fundamental rule in the method and procedures of Christian theology. There is no adequate reason for surrender of this principle. Whatever may be the outcome of the agitation and ferment brought about by the evolutionary theory of the origin of the world and man and the allied work of literary and historical criticism upon the Biblical records, no conclusions have yet been established that remove the Scriptures from the position to which the Church has accredited them, as the infallible rule for faith and life and the norm of Christian theology. Whatever weight may be given to knowledge from other sources, from tradition, philosophy, or the physical sciences, such knowledge must be but auxiliary and rank below the grade of ruling doctrinal authority. Revelation covers the essential content of the faith. Even the "Christian consciousness," which is conceded to be a proper and even necessary helping factor in understanding and defining theological doctrines, must, if it is to be reliable, be itself a product of the Scriptures, out of an illuminating experience of their truth. Its office is subsidiary.

This formal principle of theology either assumes or carries in its import a number of related truths: (I) It assumes that these sacred Scriptures are, indeed, the word of God, a divinely supplied record of a revelation of Himself, and of the things necessary to be known, believed, and fulfilled for the realization of our true life and destiny.

Their authority is grounded in this, and it is only as they are adequately and fully authenticated in this character that they attain and hold the right of umpire. The certifying proofs, to which the reason and judgment of the most intellectual and critical nations of history have bowed and which have been confirmed by the experience-testing of centuries of Christendom, will be outlined a little further on in our examination. (2) It assumes also that these Scriptures have been given under such divine adaptations that, while they are authoritative, they are understandable under the Holy Spirit and an adequate guide in all spiritual truth needful for salvation. The main facts in this relation will appear in the consideration of their inspiration. (3) In its import the principle involves a repudiation and exclusion of any supposed right or authority of the Church to enact extra-biblical doctrines or articles of faith for the consciences of men. (4) It excludes, too, a limitation of the right of interpretation by any supposed exclusive authority conferred upon an ecclesiastical hierarchy or ruling official, in derogation of personal interpretation, liberty, and responsibility in matters revealed to faith. And (5) it disowns the right of tradition or extra-biblical ecclesiastical information, to impose articles of faith or practice for which clear warrant of the Scriptures cannot be given. In asserting tradition as an authority co-equal with the Scriptures as a source of saving truth and moral discipline, the Council of Trent has defined the position of the Roman Church in contradiction to this formal principle of Protestant theology. The vindication of the principle will be made to appear in the conclusions to which the evidences of Christianity and a summary of the doctrine concerning the Scriptures necessarily lead us.

But this rule of Biblical supremacy calls up at this point the whole question of the province of reason and its work in the determinations of Christian theology. This has been one of the battle-questions of modern and recent times. It has been brought on and continued by the intellectual activity and progress of the age. Through the brilliant achievements of the human mind in the domain of science, discovery, invention, and subjugation of nature to obedient service, and its magnificent creations and ranges of metaphysical and philosophical speculation, a spirit of intellectual confidence and self-sufficiency has been begotten and grown strong. Even when and where it has taken the position of religious agnosticism, a conclusion of almost blank nescience as to theistic and spiritual verities, it has, nevertheless, assumed a temper of dogmatic positiveness as to the certainty of its own knowledge and the competence of reason to settle both physical and moral truth. It's very negations are assertive. Humility of mind has largely disappeared under the pride of scientific advance, which is supposed to have furnished new view-point and such illumination over the whole domain of knowledge as to give to the human reason alone an imperial supremacy in the realm of knowable reality. A sign of this appears in the strong disposition to discard from the conception of the cosmic system everything that the scientific understanding cannot bring under its classification in the uniformities of natural law, and to believe in the existence of nothing which formal logic cannot reduce under the category of such uniformities. It is betokened, too, by the pressure for the elimination of the term "supernatural" as properly expressive of a distinctive characteristic in the content of the Christian revelation. It is well, indeed, to rejoice in and honor the intellectual triumphs of our age. They have lifted us above some of the faultiness and mistakes of earlier science and philosophy. They have enriched life and thought with much that is valuable. But it would be premature to assume that all present scientific speculations and theories will stand the siftings of still advancing knowledge and speculation. The tendency, however, to enlarge the authority and sphere of reason in matters of religious faith is unquestionable in the spirit of the times. At the very best, our times are not marked by evidences of an anxious sense of need of divine instruction and help for spiritual guidance and destiny, or of dependence on supernatural communication and direction. Unquestionably strong rationalistic tendencies are widely prevalent and urgent. This question, therefore, of the true relations of reason with respect to the substance and form of the Christian faith must here be settled for ourselves, if we are to move consistently through the whole long range of theological examination and maintain firm footing amidst the strenuous influences of our times.

We propose no lengthened discussion of the subject. It will be enough to summarize the conclusions to which, we believe, just views and discriminations must bring us:

1. Reason, as the whole human faculty of knowledge through perception, intuition, and the logical processes, and revelation, as the disclosure of truth through the Scriptures, cannot be viewed as contradictory of each other, but as necessarily in agreement. The one may speak where the other is silent. The one may transcend the other and bring higher or broader realms or realities into view. But there can be no real and positive conflict. On this conclusion we are compelled to stand, because, ex hypothesis, both reason and revelation are from the same divine Author. And this Author is both the Absolute Reason and the unchangeable, ever-self-consistent Truth. This may seem here simply an assumption; but it is an assumption warranted, on the one hand, by the proper and sufficient evidence that the revelation is, indeed, of God, and, on the other, by the whole body of truth for the theistic origin of the world and of the human reason as a divine gift. When, therefore, this claim of revelation as of God is once verified and He is identified as the Creator of the human mind, if there appears a seeming conflict in their representations either one or the other has been misread. Such misreading may easily occur, as the history of rational judgments and of Biblical exegesis abundantly shows. And the principle is indubitably correct, as fully conceded by the soberest decisions of philosophy itself, that an article or point of faith taught by revelation, is not in contradiction of reason by being above it, i, e., by being either naturally undiscoverable or a mystery when revealed. Even within the natural sphere alone there are manifold realities beyond either discovery or solution by reason. Science, as truly as revelation, has to face the fact of mystery.2 The essential harmony between reason and revelation is but another expression of the harmony of God with Himself.

The offices of reason in this relation are justly indicated as (a) To judge and decide upon the claims of a given revelation to be of divine origin and authority. A religion which transcends the data of simply natural theology can have no authority for its higher teachings until it secures reason's favorable verdict upon its divine credentials. Faith becomes but an unwarranted superstition if it accepts an offered revelation which is without fully adequate grounds for such acceptance. The revelation must come with full proof that it is of God. Its claims must be sustained in the court of reason, sitting in most sober, searching, and conscientious examination. Until its divine credentials are thus adjudged sufficient it can acquire no legitimate standing as arbiter. When so authenticated its position of supremacy has come through the reason itself. This is the first thing in the high and responsible office of the human reason. It opens the gates of truly warranted and intelligent faith in God's redemptive truth and grace—than which it can have no higher or more sacred function. Of all men it should be farthest from the Christian theologian to vilify the human reason, since God has called it to such an office—to test and pass upon the signs, marks, and evidences of the great self-manifestation in which He has presented Himself for human confidence, obedience, and salvation. But reason assumes an unwarranted role when it undertakes to pronounce against the possibility of a supernatural revelation or against a possible proof of any. The import of such undertaking amounts, in the first case, to the absurdity of claiming that the finite human mind can have an omniscient view of the possibilities of being and event; and in the second place, demands a standard or grade of proof above that which reason itself, in all other relations and affirmations, has evermore adjudged to be fully adequate to accredit the certainty of historical or other phenomenal reality. In such demands it puts itself in conflict with its own canons of certitude, and becomes the abuse of reason, known as "rationalism." (b) The Sacred Scriptures, as the records of God's redemptory self-revelation, being thus certified as from Him, the reason properly takes the position of a pupil, bowing to their authority in the sphere in which they teach. In this, however, the office of reason continues to be a high and responsible one, because it is the office of correctly understanding their divine communications, of intelligently and accurately reading God's thoughts after Him and making them our own. While for all that is essential for a saving faith and a Christian life, the Scriptures are readily comprehended by the sincere understanding, yet in their immense ranges and reaches into spiritual truth and principles they present problems whose right explanation calls for the best powers of the human mind. As they are a record of a great providential movement in history, advancing from the earliest times through centuries of divine manifestations and guidance, ordinances and administrations, in the Old Testament, to the consummation in the coming, teaching, institutes, sufferings, death, resurrection, and ascension of Jesus Christ, and the establishment of the Church through the appointed ministry of the apostles; covering advancing revelatory communications from the beginning to the completion in the New Testament—all connected with an almost endless diversity of local circumstances, social conditions, personal character, political institutions, and national changes and contacts, with their complex influence and significance—evidently even the reason's function of theological interpretation covers an almost measureless field of difficult work, for which the most discriminating intellect, the purest heart, and the most faithful conscience are none too great an equipment It necessarily requires an ample apparatus of knowledge, historical, linguistic, archeological. Alas, how often the office of interpretation has failed to reach the exact truth or has delivered error because of the lack of comprehensive information, clear spiritual discernment, or training in logical discrimination and conclusion. How often has it been used to pervert the divine meaning and darken the truth out of sight by clouds of mystification. The history of exegesis is full of sad evidence how mental peculiarities, educational warpings, philosophical prepossessions, or other disturbing forces may interfere with the correctness and reliability of Biblical interpretation. Both the fallibility of reason and the sacred importance of its office are strikingly illustrated in this history. The theological exegete must possess not only a sincere and reverent spirit, seeking simply the divine teaching, but also a clean, mirror-like mind for reception and reflection of the pure revealed truth. But the reason transcends its office when it turns critic of that which it recognizes as the real sense or doctrine of a revelation which it accepts as such. While it may justly urge the criticized teaching in connection with the earlier question of the divine character of the offered revelation, it cannot, after accrediting its authority, shape or modify the doctrine or system of doctrine otherwise than taught, simply because of its own conceptions of what ought to be true. To do this is to transgress the right use of reason in the exegetical office, and to hand over this office to the abuse of reason which again justly bears the reproach of "rationalism." (c) To the reason belongs also the office of vindicating the doctrines of religion and theology. This it can do by tracing how they separately and together meet the deep needs of man's moral and spiritual nature; how they integrate themselves into a complete unity in harmony with the total constitution and order of the world; how they affect human life, personal, social, and national, in exaltations and fruitage of highest human virtue and divine benediction, and thus bear witness to themselves as a true and necessary part of God's provision for human welfare and happiness.

2. Through this conception of the relation between reason and faith we are prepared to mark the relation sustained to theology by the two great divisions of reason's activities, viz.: Natural Science and Philosophy.

(a) By Natural Science. Science, being but the knowledge of nature as attained and certified by our faculties of observation and systemization, must, of course, occupy a relation to theology much akin to that of reason itself. Its material is as broad and varied as the whole observable product of God's creative work. It studies substances, forces, and movement. It investigates the phenomena in inorganic, organic, and psychic nature. It rises above the earth and examines the measureless wonders of the astronomic universe. It compares, judges, classifies, and finds the laws of sequence and uniformity, and through these laws forecasts the coming of what as yet is not. It specializes its work in many particular sciences, but in its final effort it seeks to unite the results of all its investigations into a consistent conception of the full cosmic universe. It is manifest that science is thus a progressive and changing knowledge. Its work is largely experimental and tentative, adding continuously to the amount of real, true "knowledge," often compelling the repudiation of notions or theories which were counted such before. Judged by the experience of the past, at every stage of its advance it has much still to learn as well as much to unlearn. By the very root-conception of the term, i. e., scientia, that which is known, its true, actual content is always lagging much behind its pretentions or that which is set forth. By no means is it all science which even leading scientists believe and present, as the continual funerals of both new and old "scientific" formulations and theories fully attest Many of the monuments of science are gravestones. The stones, however, are memorials of truth's progress. Beyond all doubt science, despite its limitations, as a successful interpreter of the works of God gives helpful light for understanding His word and the right determinations of Biblical theology. It has indeed but little in aid of Christian "soteriology;" for nature, though conscious of its need, has no message of salvation. But by the clearness and certainty which science sheds through natural theology and the wider and more accurate reading it furnishes of God's thoughts and ways in His works, it becomes auxiliary for correct adjustment to and in the total theological view, of the completing truths of the Scripture revelation. Just as truly, on the other hand, is science itself an immense gainer from the presence of revelation. For it is only when revelation has furnished the ultimate and full intention of the world's order and system, in their moral and spiritual significance for man's welfare and destiny, that the structure and adaptations of nature appear in adequate explanatory light According to both the Scriptures and science, the construction-movement of the earth looked to man; and can be fully understood and appreciated only in the light of the teleology of his welfare and destiny. Morning light for the true vision of nature comes only when revelation shines across the horizon. This helpfulness of theology is verified not simply by the indubitable fact that the grandest scientific activity and achievement belong almost entirely to nations or peoples to which revelation has given the quickened and clarified intellect and life of Christian civilization—the Christian peoples leading all others in science—but also by the concurrent fact that its service has been best for stable and beneficent results in proportion as it has worked along the lines of revelation's fundamental cosmic and moral teachings.

The normal relation between science and theology is, therefore, that of mutual helpfulness. They should stand in friendly attitude, while maintaining independent investigation in their distinct spheres of truth. Strife can never come in the truths themselves. This can arise only through erroneous interpretations or speculative theorizing on one side or the other or both, and then asserting for such unwarranted theories an authority which belongs only to "known" truth. Hypotheses are not science, nor unrevealed dogmas theology. As science is the knowledge of nature, of the realities discoverable in the uniformities of natural existence and law, it can neither furnish articles of faith in the higher range of supernatural redemption and grace nor disproof of the existence of such a sphere, when the credentials of this, of proper and rational kind, are in fully adequate evidence. On the one side, theology has no right to deny the invincibly known realities and truths of nature. On the other, science has no right to affirm the nonexistence of a higher sphere of divine love and verities, or a supernatural administration of redemptive grace for the life and destiny of mankind, simply on the ground that these verities are not discoverable or testable by the scientific apparatus applicable alone to the natural sphere. We must even go further and say that science distinctly points to the religious sphere. Not only is its apparatus incompetent for disproof, but one, at least, of its fundamental postulates—namely, the principle of ends or "final cause," by which it guides its own movement in intelligent appreciation of its conclusions—must, if allowed just force, recognize the total teleology of the natural system as looking to these same human interests which the supernatural system makes supreme in the purpose of the world. Science, as truly as theology or philosophy, makes man's being and welfare the grand aim and goal of what it calls the cosmic evolution. It thus concedes the lofty significance and unique position of man, whose highest endowments and interests connect him with the moral and spiritual sphere. When men take naturalistic science, either as a negation of "religion," or as itself the sufficient religion, they absurdly assume that man has no interests beyond those of physical existence. And he who, on the other hand, recognizes man's relation to a higher sphere of spiritual being and interests, and yet puts these spiritual interests in complete isolation from the physical or phenomenal world, which is the sphere of science, irrationally disrupts the unity and interrelations of the cosmic system, the unity, harmony, and interdependence of which is part of the fundamental spiritual postulate. The notion that the knowledge of the one sphere of reality and interests can stand apart from and shed no light upon the other sphere of reality and interests, violates the rational demand which compels us to hold all truth as self-consistent, with all its parts in mutually interpreting and supporting harmony.

(b) By Philosophy a similar relation is sustained. As distinguished from science, philosophy is offered explanation of the reason of things, in the realms of both mind and matter, of either parts or the whole of the universe. It goes beyond the scientific systemization of the phenomena of nature in their relations of sequence and dependence, and seeks to find and exhibit the thought-relations in which nature lives and moves, the ideal in which the actual world-constitution finds its elucidation. The very idea of philosophy rests upon the assumption that the universe is a rationally ordered whole, a divine thought made actual. Hence rational thinking is fairly held to be capable of reading this thought embodied in the constitution of nature and life, tracing out the truth and significance of things. Philosophy endeavors to present not the phenomenal, but the rational reality of the world. Its sphere, therefore, lies closer to the realm of theology than does that of science. Indeed, it has much in common with it. It ought, therefore, to be a true and helpful ally to theology, as theology, if allowed, may, in turn, illuminate the problems of philosophy. Philosophic explanations, however, greatly differ, owing to the different standpoints from which nature is viewed or the use of different principles of interpretation. We have many philosophies, some more and some less true to the real thought-relations which the creational action has fixed in the physical, mental, and moral existence and order of the world.

There has always been a strong affinity between theology and philosophy, a tendency to unite their lines of thought and explanation. Philosophy tends to become theological, theology philosophical. Ever since the days when Plato's philosophy reached up into the high realm of theistic and spiritual verities, and Christianity, in turn, employed his thinking in support, and, in some degree, in elucidation of its divine truths, this tendency has been evident. The history of doctrine in the early Church shows abundantly, and sometimes only too strongly, a molding and coloring influence on theology from its contacts with encompassing philosophic speculation. To say nothing about the gnostic and other heresies which broke the peace of the Church, the Alexandrian type of theology, so influential in Greek Christianity, is a perpetual historic reminder of this molding force. In every century since, we find systems of theology shaped in greater or less degree by prevalent philosophies; and at the same time some philosophies determined in large measure by believing submission to the dogmas of the Church. Every prominent system of modern philosophy has made itself felt in theology—sometimes sending waves of influence over large spaces of the theological realm.

As theology and philosophy both seek truth as to the divine thought in, through, and for nature and life, they certainly ought to stand in mutually helpful relations to each other. To a large measure they have done so. It would be difficult to estimate the full help which theology has received from this source. It has found in it corroborating testimony for many of its leading truths. For such as lie within the range of reason's comprehension it has received the confirmatory validation of the intellectual and moral judgment. The very understanding of them becomes endorsement and assured faith. When they have been truths of pure revelation, incapable of discovery or proof by the human reason alone, the clear showings of philosophy have nevertheless availed for vindicating their credibility by exhibiting their coherence with all other certified truths in self-consistent unity. They have kept invincibly evident the principle that transcendence of reason does not necessarily mean contradiction of reason. The sphere of the possible and true may extend both above and below the reach of human explanations. Predominantly the philosophy of Christendom has been a friendly and serviceable ally of Christian doctrine. Without being itself the furnishing source of this doctrine, it has given it integration in the best intellectual cosmic systemization. On the other hand, philosophy, constructing systems in perfect freedom on many and diverse presuppositions, assuming very different and even entirely opposite principles, has often not only brought perverting and weakening elements into theology, but arrayed itself in contradiction and strife. The difference of philosophies, the variance of system with system, has been one of the most patent facts in the history of thought. While some have, to greater or less degree, set the truth of being under genuine illumination, others have misconceived it and put a false face on the phenomena of existence and the meaning of life. They have been in incessant war with each other and changing with the passing generations, as one speculative genius after another has shifted the view-point or amended the conclusions. From this contrariety and shifting of philosophical teaching, perversion must inevitably come to theology, as it often has come, by a too easy and close alliance with it. Ceaseless vigilance is necessary against false and changing systems. The philosophic form of theology, or the philosophic contribution to it, has always constituted its variable quantity.

There are two forms of philosophy with which theology can have no alliance whatever, as they are absolutely antagonistic to it. One is monistic materialism, which denies the existence of spirit and leaves no place for moral freedom. A view of the world and man which resolves all the cosmic processes into mere atomic evolution and the human mind into molecular brain interactions exhibiting "mentality," allows no place for either moral or religious responsibility. The spiritual realm is cancelled. The other is pure idealism, standing on the extreme opposite to materialism, and discrediting the existence of matter and a substantial outer world. This dissolves the realm amid which the human spirit is to exercise its life and powers, reacting in love and duty on physical conditions. It assigns to the spirit a creative omnipotence for the production of the whole world in which it lives and moves as itself "lord of all," thus denying Christianity by a virtual deifying of self as cosmic creator. "A God without a real world is not the God of theology; a spirit without the flesh to subjugate is not the Christian spirit." No monistic philosophy, recognizing only one kind of essence in the universe—whether it find the ground and sum of being in matter or resolve all into an endless evolution of absolute spirit—can ever be harmonized with the teaching and principles of the Scriptures. These everywhere presuppose a dualism of God and the world, spirit and the flesh, in actual and ceaseless relations.

There are two other forms almost as absolutely un-theological—deism and pantheism. Deism, in its false emphasis on the transcendence of God, separates Him so thoroughly from the world as to exclude revelation from Him or fellowship with Him. It not only pushes God away off into incommunicable heights, but seats indifference and heartlessness instead of active love upon the throne. Though it holds to the existence of God, He is not the God of redemptive goodness and saving help. Its theology, if it can construct one, is not the theology of the Christian Scriptures. Pantheism, by identifying or confounding God with the universe, making God the sum total of being, the all (τὸ πὰν), an eternal essence evolving by interior necessity through all the forms of existence and phenomena—all modes and forms of nature being but forms and modes of God and parts of God—at once overthrows all freedom and responsibility by denying the true personality of both God and man. This pantheistic philosophy, reducing man into an ephemeral phenomenon of cosmic evolution, a momentary wave of intelligent self-consciousness on the upper surface of earthly existence, and shearing the Absolute Being, though still spelled with capitals, of every attribute of knowledge, wisdom, holiness, love, and redeeming goodness, presents neither the Godhead nor the manhood gloriously mirrored to view in the pages of revelation, and obliterates all the conditions of religious worship, love, and hope.

Milton Valentine

CHAPTER III
THE NATURE AND MODES OF REVELATION

Seeing Revelation to be the principal and supreme source of Christian theology and what this means in relation to other authority, we must seek a definite understanding of its nature and modes.

i. What is revelation, in the sense in which the term is applied to the Bible as that source? The essential conception of it is that of a supernatural and historical disclosure by God of Himself and of truth needful for the moral and spiritual well-being and destiny of men. It covers the act or process of disclosing as well as the disclosure given by the act. The New Testament word for it is ἀποκάλυψις, a laying open of what was covered (Rev. 1:1), and its import is found in such passages as Matt. 16:17; 1 Cor. 2:10; Gal. 1:12. In its basal significance it expresses the historical movement of God's eternal purpose to provide and make known the way of salvation from the state of sin into which humanity has fallen, and thereby again to enable it to realize the true life and goal to which its creation looked. In its central reality it is God's self-manifestation in the person and work of Christ, including all the special preparations leading up to that, and the succeeding apostolic teachings which have unfolded its redemptive and saving import. It consists, therefore, in that whole providential administration and multiform instruction in which God has made known Himself, His will and grace, and human duty, opportunity, and destiny, through which Christianity has been established in the world, and of which the Scriptures of the Old and New Testaments are the permanent records.

That we may see this revelation in its right light we must recall some of its distinct characteristics and relations.

First, it is a special revelation. It is such by the very relation in which it appears. Both by its initial statement of a lapse of human life into a condition of sin, and by its whole declared redemptive or soteriological aim, it necessarily appears as a movement or stage of divine manifestation beyond that generic revelation which God's creational work at once gave, and evermore gives, of His being, thought, power, and will. It has its own distinct and definitive place. There is, unquestionably, a primary, fundamental, perpetual self-revelation of God in the cosmos itself, in the soul of man, in the intelligence of the race. God has not left Himself without declaration or clear witness. The universe reveals Him, everywhere from atoms to worlds, forever speaking into reason's ear. A general law of divine revelation is thus to be recognized through creation and history. This is to be neither denied nor ignored. It is rather to be emphasized and built upon in forming our conception of the Christian revelation. For the special revelation rests in and upon the general revelatory principle, and exhibits its advance to meet the conditions presented in the lapsed humanity for whose welfare the cosmic existence and order are meant. Thus, though not separated from generic theistic revelation through nature, it is yet distinguished from it by relations and features peculiar to itself. God, indeed, was not taken by surprise by humanity's guilty abuse of the high endowment of freedom and its self-enslavement to sin. He foreknew, and always truly knows, both the world and humanity according to their historical progression and conditions; and the revelatory progress, which belongs to providential administration, attends and keeps pace with their developing conditions and needs. The divine revealing of creation passes on into the divine revealing of administrational love and activity—both connected with and looking to the same moral purpose of the world, the first already disclosing that purpose, and the second conserving it and holding open the possibility of its attainment. And this special revelation, reflecting and explaining distinctively God's providential goodness and redemptive provision, must necessarily exhibit peculiar characteristics and adaptations. What revelation would have been, had there been only a sinless development of mankind, we cannot tell. Possibly it would have been simply the creation itself, in its ever freshly illuminated pages, disclosing the thought, the wisdom, the power, and the will of God. Possibly it might have embraced progressively instituted relations of life and fellowship with God, opening evermore clearer and more beatific vision of His character and love—affording richer and richer views of truth. But lapsed into an alienated state and sinful development, the abnormal condition and the need of recovery called for something more and different. As to humanity itself, its self-made rupture from the divine fellowship and consequent darkening of spiritual intuition left the creational revelation less effective, while the ensnarement in evil made more light absolutely necessary. As to God, only further self-disclosure, beyond creative manifestations, could exhibit Him in the fullness of those attributes by whose vision the alienation might be overcome and recovery secured. Though creation itself was a work of love, it was more distinctively a disclosure of wisdom and power than of goodness or mercy. It invited no return by assurance of forgiveness. It showed no provision for the regeneration of humanity. God must be seen in other than creative attributes. He must add a revelation of His grace, in soteriological economy and teachings, which shall maintain the order of the world's progress according to His "eternal purpose" of goodness to the race. The Christian revelation, therefore, though grounded in generic revelation, is special. It has an aim continuous with that of the divine creational thought and goodness, but becomes specialized as the advancing providence of care and love which holds the historic advancement of humanity to its rightful opportunity and goal.

And it is also supernatural. It must be this too, by its very relation. There is not the faintest reason to think of the divine activity as exhausted and ceasing with the creative form alone. God is Sustainer and Ruler as well as Creator. The deistic notion of His absolute transcendence, in which, after creation, He takes no further concern for creaturely welfare, is as irrational in philosophy as it is contrary to the Scriptures and to the whole moral and religious interest of the world. The self-disclosure through the cosmos, both physical and moral, reveals Him only in His creatorship. This creatorship issues in a given constitution of nature. This natural constitution furnishes only natural revelation—of God as the author of nature, and of His way in nature. But it has no revelatory voice of redemptive goodness and help, no word of information as to the spirit and order of the divine administration over the humanity with which God has crowned this world system, now sinning, guilty, wretched, and needing pity and direction. The generic naturalistic revelation is not withdrawn, but it is inadequate. The mere energies and uniformities of natural law furnish neither the information nor the spiritual forces for the soteriological need. Beyond the creational, natural provision and directions, a supernatural order of grace and training necessarily comes in, if God's aim of love for the race, made in His image, is not wholly to fail. The redemptive administration, the redemptive teaching, and the redemptive powers are necessarily in excess of the simple movement and revelation of the natural constitution, and they come in with, as they belong to, the providential governmental goodness and grace of God.

The whole question of supernaturalism in Christianity, agitated these late years with so much hostile endeavor, can be rightly understood and determined only by remembering these fundamental facts and principles. The distinction between the divine activity disclosing itself in the cosmic creation, including the human constitution, and the divine activity in the moral administration over the world of humanity must be kept clear. The distinction itself is real and indubitable. The first, the origination of the world with its established uniformities under physical law, is prior and conditional for the second. The second follows, and concerns the government of the intelligent, free and responsible beings for whose life the physical world has been created. The forces and movement established by creation are natural—even in respect to spiritual endowments. The principles and order of the government are moral, and therefore require, as is self-evident, that the administration be in the undiminished divine freedom that answers to the contingent needs which arise in humanity's use or abuse of its given freedom. The moral disorder, sin, coming by the abuse of this freedom, and crossing the divine aim for man's welfare and destiny, called for light and relief which were not in nature itself, but possible of supply through redemptive or soteriological goodness. God is as free for soteriological as for creational activity—for adding a supernatural administration with its spiritual forces and laws as for creating the natural system with its uniformities. The moral administration is by essential conception, forever free—God's freedom acting in relation to man's abuse of freedom. Beyond all question, Christianity presents itself as belonging to, as well as expressing, the grand aim and central principle of this providential moral administration of the world's movement. Without doubt, too, is it constituted to a soteriological design, a design beyond that disclosed in natural revelation or provided for already in natural, physical order or mere human knowledge and strength. Equally beyond doubt is it, moreover, that the records of Christianity present God as, in His providential activity, after the world's creation and human sin, giving a gracious promise of pardoning mercy and redemptive help, establishing a dispensation of arrested judgment with respect to sinful humanity; or perhaps we should rather say, a dispensation of stay and check on the forces of evil in life, instituting actual relations of reconciliation, acceptance, and fellowship between Himself and men, accompanied with clear and wonderful proclamation of the laws of human duty and holy life and no less wonderful prophetic teaching of spiritual truth and fore-announcements of the kingdom of God on earth—altogether a unique dispensation moving continuously on through centuries to the "fullness of time" when, in the incarnation and work of the divine Son, the redemptory and saving provision was completed for all the ages. Unless the entire Scripture record is utterly false, this aggregate movement, in its characteristic trend and multiform particulars, reveals God as ruling over human affairs in attributes of character and methods of goodness, and with transcendent aims for human destiny, of which simply cosmic processes and nature's revealings have no voice. The movement, though based on nature, is in excess of mere nature's provision. It forms a supernatural self-manifestation of God, a manifestation whose aim is not creational, except in the moral relation of a παλιγγενεσία, "regeneration."

The supposed strife between nature and the supernatural comes from misconception of one or the other or of both, and of their relations to each other. When correctly viewed, the strife disappears. The natural constitution of things is divinely and permanently adjusted in its existence and evolution, under the uniformities of cause and effect, as the theatre on which humanity is to live its high life of freedom and responsibility. No supernatural or special divine power need ever be invoked for the sake of mere physical nature. But the very creation and establishment of the nature-constitution, under uniform law, leads to and introduces the free providential administration of care and direction for the moral order and spiritual interests of the human race, made in the image of God, for whose welfare the world has been built. These interests must be cared for and guided according to the principles of intelligence and personal freedom. If God in His free creational activity has originated and ordained the constitution of nature, with its uniformities, what hinders the conception of His further activity, when the time of moral administration is reached, establishing a soteriological order of self-revelation and gracious help for the race ensnared in the labyrinths of sin? It is truly super-natural because, without annulling the cosmic nature-constitution, it introduces, in its own time, according to unchangeable purpose, the soteriological principle for preserving to humanity its opportunity of reaching its true goal in eternal life. The idea, therefore, that super-naturalism is inconsistent with nature is utterly gratuitous and false—as plainly so as would be a claim that the education of a child's mind is contradictory to its original endowment with mental faculties. Much rather does it imply the true use and preservation of nature, in carrying into effect the moral and spiritual purposes and adaptations for which it obtained its existence. It prevents the defeat of the very end of nature.

To be true to Christianity, theology can never surrender the supernatural character of the Biblical revelation. Its claim is sustained, not only by the clearly evident place for the supernatural in the teleological ordering of history, but by the equally manifest fact that without it the world-existence, history, and end remain, or rather revert into, an unexplained and insoluble enigma. For, outside of this revelation, the thought of mankind, striving through all the ages to solve the problem of life and destiny from nature's revelation alone, has neither lifted the darkness nor ceased to plead for some satisfying light. The state of the pagan world to-day, as in all the past, is absolute disproof of the ability of naturalism, or the mere human reading of nature's pages, to supply humanity's mighty spiritual and soteriological needs, or to furnish the race with the matchless and saving truth and grace which are given in Christianity. This fact clearly implies that it is just by this supernatural character that the Christian revelation stands as God's true self-disclosure to man, making known the unique redemptive order which it reveals, which He alone could institute, and which fully supplies the religious needs of the race, establishing right relation to God, and regenerating heart and life. Christian theology can never consent to obliterate the valid distinction between the natural and the supernatural self-manifestation of God, without giving up the special soteriological character of the latter and permitting Christianity to drop down to the rank of a mere human product as one among the simple nature-religions of the world. This would be utterly false to its whole position and claim.

This brief view of the place and significance of the Christian revelation is sufficient to show the great error of those who, under the influence of scientific and philosophic theories, especially the theories which credit the world and humanity to evolution and natural law, seek to make this free moral and redemptive revelation also a mere growth or progress of human thought and discovery, in which men find out the things of God and the principles of right living more clearly than before, simply by a better reading of the cosmic laws and the constitution of man. The error refuses the idea of any Divine self-disclosure beyond the one in nature. But the Biblical revelation is a movement of God toward us, not our working toward Him. It is no mere human discovery of God, but a further gift from Him. It is not humanity's progress into the light by its own ascent upon

"The great world's altar-stairs
That slope through darkness up to God,"

but His gracious descent to us. Without doubt much truth is gained from nature, but it is only truth of a scientific or philosophic finding. When correctly found it is, indeed, genuine truth of God and in living harmony with all other truth. But the truth of the Christian revelation is the peculiar gift of God's redemptive provision and grace.

2. This view of the essential nature of revelation makes clear the fact that while it is a self-manifestation of God, there are, nevertheless, two factors in it—the divine and also the human. The first is the real source, the second the instrumental channel of recipiency and record. The human factor is not the ruling one, but still one that

appears in the form in which revelation is finally molded. It means that God has revealed Himself, as was necessary, in ways adapted to the capacities of the human mind and in the forms of human thought and speech. He has used men's natural faculties for the apprehension of His plan and will and spiritual realities, and their language for the expression of the divine truths. These are, indeed, made the very media and instruments of the divine communication to the world. That God has thus, as seems to have been needful, allowed the human side to determine the forms of the divine self-manifestation, explains the human element so plainly and strongly brought into the Scriptures. They have become a type or reflection of the supreme reality of the saving movement—the divine-human Christ. There is an "Immanuel," God-with-us, for the Bible as well as for the Saviour. This adapts the revelation to the human understanding without diminution of its authority.

3. The specific modes of revelation must be conceived of in accordance with these fundamental views of its nature and factors. The activity of God in disclosing Himself in love and grace, unfolding the way of salvation and life for mankind, had necessarily to take forms that would distinctly certify the divine presence and communication. Whatever modes it might assume, it had to bring men, in some real, intelligible sense, face to face with that Presence and identify the communication with God's authority and will. God must open Himself as God to the human apprehension. And as the occasion and sphere of the self-revelation lay in the supernatural or miraculous, the modes of it, necessarily taking on these characteristics, bring us into the presence of mysteries or occurrences not explicable under the laws and terms explanatory of simply natural events. The Biblical accounts employ statements which look rather to certifying the fact of the divine manifestations than explaining the problem of the mode. The manner of the revealing, grounded in the principles and order of God's plan of gracious providential government for the race, appears varied and modified almost infinitely according to the historical conditions and unfoldings, but always marked by the characteristic of adequacy for the revelatory effect. All the variations, however, may be grouped under a few specific modes characterized by distinguishing features: (a)

Theophanies—putting Himself in communication with men through phenomenal appearances, sometimes anthropomorphic, sometimes angelic. These must include all the Old Testament cases in which He opened the reality of His presence through an appeal to sight in making known His will and plan and promises, whether in burning bush or pillar of fire or the Shekinah symbol or in personal theophany. According to John 12:41; 1 Cor. 10:9; Heb. 11:26, these Old Testament theophanies were Christophanies, manifestations of the Son before the incarnation. (b) Speech. This is found concurrent with the divine phenomenal appearing, though sometimes it seems to have occurred alone. From Eden onward God condescended to use human speech in addressing his message to men. This is signally illustrated in the theophanies and in the giving of the law. (c) Miracles, more distinctively so called, as certificates of the divine presence, and seals to the authority of prophets and teachers empowered to deliver truth in God's name. They were a mode of manifestation significant of divine power and potent for impressing the divine will. (d) Inspiration—the Holy Spirit's supernatural teaching and communication of the things of God and the duties of men, as in the prophets of the Old Testament and the evangelists and apostles of the New. "The Spirit of Jehovah spake by me" (2 Sam. 23:2); "And Jehovah said: I have put my words in thy mouth" (Jer. 1:9); "Holy men of God spake as they were moved by the Holy Ghost" (2 Pet. 1:21). Inspiration as a mode of revelation, at this point, is considered apart from the related truth of its guidance in the Scripture record. This truth will come before us hereafter. (e) The teaching and redemptive work of the incarnate Son of God, the central and all-comprehending reality in the self-revelation of God, about which all others cohere, either as antecedent needful providential preparations or as subsequent developmental explanations. This determined the relations of all parts of this soteriological manifestation and aggregates them into unity. In Jesus Christ, as God manifest in the flesh, making known both God and man, establishing through propitiation and the Holy Spirit, actual relations for forgiveness and cleansing from sin and a kingdom of eternal life, the full divine revelation, according to human need, is all centralized and summed up. "He that hath seen me hath seen the Father" (John 14:9).

4. Revelation was progressive—in two ways. (a) As to its substance. Being a redemptive movement for the spiritual regeneration of the race, it necessarily entered into history as an advancing process of adapted instruction and instituted relations of right life and fellowship with God. It was an order of moral training through a divinely adopted way of forgiveness of sin and recovery to righteousness, in methods in harmony with the rational and free nature of humanity. So one truth after another was made known, as it was needed and could find reception. The light was given according to recipiency—God's free grace pressing measures of it to the full of humanity's consent to use it. The light was always made to shine upon the darkness faster than the darkness comprehended it. This progress was not in addition to the redemptory reality itself, but only in revealing it. The proto-evangelium (Gen. 3:15), at once setting forth a victorious redemption and salvation over against sin, assures us, from our view-point of it under the Gospel, that the truth of redemption was all complete in the divine mind and gift from the beginning. But there was revelatory advance, through appointed significant offerings of propitiation and thanksgiving; through many divine manifestations in which God showed His mercy and declared His will; through a distinct covenant with Abraham and his seed, chosen to be a special medium for the conservation and expansion of the divine truth and grace—a covenant vouched to faith in sacramental sign and seal, pledging blessings to all the families of the earth; in the call and endowment of Moses, and his divine legation in that unique and wonderful transfer of the chosen race from Egypt to Palestine; in the great Moral Law of Sinai and an instituted Tabernacle Worship, with prescribed sacrifices of atonement to be continued for the long centuries of Jewish history as impressive types and assurances of God's provided propitiation for the sins of the world—on and on through manifold distinct Messianic prophecies, throwing into ever clearer light the coming of the divine Saviour who should unite in Himself the accomplishment of all priestly, prophetic, and kingly offices, and establish God's dominion of life and righteousness in the earth. (b) As to form. At first God revealed Himself in sensible manifestations, as a necessary accommodation to the earlier pupilage of men. With Moses He speaks "face to face, as a man

speaketh unto his friend" (Ex. 33:11; Num. 12:8). Miracles early appear, as special displays of the divine power through human instrumentality, arresting attention and accrediting the divine authority. In these miracles themselves a progress may be traced, evidently educational, from the physical to the spiritual, the spiritual miracles of inspiration and prophecy becoming the more prevailing form. Then came the revealing Presence in the Person of the Christ, disclosing the deepest and most transcendent spiritual truths, realities, and mysteries of redemption. Finally, through the gift of the Holy Spirit, to take the things of Christ and show them to men, and the completion of the inspired record of these things, revelation became an abiding presentation of the supernatural truth appealing to our higher faculties, superseding visible theophanies and sensible miracles.

The reason of the closing of the process of supernatural revelation is that the full provision of redemption and the truths for spiritual salvation have been given and adequately certified to the world. The idea that revelation is a still continuous, endless process, forgets its special aim and character. It forgets its redemptory purpose, as providing conditions for the forgiveness of sin and recovery of men to true and holy life. It forgets that it consists essentially, not in ethical truths or principles, but in a series of divine acts, moving historically at length into the incarnate manifestation of God Himself, in the Person of Jesus Christ, His self-offering as the propitiation for the sins of the world, His resurrection for justification, His ascension and mediatorial dominion, the establishment of the Church and its endowment with the presence of the Holy Spirit, and with the means of grace in the Gospel word and sacraments. It forgets the objective character of this revelation and the completeness of its soteriological provision and truths. All that it was needful that God should do to reconcile the world to Himself, not imputing their trespasses to men, drawing them back to faith and obedience by the cross of His love, and renewing their hearts by His Spirit, has been done. All the teaching needful for a saving understanding of these redemptory provisions has been given. All the means necessary to enlighten the mind and work an appropriating faith have been furnished. All the requisite truths and precepts for the order and regulation of the Christian life, have been supplied. And the same

God who has thus entered into human history in this course of redemptive activity or work has providentially mated the work and its essential truths with a true and adequate record, in an organism of Holy Scripture, preserving the given revelation for the world. Christianity stands in historical mould. Its power rests upon its historical realities and becomes void for faith if these be resolved into fictions. It cannot be severed from its historical bases and remain itself. It cannot be made a mere subjectivism. The effort of some theologians to detach it from necessary relation to these realities, so as to make it stand practically independent of its historical evidences, an absolute religion complete simply in the moral intuitions, religious aspirations, spiritual sentiments, and satisfactions in which each man may find it accredited by his own nature—a mere naturalistic idealism—is in destructive contradiction of the very foundations of Christianity. Unquestionably its verities have such self-attesting power to the human soul, to a wonderful degree. It arises from their divine adaptations to the religious need. But remove or resolve into myths the supernatural facts of the Old Testament providence and the New Testament redemption, which constitute the fundamental material of Christianity, and the very verities whose adaptations witness so assuringly are discredited and discarded. The very content of the faith is lost. The tree severed from its roots cannot live or bear its fruits. The all-embracing differential characteristic of Christianity is that it forever stands for a divine historical achievement in the past as supplying the provision and guarantee of grace and salvation in the present and the future. The continuity of Christianity is the apprehension and appropriation of the finished redemption and its redemptory truth, in the Biblical deposit, mediating, under the Holy Spirit's presence, supernatural saving forces. This apprehension is progressive, marked by increasing insight into and understanding of the Christian truths and doctrines. It involves, through the ongoing centuries, ever new applications to altered and advancing conditions of human life, giving fresh and richer view of the meaning and power of the Gospel. Every age more light is breaking forth from it—not, however, because of additions to it, but because more is found to be there.

CHAPTER IV
EVIDENCES OF REVELATION

As conditional for thus taking the Scriptures of the Old and New Testaments as the principal and decisive source of theology, we must have proof that they are indeed a supernatural revelation from God. Only thus can they acquire authority to rule our faith. For faith is not to be credulity but a firm confidence resting on adequate evidences. The Scriptures can claim our credence and rightly dominate our minds precisely in the degree in which they have such evidences. They present themselves before us as rationally capacitated to discern their credentials and meet our responsibility in relation to them. As to essence the evidences have been the same from the first, but they have been much varied in form and relative emphasis according to the changing character of skeptical attacks. From the vast mass we must remind ourselves of some of the most characteristic proofs, prefacing with some general considerations.

i. A special revelation is surely possible. The possibility becomes evident not only from our necessary conception of God as able to do what He wills, but specifically: First, from His relation to the world, as not only different from it and above it, but as also immanent in it, His eternal will and power touching it everywhere and forever. "He is not far from everyone of us; for in Him we live and move and have our being, Acts 17:27, 28. With no right whatever can the created system be supposed to form a limit to the possibilities of His power in providing and dispensing needed moral help for the creatures for whose welfare and destiny the physical order exists. Unquestionably the ruling teleology of nature looks to humanity as the goal of its adaptations; and God is certainly forever free among its powers for the sake of the accomplishment of His eternal moral purpose. Both his transcendent and immanent relation to the world is thus a guarantee of the possibility of His supernatural self-revelation. To His free omnipotence there can be no objective hindrance. Secondly, from the trinitarian being of God—the second form of His subsistence, both by designation and Scripture explanation, pointing to an interior relation for it in the Godhead. Whatever may be thought of the idea that the truth of the Trinity taught in the Scriptures, is disclosed or required by the very conception of God, as the self-existent, self-sufficing absolute Personality, we may at least say with certainty that that truth opens to view a divine reality suggestive of objective self-manifestation—a "basis of objectivity within the Godhead"—whereby the infinite One may declare Himself to creature intelligence. In the life of God is the eternal "Word," the "Logos," ever "with God" and really "God" (John 1:1), through whom and the Spirit He exhibits Himself in all the activities of creation; and in this mystery of Triunity appears distinct evidence of an interior or subjective condition for the divine self-manifestation, self-expression. "The only begotten Son, which is in the bosom of the Father"—"the effulgence of His glory"—"He hath declared Him" (John 1:18; Heb. 1:3). The infinìte and absolute Being is not am closed, unrevealable selfhood, existing in infinite exaltation above all created things, without internal adaptation to disclosure of His attributes and will to the beings whom in His freedom He creates to know and enjoy His love. And when in His providential order He adds to creation a supernatural self-revelation, He moves out through the same eternal Word and Spirit by whose creational powers and activities He established the world in open and living relations to Himself. Thirdly, from the constitution of man as made in His image. As a creature endowed with the powers of intelligent, free personality, answering to those of God, man is capacitated to know Him and have fellowship with Him. The personality of man, the highest existence on earth, answers to the personality of the Maker of man. This gives the principle of recipiency. Though not to a stone or a tree, incapable of knowledge, yet to a creature gifted with the attributes of personal intelligence and lifted thus into divine likeness, God can surely reveal Himself. He can communicate His thoughts into the human mind and establish relations of fellowship.

This possibility has, indeed been frequently and variously questioned. But when the main forms of doubt are examined, they dissolve into shadows and their force disappears; A few illustrations will suffice. (a) It is often objected that as nature's forces are fixed in energy, and act under the invariable law of cause and effect, in a movement inherently balanced and necessitated, such supernatural action as is involved in a special revelation is necessarily excluded. Since such revelation belongs to the sphere of the "miraculous," it is said to be barred out by the intrinsic and unbending constitution and order of the world. But it is enough to point out in reply, that nature's system, in its uniformity of sequence, presents in fact no such rigorous exclusion of free or special causation and accomplishment. It is so elastic and pliable as to permit the human will, which stands above mere nature's mechanism and uniformities, to act every day and hour as a special cause upon nature and produce effects which these uniformities themselves could never bring about. Human will can establish for human life new conditions, without breach or suspension of nature's inherent order of cause and effect. Surely the Divine Will, in its free omnipotence, has as much power as the human. And when, in the order of His moral purpose, God may desire to establish relations of special instruction and help for man's need, the physical system, over which man himself, as made in the divine image, has been placed in "dominion," must necessarily, without being infringed, serve, rather than bar, His revealing love. (b) The possibility is denied sometimes on the supposed ground that there can be no relations established between the Infinite and the finite. They are so apart, it is alleged, as not only to preclude communicative adjustment, but to be unrelatable. The objection arises from such forms of philosophy as imagine that to think the Absolute or Infinite as sustaining relations is necessarily to nullify its infinitude or absoluteness by the limitations implied in the existence of other things. But, as philosophy itself has abundantly shown, it is an arbitrary and mistaken conception of the Infinite to define it as being "without relations," or as excluding the possibility of other existence to which it may assume relations. In truth, the psychology of the idea of the Infinite makes it indubitable that the mind finds it related to finite things in the very possibility and necessity of the concept itself. For it is only on the occasion and basis of our knowledge of finite existences that the idea of the infinite emerges intuitively as correlate of the finite.

In the same way the idea of the Absolute appears as the correlate of the known dependent existences of the cosmos, and implies for it no exclusion of relation but the single one of dependence. Psychologically, therefore, we never have the idea of "the infinite" or "the absolute" except as correlates of the finite and dependent. Apart from this co-relation the conception would become a blank. When, then, these philosophical terms are used to designate God as the Infinite or Absolute Being, they normally present Him not without but in relation to the existences which He has created. God is naturally conceived to be "absolute," simply as dependent for what He is on no other being, and "infinite" as without limitation to His perfections. Any other conception of the terms is a Pseudo-conception. And when in His freedom He creates other being than Himself He necessarily relates Himself as Creator, Preserver, and Ruler to the product of His power. His self-revelation moves forward upon the open and divine relation thus established by His creational activity. (c) The divine immutability is sometimes supposed to exclude revelation. So maintained Jacob Grimm and David Frederick Strauss. "An isolated act of God in time," it is said, "contradicts the idea of His un-changeableness." But the difficulty with respect to revelation is of no more force than with respect to creation. And as it is conceded by all, except atheists and pantheists, that God has created the world, in the free action of His will, the cosmos itself, as a self-manifestation in time, makes indubitably clear that His immutability is no bar to free self-revelation. And in fact the divine immutability, like the divine "infinity," is misconceived when it is imagined to be inconsistent with God's self-revelation. He is indeed immutable, but is immutable in His self-revealing nature, purposes, and action. That is, in His essence and will He is unchangeable; but His immutable nature and will is self-revelation according to the needs of His children.

2. Another preliminary consideration is the probability of a revelation. The nature and relations of the race raise a clear rational presumption in this direction. For a revelation is clearly desirable and needful. To see the force of this, we need only consider the facts in man's constitution and relations, as natural information presents him—a rational and moral being, placed in unique and high pre-eminence

above all other creatures of the earth, with the lofty endowments of intelligence, sensibility, and freedom, with profound adaptations and affinities for truth and knowledge, a sense of obligation to right and duty, and instincts which even crave fellowship with the Divine thought and happiness, thrown thus into the enormous responsibilities of life with all its solemn and complex problems as to his origin, purpose, and destination, his relations to his Creator and His Creator's plan and will concerning him. Even apart from any moral fall or degeneracy of the race, the condition would have presented a manifest need of some divine instruction and direction. That God should crown His earthly creation with a race of beings of such sublime and perilous endowments, whose welfare would be dependent on their understanding and freely meeting the requirements involved in their relations and responsibilities, and leave them without any word of information and instruction as to how they might rightly achieve their life and destiny, would seem to be inconsistent with all that we can reasonably think of the character and goodness of God. In the very creation of such beings, with such responsibilities, God Himself created the need of a knowledge of Himself and His will. Under the law of need and supply, illustrated everywhere through nature, as light for the eye, air for the lungs, objective provision for subjective instincts, and the like, we would look for the light of the knowledge of God and duty to meet the human capacities and need for the spiritual direction of life. It may, indeed, be said that sinless humanity, in the unclouded perceptions of its intellectual and moral faculties, might, from creation itself, have reached sufficient truth for this self-direction, without superadded help. It is questionable, however, whether such human findings alone could have fully met the great and many-sided need or rendered a higher revelation superfluous. At any rate, the glimpse which the Scriptures afford of primitive man exhibits him as placed under open divine communication. This is certainly in accordance with the reasonable probabilities in the case. Much more is this necessary when the race has been self-corrupted and darkened under sin. In this condition of corruption new necessities of help arise. A revelation of God's compassionate love, disclosing a gracious forgiveness and a way of return to divine fellowship and blessed life, became essential, if man was still to realize the end of his creation. The condition of pagan humanity, which, in the development of the race and the progress of history, came to stand outside of the onward movement of redemptory revelation, is a most impressive witness to the sore and sorrowful need. Allowed to try its own resources in finding the sufficient light of life, whether in rudest tribes or most cultured peoples, the result has always and everywhere been the demonstration of a human want which a self-revealing God alone could supply. If, therefore, we assume, as we are entitled to, that God is good and deals with His creatures consistently, according to the necessities of their condition, this unquestionable and supreme importance of the human interests involved furnishes an antecedent probability of a divine self-manifestation for the needed help and guidance of the race.

3. The positive evidence that the Christian Scriptures are a supernatural revelation from God is fully adequate. The immense mass and variety of it preclude anything like detailed and full presentation here. The scope of this theological outline must be content not to unfold the evidence, but simply to mark its different forms and characteristics, with mere suggestions as to their force and essential conclusion. For the developed form and cogency of the proofs, the student or reader must consult the special treatises in apologetics.

The chief evidences are usually and properly classed under two heads: First. The External, consisting of such as arises from History, Miracles, and Prophecy. They stand not as identical with the substance itself of the divine message, but as attending corroboration of the divine hand in the gift. Secondly. The Internal, discerned in the very contents of Christianity as intrinsically divine, as self-evidently of God and the adequate supply of humanity's religious and moral needs. The chief of these appear in: (a) The Harmony of the Scriptures, (b) The supernatural character of Christ, (c) The supernatural Doctrines of the Bible, its transcendent morality, the exact adaptation of its disclosures to the needs of the race, and the supernatural power of its truths.

We must mark the essential relations and force of these in their order.

THE EXTERNAL EVIDENCES

The characteristic of these is that they express, not the direct self-testifying force of Christian truth, but the objective attendant testimonies authenticating the supernatural facts in which God has revealed Himself and human duty. They are the public credentials in the form of the outward events which embodied the divine disclosure. Though they are closely joined with the Internal Evidence, often blending on their marginal meeting lines, they have their own characteristic feature so strongly as to justify the distinction made between them and the latter. They are pre-supposed by the internal evidence and required by the very form, the historical in which Christianity presents itself.

Historical Evidences

Since Christianity presents itself as grounded in a providential movement in time, consisting of divine activities in which God has progressively made known to men His relations, character, and will, culminating in sending His Son as the Savior of the world, through whose ministry of teaching and propitiation a Gospel of forgiveness and eternal life has been provided and ordered to be preached to mankind, its primary and fundamental evidences must necessarily be historical. It claims to stand in great public facts, in the annals of a covenant people, in the appearance and life of Jesus Christ. The first and basal question of all must be: "Did these things, as embodying these divine self-disclosures, actually take place? Are these Scripture accounts truly and firmly historic?" The proper proof of historic events must be history. This fundamental place of the historical evidences has not always been duly appreciated. Recently—say beginning half a century age—the emphasis was so laid upon the internal self-witnessing sufficiency of Christianity as to make light of its historical foundations and to hold it as relatively independent of them. A phase of this error has been embodied in the Ritschlian school of teaching. But the error forgets both the primary nature of revelation as "in act and deed," and the logical demand that a historical religion must have its historical credentials. And with the reawakening of the historical spirit and method, in connection with the Higher Criticism, the strong accent justly belonging to this kind of evidence has been thoroughly restored.

The very effort of the Ritschlian tendency to continue Christianity while detaching it from the objective facts which form its historical embodiment, resulting often in elimination of its supernatural content, surrendering the reality while holding on to the name, has made it impressively clear that Christianity in its integrity cannot live if its historical foundations be set aside. Its general theistic view and its unique ethical system might still hold the respect and homage of the minds of men, but its "Gospel" of redeeming love, forgiveness of sin, and eternal life, as summed up, for instance, in the Apostles' Creed, would have to disappear as an imposture or as an empty dream of myth-constructing imagination.

This kind of evidences, therefore, lies at the foundation of all the evidences. Dr. Stanton well says: "The value of Christianity as a revelation, as a divine assurance of God's forgiving love, gracious help, and of immortal life, depends on its historical truth. This view of Christianity has been the secret of its power in the past."

This giving of the first place to these historical evidences is attended by the logical advantage that, with respect to the whole apologetic view, it brings us at once to that in Christianity which is most outstanding and incontrovertible—the founding of it and its actual existence. The mind is at once anchored to phenomena that allow no doubt. At the present moment, over the face of all the earth, Christianity is the greatest living historical fact of the world. Through the eighteen centuries, running back into the past, it has been the shaping reality and force in human history. If anything on earth has indubitable historical existence and power it is Christianity. The epoch of its establishment, though appearing, like all other deep divine movements, as the sequence of a long preceding history, was great and revolutionary enough to give a new enumeration of the centuries. And just as clear and indubitable is it that this establishment was grounded in the unique Person, teachings, life, and revealing deeds of Jesus Christ at the time and place, and in the general circumstances, to which history has credited it. We have thus unquestionable starting point and beginnings from which to move, through all other evidences, toward the true conclusion.

Of the essential and true historicity of the facts in connection with the life, teachings, and work of Christ, in whom and in which the divine truth and authority of Christianity stand and are vindicated, we have adequate and abundant proof in the writings which the Church has gathered together in the New Testament Scriptures, sustained and corroborated by antecedent, collateral, and consequent history. These writings, in their number and variety, in the situation of the writers and the explicitness and concurrence of their testimony, constitute a mass and weight of evidence such as is found to underlie but few of the undoubted and indubitable events of the past It is ample even according to the sacred interests involved.

If it be shown, therefore, that these New Testament Scriptures, viz: the four Gospels, the Acts of the Apostles, the twenty-one apostolic or sub-apostolic Epistles, and the Apocalypse, or even the undisputed portion of them, are truly authentic, we have in them all that is necessary for the full historical validation of Christianity in all its essential supernatural facts, truths, principles, and doctrines. To exhibit this authenticity or historical trustworthiness is the main task and service of this branch of apologetics.

And what are the results of its showing? We can here give only the main facts in outline.

i. Both the genuineness and authenticity of these four histories of Christ, the Acts of the Apostles, and most of the Epistles, are clearly and invincibly certified by numerous and varied quotations from them and appeals to their facts and teachings, from the very age of the apostles down to the present. This great fact thus becomes a twofold testimony. In its proof of their genuineness, viz: that they are the productions of the authors whose names they bear, it is the assurance that the accounts are truly from the apostles or their immediate associates, who as the cotemporaries of Jesus Christ and witnesses of His life and ministry were in the situation required for making the true record. In its relation to their authenticity, it not only implies that the writers were properly related to the events which they record, but shows that the writings were in fact accepted and used as the true and authoritative account of the establishment and teachings of

Christianity. The full import of this twofold testimony will appear further on, as the bearings of it are specified.

The quotations begin with the Apostolic Fathers, writers so called because of their immediate or close connection with the apostles themselves, viz: Clement, bishop of Rome, and an assistant of St. Paul, A. D. 93–95; Ignatius, bishop of Antioch, A. D. 107–116; Polycarp, bishop of Smyrna, died A. D. 155, a disciple of St John; The Disciple to Diognetus, A. D. 120–140; and Papias, a hearer of those acquainted with the apostles, bishop of Hierapolis, in Phrygia, A. D. 120–160. "The Teaching of the Twelve Apostles" belongs to the date of these Apostolical Fathers, probably about A. D. 100, and shares their evidential value. Considering the relations of these writers, the immediacy of their succession to the apostles, the specific and limited aims with which they wrote, facing the thorough familiarity of those addressed with the teaching and deeds of Christ from the lips of the apostles and evangelists themselves, we need not wonder that comparatively few direct and explicit quotations are made by them from the writings now gathered into the New Testament collection. Theirs was a transitional period. It suited their situation rather to base their exhortations and appeals upon the information which had by apostolic instruction become the common or universal possession of the believing community. Nevertheless, taking them only in their undoubted genuine productions, we find clear and explicit recognition of the New Testament writers and writings. In some cases reference and quotation are made directly and by name. But the chief force of their testimony, while thereby scarcely inferior in value, is largely indirect, consisting in the use of an immense number of passages, along with numerous passages indubitably quoted from the Old Testament, apparently drawn without name from the New Testament writings. These passages abound, woven up thickly sometimes into the woof and warp of their productions. They naturally strike New Testament readers as direct, self-evident quotations or references; and almost certainly they are such. If so, they testify to nearly all the histories and epistles in our New Testament But we do not wish to take advantage of what may be said to be apparent rather than real. For as the minds of the writers were saturated with the traditional oral teaching of the apostles, with its fixed forms of statement of facts and truth, it may be claimed that these passages may, after all, not really have been drawn from the New Testament writings, but from their authors' full spontaneous memories, or possibly from other written current memoranda or memoirs or "logia" made by the first disciples. But fully allowing all the proper force of this critical difficulty, we are, nevertheless, justly entitled to say two things: (a) That the passages still appear as actual quotations, made more or less literally from our Gospels and Epistles—in the same manner of quoting as is found characteristic in drawing from the Old Testament Scriptures; and (b) That even if they could be shown to be simply the traditional forms of Christian expression or taken from lost documents, their evidential value for the historical authority of the New Testament records would scarcely be diminished. For they show a thorough agreement with the New Testament as to all the essential facts and teachings of Christianity. If the apparent quotations, instead of being drawn from our present written records, are simply echoes from the apostles' lips, reverberating in the memories of the writers, they still stand as corroborative and invincible evidence of the essential identity of the events and truths which created Christianity with those recorded in our Scriptures. And the force of this testimony, taken at its least, witnesses—assuming Papias as reliably reported by Eusebius—to the genuineness of two of the Gospels and several of the Epistles, and to the historical authority of almost the whole New Testament

But the testimony as to both advances and enlarges in the Church Fathers of the second century, when the number of writers increased and the heathen assaults upon the divine truths of Christianity drew forth scholarly vindication of its historical and supernatural foundations. Introducing the period which has been well characterized as "the age of apologetics," these writers give us more explicit and abundant historic assurance. The mention of only a few of them will suffice to illustrate the nature of their witness.

Justin Martyr, the first Christian author of the sub-apostolic period, a Palestinian Gentile, well educated, a resident of Ephesus and Rome, whose writings exceed in bulk all the remains of Christian literature before his time, wrote not later than A. D. 145–150. His date and position put him in most reliable relation to the earlier Christian writings and historical sources for the beginning of Christianity. He was, indeed, no ordinary man. In his early life he was trained in philosophy, and while a pagan seeking satisfaction for his religious needs, made careful inquiry into various philosophical systems. After his conversion, it is evident, he carried his habits of learned and careful investigation over into his relation to the question of the origin and truth of Christianity. In his first "Apology," or vindication of Christianity, addressed to the Emperor Antoninus Pius, he mentions as authority for the facts and doctrines of Christ the "Memoirs of the Apostles" and their companions, composed by the apostles, calling them also "Gospels," which were read on Sundays in their assemblies of Christian worship and made the basis for exhortation. While Justin does not state the number of these "Memoirs" or "Gospels," nor the names of their writers, there can hardly be a doubt that they were our four New Testament Gospels. For his references to the evangelical history and teachings abound in passages that are manifestly actual quotations, made more or less literally from them. There are about one hundred and twenty of these—some made from each of our four. Many of them, it is true, are inexact. But so also are many of those undoubtedly made from the Old Testament Scriptures. It was evidently customary those days, as is often done still, to quote writings memoriter. "In some cases, moreover, Justin's quotations from the 'Memoirs' incorporate so exactly the specific variations of Matthew and Luke from each other, that there can be no doubt that the text of those Gospels was before him." Should we, however, set aside all the evident probabilities in the case and admit the unproved and unprovable assertion that Justin drew his matter from other and lost "Gospels," we are still justified in holding his testimony, like that of the Apostolic Fathers, under similar supposition, as thoroughly assuring the authenticity of our canonical Gospels, by its wonderful corroboration of their historical and evangelical correctness. Indeed, on that admission, the evidence would rather be strengthened. For it would mean the multiplication of mutually supporting testimonies. Could it be shown that in Justin's time there were four "Memoirs" of Christ, accepted and used as "composed by apostles and their companions," though now lost, from which he drew all these quotations tallying so fully with our New Testament Gospels and sweeping through most of the great facts of Christ's life, it would surely be a most impressive evidence that these Gospels have brought down to us the original and essential truth. But we need not take this secondary conception as the true view. For, as the result of the long and exhaustive examination of the matter by historic scholarship, especially helped by recently discovered early Christian writings, it has been incontrovertibly settled that Justin's "Memoirs composed by the apostles and their companions" were the four Gospels of Matthew, Mark, Luke, and John, as incorporated, a little later, by his pupil Tatian, into the Harmony or fourfold combination called the "Diatessaron."

Another great writer, a little later, Irenaeus, bishop of Lyons, in Southern Gaul, throws a flood of light on the already plain facts. Born early in the second century, probably sometime between A. D. 115 and 125, in Asia Minor, the region "where two such eminent apostles as John and Paul had lived and labored," he had been a pupil of Polycarp. He was a man of conspicuous ability and integrity, with the best advantages for acquiring a knowledge of the condition of the churches in Asia Minor and Italy as well as in Gaul. Besides perpetual direct references and quotations in his chief work, "Against Heresies," Irenæus names the four Gospels and gives a statement of their composition. After declaring how the risen Christ had sent, and by the Holy Spirit empowered, his apostles to teach and preach, he says: "Matthew also issued a written Gospel among the Hebrews in their own dialect.... Mark, the disciple and interpreter of Peter, did also hand down to us in writing what had been preached by Peter. Luke also, the companion of Paul, recorded in a book the Gospel preached by him. Afterwards John, the disciple of the Lord, who also had leaned on His breast, did himself publish a Gospel during his residence at Ephesus in Asia." These Gospels and no others, he assures us, were acknowledged by the churches. This testimony, written about A. D. 180, and woven into the very texture of his defense of Christianity, and accompanied with incessant quotation from all parts of the New Testament, leaves no room to doubt what were the fundamental historical authorities for the belief of the Christian churches at that date already throughout the Roman empire.

Contemporaneously with Irenæus in western Europe, Theophilus, bishop of Antioch in Syria, was defending Christianity in the East where believers were first called Christians. In his brief plea for it to Autolycus, he distinctly quotes from Matthew, Luke, and John, the last by name, classing John among Spirit-bearing [inspired] men, the authors of "the holy writings which teach us."

Passing from Asia and Europe over to Africa, we have, only a few years later, the testimony of two most eminent and scholarly writers—Clement, of Alexandria, in Egypt, and Tertullian, of Carthage, both born about A. D. 160. The former quotes numerously from the New Testament Gospels and most of the Epistles. He marks these Gospels as the "four Gospels which have been handed down to us," distinguishing them from an apochryphal Gospel "according to the Egyptians," and setting forth the order in which they were written.2 The latter, in the fourth of his five books against the heretic Marcion, mentions our four Gospels by name, and inveighs against Marcion's mutilation of Luke in his heretical interest, and affirms, in an extensive showing, that in these four Gospels alone the true Gospel of Christ had been preserved "from the very beginning," "from the apostles," "as a sacred deposit in the Churches of the Apostles."

It is needless to adduce testimony from later writers. For from the close of the second century onward the historic recognition of the New Testament writings sweeps on in broadening and deepening volume. We must not, however, omit to observe how the strength and conclusiveness of the testimony from the two earliest centuries has been recently assured by new historical and archaeological discoveries. The unparalleled researches of our day have brought, not doubt, but fullest confirmation. Some of it has come through finding, in 1887, in the Convent of St Catharine, on Mount Sinai, a Syriac copy of the Apology of Aristides. The existence of this Apology in the early Church was mentioned by Eusebius and Jerome, as having been presented to the Emperor Adrian. When thus recovered, it at once threw verifying light on the conditions and life of the Church in the sub-apostolic period, especially making evident its establishment upon the fundamental facts and teaching of the records in our New Testament. Presented to the Emperor in 125, and referring him directly to "the writings" held by the Christians as authoritative for their belief and practice, this Apology of Aristides certifies the very conditions among them which are implied in Justin Martyr's Apology to Antoninus Pius about twenty-five years later. Still happier corroboration has come from the recovery of a complete copy of Tatian's long-lost "Diatessaron." This has indubitably identified the "Memoirs of the Apostles and their Companions," mentioned by Justin Martyr as read in Christian worship, with the four Gospels of the New Testament. For it is found to be a veritable compilation from all these four essentially as we have them to-day; and, as Tatian was a pupil of Justin, he cannot reasonably be imagined to have used for his composite Harmony other four accounts than those which his eminent teacher and the churches of his day accepted as the authoritative records of their faith. The effect of this obtaining of the actual text of the "Diatessaron" is thus to convert Justin's statement about the "Memoirs" into one concerning our four canonical Gospels. It has given final documentary verification. A similar result has come from the finding, in 1887, of a fragment of the apocryphal "Gospel of Peter," a very early production referred to by some of the Church Fathers. All taken together, the recovery of these ancient documents has had the effect of throwing back the sure date of the Church's universal acceptance and use of all our four Gospels, the Acts of Apostles, and nearly all the Epistles into the first half of the second century, not more than twenty or thirty years after the death of the Apostle John, and within the lifetime of many who had received the Gospel message from apostolic lips. The decisive import of this fact can be rightly estimated only when we keep in mind the relations and wide territorial extent of the phenomenon. For this acceptance is found to be no mere temporary or local thing, but a fixed, widespread fact, resting back on abundant traditional and written evidence from out the still earlier period and passing on organically into the living movement of the after time. It is a massive fact. It marks the whole Church throughout the Roman Empire with its thousands and thousands of believers, from the valleys of the Euphrates on the east to Gaul on the west, and along the African shores of the Mediterranean. Theology must take note at this point how utterly futile is the critical theory which alleges that the New Testament Gospels are made up largely of myths and legends which, forming in the interval between the death of Christ and the writing of these Gospels, took the place of the actual history and claims of Jesus, metamorphosing Him from a human into a divine being. The time is too short for such a process; and as the apostles at once, from the day of Pentecost, began the delivery of their message, "beginning at Jerusalem," and extending their personal ministry in the establishment of churches east and west, in Syria, Asia Minor, and Greece, it becomes impossible to conceive that subsequently composed Gospels, with a transformed message, could have been palmed off upon all these apostolically-taught Churches.

2. Thus far we have referred only to the literature of the post-apostolic day for the historical authority of our Gospels. But we must go back to still earlier documents. The New Testament Epistles form an integral part of the historical evidences. Their place and value require special emphasis. The post-apostolic testimonies, as we have found, distinctly recognized them along with the Acts of the Apostles, as concurrent authority for facts and truths. They are part of that great body of records in which historical Christianity rests, and their genuineness and value having been at once acknowledged after the apostles' day, they become themselves immediate witness to the original fundamental facts. No one will, indeed, claim that the very existence of Christianity as a divine revelation depends upon a positive proof of the persoual authorship of every individual letter or book included in the New Testament collection. Yet nearly all of them, as already indicated, at once vindicated themselves to the mind of the early Church as genuine apostolic productions; and ever since, through and after all the searchings of honest and even hostile criticism during the passing centuries, the Church has seen no adequate reason to reverse its original judgment giving them canonical standing. The utmost that that criticism has effected is an uncertainty as to the real authorship of a few of them, without excluding them from the position of historical authority.

The extremest of the destructive critics themselves confess the genuineness of the four great Epistles of St. Paul, the two to the

Corinthians, that to the Romans and to the Galatians. And it has often been justly remarked that even if these alone were left us, we would still have amply sufficient to prove the full acceptance by St. Paul of the facts and truths of Christ's life as given in the Gospels. But we are not at all fairly limited to such a reduced remnant. The genuineness of the great body of the Epistles as well as of the Acts of the Apostles and the Apocalypse remains secure through the fires. Taken together, and supported by the few which, even if of unknown authorship, unquestionably belong to very early date, they form an impressive combination of direct contemporary testimonies, concurrent with the accounts in our four Gospels. In incidental way mostly, they touch upon the history and teachings of Christ so constantly and variously, in clear, distinct allusions and assumptions, as to make it incontrovertible that they wrote with the same substratum of facts as to Jesus' life, character, deeds, and teaching as is given by the four evangelists. Though the Epistles were not written with historical aim, but for practical direction and encouragement of the Churches, they abound in historical references and implications. The correspondences between them and the Gospels fit the fact that one set of the apostles and their fellow-disciples were writing the "Memoirs "of Christ and another set were, at the same time, sending letters of instruction to the Churches and pleading for the true life of faith in the same Christ. Almost all the leading biographical features of the Savior reappear as we look into the Epistles, as the great shadows from the bank on the shore-line of waters appear when we gaze into the stream—the same super-naturalism along with the life that was natural, the same marks of humanity, the same signs of Divinity, the same Son of man, the same Son of God, the same fact of pre-existence, the same assurance of resumption of glory and dominion. The Epistles thus carry back the testimony of the post-apostolic period to the same Gospels which have brought the sacred records down to us. Where is the chance for the alleged process in the mythical and legendary theories, to give us, in our New Testaments, a miracle-working and Divine Christ out of an original simply human Jesus?

But beyond this common witness of the Epistles and the Acts of the Apostles, a special and unique value belongs to that of St. Paul. For, as an apostle, he sustained a peculiar and exceptional relation. He had been superadded to the list of the original apostles. The relation of the original company, as seems to have been demanded for their appointed service, made them attendant beholders and hearers of Christ's life and ministry, on to the close in His death, resurrection, and ascension. But St. Paul stood apart from them in the mode of his call to the apostleship and the way in which he became acquainted with Christ and the Gospel. He had not been a witness of Christ and His humiliation. He dis-distinctly and emphatically declares that he received the Gospel, not from man or through man, but directly, "through revelation of Jesus Christ," the ascended, glorified, enthroned Christ. What he preached and wrote was not "after man," something evolved out of his own thought or framed from his imagination, but as his affirmation necessarily means, supernaturally communicated to him by the glorified Christ Himself. He declares, further, that the truth was made known to him through the Holy Ghost. It cannot be fairly maintained that St. Paul did not, in his intercourse with those who were apostles before him, hear them narrate much of Christ's life and teaching. But he was not dependent on this. He had other and supernatural source for the essentials of his knowledge and convictions. His Gospel was given him in direct communications from the exalted Savior and His Spirit. This makes his testimony that of a distinct and independent witness, with whatever of unique force it may and should have from the fact of its being a direct divine attestation of the same Gospel which comes to us in the canonical Gospels of the New Testament.

But St. Paul's peculiar relation carries his witness to still greater cogency. For it reaches to the part of the Savior's existence and saving activity which began after He had passed beyond the sight of the twelve. The revelation or communications directly given by Christ to these twelve, on which they based their preaching and writing, covered the term of His earthly life and limitations, closing with the ascension, and assurances of a continued invisible presence and help. But the Gospel of redemption and salvation through the earthly manifestation and work of the Son of God implies also an enthronement of Christ, a redemptive administration with all power in heaven and earth, as Head over all things to the Church. The proper sequel to His earthly work is

His heavenly dominion and the carrying of the redemptive purpose into accomplishment. During His humiliation and state of self-limitation, He declared that He had 'many things to say to His disciples which He could not say yet.' It was an implied assurance that after His departure He would "say" some things to them, inform them of the significance of His death and resurrection, give an authoritative interpretation of what He had done. It was an intimation that He would not close the term of His direct supernatural revelation until He had fully endowed the circle of apostles with the facts and truths necessary for their peculiar vocation of preaching and recording, for the ages, the whole Gospel of forgiveness and life. But it is the distinction of St. Paul that he was called to the apostleship through a wonderful and impressive post-ascension Christophany, and that thus his entire apostolic witness, in all its proclamation of the truth as immediately and supernaturally "revealed" to him, has been made a special testimony at once to the Gospel of Christ incarnate and crucified and the Gospel of an ever-living, glorified, transcendent Christ, reigning as one with the Father, in the everlasting kingdom of God. It would have been a distinct loss to the Church had there been, after Jesus' disappearance from the disciples, nevermore a word from Him, never again a single putting of Himself in certifiable and assured communication from beyond the veil of invisible existence. If it formed, as it surely did, a part of God's providential care that the portion of the Savior's work in His state of humiliation should be attested by apostolic witnesses, may it not be a part of the same providence that the call and endowment of the one great apostle added after the ascension should make him, in a peculiar and eminent sense, the representative apostle of the glorified Savior? His unique position makes his apostleship, carrying the supernaturally communicated message, the crowning testimony to the complete Gospel. Most inadmissible is the plea that theology should "go back to Christ," if by this is meant that we shall in any wise set aside the historical and didactic authority of the genuine Epistles of this great apostle.

3. The historical trustworthiness of these New Testament writings, thus thoroughly accredited to their authors, is commended by the situation of the writers. They stood in closest possible relation to

the things of which they testify. They were eye-witnesses and ear-witnesses, or only a single degree removed from such personal relation. Through the whole of Christ's personal ministry, the twelve were His attendants, seeing and hearing, having opportunities for most intimate observation. They were in the closeness of pupils to their Teacher, watching His ways, entering into His experiences, treasuring up His sayings, filling their memories with His life. They were, as all the accounts imply, men of positive personality, by no means over-credulous, but rather slow of conviction, yet desirous of finding the truth without mistake, serious, sober-minded, honest men. Of the second and third Gospels, the authors, though one degree removed from this position, were recipients and recorders of the facts and doctrines as these were communicated from the lips of those who had them at first hand. The Epistles of disputed authorship verify their authenticity by their internal essential unity with the undoubted apostolic writings. It is almost impossible to conceive of reporters or historians in better relation to the facts they narrate.

And when the time of this close association had passed, after the period of early questioning and doubt, of growing conviction, of listening to truths such as had never been spoken before, of beholding signs and wonders of kindness and power, after the shock and bewilderment of the crucifixion, the mysteries of the resurrection and ascension—after the three years of this relation and experience were ended and lay behind them, these apostles felt constrained, in the face of obloquy, persecution, and death, to bear testimony to the things they had seen and heard, the unique wonders of Christ's life of teaching, miracles, goodness, and saving power. They did not count their lives dear to themselves, but were ready to suffer the loss of all things in finishing their appointed course of testifying to the Gospel of the grace of God. No supposed earthly advantage, adequate to explain that course, is conceivable. They could have had no sufficient reason, impelling their heroic courage and self-sacrifice in persisting in proclaiming the Gospel, or even in preaching it at all, apart from their sense of obligation to the truth, and their spiritual interests as involved in that truth. In the case of St. Paul, after the arresting Christophany of the glorified "Jesus of Nazareth" whom he had been persecuting, and the revelation of the Gospel to him, a complete moral and spiritual transformation of life took place. The bitter persecutor became the most self-sacrificing disciple and most heroic witness and missionary. The very phenomenon of his conversion and his long after-life of steady, unfaltering apostolic ministry through opposition, perils, persecutions, accepting the martyr's death at last, is one that defies reasonable solution except on the ground of his own assured certainty of the truth of the Gospel thus made known to him, and the sincerity, strength, and commanding power of his fidelity to the truth as he knew it. Witnesses of such high moral integrity, with no conceivable adequate motive for falsifying, speaking out of their direct knowledge, are surely entitled to be believed when they testify to facts.

The dates of the New Testament writings necessarily become elements in the situation of the writers. The effort of hostile criticism to use this against the reliability of their statements, utterly fails under the plain facts of the case. Two points make this sufficiently clear. First, that from the close of Christ's ministry to the date of the writings, the interval lies well within the safe command of the historical recollection. Second, that in an extraordinary degree, in this case, the recollection was kept alive and certain by the constant employment of the apostles in proclaiming the Gospel, from immediately after the ascension, on continuously in their missionary labors of founding and instructing the Churches. Besides, it is surely fair to take account of written notes or memoranda, probably made and used among them in their preaching, and to recall the greater efficiency of "tradition" or oral repetition of facts and teaching in that period when, before the art of printing, the traditional method was in such popular use. The wonderful events in the history of Christ and the impressive precepts of His teaching had entered deeply into their minds, and their continual rehearsal of them in their missionary labors necessarily carried them into fixed familiarity. They built the life and teachings of Christ into themselves as they built up congregations upon them. The conclusions of the fullest investigation place the dates of the New Testament books within the period extending from A. D. 50 to 95, nearly all of them in the earlier part of this period, when the writers were in the midst of their apostolic preaching. And the trustworthiness of their direct and living grasp of the historical and doctrinal materials is strongly sustained by the fact that all along the lines on which the Gospels touch each other, or the rest of the writings touch the Gospels and one another, through immensely diversified settings and order of statement, there is an impressive agreement among all the writers as to the essential facts and teachings. At whatever date or place they wrote, from first to last, underlying the writing is found substantially one and the same Gospel in all the Gospels and Epistles, completely negativing the idea of either a gradual forgetfulness of the original truths or a metamorphosis by unhistorical changes or accretions in the course of time.

4. For, in indissoluble connection with this closeness and self-sacrificing conscientiousness of the apostolic witness, stands the acceptance of it as given in the New Testament accounts by the Churches founded and taught by the apostles. According to the evidence already given, these accounts are found referred to as authoritative for the Christian history and truth in the Churches in all parts of the Roman Empire, in the early part of the second century, shortly after the death of the apostles. These Churches had been gathered and instructed by the different apostles and their associates in missionary labor. They were familiar with the story of Christ and of His work. Their faith rested on it, and it had been incorporated into their very life. They had been grounded and confirmed in it by its original witnesses. Only, therefore, as accordant with the original history and teaching could the Gospels, Epistles, and other offered writings be received or installed in position of authority. And we must remember the combinations of concurrent testimonies which the reception, so accorded to these writings, thus implied. It meant not only an agreement of the written Gospels with the Gospel preached by the apostles, of the Epistles with the evangelical histories, of the Churches of one country with those in another, but, most strikingly, the substantial sameness of the truth of Christ as lodged by the preaching of the different apostles in the mind of the Church with the epistolary communications of other apostles. For the Epistles, so received, came not only from the hand of the apostle who had given the oral teaching. The correspondence crossed the lines of personal ministry. Skeptical criticism has sought to find a naturalistic perversion or obscuration of

the simple Gospel of Jesus through a compromise of divergent Gospels by Peter and Paul. But the Petrine and Pauline types can be magnified so as to create doubt only by ignoring the force of the facts here in view. A certain evidential value belongs to St. Paul's Epistle to the Corinthians as written to his own "children in the Gospel."2 But there is added significance when St. Peter writes to the Churches of Asia Minor, founded and taught by St. Paul and his helpers, and the Epistle is at once unqualifiedly received, and is found, while exhibiting distinctly Peter's manner of presentation, to set forth essentially the same doctrine as is given in the Epistles of Paul. Of like import is it that St. Paul's Epistle to the Romans, written before he had seen them, was received as supporting the same Gospel as they already believed, though the Church there had not been established by any of the apostles, but through carriage to the capital city by converts from other places. The total fact of this acceptance of these Gospel histories and the Epistles, therefore, exhibits, in peculiarly massive force, the essential historical agreement reached at the end of the apostolical period, viz: the agreement of the end with the beginning, of the different apostles with one another, of their written testimonies with their oral witness, and of the Churches with each other throughout their wide territorial extension. We have an almost unparalleled coherence and strength of confirmation.

5. The thorough reliability of the accounts which have come to us is sustained, further, by a verified and assuring exactness of these accounts in all matters archeological, geographical, biographical, or personal, alluded to or implied. These allusions are frequent and almost numberless. They appear mostly in incidental ways. They relate often to things quite local, sometimes to things of wide-reaching interest. The trustworthy historian, the truthful writer, is always revealed in connection with these things. The situation in Judea at that time was much in the eye of the world. Changes were going on rapidly. The religious movement was making its way in constant contact with both Jewish and Roman life peculiarities. The situation was dangerous ground for the inventor of a story, or a writer of inadequate information or without steady regard for truth. The authors of our New Testament books, tracing, amidst such changeful and complex

conditions, the ongoing course of events recorded in their histories, or giving epistolary instruction and guidance to the Christian communities, all involving continuously so many relations of place, time, customs, laws, and local circumstances, were necessarily subjected to a most severe test as to the correctness of their knowledge and careful fidelity to it. Most wonderfully have their writings vindicated them in both these respects. With an unusually large historical apparatus for the detection of mistake or the discovery of fraud, criticism has not convicted them of any positive error in these collateral or circumstantial references. Their exactness is sometimes remarkable, as in St. Luke's designation of Sergius Paulus as proconsul, though this was long assumed to be a mistake till Greek history was found to verify it;2 or his terming the magistrates of Philippi who were attended by lictors στρατηγοί, while he designates those of Thessalonica πολιτάρχαι, a distinction based upon a somewhat obscure and remote difference in their relation to the Roman government;5 or, still further, as his implication of two "taxings," or enrollments, made under Cyrenius (Quirinus), which has received verification only in recent times through the findings of scholarly research.7 Estimated merely in the character of human writings, the literature of the world furnishes no historical authorities better accredited, in this respect, than the historical books and the Epistles of our New Testament Scriptures.
6. The testimony of Pagan and Jewish writers, though small in amount, is of large historical weight. Coming from adversaries, who, in their distant and hostile attitude, utterly failed to understand the reality and spirit of Christianity, this is found only in forms of incidental and constrained allusion. The witness does not go into the minutia, but so far as it goes, it recognizes the same origin of Christianity as its own writers declare, and gives evidence of the spread of the faith and the sufferings and heroic fidelity of its adherents. The chief value of it is that it comes from a source that cannot be suspected of complicity.

Here falls into place the great Roman historian, Tacitus. Writing about A. D. 100, and narrating the burning of Rome and Nero's desperate effort to relieve himself from the odium of firing the city, by imputing it to the Christians and enacting a horrible persecution of them, Tacitus makes record of quite a number of facts as to the rise and progress of Christianity, mentioning the source of the designation "Christians," in the name of their leader, "Christus," the crucifixion of Christ by Pontius Pilate in the reign of Tiberius, the spread of the religion in Judea despite the ignominious death of its founder and the opposition met by its followers, and its propagation to other parts of the world, even to Rome, where already in Nero's time Christians had become very numerous, "a vast multitude," who, in this persecution were pursued with such exquisite cruelties and awful tortures as to awaken commiseration even in the heathen mind, and lead to the impression that they were not so punished out of regard to the public welfare, but to gratify the imperial cruelty.

We lay no stress on the passage sometimes quoted from Juvenal and Marital3, contemporaries with Tacitus, except as probably reflecting the fearful forms of punishment in the Neronian persecution, and thus becoming witnesses to the sufferings and courage of the Christians. Equally small emphasis need be laid on the records made by Suetonius, of the banishment of the Jews, under leadership of Christus, by Claudius, the punishment of Christians by Nero, and the destruction of Jerusalem by Titus.

But in the celebrated letter of Caius Pliny, Governor of Pontus and Bithynia, A. D., 107, we have an indisputable, prominent public pagan record, left for all ages, which, like that of Tacitus, clearly, as far as it extends, identifies the Christian facts, principles, doctrine, worship, and spirit with those presented in the New Testament Scriptures.

These notices, though few and remote, afford us as much as could be expected, considering the unfriendly and averted attitude of the pagan mind. They fit the situation and are quite enough for the needed historical certification. And they are followed by a rapidly enlarging number of references, as advancing Christianity developed further and broader contacts with pagan life and power. These bring us to the reports of long-continued bloody persecutions, and the published assaults of Celsus, Porphyry, and the Emperor Julian, who conducted their attacks on Christianity, not by rejection of its records, but as appealing to them and quoting them.

Of Jewish writing of that day, but little has come down to us. But of the one great author left us, Josephus, allowing the passage speaking directly of Christ to be spurious, his "Wars of the Jews" is history's great record of the fulfillment of Christ's fore-announcement of the destruction of Jerusalem, and in the Mishna of Jewish traditions, reduced to writing about A. D. 190, there are distant, but well assured allusions to the same event, and they suggest no contradictory origin for Christianity.

7. All these testimonies, with the religion whose origin they unfold and attest, are organically joined with the long centuries of precedent history and with the ages of history ever since. They interlock with the records both before and after. They present but a link in a movement that stretched from the earlier time, reaching down to our day. This is a feature of the historical evidences of the highest moment. The self-revelation of God in Jesus Christ was not a sudden isolated thing. It is indisputably and confessedly the outcome of a clear and marked development which, in the Old Testament discipline with the posterity of Abraham, had for thousands of years been promising a divine redemption, and drawing a most significant and deep line of movement and historic record through the world's preceding history. The movement made its own track inerasable forever, verified and vindicated to-day by still newly-found monuments of its progress and touch on the lands and nations along the way. It is but reasonable to believe, upon any fair theistic conception of the world, that the great ruling purposes of God would mark themselves in the leading, prolonged trends or lines of human history. Things deep in the design of God must hold their way through all human changes. We justly apply the principle here. The establishment of Christianity was nothing detached, alone, or sporadic, but the completion of long centuries of unmistakable Providence. The New Testament records are buttressed by the whole history of the covenant Hebrew people, and our Biblical Scriptures form an organism of divine as well as human witness to redemption.

Thus as to the linking of the Gospel history into firm antecedent history. The integration into that which has been made and written since suggests the magnitude and immovable strength of the aggregate historical testimony to Christianity. For, passing on from the last writers whom we have quoted or referred to, Christianity has been making history in the face of all the world, and making it a synonym of the world's best life and progress. Some special points are to be noted here. (a) That the evidence of a real revelation of God in Jesus Christ was such that, immediately and right on the spot, men, by the thousands, were constrained to believe, who, under ineradicable conviction of the truth of this revelation and their sense of obligation to it, as well as of their spiritual interests in it, confessed their faith, and maintained it in the face of opposition and danger, and at the sacrifice of worldly advantage and comfort. Their faith entered into their lives as a spiritual regeneration, the power of a new, pure, strong life of unselfish love and good works. They were ready to do or die for the Saviour, in whom they had found Israel's promised divine Messiah, the forgiveness of sin, conscious fellowship with God, and assurance of immortal life. (b) The Church also, as the fellowship of the faith, taking organization under the apostolic preaching and writing, has brought down continuously, not only its own existence, but that of the two permanent sacramental rites and the observance of the Lord's day, as perpetual witnesses to the historic events out of which they rose. These sacraments and this observance are historic facts whose origin is based in events found in the Gospel records, but which, apart from the real historicity of these events, is utterly unaccountable. Something impressively real, in each case, must explain the starting of these rites or observances. Could our Fourth of July celebration have become a national order without the Declaration of Independence? Could these rites have started without any such facts or warrant as the apostles have laid at the basis of their establishment? Or could the apostles, considering their heroic sincerity and fidelity, have fraudulently established them as devices of their own while writing as they did to the Churches? And if these ordinances stand truly based as they are represented—as seems the only credible explanation—do they not carry us into some of the realities which form central features of the divine, supernatural redemption, the atoning death and the victorious resurrection of the Son of God and the Son of man as the Church has always held?

These and collateral historical evidences lie at the basis of all the Christian evidences. Christianity is the greatest phenomenon of history—its unfolding preparations of Old Testament record, its complete constitution and full founding giving new date for the centuries, its progress and influence producing the earth's highest civilizations. Its accredited records show where, when, and how it came to exist, with endowment to work its exhibited results. Looked at in the light of the claims of these records, it has been established through a historic supernatural self-revelation of God, providing for man salvation from sin and purifying power for the holy character and immortality for which his creation designed him. Admitting this claim, the great phenomenon is solved. Denying it, no reasonable solution appears possible. Admission of the claim involves, indeed, the reception of some mysteries; yet, no more mysteries and fewer seeming impossibilities than connect themselves with rejection. Mysteries are inseparable from the limitations of human understanding, and are thickstrewn even through nature. But the point to be here observed is that, plainly, this historical evidence is properly the primary and basal evidence, to whose conclusions all other forms of evidence are contributory and confirmatory. In these other forms the historical claim, as made at the beginning and interpreted by Christendom, finds rich and abundant verification. At the chief forms of these we must glance.

Evidence from Miracles

The long strife on the subject of miracles has cleared the conception of their nature and evidential relations. Most of the difficulties brought to view in the discussion have been found to arise from false notions as to what a miracle really is and how it is related to the gift of a revelation. To this source, as has become plain, is due not only the oft-asserted impossibility of a miracle, but its severe strain upon faith even when conceded to be abstractly possible, and the consequent disposition on the part of some Christian apologists to abate from its evidential value. The clearing of the conception of it, under exact definitions, and with correct showing of its essential place in redemptory divine self-disclosure, has resulted in fixing it, not indeed exactly in its old position, but in one more vitally organic in the revelatory process, and of equal but different evidential worth.

Milton Valentine

There can be no doubt that the Biblical histories associate miracles with the progress of revelation. There are records of them in the Old Testament and in the New. They are woven into the accounts as essential parts of revelation itself or as normal accessories. They are integrated in the person and work of Christ. They continued, in a measure, in the ministry of the apostles.

For our purpose of explaining their occurrence and their bearing as evidence we may confine our reference particularly to the miracles of Christ. For the Christian view of supernatural revelation centers it in Him in His mediatorial and redemptory manifestation. The miracles before Christ were tokens of His preadvent mediatorial revelation, blossoms of the "fullness of time." Those afterward were signs of His continued invisible presence and power, working, for exigent reasons for a season, through His chosen agents. No fair treatment of the New Testament narratives can eliminate the miraculous element. This is the conclusion, summing up the verdict of German historical criticism. "Whatever view men may take nowadays of the miracles attributed to Christ, three things are practically certain: that the people among whom He lived believed that He wrought them; that this belief was a chief element in attracting men to Him as their Master, and confirming their faith in His divine mission; and that Jesus Himself meant and taught them so to believe."[2] Prof. Seeley well wrote: "The fact that Christ appeared as a miracle-worker is the best attested fact in His whole biography." The apostolic reporters of them were competent witnesses, of sober, conscientious mind, affirming not from hearsay, but from personal knowledge, assured by three years of close observation. With respect to the critical suggestion, that these witnesses, as only observers, reporting the phenomena simply as seen and representing them as divine tokens, thus transcended the reach of external observation with an interpretation of the cause which was beyond sight, and in which they may have been mistaken, it is enough to remind ourselves that they were sustained in their interpretation by Christ Himself, who, as the worker of the miracles, was consciously cognizant of their cause or the source of the power operative in them, and who, at the same time, claimed to be working them as God's clear witness to His Messiahship and divine mission. The miraculous basis of

Christianity is asserted all through the apostolic writings. Whatever may be thought of Schleiermacher's concession that a belief in miracles is not directly involved in the faith of a Christian, he was certainly right in regarding a denial of them as destructive, because of its blightening effect in overthrowing confidence in the reliability of the apostolic account of Christ.2

The chief aspects of the function of the miracle become plain through a glance at the following points:

I. DEFINITION. The New Testament designates them as "signs" (σημεῖα), "wonders" (τέρατα), "powers," or "acts of power" (δυνάμεις). But these designations do not give a definition. They present only certain aspects or uses of the phenomena. A miracle may, in general, be said to be an unusual event in physical nature wrought by direct action of God working for a moral end. More specifically, it is defined as "an event in the physical world wrought by God independently of the sequences through which He ordinarily works" It is the production, by the exercise of divine power, of a definite effect which could not otherwise take place.

Analysis of this definition discloses its included elemental conceptions.

(a) It is based on the theistic conception of the world. It views the universe as the work of God, who is a personal Being of infinite power, creating and sustaining it in rational and worthy purpose. And it declines to conceive of His power and efficiency as all transferred into the forces and laws of nature or as restricted to its established uniformities. We must avoid, as the Scriptures require and the best philosophy demands, both a pantheistic confounding of God with nature and a deistic separation of Him from it. Nature does not move on as an independent or inflexible mechanism. While God is above it as its Creator, He is also immanent in its forces and order, which depend and move in and on His abiding omnific Will. His free but permanent Will is the reason and source of all forces and their order. God and nature do not stand to each other in merely external relation, but He is in ever-living communication with it. "He upholds all things by the word of His power." "He is above all and through all and in all." "In Him we live and move and have our being."

(b) The definition assumes the reality of the distinction already made between nature and the supernatural. Much of the difficulty in the case comes from obscuring or refusing this clear and fundamental distinction. But just as soon as it is clearly seen and distinctly remembered that physical nature, with its divinely fixed uniformities, exists for an end beyond its own being and motion, viz.: as the presupposition and basis of a divine free moral administration for the life, welfare, and destiny of mankind, the difficulty ceases. For, at once, in connection with the further fact of humanity's lapse into sin, there opens to view both room and need of the whole supernatural providence of redemptive provision and help, in connection with which alone the miracles are declared to have been wrought.

(c) It implies for miracles no "violation "or "suspension" of the laws of nature. Definitions have often been given which involved such a conception of them. Hume and others have endeavored in this way to put them beyond the range of rational belief. But they imply no such antagonism to nature, and are not to be thought of as clashing with its proper order. They are due to a special and direct exertion of the divine will-power, without annulling any natural force or its sequences of cause and effect. God inserts His direct power for its own effect; and the natural forces admit the effect without either annihilation or interruption. The reality may be fairly illustrated in the operation of the human will-power. When this, through science and skill, inserts its directive touch in nature's ongoings, and turns water or electricity into driving forces for industry or commerce, or shapes the transparent glass into lenses for bringing the distant stars into view, no law of nature is violated or suspended. The result is accomplished by a special free causation—the free causation conforming its directive power to nature's laws, yet transcending them—for the special effect. When this free human power lifts a hand or casts a stone into the air, the law of gravitation is not infringed—every particle of matter in hand or stone still gravitating as before. The weight that is felt in lifting the stone or holding up the outstretched arm at once measures the continued gravitation and becomes proof that it does not surrender its rights while free-will causation seems to violate them or interrupt their action. When the sons of the prophets cut down a stick and cast it into the water and the ax-head swam (2 Kings 6:6), neither the specific gravities of the water or iron were altered, nor was the law of gravitation suspended.

(d) This conception of miracles at once answers all allegations of their impossibility. Such allegations have been made to rest mostly on a supposed contradiction of miracles to the scientific principles of cause and effect and the consequent reign of the law of uniformity in nature—sometimes viewed as an a priori presupposition of science, though generally held rather as a conclusion inductively established by it. This law of continuity has sometimes been interpreted as constituting the physical universe in a balance of forces and necessitated movement that allows no break or disturbance whatever. How this continuity of ongoing forces in the universe is conceived of is illustrated in Fichte's well-known supposition about the sand-grain on a seashore: "Let us imagine this grain of sand lying some few feet further inland than it actually does. Then must the storm wind that drove it in from the seashore have been stronger than it actually was. Then must the preceding state of the atmosphere by which this wind was determined have been different from what it actually was, and the previous changes which gave rise to this particular weather," etc.2 And Fichte goes on to picture the disasters which such a range of antecedents different from the actual ones might have involved, all "in order that a grain of sand might lie in a different place." The overdrawn illustration suggests the Buddhist philosophy which identifies every human act, as well as every physical event, as the unescapable effect of all precedent causation operating in unbroken line. Rhys-Davids puts it thus: "The history of an individual does not begin with his birth, but has been endless years in making; and he can never sever himself from his surroundings, no, not for an hour. The tiniest snowdrop droops its fairy head just so much and no more, because it is balanced by the universe. It is a snowdrop, not an oak, because it is the outcome of a Karma of an endless series of past existences, and because it did not begin to be when the flower opened, or when the mother plant first peeped above the ground or first met the embrace of the sun, or when the bulb began to shoot above the sod, or at any time which you or I can fix."2 With respect to this conception of man and nature, offered by the atheistic philosophy of Buddhism, with its dismal fatalism, it is enough to say that it stands utterly apart from the Biblical and theistic conception of the world. It knows of no personal God for self-revelation. With regard to the force of Fichte's illustration, implying a materialistic fatalism almost equal to the Buddhistic, it is sufficient to remind ourselves how entirely the difficulties suggested disappear, if we simply think of the sand-grain, not as carried by the storm or wave, but as thrown by the hand of human freedom those few feet farther inland. In this case, what becomes of the imagined necessity of all those different physical antecedents, or the destructive consequences of their removal? This conception of nature is constructed, not by science, but by fancy, when it is represented as moving in such close-linked sequences as to exclude free causation from effecting alterations. As a matter of fact, assured by universal experience, nature's system, though under the "reign of law," openly shows a flexibility or elasticity in which it becomes delicately susceptible to even human will-power, submitting itself marvelously to the dominion and uses of man. Human free-will is all the time laying hold of matter and force, inserting its efficiency into the midst of nature's ongoings and working thousands and millions of effects which nature, left to itself, could never work. Nature makes no watches, builds no steam engines, constructs no telegraphs, tunnels no mountains. But truly understood, it is so plastic and yielding to intelligent will as not only to suffer a sand-grain to be moved without ages of linear physical causation, and without consequent disorder, but to permit human freedom to mass together the weight of cities, change the face of continents, harness steam for the transportation of commerce, and make electricity an obedient servant to bear our messages around the world. In constructing the physical world in this combined invariable uniformity of its own forces and this plastic susceptibility to volitional force, God not only adapted it as a proper dwelling-place of man for his use and the exercise of his free activity, but at the same time provided room for the display of miraculous powers—one and the same system of nature, open in limited measure to the action of the human will, open without limit to the Infinite Will. Used within the human limit we do not call the result a "miracle," because it is simply a human affair, made possible in the natural constitution, yet a "sign" of man's "dominion." Used by God it is superhuman, divine, a witness to His truly supernatural presence and power. The point certified and illustrated in these facts is the facile and thorough openness of nature's system to action of free willpower. If so to the human will, then certainly to the Almighty Will.

2. THE PLACE OF MIRACLES. This is rightly seen only in the light of the teleological principle. God has a supreme purpose in the world, in connection with the moral life, welfare, happiness, and destiny of mankind; and miracles manifestly have their place in the soteriological redemptive economy, with which alone the Scriptures associate them. They are no part of the natural system with which science deals, and belong not to any necessity for the order or completion of the physical cosmos; hence no objection can be raised against them as derogatory to God in implying such a failure in His creative wisdom and power as to require the help or correction of after-intervention. It is only when we recall the great truth that through the aggregate natural world God is aiming at a moral product in the free life of man, and further, that there is such a thing as sin, which has disturbed the true life, order and happiness of humanity and created a need of God's coming forth for relief and help, that we see the true position and import of miraculous action. It is part of the supernatural administration, in which, without destroying the natural system established in creation, God, in His freedom, adds a remedial system to meet the condition brought in by human freedom, and to conduct the world onward to its true design.

And it has place only in creating and inaugurating the supernatural remedial administration. The truth in the case requires us to distinguish miracles as only a limited and temporary part or feature of the supernatural system. They were necessities for its initiation and establishment. They all center, as already said, in Christ, bringing, introducing, and setting up redemptory provisions and conditions, whose work was marked necessarily by "powers," "wonders," and "signs." Those of the Old Testament were the preadvent steps of the supernatural preparation of His coming. Special periods in that preparatory economy were particularly marked with them. In the Mosaic period, when the authority and supremacy of Jehovah needed assertion and display, and again in the days of Elijah and Elisha, when the truth of monotheism required vindication against the encroachments of idolatry, they appear in striking prominence. Those of Christ were the appropriate manifestation of His supernatural person. Those of the apostles were from the same source. Around the person and ministry of Jesus Christ, the eternal Word made flesh as the Savior of men, the full presence and action of miraculous power culminated and accomplished its work. When the complete provisions of redemption were wrought out and the new kingdom of grace was certified by miraculous activities, the miracle, as a special extraordinary event, ceased and disappeared in the regularly constituted supernatural action of grace through the word of the Gospel under the power of the Holy Spirit. The miracle is never to be considered something isolated, apart from this supreme, divine purpose with respect to humanity.

3. THEIR CREDIBILITY. The abstract possibility of miracles being conceded, the question of their credibility stands in new light. It becomes simply a question whether any adequate reasons appear for God's working them. They cannot be understood in vacuo, void of all relations to a rational, worthy purpose, or as idle or useless exhibition of divine power. This is one of the emphatic points which Origen made concerning the heathen prodigies or marvels which Celsus sought to set in opposition to the Christian miracles—that those fabled wonders or exploits of sorcerers were of no use, had no serviceable aim or power for human welfare, no such force for the establishment of beneficent institutions for the moral benediction of the race, as would show them to be part of the counsel of Heaven; whereas the mighty works of Christ showed an aim and actual benediction worthy of God. We may well regard as incredible and unworthy of belief the thaumaturgic deeds of men, wrought for applause or gain, often immoral, always manifestly apart from any living connection with God's moral purposes in the world. They could have no claim on our faith. Reverence for God requires repudiation of the vain trifling. But the miracles of Christ belong to the grandest conceivable moral purpose, a purpose meeting the greatest and most deeply felt need of the human soul, and showing itself efficient for the true life and highest interests of mankind.

They look to the end for which even the whole physical system has been constructed and preserved. Nature is teleologically ordered, in ascending grades, to that which is designed to stand as highest. Matter is for spirit. The material world is not for itself, but for the life and immortality of the race made in the "divine image," the heavenly Father's children, meant for likeness of character with Him, high in spiritual excellence and happiness. The supreme moral aim of the world, in connection with whose realization, despite even the human lapse into sin, miracles are presented as finding their only place, is already incorporated and certified in the teleology of the physical constitution itself. The likelihood of a miracle, or a series of miracles, can never be fairly estimated if shut off and held apart from the whole moral aim and adjustment of the world. For it is not for the rectification of physical nature, but for introducing means of rectification of man's perverted views of God and his ways of sin and misery—rectification in the realm of moral and spiritual life, the supreme realm to which the cosmic constitution as well as God's providential purpose looks. The same degree of credibility must attach to miracles as attaches to the idea of the superiority of moral order and spiritual good over the mere mechanism of nature. If there is no invincible improbability that God as Holy Love should give to man needful information as to his duties and the conditions of his welfare, beyond that which may be gathered by reason; and, further, should make known a way of forgiveness of sin and redemption from its bondage and misery, concerning which nature is silent, there can surely be no insuperable improbability of supernatural revelation. History and ethnology unquestionably show that men, outside the circle of special revelation, have striven for more light as to human duty and destiny and salvation from the woes of moral evil. But such special supernatural revelation is itself intrinsically miraculous. The alleged incredibility of miracles, therefore, entirely disappears, in this true, broader view of the question, taking in the facts as a whole. The proper proof of them is simply adequate testimony. Hume's argument, that no amount of testimony could prove them, is now universally recognized as shallow and sophistical.

4. THE PROOF OF MIRACLES. The supposed impossibility of miracles having disappeared in the light of correct definition and a

deeper view of the open receptivity of nature to special causation by Will Power, both human and divine, and their credibility made clear by the manifest and almost infinite moral reason for them in the human need of a divine redemption and help, the proof of them plainly depends upon, while it requires, adequate testimony. Like the whole supernatural economy in connection with whose establishment they are reported, they may be duly certified to rational faith. The evidence which attests them is of one piece with that historical testimony which assures the aggregate facts in which Christianity has been founded. They are interwoven with the very warp and woof of the history of redemption. As divine "powers," "wonders," and "signs," they blend with the revelation idea that runs in transparent clearness through it all. The Biblical history is found, in fact, to yield to no history in the world in the clearness and accuracy of its statements. Investigation in the archaeology of the long-buried past is still continually coming upon memorial evidences of the veracity of its records.

No historico-critical endeavor has been able to impeach the credibility of the testimonies to the miracles without discrediting the entire history of which they form an integral part. The testimonies were given with a calmness and conscientiousness that remained unshaken in the face of suffering, persecution and death. If such testimony is worth nothing, no testimony on earth is of valid force for facts, and any human witness may arbitrarily be set aside. To the alleged incompetence of mere spectators to assure the invisible cause of the phenomena, we must remember Christ's own testimony from His immediate knowledge. Similarly, in case of the apostolic miracles, it is the worker of them who reports them, not as human deeds, but as wrought by the divine power of Christ. To reject Christ's testimony, and that of the apostles in this relation, amounts to the absurd allegation that both He and they were impostors carrying on a scheme of deception. This charge would be valid against Christ even if He, knowing His disciples to be crediting His mighty deeds to "the finger of God," had simply allowed them to remain under a delusion. Moreover, the objection that as witnesses they, in their unscientific age, were uncritical and disposed toward the marvelous, and therefore easily mistook appearances for reality or reported false perceptions, or misinterpreted phenomena for miracles of God, has but little force, if we remember two things, viz: First, that they were, in fact, ready to accept miracles at all only as they were to accept the reasonable truth that God is present in supreme power in the world, and at hand with the help for His people which the great moral emergency required, and which they warrantably believed had been promised. Secondly, the phenomena, in large part at least, were of such a kind as to stand clearly above the reach of human ability. They were forced to locate them in superhuman power. And with what judgment and justice they placed them there becomes evident in that through all the progress of science revealing the laws and possibilities of nature, and the ability of the human intelligence to effect wonderful phenomena, those miracles have not to this day been brought within the sphere of natural or human working. The advance of science, with its marvelous achievements, instead of reducing Christ's miracles to natural or human products, tends to confirm their supernatural character. For, as science goes on toward an entire and exhaustive disclosure of nature's laws and possibilities without revealing the secret of Christ's miracles in natural force and opening them to human repetition at will, it lessens the likelihood that it will ever be able to do so.

But the full strength of the proof is seen only when the miraculous history is taken all together and viewed in its unity. It is not a question of the proof of this miracle, or that miracle, or some other, isolated and considered in itself, but of the whole supernatural redemptive providence and working which have established and endowed Christianity with its saving power. Adverse criticism has been wont to take advantage of an unfair way of calling out the Christian miracles separately, for single assault, or broken apart from the great age-long revelatory movement for human salvation. It has become abundantly evident that it is impossible to repudiate the miracles as false perceptions, misinterpreted natural phenomena, merely human marvels, or myths or legends manufactured by the religious temper of those far-away times, and still hold to the generic supernaturalism and redemptory character of Christianity, including the divine call of Israel, the gift of the Law, the institution of a typical worship, the inspiration of prophecy, the incarnation of the Son of God, the aggregate "wonder" of His life and teaching, the crowning miracles of the resurrection and ascension, and the living Christ of history since. The subordinate supernaturalism of the miracle-records is so integral a part of the whole redemptory revelation and provision that they inevitably stand or fall together. To repudiate the reality of incidental miraculous phenomena logically carries with it a repudiation of the entire supernaturalism of Christianity, as is constantly illustrated in the case of deniers of the Gospel miracles. But as long as Bible Christianity stands, belief in miracles must form part of the Christian faith. And the point to be particularly observed is that the strength of the proof justifying this faith is seen only in the clear and thorough transcendence of the structural contents of Christianity taken as a great whole, so that without miraculous action of divine power its establishment is unaccountable and its doctrinal content is lost. The proof of a miraculous founding of Christianity is Christianity itself, grounded in its fundamental miracle of the incarnation, "God manifest in the flesh," the miracle of miracles and the explanation of all others. Christ appeared as a supernatural Person in whom the natural continuity of human sin was superseded by a moral perfection that knew no sin, a teaching superhuman in its reach and divine in its adaptations, offering effectual sacrifice and propitiation on the cross, crowned with the sealing miracle of resurrection from the dead, the divine ascension and enthronement in a kingdom which is not of this world but whose extension carries regenerating power to humanity's moral and spiritual life wherever its light and power are accepted. All this beneficent reality, all this grand phenomenon through the centuries, supplying the necessary light and forces for humanity's highest welfare, which no resources of nature have otherwise or elsewhere furnished—all this is the great "sign" and "wonder" and "power" that demonstrates that the foundations of Christianity were laid in God's miraculous working. Christendom itself in the high moral and spiritual products and benedictions it exhibits, and the mighty powers and adaptations it shows for character, life, and blessedness, incomparably above all the products of the world's efforts, is indeed a permanent miracle. In its original reality, in both event and doctrine, Christianity is penetrated all through with the miraculous. The incidental manifestations were but the normal witnesses to the Divine activities that were establishing it.

5. THE EVIDENTIAL VALUE OF MIRACLES. This has been differently estimated at different times. In the early Church, Middle Ages, and Protestant theology, apologetics made large use of them as proof of the divine authority of Christianity; but since the rise of modern deistic and pantheistic philosophies, and the recent development of physical science with its emphasis on the conservation of force and the reign of law in nature, energetic and persistent assault has been made upon the Biblical miracles, and the appeal to them has been less used—not because not valid, but as less available. Opponents of Christianity have represented them as not the triumphant proof of its truth, but the greatest impediment to its reception. Hence apologetics has tended to rest the proof more on other forms of evidence. They have, thus, often been thrown into the background, as tenable, indeed, by faith, but not its support or warrant. But this persistent and many-sided assault and depreciation have stimulated Christian thought to deeper study and led to profounder views of the real import of miracles and of their position in the redemptory economy. The advance not only corrects the false forms of definition which long allowed them to be thrust into untrue antagonism to nature, but holds them in closer and more living relation to the whole divine activity for the spiritual regeneration of man, and especially emphasizes their indissoluble union with the very life and work of the Mediator as God manifest in the flesh.

The truth in the matter, as now thoroughly vindicated, concedes, indeed, that while as to the original witnesses, in the state of mind into which their training had brought them, the very sight of the miracles was power fully adapted and actually efficient for evoking faith, as to the world, since the full institution of the Church, faith is required for their acceptance, i. e., the historical faith that responds to adequate historical testimony to their occurrence, in connection with conditions and historical movements which furnish a reasonable ground and justification of them. It concedes, too, that in themselves, as isolated phenomena, they are not to be held as the alone evidences of the divine truth, or as per se necessarily effecting faith. Christ Himself called attention to the self-witnessing power of His teaching, the self-verifying divinity of His truth, as an evidence which ought to have made a "sign-seeking generation" less dependent on the attending miracles—reproaching them for their low spiritual sense that would not believe except on sight of these objective "wonders," or that would, perhaps, remain unbelieving though one would rise before them from the dead.'2 Nevertheless He asserted their real evidential value as proof, and wrought them in explicit connection with this purpose, even staking His Messianic claims and divine authority upon their reality.2 When faith was not evoked through the higher moral force of the appeal of self-verifying truth, He still pointed to the attesting miracles: "Though ye believe not me, believe the works." These "mighty works" were a means of carrying the beholders' minds up to the divinity of the truth taught, and causing the view to rest upon the divine Christ Himself, upon His whole supernatural claim, office, and work as the Redeemer and Savior of the world. Their evidential value was not in what they were in themselves, but as "signs" of what He was as "God manifest in the flesh," accomplishing redemption and teaching the way of life. And it is only when Jesus is viewed in the illuminating light of the miracles, which show themselves in His Person and ministry, that we are impressed with their transcendent value for assuring His full divine authority.

Only a comprehensive and discriminating view of the miracles of Christ will bring this relation and significance into clear relief. (a) The first and lowest relation was that of given credentials to a divine commission or office to teach or act in the name of God. In this sense miracles might be attached to the ministry of prophet or apostle, as bearers of God's truth. In the case of Christ they were certificates of appointment and authority. As such they were of great weight, as guarantee for faith in the message. (b) In the life of Christ they were the normal or natural manifestations of His supernatural Person. If the whole conception of the Old Testament promises and the New Testament claims was realized, the Messiah was the Eternal Word "made flesh," the incarnate Son of God, living and acting in the presence of men. That this supernatural Person should exhibit supernatural deeds, as well as teach supernatural truths, is but according to the law of cause and effect and the principle of self-consistent personal action. Allowing for the difference between physical and free causation, the supernatural would ray out in His activity as naturally as light from the sun. When out of His personal divinity Christ wrought miracles, He was but expressing Himself. It was a part of His teaching, teaching concerning Himself, the same truth that His words were frequently uttering, and with an added verifying power beyond the capacity of words alone to give. Had Jesus confined Himself to verbal teaching, and day after day and year after year of His public ministry there had never appeared in His action a sign or token, a manifestation or suggestion of supernatural power, what a large, if not fatal, loss it would have been to the evidence that He was, indeed, the Son of God, as He claimed to be! What a loss to the impressiveness of the demonstration of His divinity! But by as much as the loss would have dwarfed the proof, by so much do His miraculous deeds sustain His teaching and accredit His whole supernatural claim and authority. They be come a vital, essential proof of what He was, completing and crowning His divine self-expression. (c) They stand, also, in direct connection with the highest and divinest moral ends. They are articulated into a spiritual aim than which none of larger moral grandeur has ever been conceived in human thought—the entrance of men into a state of peace and fellowship with God, the regeneration of life under the divine truth and Spirit, and the establishment of a spiritual kingdom to bring righteousness and love into sway through the earth, with entrance thence into everlasting life. According to the whole picture given by the evangelists, Jesus' entire personal life was pervaded by the love and kindness, the goodness, holiness, and moral elevation which accorded with this beneficent purpose. His miraculous activity, therefore, stood in unity with His whole beneficent aim, and took on all the value which belongs to the great object toward which His ministry was directed. (d) They certify the power needed to redeem. The purpose of Christ's coming extended to deliverance from the physical as well as the moral evil which sin had wrought. The system of nature is an organism, and man's physical well-being is tied close to the direction which the spiritual movement takes. Human sin bore fruits of physical disorder—disease and death. The Deliverer must be Lord of all nature. The "kingdom of heaven" must not only bring forgiveness and renewal of heart, but include arrest and reversal of the physical fruits of transgression. Hence Christ's ministry showed dominion over nature. Wherever He touched it or spoke to it, it was obedient to His power—in storm and sea, in tree and man, in disease and death. Had Christ been helpless before the physical consequences of moral evil, which exact "the uttermost farthing of penalty," had no "signs" of saving "power" in this relation appeared in His person, the absence would have been fatal to faith in His claims. But the loss by such supposed absence only measures the sublime value of their presence. And this consideration leads to a further: (e) His miracles form the beginning of His actual redemptive work. They are more than signs of power. In rescuing from sickness, suffering, and death, as well as in forgiving sins and restoring to fellowship with the Father, He is seen at His redemptive work, presenting first-fruits. His deeds, therefore, complete the view of His person and saving work, and carry all the evidential value which this necessary relation gives.

Most indubitable does it thus become that the miraculous activity of Christ is normal and essential evidence of the divine foundations of Christianity. It is synonymous with the proof of His supernatural Person, and of the supernatural redemption He was accomplishing. The assertion, sometimes made, that "the Bible does not need the attestation of miracles," is utterly misleading, if the supernaturalism of the Christian revelation is not to be surrendered. The absence of these supernatural "signs and wonders," in teaching, life, and deeds, from the alleged revelation and from the life of Christ, would leave them without their proper and essential divine signature, and without correspondence with the fundamental claims and mission of Christianity.

Evidences from Prophecy

As a miracle of knowledge, prophecy, especially predictive prophecy, has an evidential value closely akin to that of other forms of miracle. Two things underlie and vindicate its force in this relation. First, the fact that it gives a clear and specific fore-announcement of events utterly beyond the reach of simple human foresight, and secondly, the sure principle that God would not authenticate falsehood by bestowment of the prophetic gift. It becomes God's seal to His messenger and message.

A clear vein of prophecy runs through the Scriptures. A divine forecast enters into the very texture of the Biblical revelation. It becomes organic in the revelation because the revelation is a historical movement whose inspiring goal is opened to the apprehension of faith at every step of the progress. Sometimes the prediction is of events in the near future, marked by very definite features and bounds. This form is well illustrated in the prophecies of Isaiah and Jeremiah foreshadowing the Assyrian and Babylonian captivities of the Jews and the destruction of Babylon. Such predictions, with their clear and indubitable fulfillment, stand as impressive proof of the divine revelation of which they form a part. But of far greater force are those prophecies that, in Messianic forecast and promise, directly pre-announced Christ and Christianity. Beginning with the first Gospel declaration concerning a conquering "seed of the woman,"2 on through the Abrahamic call at the root of the Jewish separation, and the multitudinous assurances of a coming Deliverer and Saviour, lighting up the advancing pages of the Old Testament Scriptures to their close—all accompanied by a distinct corresponding historical, national, and religious organization and movement in the Hebrew people—these Messianic prophecies appear in increasing frequency and clearness. They have an augmented impressiveness from the very fact that they attend and explain that great historical Hebrew development in which they are a constituent part. They justify the movement by holding forth the goal of it The New Testament exhibits the fulfillment of it all as undoubtedly as fruit exhibits the prophecy of the blossom, but with the difference that while the fruit comes from the blossom by regular course of nature, the New Testament fulfillment stands entirely apart from any simply natural law to account for it.

It will suffice for presenting the value of the evidence from prophecy simply to adduce from the great continuous web of it and its fulfillment a few illustrative examples.

1. From Gen. 12:1–3: "Now the Lord said unto Abram, Get thee out of thy country and from thy kindred, and from thy father's house,

unto the land that I will show thee: and I will make of thee a great nation, and I will bless thee, and make thy name great; and be thou a blessing: and I will bless them that bless thee, and him that curseth thee will I curse: and in thee shall all the families of the earth be blessed." This assurance that in Abraham all the "families" or "nations" of the earth should "be blessed" was repeated to him in different relations—first in connection with the promise of a son in his old age, and again when his faith was tested on the mount of sacrifice (Gen. 18:17, 18 and 22:15–18). As the heirship of Abraham's covenant position fell to his son Isaac and then to Jacob, it was renewed and reiterated to them, confirming the descent of the promise through his seed (Gen. 26:4; 28:10–15). The promise is found to lie, in fact, at the root of the peculiar historical development exhibited in the Jewish race, shaping the course of events for thousands of years and giving direction to the pens of the long list of Old Testament writers in the profoundest thought and structure of their productions.

The true historicity of this covenant fore-announcement is firmly accredited by the whole unquestionable, unique development, position, and literature of that peculiar race, to which that announcement forms the fitting initiation, and which repeats itself in ever onward-looking prophecies. The Hebrew mind, indeed, seems never to have taken in the full scope of the "blessing" or the way in which it was to reach "all nations." It did not comprehend all that the Spirit within "did signify" in thus testifying beforehand. But from our position for reading the meaning and reality of history, it is certain that the advancing development of the national existence was still carrying the promise and the divine design it expressed on toward fulfillment.

It is absolutely certain that no fulfillment can be traced under any interpretation that would apply the promise to Abraham's seed or posterity in the natural sense, or simply as a people collectively. For, though they possessed a higher and better knowledge of God and His will than surrounding peoples, they were isolated by their civic and religious organization and narrowed into a dominantly exclusive temper. Though they made some proselytes, incorporating them into Judaism, they remained bitterly hostile to the idea of any extension of the prerogatives and divine favors of the "children of Abraham" to the alien Gentiles. Nor did the narrow and dwarfing separateness, which indeed guarded and preserved the divine truth and purpose incorporated in their existence and mission, allow them to become a mighty, conquering world-power, that by arms and victories might extend its higher faith and beneficent administration into a universal dominion, as some in our times seem to think a Christian empire may do. Neither during the continuance of the Jewish commonwealth, nor since its extinction at the beginning of our Christian era, can the prophecy of that covenant race be shown to have had a merely naturalistic aim or accomplishment. Down to the present time, apart from the opening of the fountain of spiritual truth and life in Christianity, there is hardly a people on earth whose incoming and presence are less accepted as a blessing "to all nations." While, in their strange dispersion and unparalleled exclusive separateness, they have gone everywhere through the world, almost everywhere they have been put under bans of legal repression and pursued with persecuting antagonism.

But just as true and indisputable is it that human experience and history have traced and are still tracing a clear and high fulfillment, through the Messiah, "the Christ," that "seed of Abraham," whose coming the Hebrew Scriptures, under their true interpretation, throughout held forth as the end of the specialistic Jewish development. "The Scripture, foreseeing that God would justify the heathen through faith, preached before the Gospel unto Abraham, saying, In thee shall all nations be blessed." "If ye be Christ's, then are ye Abraham's seed, and heirs according to the promise." That most peculiar development of the covenant and Jewish life was conducted to a divine fruit in Christianity, which has ever proved and still proves the rich benediction of reconciliation with God, renewal of heart, and all the blessings of the higher civilizations, culture, welfare, and happiness, to all the families, individuals, and nations to which its message and power come. The progress of the earth to-day, in all that lifts human life to what is best and worthiest, and strong in the elevating anticipations of immortality, is, as a matter of fact, witnessing fruits of the actual fulfillment, and still progressive fulfilling, of that divine promise and Jewish unfolding. There is, therefore, a mysterious link connecting that pledge to Abraham in Haran with the times of Christ and the course of history ever since—the divine foresight and superintendence stretching across the long interval and certifying itself as divine to-day. It illustrates the evidential force of prophecy.

2. Isa. 43. This chapter is too familiar to require insertion here. While Isaiah abounds in predictions of Christ, this is the most remarkable of them. Some facts in regard to it must be borne in mind. (a) The prophecy was written about 700 years before Christ. (b) It was translated into the Greek of the Septuagint version about two hundred years before the birth of Christ. So no criticism can question the priority of the prophecy to the events of the New Testament. (c) The "Servant," of whom the prophecy speaks is interpreted even by the Jewish Targums as the Messiah. This shows an agreement by the early Judaism with the Christian interpretation of the reference. Jewish expositors who reject Christianity find the reference a crux; and the variety and vanity of their attempts to discover a solution adjusted to their rejection have made their failure thus far a most convincing proof of the impossibility of doing so. Indeed, many Jews have been brought to faith in Jesus Christ by the force of this prophecy.

Its divine application to the Messiah is immovably sure. It is woven, orderly and closely, in the texture of the total Isaianic representation of the Coming One, the anointed Deliverer of Israel—a representation that, while giving due recognition to the Messianic vocation and position of the whole posterity of Abraham or the Jewish people collectively, as holding and assuring spiritual deliverance and high exaltation, yet carried on the view beyond that subordinate and subsidiary range and concentrated it finally upon the Messianic office in the single Divine Person who should arise in the midst of Judah, the special "seed of Abraham," and "of David," in which it was to be really and fully accomplished, not simply through the functions of prophecy and rulership, but also that of priestly propitiation. And the delineation stands in the mold furnished elsewhere by the entire body of Messianic prediction and promise by the prophets before, contemporaneous with, and after Isaiah—all together completing and irrefutably assuring the application to Christ. Jewish ingenuity has been able to find the counterpart to the description in no other personality of Hebrew history; and its chief resort in applying the description to the nation as a personified whole breaks up into utter confusion through refusal of the language to unite in grammatical coherence and relevancy, or tally with any experience of the Jews as such. But the whole portraiture becomes a clear mirror, reflecting in every part, in almost startling distinctness, the position, character, experience, aim, meekness, vicarious suffering, and propitiatory death of Jesus Christ, making of Himself an offering for sin and an intercession for transgressors, through which He passes into an exaltation and triumph in which He realizes His high joy in seeing many justified in His righteousness. Across the interval of those centuries the Spirit of prophecy traced in terms of explicit history, the unparalleled realities which, so long a time after, became conspicuously actual in the rejection and crucifixion of the divine Messiah and the saving power that has come from Him ever since. This Scripture is thus another illustrative example of the evidential value of prophecy.

These two are types of the Old Testament method. The individual prophecies are too numerous and varied for rehearsal here. But we can see the full force of the evidence they furnish only when we recall how many distinct things were thus foretold of Christ. Of these we must note His descent from Abraham (Gen. 12:1–3); from Judah (Gen. 49:10); from David (Jer. 23:5); the time of His coming (Dan. 9:24); His divine and human natures (Isa. 9:6); the place and circumstances of His birth (Micah 5:2; Isa. 7:14); His threefold office, as Prophet, Priest, and King (Deut 18:15, 18; Ps. 2; Ps. 110; Zech. 6:13; Isa. 61:1); His preaching (Isa. 9:2; 61:1, 2); His miracles (Isa. 35:5, 6); His sufferings and death (Isa. 53; Zech. 13:7); His resurrection and ascension (Ps. 68:18); the consequent gift of the Holy Spirit (Joel 2:28); and the extension of the Gospel (Isa. 53; 9:7; 35).

If we consider how grand is the concert of the Scriptures, historic, didactic, and devotional, by so many writers widely separated and extending through more than ten centuries, all keyed to this Messianic idea, imbedded at the same time and carried forward continuously in peculiar institutions of government and worship, typical sacrifices, rites, and festivals, forming a distinct, unparalleled movement unfolding into the events of the Gospel histories, and the

Church and life of Christendom, it becomes impossible to doubt that the Old Testament really foretold Christ and Christianity—so sealing both the Old and New Testaments as of God.

It may be said that the rejection of the Christ by the great body of the Jews when He appeared discredits the validity of this conclusion. But the conclusion rightly rests, not on the conduct of the Jewish leaders and the mass of the people when He came, which then, as often before, failed to reflect the full light of their training, but upon the whole prophetic view, embracing the entire range and combination of Messianic forecast, in all its forms, as now seen to have been actually fulfilled and to be actually fulfilling still, in the historical Christ and the establishment of Christianity. The reality and reach of prophecy become clear and certain, not by its being viewed prospectively or in contemporary movements, but especially, if not only, after the historical fulfillment has thrown the light of clear interpretation and verification on it, and it lies unmistakably defined and fixed in historic retrospect. The question is not what the Jewish rulers did, nor even what they might have known, enabling them to see in Jesus Israel's long-promised Messiah, but what we now may see and understand in the light of the whole New Testament record and with the entire history of Christianity before us.

The rejection of Christ by the Jews is easily explained by incontrovertible facts—facts which leave the actual fulfillment of the Messianic assurances untouched. One fact is that these prophecies had lodged in the Jewish mind of that period a deep and strong expectation of the Messianic appearing. Proof of this is abundant in the post-canonical Jewish literature, apocryphal, and pseud-epigraphic. The hope burned intensely in the national life. Another fact is that in the troublous times of the Maccabean wars and under the chafing bondage of Roman wrong and oppression, the highest spiritual features in which the prophets had delineated the coming Messiah were obscured and lost sight of in notions which resolved the promised blessing to Israel into political and national deliverance and the divine Deliverer, if at all viewed as a person, into a God-sent, heroic Leader or Prince, who should consummate the victorious power of Israel and exalt it into an attractive world-dominion. After the voice of prophecy had ceased in the land, the spiritual and true import of the Messianic idea passed under a deep, dark eclipse, through the perverting national longings and varied misleading influences. The features of the Messiah of the prophets faded out from the vision of the people and their religious guides. The whole stress of the Messianic conception was centered in the kingly function as mighty heir to David's throne. In the blindness of passionate longing and fanatical expectancy for a kingly ruler, the face of the Messiah could not be seen in the meek, gentle, patient Teacher and suffering Savior. They naturally failed to recognize Him when He came. "He came unto His own, and His own received Him not"—though to "as many as received Him He gave power to become the sons of God." But the veil of obscuring, blinding influence has been removed from the minds and hearts of men, who now can trace under the clear illumination of fulfillment the whole prophetic delineation in the divine Son of God and Son of man and the "kingdom of heaven" as established on earth.

3. There is a great and indisputable New Testament prophecy that integrates itself in the Biblical system and further illustrates the prophetic reality. We refer to Christ's fore-announcement of the destruction of Jerusalem and the Jewish nation (Matt. 24:1–34; Mark 13:1–23; Luke 19:41–44; 21:5–24). This stands as a connecting and transitional link between the fulfillment of Old Testament prophecy in Christ and the consequent onward prophetic realizations after Christ had incorporated in the revelation His own far-reaching unfoldings for the verification of the Christian centuries.

It is indubitably certain that this pre-announcement of the approaching utter overthrow of the sacred city was made and published before the event took place. No plea that the overthrow preceded the prediction can be sustained. Almost the entire weight of historical and critical authority affirms that the three evangelists who record it wrote before the year A. D. 70, in which the event occurred, and this is confirmed by the fact that in none of them is there the least intimation, even by incidental implication, of the fulfillment of the prophecy. An equal silence, it is true, obtains in the Gospel of John, who did write afterward; but John made no record of the prophecy itself, and his entire silence on the whole subject is easily explained in the fact that it lay outside the scope of his purpose in his particular delineation of the Master. But in view of the mighty impression made by that woeful destruction, it is manifestly incredible that the three evangelists who record the prediction at length should, or could, have failed to add a hint of the awful realization. So the priority of the prophecy to its fulfillment cannot be questioned.

And the warning pointed out the overthrow not merely in general terms, which might suit various dissimilar cases of possible occurrence, but in distinct, specific, minute, peculiar features, a succession and combination of particulars never before drawn. The terms can be made to tally with no experience in Jewish history save the one named in advance. And beyond the particularistic declaration of the complete destruction stands the fatal, far-reaching word: "They shall be led away captive into all nations; and Jerusalem shall be trodden down of the Gentiles, until the times of the Gentiles be fulfilled."

The actual destruction of Jerusalem, corresponding to the prophecy, is one of the unquestionable and outstanding events in the world's history, and the effects and memorials of it are still visible throughout the world. Josephus, the great Jewish historian, who has included a full detailed account of it in his "Wars of the Jews," written at Rome, writing as an eye-witness of the long and dreadful tragedy, and as an enemy to Christianity, has yet left a description of it which covers all the terms of the divine prophecy. Under the tracing of his historic pen we read to-day the details of the cruel siege and terrible famine, the strange successions and unparalleled combinations of suffering, horror, and desolation, in which we see every feature of Jesus' prediction, even the most improbable, completely fulfilled. The calamity swept on till the site of the city was turned by the plowshare, and the remnant of its inhabitants captive and scattered into an exile "among all nations," a dispersion in which they still wander—an unequaled phenomenon of race separateness and persistence, a living monument to the divinity of that fore-knowledge to which this whole history lay in open, infallible vision.

THE INTERNAL EVIDENCES

It should be expected that a religion or revelation from God, given through a course of divine self-manifestations historically accredited, would at the same time shine in its own light, authenticating and commending itself directly to the intellect and heart of the race. The divinity of its Source must be reflected in its contents. Its origin must appear in its intrinsic power and fruits. This evidence Christianity possesses in clear and triumphant measure. We must remind ourselves of some of the chief forms of it.

1. The Peculiar and Profound Harmony of the Scriptures. To see this clearly and to estimate its force correctly, we must keep in mind the actual facts in the case. These Scriptures consist of sixty-six books, written by about forty different writers, of different degrees of culture and in different positions in life, from kings and statesmen down to herdsmen and fishermen, in regions widely remote from each other, some in Central Asia, some in Judea, some in cities of Greece, some in Rome, at different periods extending through about fifteen centuries. They reflect widely different environments, the presence of diverse types of personal, industrial, and social life, habits, customs, and influences, variously modified and changed, often through sweeping revolutions, as time went by. But though the authors, so numerous and separate from each other, wrote independently and with an individuality that appears in thought and style; and though the books comprise history, biography, poetry, and letters, dealing, under the most varied circumstances, with the great subjects of God, creation, man's place and relations, religion, law, government, human duty, opportunity, and destiny, they are found to harmonize as a record of one movement, presenting and developing the same fundamental or ruling truths and principles, progressively constructing a single system of theistic teaching, divine providence, and human salvation—a movement penetrated and dominated by one great unitary aim, which appears at last in the establishment of Christianity. The concert in the strains of the many and distinct writers must have been keyed by a divine inspiration; for it is not after the manner of human writers thus to agree—so that the notes heard in the opening utterance reverberate through the long progress and come to clear and ringing resonance when the revelatory voices proclaim the conclusion. If we take any

similar collection of writings extending over an equal space of time, and composed by an equal number of authors, we shall find nothing like this in history."

This unity and harmony of the Biblical revelation has been set in fresh light by the distinctness with which all modern scholarship has recognized and presented the progressive character of that revelation. We are thus no longer perplexed by the seeming discrepancies between some passages in the Old Testament and the New. They are only the normal phenomena resulting from the advance from the earlier and partial to the later and full disclosure of spiritual truth, or the advancing training toward and into the full standard of moral relations and life, as men could be prepared for reception of the perfect law of duty. The unitary harmony is not a formal one but vitally pervades the record of a great divine, providential, practical movement, progressively lifting spiritual thought and moral life, through redemptive provision and adapted instruction, all based in fundamental truths which from the first implicitly embraced the conclusion—a moving light which, like the rising sun, shines "more and more unto the perfect day." This harmony of the Biblical literature, organizing itself upon the one great fundamental idea of spiritual salvation and an eternal kingdom of God for man; centering in a complex and prolonged system of prophecies, types, sacrificial rites, laws, social institutions, history, and promises of a divine Messiah and Saviour to come; closing at last in the fully accredited New Testament records of the birth, life, teachings, sufferings, death, resurrection, and ascension of Jesus Christ, in whom the whole Old Testament movement was completely realized, thus proving itself the full provision of a regenerating power for universal humanity—this is not only a literary phenomenon without a parallel on earth, but is in itself so manifestly superhuman as to attest itself as divine to the reason and the heart.

2. The Supernatural Character of Christ. As Jesus Christ is the center of Christianity, at once the realization of the Old Testament preparations and the substance of the New Testament truth and authority, it is fair to concede that if, as He claimed to be, He is truly the Son of God and full revelation of the Father, the evidences of it must necessarily appear in His own personal character and life. The

divine life must needs be self-evident in its own divinity. As we need no other light than its own shining to see the sun, so we should recognize the supernatural light in Him who can truly say, "He that seeth me hath seen the Father."

The advance of learning, the discoveries of science, the progress of knowledge, though often conducted in critical temper, have failed to furnish a naturalistic explanation of the unique personality of Jesus Christ, or bring His total personal character, in mind, heart, and life, within the measure of mere humanity. Unbelieving thought has worked at the task through all these centuries, but the longer and more fully the gaze of the human soul has been calmly and honestly fixed on the problem, the more evident has become the impossibility of classing Him as only and simply a man among men. United in a life most genuinely human are the ineffaceable features of a supernatural presence and superhuman thought and movement. This is a "sign" that has not been cut off.

Increasingly impressive, for instance, abides the wonderful originality of His character. This marked, primarily, His intellectual life, but it showed itself in His whole bearing. In a profound sense and large degree, men are the product of their times, place, and conditions. The forces of ancestry and environment, the limitations and trends of circumstances, give and explain the mold of their thought and lives. This does not destroy free personality, but usually greatly narrows the range in which it acts. It does not necessarily prevent originality, but it ordinarily limits its action within easily accountable variations. Long centuries of observation and science have well certified both the possibilities and the limits of humanity in this respect. In Jesus Christ the movement was on transcendent lines. Measured from the point of observation from which we now view Him, it is clear that while He truly fitted the need of His place and times, His circumstances and times could not have produced Him. Born and reared a Jew, inheriting the result of influences which for many generations had been making Jewish thinking and character distinct and intense; circumscribed within a narrow, humble sphere, without contact with schools or training other than of the traditional and current views, He nevertheless moves before us in His ministry, from first to last, in a range of thought so free and lofty as to enlarge, elevate, revise, and transform the whole realm of moral and spiritual truth. It could not fail to call forth the conviction: "Never man spake as this man," and awaken the wonder: "Whence hath this man this wisdom?" Though He underlaid His teaching deeply and fundamentally with the great spiritual, religious and ethical truths of the Jewish Scriptures, assuring that one jot or tittle of these could not fail, He threw upon them a radiance that never shone on them before and gave them a depth and largeness of meaning beyond the apprehension of His age or any earlier age, thus furnishing a fresh and higher revelation while interpreting what was involved in the revelation divinely bestowed in the past. He gave a new faith to His day and a new type of character to the world. If it be said that in this He was but the product of the intense Messianic hope that, out of the Hebrew Scriptures, filled the mind of His generation, it suffices to remember that that Jewish hope, so prevalent and passionate, embodied none of the features presented in the lowly, gentle, suffering Jesus of Nazareth and His teachings, but so darkened out of view the prophetic delineations as to secure an emphatic national rejection of His claim. His conception was the opposite of that which prevailed—peculiar and original. If, then, it be suggested, that Jesus' views were shaped directly by the Old Testament Scriptures instead of through the false notions of His nation and times, even this explanation reminds us in what a strange and pure elevation above His generation the mind of Jesus moved—a superhuman superiority to formative conditions, utterly unaccountable in the simply natural life of the Nazarean Carpenter. Though a Jew, with only Jewish environment, He rose into a range of conception and teaching in which He becomes the one catholic man for all human races. And this intellectual transcendence becomes more impressive when some of its particulars are traced out. It has features that make it stand alone. For instance, Jesus' thought maintained a luminous, distinct, undisturbed self-consistency throughout His ministry. It advanced in straight lines from beginning to end. He took no tentative positions. He never revised any of His views—never corrected earlier judgments. Though His teaching was progressive, when the cumulative advance presented His completed thought, every truth declared from the first was found corporate in the total doctrine—an aggregate teaching that made a new epoch in the knowledge and intellectual progress of the world. That the humble son of Mary, from His lowly Galilean home and Jewish training should thus stand forth intellectually so superior to and apart from the spurious Messianism of His age and country, so clean of the inveterate exclusivism of the Jewish race, so clear of their prejudices and misconceptions, so independent of Rabbinic interpretations and Pharisaic errors; announcing Himself so calmly and positively as divinely sent to establish among men the kingdom of God—which would, through Himself, gather up and unify all the Sacred Scriptures and realize their foreshadowings of grace and redemption—whose establishment, as openly declared, would be marked by the fall of the Holy City and the end of the Jewish commonwealth, and then reach on in a universal extension through the earth—that He should do all this simply as a man, without superhuman endowment or mission, is plainly inexplicable on the basis of all that we know of human possibilities and limits.

This transcendent originality is further assured by remembering another of its marked characteristics—the calmness, sereneness, and effortless spontaneity of His thought and teaching. It in no way appears as a tax upon inadequate resources. It was unlabored, inartificial, the easy expression of the normal mind, the quiet flow of the elevated fountain. Nowhere is there the least appearance of strain or mental endeavor, studied elaboration or maneuver. But everywhere the transcendent thought and truth manifestly came freely, or as we may say, naturally from the high, full life that was in Him, the exalted level at which He saw and explained all truth. This unique feature of unlabored spontaneity and calm certainty is attested by the evidence, everywhere arresting attention in the biographical delineations of His teaching, of the astonishing reserve resources, ready in His mind and serving all sudden occasions day by day with the same quiet ease and appositeness, on the sublime range of His intellectual and spiritual vision. This whole marvelous reality is not after the manner and measure of men. Compare Jesus, in this respect, with the most renowned thinkers, originators of widespread pagan religions, say Gautama Buddha, with his long years of painful self-discipline, ascetic seclusion, laborious study, and artificial elaboration, or Confucius, or Zoroaster, with their recondite speculations and studiously wrought-out rules. All fair reason and just spiritual insight cannot but become conscious, through the comparison, of the immense transcendence of the mind of Jesus, moving ever in a unique elevation, freedom, readiness, clearness, breadth, and spontaneous self-consistency, giving to mankind a full vision of theistic, religious, and spiritual truth such as humanity elsewhere has been unable to present, and which holds, in ever-enlarging space over the world, the reason and confidence of the race.

Beyond this superhuman intellectual character, Jesus' moral transcendence is even more impressive. Before the ethical consciousness of mankind the elevation of His spiritual life compels the recognition of the wonder of a human life "without sin." This reality of sinlessness is not something simply assumed or unwarrantedly accepted on the basis of a non-historical or mythically formed report concerning Him, but is a truth of the web and woof of the whole account of the man, and verifiable to the view of all times. If it impressed itself ineffaceably upon the souls of His chosen disciples, it impresses itself, out of the artless portrayal of His acts and words and temper, upon us as well. If we know anything about Jesus at all, this is one of the most certain of all the facts of His history. It fits the whole claim made by Him of being the Messiah and Son of God. It is involved in His asserted supernatural virgin birth. It is one of His own specific and emphatic claims, put forth with challenge for disproof in the presence of His enemies.2 The apostles, who were with Him through all His ministry, in closest contact with His inner as well as outward life, testify to His stainless holiness. But these special testimonies are simply the vocalization of the witness of the life itself of Jesus as He moves in act and speech, in temper and spirit, in aim and motive, in attitude and endeavor, in the simple accounts of the Synoptists and the fourth Gospel. The accounts present not a single action or word or feature of character that can be justly catalogued as sin or lacking in true conformity to the law of righteousness or goodness. Strained effort has sometimes been made to find fault in His conduct. But it is only by forced and illegitimate exegesis that these passages can seem at strife with an unstained holiness. And the marvel of this personal sinlessness grows upon the view as it stands out in the light of the peculiarities which it naturally and necessarily involved. It cannot be doubted that Jesus had a clear, deep, moral consciousness. His spiritual discriminations were distinct and strong, throwing such pure light as to uncover to those who were about Him their faults and sins that lurked in their temper and lives. His ethical sensibility was undoubtedly quick and comprehensive. And yet in all the Gospel records there is not found, as falling from His lips, a single expression that betrays the least consciousness of sin or guilt, or any compunction for any deed or word or thought in His own relations to God or men. He shows no sense of any shortcomings. He prays much, but there is no indication that He ever sought forgiveness. He said to His disciples: "After this manner pray ye:" "forgive us our debts," but there is no instance of His so praying Himself. There is no evidence that He ever joined them in common prayer. While His sympathy drew them to Him, His mysterious superiority and spiritual elevation awed them and held them in worshipful regard. While a sense of sin and unworthiness has ever marked the genuine piety of the devoted souls of men, and Christ made this feature, with its petition for pardon, fundamental in the order of Gospel grace and salvation, there is a total absence of it all from Him who is the founder of Christianity. While the true and real humanity of Jesus is an essential truth of His personality, and so prayer was involved in His incarnate position, this absence of sin and His positive harmony with the divine holiness nevertheless allowed no place for this element of human prayer. His soul was "like a star and dwelt apart" from the blight of depravity. The note of contrition evermore marking the most saintly men is totally alien to His life; and yet He consistently stands as the highest pattern of saintly piety.

We need to remember, moreover, the fitness of this fact and the evidential force that belongs to it. It is the primary and continuous moral miracle of His personality, in which the continuity of depraved nature is interrupted in human life, suggestive of the redemption which His presence and work were meaning for mankind and illustrative of its saving power. It agrees with His ceaseless consciousness of being the Son of God, "one with the Father,"2 and with His law of obedience: "I have kept my Father's commandments and abide in His love;" "I do always the things that are pleasing to Him." It accords with the fixed rule that only one that is without spot or blemish can be the true "Lamb of God," giving His life a ransom for the sin of the world. It accounts for the attractive, mysterious moral impression made by His personality upon all His disciples, awing them into reverence while holding them with cords of love. It explains that unity and coherence under which all His personal claims of Messiahship, divine sonship, spiritual supremacy, authority, and judgeship, everywhere assumed, blend in complete harmony, and attest themselves as the revealings of the character and redeeming love of God. It holds together in beautiful symmetry all the parts and relations of the everywhere proclaimed purpose to found a "kingdom" in which, through human restoration to holiness, the will of God may be done on earth as it is done in heaven. This image of the sinless Christ, everywhere visible in each separate narrative of His life, as well as in the total portrayal of the four Gospels, enforces upon every open-minded reader the recognition of a character mysteriously wonderful and supernatural.

These two leading characteristics, marked in the thought and moral perfection of Jesus, run out into various particular manifestations, and form many special features of His life, which intensify this sense of His supernatural pre-eminence. But there is no need of tracing these here. The two, in their simply general form, suffice to stamp His personality as utterly unaccountable on naturalistic principles. While so truly and nobly human, He yet rises so far above the human as to stand uniquely alone in the race. His thought transcended all the master minds of the ages, giving to human vision a new and imperishable horizon, and, through His spiritual quality, touching the life and progress of mankind with regenerative force and victorious spiritual powers over sin—powers which, so far as accepted and yielded to by men, actually lift them into a transforming fellowship with God and unite them into the true human brotherhood of love and good-will.

It is of prime importance to remember that the evidential force of the character of Christ is direct and sure, and independent of all confusions from Biblical criticism. It depends on no particular theory of inspiration, nor, indeed, upon the inspiration of the Gospels at all. It rests not on perfect integrity of the text. All this is easily made apparent. For, unquestionably, this picture of Jesus' transcendent thought and superhuman character is transparent and indubitable in the records of His life as they are before us, however we may account for the writing of them. We are face to face with it in reading the simple story of His teachings and conduct, the plain recital of what He said and did. Leave aside all theories of inspiration, examine every suggestion concerning the origin, authorship, dates, sources of composition, manner of production, and integrity of text of the Gospels, still the essential portrait remains the same, and no adequate naturalistic explanation of it is afforded or comes in sight. For all theories of a manufacture of fictitious portraiture by the evangelists, helped, perhaps, by addition of legendary or mythical idealizations, go down before the evident fact that neither the evangelists nor others could have produced the picture in any such way, or apart from the actual life, as essentially sketched. No single one of them was competent for the invention of such a character. It was an indisputably sane and just judgment of J. S. Mill when he wrote: "It is no use to say that Christ, as exhibited in the Gospels, is not historical.... Who among His disciples or among their proselytes was capable of inventing the sayings ascribed to Jesus, or of imagining the life and character revealed in the Gospels. Certainly not the fishermen of Galilee, certainly not St. Paul, ... and still less the early Christian writers." Equally certain is it that many writers among a narrow and credulous people, separately inventing memoirs of Jesus, could not originate the material or transmit legendary traditions whose possible combination or juxtaposition would enshrine and reflect the unity, purity, elevation, symmetry, and faultlessness of Jesus of the Gospels. Leaving thus all questions of inspiration aside, and over and above all theories of criticism, there is no possible explanation of the portraiture except as a genuine delineation of a historical reality, a true and consistent record of a personal history. This historically assured character, to which there is no antecedent or subsequent parallel, the supreme miracle, self-testifying before the gaze of mankind, is an imperishable witness to Christianity.

3. The Supernatural Truths and Doctrines of the Bible. The value of truth, in our times, has received its supreme emphasis. This is because it means reality, and realities are the things with which life has to do and in which all welfare and destiny are concerned. Doctrines, as exhibitions of truth, must, therefore, bring us into the presence of God who is the ground and source of all truth. As, by concession of all theists, man, as "the offspring of God," is a creature with rational personality in His image, he is capable of reading God's thoughts after Him in nature and history, and also of recognizing His thought as it may be given in special self-revelation. It is particularly to doctrines and truths distinctively religious that we here refer. Some of these, indeed, impress themselves upon the human mind through the light of nature. Others may be wholly undiscoverable by reason merely from the natural constitution of the world. But through whatever channel they reach us, they bear in their own character the divine signature. A few illustrations will suffice.

For instance, the pure theism of the Scriptures shines in unmatched pre-eminence. The result of the last century's almost exhaustive investigation of all the ethnic religions of the world has been to make this pre-eminence more striking and indisputable. Take the best of them, in their highest reaches, among the most developed races of ancient or modern times, and their conceptions of God, crude, confused, partial, everywhere passing into the corruption of multitudinous polytheisms, are found to be in every way inferior. They cannot be compared with the lofty and pure theism that shines out of the Biblical disclosure, whose very first pages exhibit Him as, through the free word of His power, the Creator of all things, almighty, holy, and good, and then in progressive teachings illuminate the conception with all the attributes of perfect being and character, until in the New Testament Scriptures He is seen in the full, precious, inspiring light of His eternal fatherhood, love, and redeeming goodness. There is nothing like it round the world. Even the Christian thought of many centuries has been only gradually comprehending the full meaning of this revelatory teaching. Measuring the possibilities of the natural human reason for forming a doctrine of God by the outcome of its world-long endeavor, as found in the crudeness, uncertainty, and inadequacy of its best achievements, we are compelled to regard the Scripture doctrine, in its distinct, positive clearness and unequaled elevation, as supernatural. Our reason, created as an open recipiency into which the divine may reflect itself, distinctly recognizes the "true God" in this teaching, and the teaching itself as from above.

Similarly the Scripture doctrine of God's relation to the world bears witness to itself. Outside of the illuminating reach of these Scriptures even His relation as Creator has ever remained under darkness or confusion. Where creatorship has been attributed to Him, His position has been reduced to mere demiurgism, fatalistic necessity, or something else far inferior to the truth of His being the free and absolute Author of the entire cosmic existence and order. With respect to the further truth of His continuous and abiding relation to the universe, non-Christian thought or theory has ever oscillated between pantheistic identification of God with nature, substituting blind, unpurposive energy for the divine personality; and the extreme contrast to this, a deistic separation of God from the world, placing Him off somewhere in empyrean isolation, without active connection with cosmic progress or human history, an "absentee God" simply observant of the movement, exercising no purposive providence for the welfare of mankind, revealing Himself in no instruction, answering no cries of prayer, drawing near in no help against want or misery. Between these two extreme tendencies, the conception has run into almost endlessly diversified forms, alike degrading to the nature and character of God and wanting the prime and essential adaptations to the condition and necessities of His bewildered children, groping through the mysteries of life and anxious concerning the mysteries that may lie beyond. But when we open the Christian Scriptures and receive their teaching, new and definite light breaks over the momentous question. God has not withdrawn nor forgotten His creation. The contrasted transcendence and immanence come into unity in the reality of omnipresence. Everywhere in these Scriptures, as the Creator of the world, God is both before and above it—a supreme transcendence. Everywhere, as its Preserver and providential Ruler, He is also in it, a living immanence—the power of His abiding Will being the energy that upholds and continues the whole created system, the so-called "laws of nature" expressing the uniformities of that Will for the physical universe. He is free to act everywhere—for moral and spiritual purposes with respect to man for whose use, well-being, and happiness He prepared the earth, and to whose right destiny He is looking in the preservation and government of it. It is made clear that in His supremacy over nature and pervasive efficient presence in it, He has come so near to us that "in Him we live and move and have our being"—that while He has made nature plastic to our touch and use, He has kept it responsive to His own touch, and has been approaching mankind from His transcendent place with supernatural moral and spiritual instruction, soteriological provision and administration. We are assured that He has related Himself in an attitude of unspeakable love toward the world, revealing the laws of duty and welfare, guiding with precepts and warnings, sending grace and truth for safety and holy life, and exercising such a providential care that, while holding the issues of the earth's whole history to His plan of love, He numbers the hairs of His children's heads.

No equal to this doctrine of God's relation, in its specific parts or as a whole, can be found elsewhere in the literature of the world. It is above all the sages of naturalistic philosophies and religions. Its pure preeminence attests the supernatural source of Christianity.

A like superhuman light brightens the Biblical doctrine concerning man. His origin, as the "offspring" of God; his endowment, in the "image" of God; his position, as meant to establish a dominion of reason and goodness over all order and life on earth; his destination, as formed for an immortality of blessedness, lift up the anthropological view into a definiteness and elevation nowhere else found. While pagan peoples have ever groped in bewildered uncertainty as to whence man came and whither he is going, hearing no assuring word from nature as to his destiny, the revealed doctrine at once exhibits his divine lineage, and completes its showing by giving to this brief life a horizon that reaches beyond and widens under eternal skies. The divine constitution of the family, the value and sacredness of the individual in his rights and responsibilities, the law of natural brotherhood, which, with its unitary force and harmonizing power, is adjusted to bind the whole race in bonds of good-will and peace in an all-embracing happiness—these are teachings that distinguish Christianity above all non-inspired anthropologies. Man has never been adequately revealed to himself apart from this Biblical revelation.

But it is especially in the great doctrine of redemption that the superhuman range and quality of teaching become self-evident. There is no necessity for human life and character more profoundly recognized in the consciousness of the race than that of deliverance from the bondage of moral evil and its blight upon the nobler attributes of character and welfare. There is nothing felt to be more inveterate than this bondage and its ever-wasting miseries, or that so excludes the race, in mass or as individuals, from a realization of the noble manhood, well-being, and happiness clearly meant for them in the endowments of their nature. There can be no doubt that though the better life in man, under higher aspirations, has struggled against the alien thraldom, it has, nevertheless, found itself incapable of winning the necessary emancipation for the unhindered true life. The natural religions, without exception, are mute as to any redemptive provision for moral deliverance. Man is left to his own resources.

PART I
TRUTHS ANTECEDENT TO REDEMPTION

CHRISTIAN THEOLOGY, in the distinct sense, and from the sources explained in the introductory discussion, begins its specific and proper work in a consideration of the two great truths of GOD and MAN. These two truths are the essential presuppositions for all the other truths or teachings of Christianity. They have a fundamental position. All others rest upon them. Apart from the existence of God and mankind, the whole matter of theology would be a blank. Christianity, in all its doctrines, expresses truths concerning them and inter-relations between them. Theology, therefore, puts them in the forefront.

DIVISION I
The Christian Doctrine of God and His Relations to the World

The truth concerning God reaches us from both the sources of information already indicated—the light of nature and the teachings of the Christian revelation. In both of these we have real divine self-disclosure. The Scriptures themselves affirm the distinctively revelatory character of nature. Apart from some disclosure which God makes of Himself man could not know anything of Him. But the whole realm of nature itself, the divine work forming the cosmic universe, necessarily to some degree reveals His being and thought in creational activity, as we have seen, He has opened a way in which our knowledge may find and interpret Him. Out of the cosmic existence and order comes the constant witness to His eternal power and deity. Beyond all doubt, however, our best and fullest knowledge of God reaches us through His supernatural redemptory self-revelation.

ETYMOLOGY OF THE TERM

The English appellation, God, has been commonly derived from the same Anglo-Saxon root as good, and has been supposed to designate the Good-Being. But a comparison of the various forms of the root discredits this derivation. Moreover, the idea of "goodness," whether in the sense of love or in an ethical sense, had too small a place, if any at all, in the pagan conception of gods, to determine their designation. As shown by Max Müller, the term has probably come from the Sanscrit *jut* or *dyut*, through the Gothic *gutha*, to shine.

The etymology of the Greek, Θεός, is uncertain. Herodotus derived it from τίθημι, to place, under the idea that the gods placed or determined all things in the world. But this account is unsustained. So is also the view of Plato, deriving it from θέω, to run, because the earlier worship was largely offered to the sun, moon, and stars in their courses. The supposition of Curtius, that it may have come from a root θες whence θεσ-σάμενοι, supplicated, is too remote and uncertain. The most reliable view seems to be that of Max Müller, tracing it from the Sanscrit deva, bright, shining; Zend, dæva; Persian, dew; Latin, deus—reflecting the early Indo-European worship as identifying God with the bright, resplendent heavens.

It is thus apparent that both our English appellation, God, and the Greek term Θεός, are carried as a linguistic inheritance from our ethnic or Gentile descent, and not from the Hebrew tongue, which was the medium of the preparatory unfolding of our Christian theism.

THE IDEA OF GOD

1. The content of it. For Christian theology the idea of God must be the Christian idea. Until we have reached this, in the measure in which the Christian Scriptures present it, we are short of the true conception. Christian theology can integrate its entire doctrine concerning God only when it has comprehended and united all the realities and features which the full redemptory revelation has made known. It can never consent to less than this as the aim of its elucidations. Nevertheless, it justly recognizes, or at least takes account of, the inferior and inadequate ideas in which the natural religious and theologic endeavors of mankind, feeling after God, have embodied their thought of Him.

The content of these has been almost infinitely varied. Historically, among pagan peoples, it has been found to range from the lowest and crudest notions of the most ignorant and degraded tribes up to the highest and best conceptions in which the sages and thinkers of cultured nations have idealized the Supreme Being as an intelligent and personal Spirit, and as the Creator and Ruler of the world. In the writings of the Old and New Testaments, also, while God is from first to last identical with Himself, and from the very beginning the concrete personal Creator as well as the almighty and righteous Ruler of heaven and earth, there is an advance in the revealed view, which enlarges the content to the completeness in which He is revealed as love and a Savior in Jesus Christ The Scriptures, therefore, are the norm for this full content. It is the high aim of theology to realize and exhibit it. Without doubt, the sincere mind of the Church, looking with open face into the word of God's supreme self-revelation, through the Christian centuries, has been making advance in comprehending the revealed idea. It is penetrating the whole thought with increasing clearness and closer approach to the Scripture intent There has been progress in the doctrine. There have been periods in which, from spurious sources or speculative philosophies, the pure, full idea has been obscured or false conceptions inserted. Partial or one-sided interpretations of the divine self-revelation have to some degree held sway. Misplaced or undue emphasis on particular attributes has often beclouded the full ordered reality or given faulty view. Christian theology can be satisfied only when it has succeeded in uniting, in true place and fullness, all the features of God's essential and moral perfection as disclosed in His self-revelation in nature and the Scriptures and made clear by the explaining force of advancing Providence and the life of the Church. But even this must not be regarded as giving the idea of God in the completeness of the divine reality. When the human mind, in its utmost receptiveness, has appropriated the disclosures of the double revelation of nature and redemption, it has grasped the content which belongs to the being of God in only limited comprehension. God is forever more and greater than the fullest measures of even the best Christian thought.

2. The origin or genesis of the idea in the human mind. Though there are still some differences of explanation among those who accept the validity of the idea, there is now a near approach to essential agreement as between the two general views that long have been maintained. The view, often urged, that it was given by a primitive supernatural revelation, and abides, often in obscured and corrupted form, as an inheritance in the race, the broken, scattered rays of that original disclosure, has been losing ground through modern historical, ethnological, and philological researches. Besides the difficulties in crediting so uncertain a thing as tradition with the universal conservation and communication of this truth, the laws of psychology forbid its acceptance as the actual and adequate explanation. For the "idea "being a psychic product, as all ideas necessarily are, something beyond mere sense impression, could not possibly come from without except in the sense that the mind formed it simply on the occasion of some divine manifestation. As even "words "are merely occasion or suggestive force on which a hearer or reader constructs or reconstructs ideas, so even a divine self-disclosure would leave the human mind blank of the idea of God except through the mind's own interpretation and identification of the external phenomena or revelatory manifestation. Indeed, the internal idea of God, however and whenever reached, is a pre-supposition for the recognition of the supernatural phenomena as of God. For these reasons it seems best, without necessarily denying a primitive revelation as a possible or probable fact—as the Biblical view implies a relation of immediate open divine communication with man—to hold that the idea of God is natural and normal to the human mind, acting in the presence of the world of nature, with its perpetually suggestive force, for this great thought and truth. In virtue of man's lofty and mysterious endowment with a capacity to know reality, both within himself and in the realm of existence around him and above him, the world of nature itself is an adequate supply of the suggestive material for his intelligence to form the idea through acts of intuition and judgment In this sense, it must be maintained, human nature is not atheistic; in its fundamental constitution its faculties are adapted to know God. In harmony with this principle also stands the recognized truth of the essential

"religiousness" of human nature. In the deepest needs of his being and life man was "made for God"—as tested by the profoundest philosophy of human experience. As a pre-condition, therefore, for meeting the fundamental demands of his nature and living his true life, his rational capacity to think and know must have included the normal ability and tendency to form, from the contacts and suggestions of his environment, the idea of a being with the power, relations, and prerogatives denoted by the term God. The witness of history and ethnic life directly supports this view, showing the presence of the idea, in endlessly diversified construction, wherever man has been found with his capacities in natural development and action. So normal is the idea to rational thought, that we are justified in thinking that could it be for a time blotted out from the earth, the human reason would renew it and fill the world with it again.

Of the various explanations which treat the idea, either theoretically or practically as a pseud idea, whether presented in the name of history or science, no one has more than a superficial and illusory plausibility. The effort to account for its genesis through a transformed reverence for dead ancestors or departed heroes, though made to look specious by discovery of various cults of ancestral and hero worship, sometimes of remote antiquity, is plainly futile by reason of its manifestly false assumption that the idea in reverence of ancestors is the same as the idea of God, or can generate it For such reverence for human forefathers or heroes does not rest on any notion of their divinity at all. It may, and when left to its own simple self, always does, permit the mind to remain a blank as to the conception and reality of God. It is only when the mind attains a new and different conception, adding from some other source the idea of a God, that the act of apotheosis, i. e., the exaltation of human beings to the rank and prerogatives of deity, becomes possible. The idea of God, therefore, is a prerequisite to the movement of apotheosis—not a product of it. The theory affords neither the reality of the idea nor the process of its origination.

The explanation which attempts to account for the origin of the idea in the ignorant and superstitious fears and dread of mankind in the presence of the terrifying and mysterious powers of nature, though often and elaborately presented, is equally illegitimate and inconclusive. It is sufficiently confuted by the permanence of the idea. For, a notion that is the product of ignorance and superstition, a phantom born of dread and darkness, ought to dissolve and disappear in the light of knowledge. The specters of night must evanish when the day comes. But the conception of God has grown clearer and stronger with the progress of intelligence and science. Nowhere is it so full and authoritative as in the highest and most advanced civilizations, in the heart of the centuries and lands where nature and reality are investigated and certified under the acutest scientific research and philosophic scrutiny. It is positive and regnant to-day as never before. It is found, indeed, that this idea is the guiding light for human progress and elevation, and for penetrative and victorious interpretation of the cosmic existence. An idea so normal to thought and so self-authenticating to the intellectual life and moral judgments of mankind endures by virtue of its standing, not as a pseud idea, but for an immutably sure reality.

3. The earliest form of the idea. The point of inquiry here is not the degree of its original fullness or completeness of content, which confessedly must have been very imperfect, but whether it was monotheistic or polytheistic Through the speculations of the "Positive Philosophy "and of various types of evolutionist science, the view has been widely put forth that back of all monotheistic thought, polytheistic notions and practices held sway. "No trace of monotheism," it has been said, "is to be found anywhere in the world except with a polytheism behind it." The genesis of the idea being supposed to take place from a time and condition of so-called "nature-worship"—the fetishism of reverencing or propitiating the different powers of nature—it is urged that this naturally at first gave it polytheistic shape in different invisible divinities behind the various cosmic powers. The question is essentially a question of fact, and the siftings of historical research, as well as of rational thought, have given an ample refutation of the theory. It must suffice simply to point out the line of decisive evidence.

Psychologically the polytheistic form can hardly be conceived as co-incident with the origin of the idea. "The singular in thought must precede the plural.... It is too often forgotten by those who believe that a polytheistic worship was the most natural unfolding of the religious life, that polytheism must everywhere have been preceded by a more or less conscious theism. In no language does the plural exist before the singular. No human mind could have conceived the idea of Gods without having previously conceived the idea of a God.... It might seem, indeed, as if in such a faith the oneness of God, though not expressly asserted, was yet implied, and that it existed, though latent, in the first revelation." Max Müller recognizes this notion: "There is a God," as one kind of monotheism, but prefers the designation "henotheism"2 as specifically expressive of the thought until the mind makes the further affirmation: "There is only One." Primitive thinking might, indeed, having the thought, "There is a God," move in the direction of saying, "There are many or more than One," but, psychologically, the essentially monotheistic thought must precede a polytheistic notion or faith.

Philological research has disclosed the further fact that the various terms and names for God in all the branches of the Aryan or Indo-European family of races when traced back exhibit a common root, a single word, as designation of the idea, carried from their original home in central Asia from which they migrated. In the early period, prior to the dispersion, they had an individual conception expressed by one term and a common name, still found embedded in the root-forms of the various languages sprung from that ancient tongue. Under that single term the deity appears to have been worshiped by the Aryan race as a whole.

The same investigation brings to view the fact that in all these races the polytheism becomes simpler and less, and approaches monotheism, the further it is traced back. "The younger the polytheism, the fewer its gods." This fact, joined with the psychological order of the precedence of the singular in thought and the oneness of the root-term, evidently becomes expressive of the direction of the movement under which the manifold luxuriant national pantheons have been produced. They appear as a growth under the process of specialization of the original idea and false applications of it to invisible nature-powers and apotheosis of heroes.

This conclusion is fully sustained by historic and critical investigations which distinctly discover and report monotheism (counting the so-called "henotheism" as possibly its initial type) as having been in fact the earliest form of the idea among the three most ancient peoples or nations in the world, whose records open our deepest view into antiquity, in India, Egypt, and China.

As to India, Max Müller, after comprehensive scholarly research, has voiced the testimony of its oldest literature in affirming the singular as preceding the plural in its theistic conception. In his "Origin and Growth of Religion," while giving the origin of the idea an inferential rather than a revelatory basis, he distinctly repudiates the notion of a polytheism at the roots of the conception in the religion of that land.

With respect to Egypt, this conclusion is given with emphasis by most of the great Egyptologists. P. Le Page Renouf, in the "Hibbert Lectures" for 1879, answering the question of the earliest form of religion there, as shown in archaic documents, says: "The whole mythology of Egypt may be said to turn upon the histories of Ra and Osiris, and these histories run into each other, sometimes in inextricable confusion, which ceases to be wonderful when texts are discovered which simply identify Osiris and Ra. And, finally, other texts are known, wherein Ra, Osiris, Ammon, and all other gods disappear, except as simple names, and the unity of God is asserted in the noblest language of monotheistic religion. There are many very eminent scholars who, with full knowledge of all that can be said to the contrary, maintain that the Egyptian religion is essentially monotheistic, and that the multiplicity of gods is only due to the personification of the attributes, the characters, and offices of the Supreme God." Renouf quotes the matured testimony of Rougé, than whom, he says, no scholar is better entitled to be heard: "No one has called in question the fundamental meaning of the principal passages, by the help of which we are enabled to establish what Egypt has taught concerning God, the world, and man. I say God, not gods. The first characteristic of the religion is the Unity [of God] most energetically expressed: God, One, Sole, and Only; no other with Him. He is the Only Being—living in truth. Thou art One, and millions of beings proceed from Thee. He has made everything, and He alone has not been made.... But how reconcile the Unity of God with Egyptian polytheism? History and geography will perhaps elucidate the matter. The Egyptian religion comprehends a quantity of local worships. The Egypt which Menes brought together entire under his sceptre was divided into nomes, each having a capital town; each one of these regions had its principal God designated by a special name; but it is always the same doctrine which reappears under different names. One idea predominates, that of a single and primeval God, everywhere and always it is One Substance, self-existent, and an unapproachable God.... Are these doctrines, then, the result of centuries? Certainly not; for they were in existence more than two thousand years before the Christian era. On the other hand, polytheism, the sources of which we have pointed out, develops itself and progresses without interruption until the times of the Ptolomies. It is, therefore, more than five thousand years since, in the valley of the Nile, the hymn began to the unity of God and the immortality of the soul, and we find Egypt in the last ages arrived at the most unbridled polytheism. The belief in the unity of the Supreme God and in His attributes as Creator and Lawgiver of man, whom He has endowed with an immortal soul—these are the primitive notions, encased, like indestructible diamonds, in the midst of mythological superfetations, accumulated in the centuries which have passed over the ancient civilization." Prof. Tiele, of Leiden, explains that though it was distinctly taught that 'the invisible God by whom all things came into existence is a Being who is One and alone, He yet revealed Himself afterwards in innumerable manifestations, and symbolic representations were easily imagined and multiplied. Through different forms of local representation, without felt inconsistency with the emphatic assertion of the oneness of His being, polytheistic language and practice obtained place and propagated itself until the latter obscured the former.' "Men had long been accustomed to regard these various divinities as nothing more than different names for the same God."

In respect to China, Prof. James Legge, in the department of the Chinese Language and Literature in the University of Oxford, is a competent and sufficient witness. In his "Religion of China," speaking of the two primitive Chinese characters, Tî and Fíen, as affording a clue to the original form of belief, he says: "Thus the two characters show us the religion of the ancient Chinese as a monotheism. How it was with them more than five thousand years ago, we have no means of knowing; but to find this among them at that remote and early period was worth some toilsome digging among the roots of primitive written characters. I will only add here that the relation of the two names which we have been considering has kept the monotheistic element prominent in the religion of China proper down to the present time, and prevented the prostitution of the name Tî, as Deus and other corresponding appellations of the Divine Being were prostituted. ... Five thousand years ago the Chinese were monotheists—not henotheists, but monotheists; and this monotheism was in danger of being corrupted, as we have seen, by a nature-worship on the one hand, and by a system of superstitious divination on the other."

Only a few words more are needed to indicate the force and validity of the evidence from these examples. They present not the dicta of a priori speculation, but the witness of history and archeology. The points in which they appear on the horizon of the past mark the three countries whose monuments open the longest and deepest retrospect into the natural religious thought of humanity for the study of the subject Their testimonies are reported to us by the most learned and competent scholarship, alter special and prolonged study of the fullest resources available in each case—resources not likely to be superseded. These evidences, therefore, have the right of way against theories based in speculative philosophies, superficially sustained by references to the existence of present polytheisms.

CHAPTER I
EVIDENCES OF THE EXISTENCE OF GOD

As all Christian theology rests in this idea of God, the validity of it needs to be sustained and vindicated against all atheistic denial and agnostic distrust Hence the necessity of keeping in view the evidences that the conception is not illusory, but stands for a reality that is fundamental and forever certain in connection with the existence of the universe. After being subjected to the most rigorous tests under our modern scientific and philosophic progress, these evidences remain in undiminished fullness, though the formal presentation of them has been shown to be sometimes faulty. We do not claim, indeed, that this great truth is susceptible of the kind of proof which belongs to the demonstrations of pure mathematical science, immediately compelling the assent of the understanding, but that, nevertheless, it is capable of being established in the same sure, rational certainty which assures all the great duties and practical interests of human life and welfare. Christian theology necessarily holds to a double source of these proofs, because, of necessity, it connects both the world of nature and the phenomena of the redemptive revelation with the being and activity of God. They divide themselves, therefore, under such as appear in the realm of nature and such as are afforded by the special divine self-disclosure in Christianity.

It is not the purpose of this work to present these evidences at length or in detailed fullness. They are properly studied only in special treatises. It must suffice to indicate simply their general nature and leading forms, suggesting thus their immense range and completeness.

PROOFS FROM NATURE

By these are meant all that may be discovered by reason from the natural constitution of the world. If the idea of God is legitimate at all, the world must be recognized as His creation and its constitution and order be credited as the product of His power. Any other relation than this would vacate the fundamental conception of God—especially as it stands in Christian theism. To be God He must be Creator, to whom the earth and man owe their existence and men sustain religious relations. If deity thus involves creatorship, then everything that is made naturally reflects His being and thought The expression of Himself is to be found everywhere—from atoms up to starry worlds and to the still loftier wonders of the realm of mind.

> "The earth is crammed with heaven,
> And every common bush afire with God."

The proper proofs of His existence, therefore, are the sum of all the indications given of Himself in the physical universe, the constitution of the human mind, and the history of mankind. Nothing could be more unreasonable than the notion sometimes suggested, that the truth of theism is dependent on some single argument, or this, that, or the other form of demonstration. The evidence is as immense, diversified, and cumulative as the inexhaustible range of phenomena which the universe opens to study and interpretation—as boundless as the realm of nature and the reach of reason. If it is fair to affirm a single evidence, there must be innumerable evidences. They appear in thousands of different ways to different minds, approaching the question from different angles. Theism thus rests its conclusion, not simply on one or several formal arguments, but upon the aggregate testimony of the whole world-system and all its particulars, upon the force and consilience of all the indications in nature, thought, and life, as they are found running up and compacting their varied logic in one common demand.

Before marking the chief forms into which the evidences have been most conspicuously and fairly cast, it is proper to note some considerations which, though not amounting to positive proofs, create distinct and strong presumptions in the direction of the theistic conclusion. They are not the final word, but they open the right of way, and establish an evident and impressive probability as to the sure issue of the completest examination.

1. The first of these is the universality of the idea of God, The fullest historical and ethnological inquiry justifies the statement that this idea is connatural to man. Wherever the human mind has had its normal and healthy unfolding the idea has appeared. We are safe in saying that there has been no well-authenticated case of a nation or race found utterly without some conception of deity or conviction of a Supreme Being. Even among the lowest tribes are found objects of worship to which divine powers are supposed to belong. Not only has the human mind shown no repugnance to the idea, but has developed it and persisted in it, seemingly under the necessities of human thought This is a strong presumption of its truth. A conviction that springs so inevitably from experience and the action of reason in the presence of the phenomena of the world, and is so perennial in vitality, is justly viewed as founded on reality. That an idea should be so thoroughly normal to the human mind as this has proved to be, forcing itself into recognition everywhere and in all ages, asserting a virtual omnipresence in the thought and belief of the race under all conditions and changes, and yet be wholly false and illegitimate, a universal but necessary mistake, is against all natural and reasonable probability.

2. Another fact of this kind is the religious instinct of the race. This must be mentioned separately, because it is essentially different from that just noted. Beyond the idea of God, found to be so universal, there is the further principle of human nature that shows itself in religious feeling and acts of worship. Deeper than that idea, and operating through it, is the ever-conscious sense of dependence and the need of favor and guardianship such as is involved in the idea of deity. If the relation of creatorship is legitimately included in that idea, as we must admit that it is, man, made by God, was made also for God, with a nature calling for fellowship with Him and life sheltered in His care. We may rightly call the religious principle, thus grounded and forcing expression of itself everywhere, a religious instinct, as it evidently comes spontaneously out of the very framework and set of the mental and moral sensibilities. Not only the intellect with its idea of God, but the heart with its feeling of dependence and impulse to worship, shows a constitutional organization for religion. Man worships something everywhere; if he fails to reach a conception of the true God, he gives

homage to imaginary divinities and seeks favor from them. This principle of worship appears to rise with the characteristics of an organic psychical instinct Its persistence is even more impressive than its genesis. For it cannot be annihilated. It is true that persons averse to the self-control required by spiritual duties and held by love of godless indulgences may live, practically, "without God in the world." But this practical atheism, ignoring the claims of the religious life, is no more a disproof of the constitutional organization of the human soul for it than is the like practical immorality of thousands of men a disproof of the existence of an inherent moral demand. It is also true that speculative philosophies may adopt atheistic theories of the world, but right in the face of these speculative denials, the deeper constitution of man's essential nature, left thus unrecognized and wronged, re-asserts the law of religion, persisting in worship and framing strange cults. History presents conspicuous instances that show how human nature throws back deniers of religion into acknowledgment of religion. Though Buddhism is theoretically atheistic, all the oriental lands over which it has spread are marked by the most developed and multitudinous idolatry. August Comte, who built his "Positive Philosophy" on atheism and a denial of all religions verities, in the end, led by his own emotional nature which his system had defrauded, appended his scheme of deifying ideal humanity and framing an elaborate system of worship and rites. Though he rejected religion in the beginning, the necessities of worship of some sort forced the manufacture of a new religion at the last Similarly, materialism and materialistic philosophies are found returning on their own path. Displacing God in favor of simply matter and force, evolving from these all the physical and mental phenomena of nature, recognizing no spiritual existence in man or supernatural Power above him, they yet in the end consent to the fact of the religious necessities of human life, and even proceed to tell us how men may still worship. Failing by their theories to eradicate the religiousness that lies in the very depths of the soul's constitution, they invite it to exercise the religions sensibilities in reverence, homage, and trust in nature, in the universe, as the highest reality of power. The idea of God is replaced by the cosmos. "We demand," say Strauss, Haeckel, and others, "the same piety for our cosmos that the devout of old demanded for his God."

What is the meaning of this instinct, acting apparently with the uniformity of a psychic law? Do these deep cravings reach out forever only into blank vacancy and to nothingness? Is this necessary worship, clustering around this necessary idea of God, only the acting out of a necessary dream? Is there really no Father in heaven at all, whose hand these needy children are seeking to find, and believing that they do find? These deep and abiding instincts must imply the existence of the Divine Being, unless human nature be fundamentally false. That it is thus false, it is utterly unreasonable to believe. For one of the most incontestable facts, established by observation and inductive science, is that every well-defined instinct, wherever found, implies and points to a corresponding reality. Whatever theory as to the origin of things men may adopt, they recognize the fact that a law of adjustment and correspondency everywhere prevails. Nature makes no halves, leaves no parts standing alone, presents no monstrosities of structure in which subjective constitutional necessities and cravings are left without external complement or supply. The eye is answered by the light, the ear by the atmosphere, the lungs by the air, the appetite by food; over against the intellect, and fitting it, are the objects of knowledge; the sensibilities find their subjects ready for them; the will looks out on a real world of voluntary action. Passing on to the instincts, the certainty of their indications and directive action has ever been one of the things for wonder and admiration. As far as scientifically examined, they are not misleading. Whether they teach the bee to construct its cell, or the beaver its house, or the bird its nest, whether they inform the pigeon of the time and way of its migration, or direct the fishes to the distant waters to deposit their eggs, they are followed safely. They do not mock or point to nothing. Every positive normal instinct expresses a truth and looks to a reality far beyond itself, pointing out the reality through the darkness with almost unerring ray. Not more truly does the lake, reflecting stars from its deep bosom, certify the reality of the starry heavens above it, than do these universal instincts assure the objects which we behold mirrored in them. To look upon the deep religious instincts alone as deceptive and spurious would be utterly unreasonable and unscientific. They, therefore, form a clear and valid presumption for the real existence of the infinite Supreme Being whom they necessarily imply. Reville was right when he said: "It would be irrational in the last degree to lay down the existence of such a need and such a tendency, and yet believe that the need corresponds to nothing, that the tendency has no goal. Religious history, by bringing clearly into light the universality, the persistency, and the prodigious intensity of religion in human life, is, therefore, to my mind, one unbroken attestation of God."

3. Of like import is the benign influence of belief in God. Though utility and truth are different conceptions, and utility does not make truth, yet it often serves to prove it and helps to find it For, to a degree that has made the fact both clear and impressive, truth is promotive of man's welfare, while error misleads and blights. Falsehood kills, like frost, every precious thing it touches. The channels of error can bear no refreshing streams for virtue, order, or happiness. But truth is light, sunshine, and blessed power to the world. It is health and vigor to the mind. It is elevation and progress to society and every human interest. Belief in the existence and government of a Supreme Being has this clear seal of utility. The ideas of God, responsibility, divine favor, and divine displeasure, have been potent for justice, veracity, honesty, temperance, purity, and order. They have tended to repress wrong. They have given nerve to moral character—in individuals and communities. Long before the days of Plutarch, who wrote: "I am of opinion that a city might sooner be built without ground to fix it on than a commonwealth be constituted together without any religion or idea of the Gods, or, being constituted, be preserved," moralists had been feeling that neither personal life nor society could bear the loss of this faith.

The strength of this benign influence has always been in direct proportion to the clearness and fullness of the theistic belief. Prevailingly, indeed, the idea of the Supreme Being has been so overlaid by distorting polytheisms, and His relations to the world and man have been so shrouded in darkness and error as to turn the true fruit, in large measure, into false. Often the notion of God has been so dreadfully misconceived as to pervert religion into conflict with even morality and make it a wasting power. But this result attends the falsification of any great and potent truth. The blight becomes proportionate to the greatness of the truth perverted. But whenever the conception of God has been clear and well developed, discerning Him as the self-existent Maker and Governor of the universe, infinite in wisdom, power, holiness, and goodness, this faith normally strengthens all the best forces of human life and purifies and elevates its joys. The best and loftiest ethical systems the world has ever known are found under the light of the clearest and most positive theism. Under this light the human mind shows its healthiest vigor, the conscience its clearest affirmations and most regal authority. Under it manhood grows to its noblest forms and shows its finest possibilities. Under it science and philosophy are achieving their grandest successes and nations are growing the freest and strongest. It is hardly a falsehood that is bearing these happy fruits, a thorn that bears these grapes.

4. Of real presumptive force, also, is the further consideration that all the facts and phenomena of the world are best accounted for under belief in God. No principle of scientific procedure is more fully recognized than that a theory is proved true by thoroughly explaining all the phenomena concerned. It is discredited when it fails to solve all the facts. If it accounts for all, or best accounts for them, it gains scientific authority. Thus a conjecture as to the sun's place in the solar system passed from a mere hypothesis to the rank of scientific truth in astronomy. So, too, a supposition in Newton's mind has come to stand as the truth of the law of gravitation. As it explains all the phenomena, it is accepted as true, despite the fact that gravitation itself is inscrutable.

Now the doctrine of God affords the most direct interpretation of all the phenomena of the known universe—and the only explanation of many of them. Not to speak of the strained methods and manifold incredibilities which mark materialistic and atheistic science in its attempts to trace the self-evolution of matter and energy from chaos to the present world-order, with all its endlessly diversified structures\, replete everywhere with myriad marks of mind and adaptation to the service of mankind, it is enough to remember that there are not a few of the most integral and essential facts of creation which have thus far utterly baffled all non-theistic solution and before which its science is confessedly helpless. Illustrations of this helplessness are found in the attempts to explain the transitional steps of nature's ascent at the origin of life, of consciousness, and self-determination. With its most searching light it has neither found nor shown, in the mere energies of nature, how the non-living could create life, how unconsciousness could generate consciousness, or how force, acting in necessity, could develop self-determination or the free-will of personality. This failure at these great points, at which the world-existence ascends to its highest and grandest realities, is frankly acknowledged by representative scientists. But we may fairly maintain that the direct solution which the doctrine of a self-existent, ever-living, intelligent free Creator furnishes of these otherwise insoluble problems, is an almost decisive presumption in its favor. To use the words of an able thinker and writer: "It is not rash to say that it is beyond all comparison stronger as an hypothesis which accounts for all phenomena under it than any accepted theory in the science of the physical universe in any department—that of heat, or light, of primal atoms, or of gravity itself." "The simplest conception which explains and connects the phenomena," writes Prof. Henry, of the Smithsonian Institution, "is that of the existence of one Spiritual Being, infinite in wisdom, power, in all divine perfections, which exists always and everywhere."

But the evidence for this great truth is not permitted to rest alone on these presumptions, strong and impressive as they are. There are various evidences that carry a positive demand, in the court of human reason, for recognition of the divine existence. They have taken four chief forms, characterized by distinctive features which come from the parts of nature used as sources of argument and from the logical methods employed. These stand simply for generic types of formal view of nature's witness with respect to the being of God. Sometimes the method is a priori, proceeding directly from the ideas which are held to be necessary in the mind's own insight and consciousness. Sometimes it is a posteriori, as necessary inference or logical conclusion from observed facts. Commonly the reasoning is found to unite the two methods. Sometimes the argument is based on the existence and phenomena of mind; sometimes on the facts of order, adaptation in physical elements and structure in the natural world.

1. The COSMOLOGICAL, or more exactly, the ÆTIOLOGICAL ARGUMENT is, perhaps, logically the first This reasons from the existence of the world as finite, originated, and dependent, to the existence of God, as the necessary unconditioned self-existent cause. It rests upon the rational law of causation—that everything that occurs must have an adequate cause. The law does not assert that being, or all-existence, must have a cause, but only that originated or begun existence must. That the world has had a beginning is indisputable, and science and philosophy are busy only with the question how it came to be. Scientific effort has been intently searching the earth's self-contained records, trying to read the history of its progress and discover how it has become what it is. In all its parts, and as a whole, nature is found finite and conditioned in its being and changes. In this search for the cause of it all, the inexorable demand of the law of causation can never be satisfied till a cause is reached that is not an effect, a first cause, a self-existent, absolute cause, one that is not dependent for its being upon anything else. The first cause cannot be in the world itself, in any phase or stage of its evolution. An "eternal series" of effects without a cause is as utterly unthinkable as a single effect or change without a cause. Hence the law of causality is satisfied only when the cause of the entire movement and product is reached. This "first cause," thus satisfying the whole world-series of events, being necessarily self-existent by the very fact of its being the first and source of all, must, therefore, be identical with God as the Creator of all. Thus, if self-existence, absoluteness, and creatorship are true elements of the divine idea, inexorable logic demands God as the cause of this finite, contingent, dependent universe.

This argument thus draws the line clearly and sharply between self-existent being and all originated and dependent being, and insists that the logic that ascends from the existence of the one to the existence of the other is legitimate and firmly valid. And modern thought has not discredited, but, if possible, strengthened and confirmed it. For it has left no place for the notion of the eternity of the world; and despite metaphysical questionings, science has come to recognize, with most absolute confidence, the validity and universality of the law of causation for the real system of the world, taken as a whole, as having had a beginning in time.

This reasoning is usually lacking in force for direct proof of the personality of God. Its immediate demand is for a "cause," which, it seems, might be interpreted as merely a self-existent something, possibly a blind, unconscious, non-intelligent force, or matter itself. But when the argument is analyzed in its essential implications it is, in fact, found to carry its force far toward decisive proof of a divine Personality. For, first, the first cause must be a free cause; for that which is first alone is, and can be, truly unconditioned, self-existent, and self-determining. Secondly, a free Cause must be an intelligent Cause. For we never reach the sphere of freedom, or self-directive choice, until we emerge from the material, until we leave matter and reach mind. By consent of all great thinkers, self-determining being, being containing in itself the cause of its own activity, is necessarily conceived of as Mind, or intelligent Will. Matter, so far as known, acts under the fixed laws of necessity. Hence a self-determining personal Spirit or Mind, an intelligent Will, must be the first or originating Cause. Logical requirement thus compels us not only to assert the existence of a first, independent Cause, but to regard that Cause as a self-existent Personality. The cosmological reasoning thus prepares the way and suggests the truth which the teleological argument more definitely reveals and establishes.

2. THE TELEOLOGICAL ARGUMENT. Found among the earliest forms of theistic reasoning, this remains one of the most prominent and impressive. It is usually known as the proof from "design "or "final causes." Its peculiarity is that, while based, as is the cosmological, on the principle of causation, it considers specifically the marks of order and purpose everywhere in nature. Teleology, or clear adjustment of structure to predetermined ends, is so omnipresent a reality in the world that we are never out of sight of it. It is traceable in every part of nature, and in many parts so clearly and definitely that there can be no denial of it without violence to the spontaneous and normal judgments of the human understanding. It seems to be co-extensive with the highest law of the universe. Teleology is, indeed, the

great fact which makes the universe a cosmos instead of chaos, adapted to the comprehension and uses of the intelligence with which it has been crowned, and through which it becomes an intelligible and justified creation. Tracing the harmonies of nature's order, the regularity and constancy of its processes, and the subserviency of each part and of the whole to the use of the race, we are warranted in looking upon the world, and even the universe, as a "thought," the realization of a mental ideal, with purpose or intent shining through it everywhere, from its primary adapted atoms, acting like "manufactured articles," up through all the aggregations in which the atoms are built into a cosmos. The argument simply arrays before the view these clear marks of design, these previsive adaptations, with which nature is jeweled, as found in common observation and revealed by the various sciences, and draws the direct conclusion. For the necessary correlate to all this is a Thinker, as the Creator of the world. The excellence of the argument is that the conclusion is directly and inevitably to the intelligence and personality of the self-existent First Cause.

It is fair to say that this form of proof, so conspicuous in the history of theistic reasoning, has been assailed by severe criticism in some modern philosophies and forms of speculative science. Most thorough examination, however, bestowed upon the three chief objections to its validity has made it clear that the criticism has failed either to remove the foundations of the argument or weaken the certainty of its conclusion.

The first objection sought to impeach the correctness of the major premise of the teleological syllogism, viz.: "Whatever bears marks of design had an intelligent author." This has been alleged to be a mere inference, hastily drawn from experience with respect to the products of human industry. It has been declared to be "an outrageous stretch of inference," and the allegation is made that we have no right to assume that because we know from experience that houses, ships, watches, etc., are due to purpose, this, therefore, is the only cause that can produce orderly arrangement, and that, for aught we know, there may be other causes besides mind for it. But over against this suggestion of some other source than mind for nature's "orderly arrangement," stands the unquestionable fact that intelligence is at once the natural explanation of adaptation of means to ends and the only source of it which we know. We do know intelligent will as the source of purposive structures, and we know of no other. No search through all the domain of experience, nor around the entire horizon of the realm of rational thought has helped us toward discovery of any other. No other is conceivable. The suggestion of it is absolutely gratuitous. Mind is left as the only known cause of specialized adaptations and structure. It is surely scientific to follow where the whole induction points. It is absurdly irrational to reject this in favor of some utterly unknown and inconceivable possibility.

A second objection has assailed the minor premise of the syllogism: "The world shows marks of design." This criticism has called in question the trustworthiness of these "marks "by an effort to interpret them as but illusory appearances transferred and imposed by our subjective experience. Numerous speculative hypotheses, breaking away from popular and normal thinking, have treated them in this way, and sought to depict the world-existence, both inorganic and organic, including man, as formed without the agency of purposive intelligence in its construction. They allege that nature may be all that it is at present without the action of any predetermining thought. Physical organs and organisms are not made for use; the use is only a result of what the organ has come to be. But from the ancient notion of crediting all these things to the "fortuitous concourse of atoms" down to the latest form of materialistic evolution, there has not been the least success in hushing universal nature's teleologic language nor in changing the normal judgment of human reason as to the truthfulness of that language. The earth has been too deeply and distinctly molded into the forms of rational adaptation to useful ends to allow belief that it is all only an illusory imposition of our too busy constructive fancy. Moreover, the human mind has too strong a recognitive sense for the peculiar working and products of mind as such, to fail to recognize and own its own everywhere, discriminating it by direct insight and fellowship from every other kind of working. The failure of the evolution hypothesis, in its pure materialistic and atheistic formulations, to obtain or hold confidence, has not been due only to the large fact that it has utterly failed to account for the various great steps of progress and ascent in the world's order, but much more because it contravenes the normal and invincible teleological judgment of the world's scholarship. Only as evolutionism has incorporated a thorough and emphatic teleology has evolution found extended acceptance.

The third criticism has aimed its effort against the conclusion as unwarranted by the premises. Even admitting nature to abound in true marks of design, and conceding the full demand of the law of causation, it asserts that these premises do not reach to theistic proof. There are two types of this criticism. One of them, based purely on the fact of "design" in nature, alleges that, as the amount of design is limited, it applies only to the "forms" of creation, not to the question of "substance," and hence its logical conclusion calls only for an artificer for the world and not a Creator, a former and not an absolute First Cause. The other, basing itself on the reality of the cosmos viewed as a total, with respect to both form and substance, and reminding that, after all, the universe is only finite, affirms that we go beyond warrant of the law of causality when, from this limited product, we conclude to "the Infinite" as the necessary cause. So far as theology employs the metaphysical "Infinite" as the designation of God it falls short of proof. All that the finite world demands is an adequate cause. But admitting the force of both forms of the criticism as far as they are valid, they by no means annul the teleological argument, nor set aside its decisive reach. For it still gives an intelligent author or "creator" for all the "design" or purposive reality in the universe; and the best scientific and philosophic judgment is obliged to make this "design" omnipresent in nature's material, structures, and action, holding it to be a reality of the substance as well as of the "forms" of existence. This makes design coextensive with the universe—it being radically, and, as a whole, the embodiment of a thought—and transfers its Maker from the position of an architect to that of a Creator in absolute sense. And though this universe is still only finite, modern astronomy shows it to be in truth so great that no limits are found to it; in fact, it is the most impressive suggestion of infinitude the human mind possesses, and hence the "adequate" First Cause and intelligent Creator becomes inconceivably great. And thus since the argument still legitimately gives us the Creator of the heavens and the earth and our Creator, it fully suffices to establish the essential element in the theistic conclusion. For, the whole question here is simply whether the actual existence of the universe, with signs of conditioned being everywhere and pervaded from atoms to globes and highest organisms with purposive adaptation, requires the existence of a Creator. "Creator of the universe" to which we belong is but another name for God. The question how great He is, and whether He is to be identified with "the Infinite," of idealistic metaphysics, is a further problem which is to have its own answer without disturbing the sufficient conclusion already certified.

The effort of non-theistic evolutionism, though worked with great talent and all the apparatus of science, to show how the seeming teleology of nature may be illusory, and all its order and teeming adaptations may be due to a blind self-contained evolution of matter and energy, from homogeneity to heterogeneity, through immense ages of time, out of inherent potencies, through survival of the strongest or best forms of existence, generating life and consciousness and intelligence, and reaching the present world-order and man, cannot justly be characterized otherwise than as a failure. To say nothing about the other innumerable blanks and breaks and chasms which have to be crossed or bridged by the use of constant "suppositions" or hypothetical possibilities, idealized as make-shifts in the absence of facts, all along the theoretical world-building, science confesses that this naturalistic evolution has been able to give no explanation of the great and most certain of all the ascending transitions, from lifelessness to life, from unconsciousness to conscious, intelligent mind, from necessity to free-will. Surely this purely materialistic evolutionary hypothesis, with all its constituent and immense assumptions, suppositions built on suppositions, cannot be claimed to possess a tithe of the force that belongs to the teleological argument, which it is invented to set aside. But its absolute futility becomes evident in the further fact that the hypothesis rests upon the absurd assumption that all nature's order, beauty, and utility are the product of chance. For, the explanation that it gives for nature's progress and improvement in organizations, from the lowest to the highest, is based on accidental variations, preserved and strengthened by the blind action of environment under which the useful survive and the inferior perish—

"haphazard improvements upon haphazard variations preserved by haphazard conditions." No design whatever guides the movement. Chance is no denial of cause, but of design. It means mere coincidence, a fortuitous result of forces without purpose. Put under the light of a mathematical exposition of the play of chance permutations, it becomes sure that there would be countless millions to one against the possibility of all the molecules and parts, say, of the human eye, coming together in construction of this organ of vision. This even for the production of a single eye; but for the continued regular formation of billions of eyes, generation after generation as ages pass on, and for all the other constructions and uniformities of the total human organization by which we live and move and have our being, the chances against it mount to positive infinity, and show this chance doctrine to be infinitely absurd. Yet this infinitely absurd notion of chance is the only alternative to the admission of design. There is no rational evading of the recognition of design, and so all the rest of the argument stands.

3. THE ONTOLOGICAL ARGUMENT. The germs of this were involved in Plato's doctrine of "ideas," but it was first formulated by Anselm in the eleventh century. From the existence in the human mind of the idea of a "most perfect being," it concluded that the most perfect being exists—because real existence is a necessary part of the idea of the most perfect being. Descartes, Bishop Butler, Leibnitz, Cousin, and many other eminent writers have used this method of argument; but, standing alone, it has often been shown to be unsound, in confounding real objective existence with the simple idea of it in the mind. A mental concept in itself by no means always assures the corresponding objective reality, whether the concept be of a most perfect being or of any particular lower grade. Existence in re is not a quality of an idea, as the idealizations of men perpetually make manifest. But, though radically deficient in itself, the argument obtains valid force when the concept is viewed not merely with respect to its own content, but especially with respect to the necessity of the human mind's thinking it. Not only must the mind, in order to think of God rationally and fully, think of Him as a being of highest perfections and self-existent, but from the indubitable existence of the finite and dependent world, as

forced upon universal experience, the thought is a necessary one. The mind is compelled to think of such a being as the intuitively necessary correlate of the world-existence. So, what the mind must necessarily think and must think as necessarily existing, can hardly be doubted. This inclusion, however, of the element of necessity in the concept, which thus gives validity and cogency to the argument, while completing it, also modifies it into close assimilation with the cosmological proof and the presumption from the universality of the idea of God. The whole force of the proof, as becomes evident, rests in the fact that, the mind being what it is and the world being what it is, the idea of God as a self-existent being necessarily arises. For the actual existence of real being necessitates the reality of self-existent being somewhere—either in the actual of experience itself, or back of it. Thus, from the notion of "being," taken as real being, must arise the truth of self-existent being. That self-existent Being is God. He is the fundamental necessity of human thought. But thus, as is apparent, the ontology of this argument must cover that of the finite cosmos as well as of the idea of the "most perfect being."

This method of reasoning, however, besides being too metaphysical for general apprehension, fails to exclude pantheistic conceptions, or make clear the distinction between God and the universe.

4. THE MORAL ARGUMENT, drawn from the facts of conscience and ethical law in the world. It may take different shapes, according as it reasons directly from the existence of conscience or from the course of history, with their realities of moral law and necessary presuppositions of a moral law-giver.

The first form takes the simple fact of conscience in man, the perception of the distinction between right and wrong, with sense of obligation, a law of duty incorporated with and made constituent of his own nature, as a direct evidence of the existence of a moral Ruler. For the constitution of human nature, rising through the capacities of knowledge, sensibility, and self-determination, reaches its highest ascent in this endowment enthroning the principle of duty and responsibility. Examination of the nature and action of the endowment makes it plain that this law of righteousness is not a fiction created by the mind or at the will of men, but a reality belonging to the order of the world as objectively constituted—not produced, but perceived by the conscience. It is not made by man, but finds him—finds him through the intelligence by which he is informed of the realities to which he must adjust his life. Moral law stands for a reality that rays itself into view in the human reason, whether men will or not. It does not come at the call or desire, or even at the consent of man. It imposes itself and its high behests upon him. It speaks to his intelligence; it appeals to his will and commands his obedience. This moral law, the grandest phenomenon in the human consciousness, calls for the recognition of a divine Lawgiver in the Creator.

The second form turns its eye upon history, and traces the presence and action of moral law in the broader relation of consequences. It takes note that these consequences make certain that there is "a power above us, not ourselves, that makes for righteousness" in the world, and a clear retributive principle which fulfills the ancient affirmation of a "Nemesis" for wrong doing. History becomes a revelation of God, not as exhibiting within the limits of present human life a complete recompense to virtue or punishment upon guilt, but as disclosing a world-constitution established and maintained in the interest of righteousness. Goodness evokes esteem and favor, while crime awakens reprobation and entails loss of respect and confidence. Righteousness unites society in the strength, happiness, and prosperity of good order; wickedness brings the strifes, collisions, and desolations of anarchy and violence. Virtue is made strength and power to nations; vice and immorality insure decay and overthrow. The funeral of the nations has been the witnessing procession of avenging consequences for violations of moral order. The voice of history is a perpetual testimony that above the tumultuous wrongs and confusions with which human freedom fills the advance of time, there presides a Power that seeks the ascendency of the principle of righteousness, smiling on its observance, and often smiting its violation with rebuking judgments. In all fairness of logic, this moral rulership must be regarded as one with the Supreme Mind, whose thoughts and purposes are so incontestable in the aggregate cosmical plan and movement.

A third form considers especially the mixed condition of things under the moral administration, in which righteousness so often fails to receive its due measure of happiness. Man finds in his own being a clear and indubitable organization or intention for two ends—character and enjoyment, or happiness. To the one end, "character," he is bound by a "categorical imperative," the "conscience," which holds him sternly under a law of righteousness and duty. This expresses a purpose wrought into the constitution and intent of his being. On the other hand, he is just as truly, though with less absolute bond, adjusted, in the essential cravings put into his nature, to pleasure or enjoyment. He justly judges that he is made for happiness, coordinated in the sentient and craving capacities of his soul for felicity. He is tied to it by structural, invincible desire. In the normal experience of life, therefore, these two ends should unite in a true realization. But this demand of human nature largely fails. On the one side, surrender to enjoyment leads astray from the way of duty into utter wreck of character. On the other, obedience to the supreme moral demand, in free fidelity to righteousness, is often compelled to forego pleasure, to bear persecution, to suffer woeful wrong and want. This apparently contradictory experience of life is thus abnormal, failing to present the true realization and consummation of what rightly belongs to humanity. There is a supreme good for man, which stands in the unity of both holiness and enjoyment. But since the moral demand is primary and supreme, the obligation to it is highest and absolute. A will controlled by moral law necessarily must, in the end, realize also happiness. Fidelity to righteousness deserves it, and the absoluteness of the moral command is an implication that it will be realized. Its realization, however, requires the existence of God, whose moral administration alone can carry righteousness into its proper rewards.

This formulation of the argument—which is essentially that of Kant, who, after his destructive criticism in his "Pure Reason," sought in his "Practical Reason" to restore valid ground for belief in God—is less direct and conclusive than the preceding forms. It has the weakness of being more complex and including some steps which are not made absolutely certain, either a priori or by experience. For it tacitly admits that this *summum bonum* for man can be realized only on condition of the soul's immortality. Hence immortality is Kant's first postulate. Further, in resting its conclusion upon the moral demand, it assumes that moral ideals will necessarily, sooner or later, be fulfilled, thus ignoring the plain fact of experience that these ideals in many cases are not made good. Nevertheless, the imperative character of the moral claim, and the experienced as well as evident adaptation of righteousness—adding the teleological element—for the highest type of happiness, are sufficient to warrant the conclusion that this absolute moral demand means a moral Lawgiver who, in a future life, will adjust to worthy character its rightful meed of enjoyment. The conclusion comes, however, as a warrant and inspiration to faith rather than as giving a demonstrated certainty. It presents what is highly probable, because of the actual law of duty, enforced by our highest aspirations.

Against the whole moral evidence the only objection requiring notice comes from certain types of evolutionist contention, which dissolve the moral law into mere custom generated from experiences of utility and incorporated as instinctive tendencies of thought and feeling into the mental habits of the race from the remote past. The moral demand is made an illusion. No absolute morality or law of unchangeable righteousness is left. It is doubly obliterated. For, first, the incorporated illusion called "conscience" is made wholly subjective, falsely projecting its notion as if an objective and fixed order of the universe. And, secondly, the distinction of right and wrong is made at bottom only a question of utility or the agreeable. But this objection altogether fails to invalidate the moral argument. For, its whole plausibility comes from its confounding the broad and ineradicable distinction between the idea of the right and the idea of the useful or pleasurable. They are immutably two different notions. For whatever decision we may in any case make as to the profitableness of a particular act or course of conduct, we necessarily raise the further question: "Is it right?" And the highest moral heroism of the race is often exhibited in following "the right" in the face of the contrary appeals of pleasure or gain, selfishness or ambition. Nothing but the shallowest superficiality can accept the notion that the moral demand is nothing but a subjective feeling, in the face of all the perpetual and impressive historic retributive manifestations and movements which the records of human life are forcing on our knowledge. An objection that offers nothing more valid or sound than this indefensible theory as to conscience can never overthrow the legitimacy and force of the moral argument.

It is proper to observe that though the theistic arguments have usually been cast into the foregoing types, the evidences in themselves are much more numerous, and, indeed, are capable of receiving an almost infinite diversity of form. For every part and point in nature, thousands on thousands, offers some peculiar reality that demands God for its explanation. The single existence of life, appearing after the azoic period of geology, is inexplicable without the living God, having "life" in Himself. The existence of the human mind, in itself, makes sure the existence of a creative Mind. The order and laws of the heavenly bodies give us an impressive astronomical argument. The science of numbers, being but the necessary product of possible relations in time and space, when applied to the size, orbits, distances, and periods in celestial and earthly systems, furnishes a striking mathematical argument, illustrating the geometrizing work of the Great Author of nature. So, from other special sections of creation. There is hardly a point to which we can turn our eyes that does not offer its plea for God. The full theistic proof is, therefore, almost infinitely cumulative, consisting of the consilience of all the myriad lines of evidence from the seemingly illimitable universe. In view of it all we may justly claim that if there is any one truth in the world invincibly assured, it is that of the being of God.

It is well here, in view of this overwhelming adequacy of the proof, to point out the inadvisability of invoking three or four forms, often offered, whose validity cannot fairly be accepted. We should set them aside.

(a) The claim that God is known by direct consciousness, Only the confusion of loose and mystical terminology can accept this. In large measure it is connected with a monistic pantheism which identifies the divine and human essence or substances and holds the divine as coming into self-consciousness in man. It says that to be conscious of one's self is to be conscious of God. But this obliteration of the distinction between the self-existent Creator and the originated being of man is intolerable in Christian theism. Disconnected from pantheism, the claim confounds consciousness with other forms of knowing, and attributes to it a function that does not belong to it, according to all exact definitions. Psychology shows, indeed, that the consciousness may include objective realities, in certain way and to some degree. Some Non-Ego is a co-agent in giving existence to every mental state. But this is through the sense-perceptions. In every act of such perception our consciousness properly includes three objects, viz.: the mental act or state, the ego acting, and the outer object which determines the act. We may, therefore, in a sense, speak of being directly conscious of the material world about us and of our fellow-men. But this knowledge of external objects is more properly credited to sense-perception consciously exercised. Moreover, with respect to knowing God, reference to this only known human faculty for direct perception of external non-egoistic objects, is entirely inapplicable; for no one will claim that God is an object of sense-perception. Of course, after a person, by some faculty of intellectual apprehension has conceived the idea of God or learned about Him, the idea or the information about Him forms part of the personal consciousness. But, manifestly this is not a direct consciousness of God, but only a consciousness of the idea, of a state or act of mind. But the real question at this point is quite another, viz.: how the idea or knowledge was given to consciousness. Consciousness is not the discoverer of knowledge or the creator of ideas, but only the inner vision in which men are aware of the ideas and knowledge which the apprehending and rational faculties perceive and present to it. The idea of God comes into consciousness only through the idea-forming faculties of the mind, as awakened to thought by the phenomena of the world and the experiences of life, and as the reason acts in turning the idea into belief. And it is remarkable that the writers who urge this direct "God-consciousness," nevertheless, when attempting an account of it, proceed to offer only suggestions that correspond to no known laws or capacities of the mind and mystify by inapplicable phraseology. The whole method so transcends or inverts psychology and allies itself with semi-pantheistic mysticisms as to bring doubt instead of certainty into the theistic proof.

This criticism of the claim in this relation is not meant to be understood as at all questioning the truth that the Christian believer, after he has been made to know God through His message of revelation and grace and has been brought into a state of fellowship, prayer, and service, may have such conscious experiences of illumination, regeneration, spiritual life, and help, through the divine word, as shall become certification, even the strongest, both of the being and love of God. But all this is an experience, with a consciousness of it, which is the effect of obedience to precedent knowledge reached by the intelligence.

(b) The assertion of an immediate intuition of God. However evident the divine existence may become under proper showing, it is not self-evident. It is not a truth seen to be clear in the simple terms of its statement. Even the ontological argument does not claim that it is so; else no argument would be used—none would be needed. If men stood face to face with God, perceiving Him directly in immediate vision, the whole history of this effort to certify His existence to reason would be inexplicable. There are, indeed, various a priori elements involved in the apprehension of God, such as the intuitions of Causality, Infinity, Self-existence, Time, and Space, but these alone, and simply as intuitions, are neither the concept of God nor of the existence of God. They are simply the material out of which, in connection with our knowledge of the facts of external nature, the judgments of the reason may affirm the existence of God to be necessary. A combination of both intuitional and experiential elements is involved. The very idea of God is built up cumulatively, and the certification, "God exists," stands only as a conclusion from the premises.

(c) The notion of knowing God by an immediate feeling of Him. Though the absurdity of this notion renders it unworthy of notice, the frequent repetition of it calls for a word of repudiation. Psychology makes no truth plainer than that feeling or emotion, i. e., the action of the mental sensibilities, depends and waits on knowing, and that a man feels, or can feel, only in so far as he perceives or knows something that excites feeling. Simple feeling, without knowing, is a purely imaginary and really impossible experience. To put it in the forefront as a direct apprehension of God only illustrates the nonsense which good men sometimes substitute for legitimate evidence.

(d) The agnostic allegation that the divine existence is wholly a matter of faith—faith as distinguished from knowledge, and instead of it. Led by false metaphysics many writers have declared that God cannot be known by the finite mind. Some of them claim that we should yet believe in Him. Holding that His being lies wholly beyond our knowledge, that we can know neither that He is or what He is, they claim that we can and ought to apprehend Him by faith. Despite endorsement by great names, this view is utterly misleading. It entirely misconceives the real relation between knowledge and faith. A mere belief, without a reason or knowledge to warrant it, is arbitrary, and rests on nothing. Faith always requires some knowledge or evidence to justify it. This evidence must precede, to beget faith. Belief, unsupported by reason, resting only on and in itself, without warrant and not implied by real knowledge, is irrational and without authority. The real relation between faith and knowledge is that faith attends and blends with knowledge. In all human thinking—e. g., in sense-perception, by which we know external objects, or in memory, in which we know again past events, we cannot prove the truths involved, but must rest on faith in our faculties, and depend for certitude on their trustworthiness. But we clearly observe that faith arises only in our knowing, and attends it. The knowing is the initial, primary, basal point in the mind's action. This faith in our knowing, or warranted by it, is always a very different thing from the so-called faith which it is proposed to substitute for knowledge, where knowledge is declared impossible. True faith moves on the certification of knowledge—because we are to live as intelligent beings, children of light and the day.

PROOFS FROM REVELATION

These confirm and establish the evidences from nature. They specially and distinctly certify the existence of God in the Christian idea of the divine Being.

It is remarkable, however, that the manner of this proof is scarcely at all that of direct dogmatic declaration of the divine existence. This is tacitly assumed, at the beginning, as a truth that already has a natural certification and recognition. And the Scripture revelation begins with at once connecting the creation of the world, man, and the heavenly bodies with God's will and power, and presenting the movement of human life and history as under His government and meant for ends of love, righteousness, and spiritual welfare. As God's creational work had already revealed His existence, the supernatural soteriological revelation assumed fundamentally and mainly the form of a redemptive and historical working that should reflect His character and express His will. It was not the truth of His existence particularly that He meant to make known, but to give that view of Himself and of man's relations to Him in which men might be won back to holiness and be saved to the destiny of eternal life. Again, it is God's working that reveals Him. Whatever direct and formal teaching of truth as truth accompanies the movement, the main demonstration of God by this special revelation shines from what He has been doing in the world.

Hence, to specify how, in positive way, the Scripture revelation gives proof of God's being, it is evident that every manifestation of Himself in the facts of the redemptive work and history becomes testimony that He is. Therefore, not only the entire body of evidence that proves the very fact or reality of a supernatural revelation as a whole, but all the specific supernatural phenomena verified by its records, individually, become evidence of His existence. Thus, the miracles recorded, the prophecies made and fulfilled, the supernatural truths and doctrines disclosed, the supernatural morality taught, the whole phenomenon of Judaism and its history in the world, the supernatural character of Christ, the founding and progress of the Church, the conscious fellowship with God found to attend experience of Christianity, the wonderful and beneficent effects of Christianity on personal, social, and even national life, the whole miracle of Christianity as a unique, supernatural, saving, guiding, permanent power on the earth—all throw their immense and final confirmatory witness to the being and government of God, already assured by the evidence of nature.

CHAPTER II
THE NATURE AND ATTRIBUTES OF GOD

We are confronted here on the threshold by the question, pushed into prominence by recent and current agnosticism: "Can God be really known?" Admitting that He exists, can we in any reliable degree know what He is, or understand His nature and attributes? The speculative philosophies which denied the possibility of the proof of the divine existence have been followed by a "synthetic" philosophy, which contends that while, by inexorable logic, a Power back of the evolved universe must be conceded as its First Cause, the Absolute or Infinite, that Power is utterly "inscrutable," and that we cannot predicate anything whatever of it. However, the analysis of the essential conceptions of "First Cause," "The Absolute," and "The Infinite," by equally inexorable logic, shows it to be synonymous with the idea of God.2 In essential thought and practically, God is the First Cause, Absolute and Infinite. We are at this point, therefore, not at all concerned with the question whether we may know that God exists. The whole theistic evidence, as well as the agnostic tacit admission, assures this knowledge. But must God, conceded to exist, be still held to be, with respect to His nature and attributes, utterly "inscrutable," the "unknown" and "unknowable"? Is He, the great Object of religious thought, so absolutely transcendent that we can form no true conceptions of His being and character, answering to the divine reality? Is the necessary Object of our homage and dependence to stand forever blank in our intelligence, so that we must worship we know not what? Are we excluded from reaching any definite idea of Him?

For the sake of clearness we must definitely distinguish this question from another with which it is easily confounded. It is not whether we can know all about God, know Him fully, comprehend Him completely. Theology does not need or pretend to do this. In this sense the finite cannot understand the Infinite. But it does assert the possibility of a true and adequate knowledge of God—that He is neither the unrevealed nor the "utterly inscrutable."

For its rejection of the agnostic claim, theology has a clear warrant in the method or reasoning of the very philosophy which has put forth the agnostic conclusion. For, as its premises it adopts the position inexorably demanded by the necessities of thought and of being, that the Power revealed in the universe must be the "First Cause," "the Absolute," and "the Infinite." Though it proceeds to deny our right to affirm "personality" of the First Cause, it has already, in the very terms of designation, affirmed the predicates of power, causality, absoluteness, infinitude, and elsewhere, of the capability of becoming manifest. If it, reasoning in obedience to the call of logical necessity from the sole fact of the existence of the world, has felt constrained to mark these great predicates in order to assert truth, what hinders us, in view of other facts that are about as deeply pervasive and certain in nature as is the single point of finite existence, from legitimately adding further predicates demanded by equal logic for the truth of things? The marks of intelligence, purpose, and consequent Willpower in the order of the intelligible universe, may as imperatively require the predicate of personality, as simple, finite, changing existence requires that of absoluteness. The manifested "power" making for righteousness, in the conscience and in history, may just as truly call for moral predicates, under the same obedience to logic. In truth, the entire theological agnosticism of this nescience philosophy is due to the arbitrary and false limitations it fixes for itself with respect to the use to be made of the realities of cosmic nature in finding the nature of the Power disclosed in the universe. It willfully refuses to advance upon its own premises and beginnings. If it is correct, as it surely is, in saying that the "universe manifests this Power to us" by its simple existence, and on this fact predicates four or five distinct attributes, certainly we are entitled to claim that the entire manifestation, in all its essential characteristic parts, as well as in its unity, must be read, and all the attributes of the manifested Reality be included in the predicates of the Power. When this is carefully and justly done, something of the nature and many of the attributes of God must become rationally and legitimately certain, as many natural theologies have clearly shown.

We are sustained in this view by what must be regarded as the actual facts of history and human belief. Whatever gross crudities and intolerable absurdities are exhibited among pagan peoples, it is yet historically certain that when, on the basis of their common recognition of the existence of a divine Being, they come to describe Him, some great features of His nature and character have been at least dimly discerned in their best thought, among their philosophers and sages. Though popular mythologies failed even to recognize their gods as creators, or to distinguish between nature and the Power revealed in it, nevertheless a Plato could and did discern in the primal Source of all being a perfect "Mind," ever existent or without beginning of being, uncaused, with intelligence, goodness, and will, who formed the world according to ideals of His own reason, an "eternal Deity," "Creator and Father of this universe."2 Similar results of thought come from other parts of the ethnic horizon, bringing to view collectively a fair list of divine attributes which the best intellect of the world has agreed must stand for essential truth. As a matter of fact, human thought has penetrated in some degree the nature of the Power which the universe reveals. In this affirmation the voice of science is at one with the claims of religion.

The possibility of this knowledge is provided for in the truth, maintained alike by Christian and by scientific postulates, that the mold of human nature has been cast into that of the divine, and can think God's thoughts after Him, within certain finite reaches. Science assumes nature's intelligibility, and in finding the truth of things comes into contact with the divine mind everywhere. In the application of this sure principle, as in science so in theology, our knowing faculties find avenue up to God. The realities of thought within, when reached through our mind's necessary and normal cognitive action, reflect realities that are true for universal mind. All our conceptions of being which enter into our necessary notion of God, and together make up what we call our "knowledge" of His nature, come to us as unquestionably genuine concepts which stand for true knowledge or actuality. For instance, take the idea of real being, which we affirm for God; we know what this reality is from the depths of our own consciousness of real existence. Or take the idea of intelligence; what "intelligence" is we know directly and surely through our own conscious sharing of it. Or, still further, take personality; in our own personality we have an immediate knowledge of the essentials of this reality as we predicate it of the Supreme Being. If other properties or characteristics, such as wisdom, power, righteousness, and goodness, are revealed as divine attributes, these words all stand for concepts of qualities which we know by the necessary action of our minds, to be justly predicable of intelligent personal existences. From first to last in these instances, these concepts are not pseud products, but are formed directly from the most indubitable realities recognized in human knowledge. It is not at all of fictions that theology constructs its portraiture of the nature and attributes of God.

If it be objected that this process simply makes an anthropomorphic God, a being fashioned in the mold of our own minds, it is sufficient to reply that our knowledge does not cease to be knowledge, when we know, as we must, according to the laws and measures of our own faculties. Our faculties are not proved false by their being human. Our knowledge on every subject must be human or anthropomorphic. The firm basis on which, nevertheless, we may still assert the competency of our faculties to reach all the way up to God, is in the great truth of our being made in His image—in the likeness of His personality. The real process in the case is just the opposite of that implied in the objection—that of making a fictitious anthropomorphic God. In the creation of a theomorphic humanity, the human knowing was adjusted, in its finite measure, to the divine, the human capacities becoming an open window for reception of the revealings of Deity.

Accordingly the Scriptures distinctly maintain that we may "know God." It is assumed and placed as the basis of their offered guidance. It is distinctly affirmed (Job 32:8; Ps. 19:1–3; 90:2; Matt. 11:27; 5:8; Rom. 1:19–22; 2:15; 1 Cor. 13:12; John 17:3; Phil. 3:10). This capacity is fundamental to the idea of our being created to be children of God and to live in fellowship with Him. But the Scriptures, with equal plainness and emphasis, assure us that we cannot know Him fully (Job 11:7; Rom. 11:34; 1 Tim. 6:16). When our cognitive powers have done their completed work of thought and comprehension, they know Him only in part, in limited measure. While this knowledge supplies us with real truth, and may suffice for the religious direction of life and the attainment of its true destiny, there are in God realities of being and altitudes of perfection which are beyond human conception. It is a suggestive statement of the Roman Catholic theologian: "As the Infinite, God is seen and not seen by us, as we see and do not see the ocean and the heavens."

The two one-sided or extreme notions on this subject are carefully to be guarded against. On the one hand, a failure to keep in mind the impossibility of fully knowing God has always tended to a worship of Him under a false anthropomorphism, in which some of the supreme attributes of Deity either fall away or are lowered into the finite types and measures found in men. The partial, and often faulty, conception is treated as if it were the whole and full reality. Allowed full sway, it opens the way to the worship of false gods and into multiform idolatry. On the other hand, through failure to recognize the true knowableness of God in the measure of our need, men hold Him as out of all relation both to our finite faculties and to the practical ordering of life. This is the "unknown God" of deism and irreligion, which put Him so far off from the world and interest in our race that practically He is as if He were not. The interests of religion are met only when God, in His nature and relations with which we, in our freedom, are required to adjust ourselves, is revealed and understood. At the same time, we can render homage and adoration, bowing in true awe, only as we also realize that in Him, so revealed and known, there are yet heights of perfection, realities of existence, beyond all the elevations and circumferences measurable in human thought. The warrant of theology to take this position has never been shaken, unless it be only the shaking which settles it upon its immovable right.

THE NATURE OF GOD

How are we to think of this? By the nature of anything, we mean the thing in itself as substance and attributes. In this sense we apply the term nature, although derived from nascor, to be born, or arise, to God. Irrespective of all questions of origin, it is applied simply as a designation of the essence and qualities of an existing being. A distinction is legitimately made in the schools between *natura naturata*, meaning originated entities of both matter and mind, and *natura naturans*, applied to the Author of originated nature. Though this distinction comes to us from pantheistic Spinozism, it serves a good use, severed from monism.

The effort to state the nature of God, therefore, seeks to state what He is. Theology has often put the statement in the form of a definition. A definition, to be complete, would have to both name His substance and include all His attributes. But, because even now, with revelation given, we see only in part, every definition must come short, showing only a partial conception of God. It is necessary, therefore, to note how far such definitions, and even all the most lengthened explanations, are to be considered as expressing Him to our apprehension, viz.: only so far as, in His self-revelation in His works and word, He has declared Himself, and taught us how He wishes Himself to be recognized, thought of, and worshiped. The representations theology gives of His nature are valid only as they express the divine self-declaration. They must suffice not only to distinguish Him from all other beings in the universe, but to exhibit Him in all the essential realities of His nature and character in which He claims human recognition, homage, faith, and love.

The fundamental truth to be affirmed concerning the nature of God expresses the essence or substance of His being—that to which all His attributes belong. As to this, the Christian revelation is direct and unequivocal: "God is a Spirit" (John 4:24). This affirmation is by Christ Himself. In it He made clearly explicit the implications of the Old Testament teaching, which had already involved this truth in its representations of God as the self-existent (יְהוָה, Ex. 3:13–16; Isa. 44:6), and as the living God (Deut 5:24; Isa. 37:4, 17; Jer. 23:36), acting, as always represented, as a personal Creator and Ruler. These Old Testament representations unquestionably contained the elements of the conception of God as a Spirit, a purposive Intelligence and free Power. The explicit assurance of this truth of the spirit-essence of God opens to full view the essential condition for genuine worship. The Object of worship must necessarily be, not matter, but Mind, the Spirit-Being to whom belong supreme knowledge, goodness, and dominion. Otherwise there would be no point of devotional contact Religion would be a link uniting to inanity—a *caput mortuum*—to nothing that could understand or help, answer our prayers, be pleased with our homage, or afford any fellowship.

It has been much the custom of theology to state the essence of God under the term "spirituality," using the word attributively and placing it among the attributes. But the use of this method and placing is discrepant and hardly just. It takes the Essence, which is the subject of all the divine properties and predicates, and classifies it among the attributive predicates. It is better, since the reality concerned is not an attribute, but the substance of God—pure Spirit—that it should have its own fundamental position, undisturbed by a confusing classification.

THE ATTRIBUTES OF GOD

How are we to think of these? We are compelled, under the laws of mind, divinely given, to think of every being or entity under the category of substance and attribute. The term thus expresses the qualities, powers, or properties which mark and define any substance or essence. Substances are distinguished from each other by the complex or total of their attributes. No substance is known directly in its interior essence or reality, but only through the qualities or properties, open to perception or scientific determination, which belong to it and manifest it. Apart from its attributes manifesting it, it would be unknown and unknowable.

The relation between substance and attribute needs to be clearly borne in mind. A substance is not made or constituted of attributes—not a mere aggregation of them. Nor do the attributes exist, save conceptually or in notion, apart from the substance. But the substance is the subject of attributes or properties which inhere in it. A substance without attributes is a mere figment of fancy—is, in fact, unthinkable. Attributes likewise do not exist apart from substance, save as mental products by abstraction and generalization. The attributes of God are, therefore, the real qualities of the divine essence and mark its being and character. They belong to the essence and reveal its intrinsic nature. God's attributes are the immutable perfections of His being.

The old nominalistic notion of the "absolute simplicity" of God, denying to His nature all internal distinction between essence and attribute, between attribute and act, or between one property and another, or between knowing and willing, and affirming all such distinctions to be only our subjective modes of representing Him to ourselves, is not only in contradiction to the necessary laws of thought, but is without warrant of the Scriptures, and amounts to a denial that we can know God at all. The correct conception of his "simplicity" is merely exclusion of all composition and inconsistency. It must be compatible with the fullness of divine attributes. The true conception of His attributes must hold them, not as mere forms of our subjective thought under which we naturally seek to represent Him to ourselves, and which we, therefore, attribute to Him, but as intrinsic properties and characteristics of the divine nature, which are disclosed to us in God's self-revelation in order that we may know Him as He truly is.

It is advantageous to make some classification of the attributes. Sometimes they have been divided into negative and positive, the negative being those by which certain limitations have been denied, the positive those by which perfections are affirmed. Sometimes they have been classed as immanent and transitive, the former relating to God as He is in Himself, internal and quiescent; the latter having respect to His activities in which His nature passes over into manifestation in the constitution and administration of the world. A third division classes them as communicable and incommunicable, those which can be imparted and those which cannot. The best division, the one most generally followed, groups them under the terms natural and moral, the natural being such as pertain to Him as pure essence or being, the moral, such as belong to Him in His ethical perfections, expressing what we specifically speak of as character. The advantage of this division is that it is based upon a very clear distinction with respect to God; it also throws the theological treatment and view in closest, most constant, practical relations with the way of salvation and the duties of the Christian life.

NATURAL ATTRIBUTES

These mark the divine nature considered simply as pure being. They express its properties viewed only with respect to God's essence and altogether apart from any thought of His moral character as good or evil. They desiguate the properties that, taken together, distinguish the substance of God from all other essence in the universe of existent being. They include the following:

1. LIFE. This connects itself directly with the truth that, as to essence, God is a Spirit. For it seems to be of the very nature of spirit to be living being, in contrast with matter which may be void of life. All through the Scriptures God is revealed as "the living God," Jer. 10:10; 1 Thes. 1:9; John 5:26. The finite life in nature implies life in its divine Source, as otherwise its origin remains inexplicable. The contingent life of the world cannot be the product of dead or nonliving existence. Though, despite all our science, life remains mysterious and beyond analytic explanation, our consciousness brings us face to face with it as a high unique reality, marking a grade of being different from all without it. The very conferring of this quality of being reveals God as the ever-living God. In Him life is perfect—infinite, absolute, original, and endless: "Who alone hath immortality" (1 Tim. 6:16), deathless, "from everlasting to everlasting." All the life existent in the universe reflects this truth of "the living God."

2. UNITY—in the absolute sense of being indivisibly One and alone. God is not one of a class of beings. There is no class. There is but One being possessing the attributes of Godhead. He is an indivisible unit, and there can be no duplicate. In this light and with this claim God has revealed Himself in the Christian revelation, from the beginning to its close (Deut. 4:35, 39; 6:4; Isa. 44:6, 8; 45:6; John 5:44; 17:3–5; Mark 12:29; Rom. 3:29–30; 1 Cor. 8:4; Eph. 4:6). The affirmations are unequivocal, and there are no opposing statements or implications. The frequent allegations that the Jewish faith made Jehovah but a national God, only greater than the gods of other nations, is unfair to the teaching of the Hebrew Scriptures, which distinctly repudiate divine reality for the objects of idolatrous worship. There is no Scripture allowance or toleration of polytheistic notions.

An appeal to reason and nature fully sustains this teaching. The necessities of ontological and cosmological thought make the first cause

One—the "first" being the unit of energy back to which the entire multiplicity of cosmic causation is traced, and in which it is satisfied. If the first cause stands for God at all, i. e., for the Being who has the full attributes of Creator of the universe, it is manifestly irrational to think of a duplicate or a plural of Cause. And this is further sustained by the scientific fact of the harmonic unity of the cosmos, its order, adjustment, purposive adaptation, and a rhythmic movement, that show it to be a unitary plan, an actualized thought, from atoms to worlds, from worlds to systems, all circling and advancing in the beauty and music of the spheres. The unity of the creation testifies to the unity of the Creator.

3. SELF-EXISTENCE. This is suggested in the name under which God early revealed Himself, Jehovah (יְהוָה from הָיָה, to be or exist, Ex. 3:14; 6:3), signifying the One who in the supreme sense exists and manifests existence, the One whose existence is in Himself. "And God said unto Moses, I AM THAT I AM: Thus shalt thou say to the children of Israel, 'I AM hath sent me to you.... This is my name forever, this my memorial to all generations.' " The statement of Jesus, "He hath life in Himself" (John 5:26), asserts the same truth. The meaning of it is that the being of God is not originated, is due to no cause back of itself, is not conditioned on any other being, is without beginning, absolute and independent in selfhood as deity. It is the nature of God to be. His existence is grounded, not in His volitions, but in His nature. The frequent use of the terms "the Absolute" and "the Unconditioned" as designations for God cannot, as we have seen, be rightly accepted as implying, as often claimed, that He is necessarily wholly "without relations" to other being; for that would be inconsistent with His being the Creator of all things. For He necessarily relates Himself to what He creates. But it means only that He is absolutely free from all relation of dependence for His own being, which is the eternally existent Ground of all the finite universe. The Latin term *aseitas*, from *a se*, with its English, aseity, the coinage of the theologians, is of doubtful service. So, also, is the Latin designation *causa sui*, in which the word *causa* does not stand for a cause at all in the sense of productive energy, the phrase being simply a form of denial of any cause or origination of God whatever, and an assertion of His absolutely primal existence.

This attribute, like those of life and unity, taught by revelation, stands accredited by the best intuitions of reason and warrant of logic. Ontologically the necessary thought of perfect Being requires self-existence, as needed to fulfill the idea. Cosmologically, as, from actual being now we are compelled to believe that there has always been real being, since the arising of existence from non-existence by no cause is unthinkable, the demand for a First Cause of the universe must mean an unoriginated, self-existent Cause.

4. PERSONALITY. That God is a personal Being is fundamental in the view given of Him in the Scriptures. He is not blind, unconscious energy or force. Everywhere He is represented under personal characteristics—conscious intelligence, purpose, and self-determination. In every disclosure of His power and activity He is seen acting in knowledge, plan, aim, and holy freedom. All pantheistic negations of personality, or resolutions of God into impersonal, unconscious energy, are utterly foreign to true Christian theology.

Personality, like life and unity, rests in the spirit-essence of the Divine Being. For only a living spirit can be a self-conscious, intelligent, and free being. Human personality inheres in the human spirit, not in the physical organism. Those who deny rational spirit and freedom in man show little hesitation in denying personality in God.

The difficulties alleged against the truth of the personality of God, when carefully examined, are found to be based on the unwarranted assumption that personality is in contradiction to His infinitude and absoluteness. It is contended that the ascription of personal attributes to Him is to define His being, and that all definition or specific determination is limitation. Such ascription is supposed to be inconsistent with the necessity of holding Him to be "the Absolute" and "the Infinite." The error is akin to the ancient and mediæval representation of the "absolute simplicity" of God, in which all distinction between essence and attribute, and between one attribute and another, disappeared, except as mere notions of human making. But the seeming contradiction is wholly due to an ambiguity inherent in the use of the abstract terms, "the Absolute" and "the Infinite," as designations of concrete being, and to false conclusions from imaginary implications. When we eliminate the elements not necessarily or rightly included, the conception of "Absolute" being does not necessarily mean a being void of all internal and external "relations," but simply One so subsisting in selfhood as to be independent of all other being for His own existence and power. Thus, "the Absolute" excludes only such relations as are inconsistent with complete independence and self-sufficiency. Also, the designation "the Infinite," when, as required by both Biblical teaching and just metaphysics, it is held apart from pantheistic confusion, expresses not simply in negative, but positive way, the full perfection of the divine nature and attributes. God is "infinite" in all His perfections—is the Perfect Being.

These considerations open the way to a correct answer to the question whether personality is in contradiction of the divine absoluteness and infiniteness. It is evident, first, that personal being is of higher rank than impersonal existence. In the grade of the impersonal we have only things—an order of existence, whether inanimate or physically animate, unquestionably inferior and teleologically subordinate. In truth, personality stands for the loftiest ascent in the constitution of being that we know of. We know of no rank of being above this. We can conceive of none. To see in this loftiest form of being of which we know or can conceive, the form real in our own existence, a finite reflection of the reality in God, is not to reduce or diminish the conception of the divine nature, but to give it the highest conceivable rank. It is evident, secondly, that the ascription of the predicates of personality to God is not in the direction of imposing limitations on His nature, but of recognizing the supreme fullness and completeness of His life. Indeed, the ascription adds, beyond the content of impersonal existence, all the attributes of which we may in the fullest sense affirm "absoluteness" of being and "infiniteness" of perfection, It thus becomes clear, thirdly, that personality, instead of being in derogation from the absoluteness and infinitude of God, is that which is essential to the true affirmation of them. God, to be thought truly, must be a pleroma—a fullness, in Himself, of self-existent, living, intelligent, self-determining, self-sufficing being and powers, or unlimited perfection of all attributes. He is this only by being the absolute and perfect Personality. It has been well written, "Instead of losing His absoluteness by possessing and exercising self-consciousness and self-determination without passing beyond Himself, it is just in this that God vindicates the reality of His absoluteness. He would not be the absolute One were he not the absolute Personality"; and "Though you might deny His infinity without prejudice to His personality, you cannot deny His personality without sacrificing His infinitude." We add, further, that He is the absolute Personality, because there are in Himself the intelligence and free-power that have conferred or created all the external forces and influences by which He is then affected. "Everything that the world means for Him is at bottom an expression of His own self-activity; and whatever of the movement reacts upon Him He recognizes as the recurrent sweep of that reality which is possible through Himself alone."2 It but exhibits the free self-activity in which He goes forth for the creation only of what He has before and eternally taken up in His own personal purposes and plan. The predicates of personality, in truth, necessarily belong to 'the Absolute' and 'the Infinite' in the highest and fullest sense, and are applicable to finite beings only in an inferior or limited sense.

The necessity of keeping the divine personality distinct and clear is seen in the fact that a denial of it means atheism. For an impersonal, unconscious thing, without knowledge or free-power, is not God—cannot be God. Not a single relation, work, or office from that involved in creation, on through preservation, providence, redemption, fellowship, love or help to creatures, could be possible or conceivable if a personal Supreme Being did not exist. In vain would mankind direct worship up to an unconscious sky or make appeal to a pantheistic, impersonal universe. In no particular, however, does the supreme importance of this attribute come into view more impressively than in the fact that a denial of it negatives the whole possibility of the ethical character of God. For ethical character is unthinkable apart from conscious intelligence and freedom. It is one of the mysteries in confusion of thought when Matthew Arnold is satisfied to leave the idea of God simply in the sphere of impersonality: 'a tendency,' 'a stream of tendency,' 'a power not ourselves, which makes for righteousness.'

5. ETERNITY. Being self-existent, God must be eternal—without beginning or end. He is superior to the limitations of time. He is "from everlasting to everlasting" (Ps. 90:2)—without commencement, without termination. He never began to be and never can cease to be. He is the Absolute Eternal Life. This is the essential import of this wonderful attribute; and it is probably about all that ought to be unequivocally affirmed concerning it. The many curious assertions about its involving, for God, 'a successionless consciousness,' an 'eternal now' of view, 'an absolute simultaneity of knowledge, without distinction of past, present, and future,' are probably but futile attempts to establish definitions beyond not only the revelations of the Scriptures, but the reach of the human faculties. At best they are mystical and uncertain. In some respects they are confusing and misleading. We will notice some of their bearings when we come to consider the divine omniscience. At this point it seems best to let the eternity of God stand in its own single, specific divine reality, unconfused by doubtful feats of metaphysical speculation.

6. IMMUTABILITY. This must be understood as excluding all change, either in the divine essence or the divine perfections and purposes. In the essence of His being and in all His character God is eternally equal and self-identical (Ps. 102:25–27; Mal. 3:6; Heb. 13:8; Jas. 1:17; Eph. 3:11). This truth rests in the absolute and infinite perfections of His nature and character. There is in Him no imperfection to overcome; there are no errors to correct.

That the Scriptures sometimes, especially in their earlier records, represent God as 'repenting' (Gen. 6:6; Ex. 32:14, etc.), or dealing in altered way with men, is not legitimately taken to mean any change in His nature or purposes. The expressions are simply anthropomorphic, adapted, after a common manner of human speech, to declare the immutable divine aversion to sin or wrong-doing, when men depart from righteousness. They reflect the changed relations made by transgression in which the divine dealing with men necessarily becomes different. It is just because God changes not, that men corrupting themselves in wickedness experience the change—as if God had repented of all His earlier love and favor.

The difficulties sometimes suggested in connection with the work of creation and with the Christological truth of the incarnation, seem to be more real and perplexing. As to the latter, it has often seemed to involve some change in the interior life of God, through the assumption of human nature into union with the Godhead. Peter Lombard's perplexity with the question, bringing on the nihilian controversy, is well known. The difficulty seems fairly to disappear under the light of the two certain truths: first, that the seeming change was no real change in the divine nature or essence. The divine "nature" in the incarnate union maintained its own pure self-identity, without alteration or confusion. The assumption in the act and state of the union was, and is, rather the taking of a new 'relation,' a new 'manifestation,' than any change of being—a redeeming manifestation and relation, instead of the relation and manifestation of divine displeasure brought in by human sin. And this, as it made the 'nature' of God neither more nor less than before, was, secondly, no alteration of His "purpose"; for the incarnation was part of His "eternal purpose" (Eph. 3:11), "without variableness or shadow of turning." The difficulty with respect to the act of creation, as involving a passing of God from an inactive, quiescent existence into one of activity, if not satisfied by Origen's offered solution of an "eternal creation," can easily be explained along the same lines of distinguishing, as above, between what God is immutably in Himself and as realizing, in time, the order of His eternally self-consistent purposes. His acts are not identical with His essence or attributes.

7. OMNIPOTENCE marks a feature of God's nature, both as to what He is in Himself and in relation to the universe. While expressing a reality in His inner being, it stands for transitive energy, which moves forth and appears in the forces of creative existence. We are assured of it in the Scriptural revelation (Gen. 17:1; Job 26:7–14; Matt. 19:26; Rom. 4:17). It is witnessed to in nature. It is that attribute by which God is the absolute and supreme causality, the Cause of all causes and effects within the range of His acting, or by which He can do, and does, whatever He pleases.

We cannot have a correct view of this attribute without bearing in mind that it, with all the rest, belongs to God only as He is the self-existent, eternal Spirit, Mind, the absolute Personality. Apart from this, as will become apparent, He could not be omnipotent. For the very conception of omnipotence, as required both by Christian revelation and the demands of reason, becomes a possibility only under the ideas which mark and define personal being. An impersonal power stands infinitely apart from God's self-portraiture in His word. In the theories of reason, such impersonal power gets apotheosis only in the irrationalities of materialism or the pantheism which dissolves into atheism.

The divine omnipotence, therefore, stands for the divine Will as Power, and must be viewed under this double conception. Under the conception of it as Will, careful definition is necessary for clearness. Will being Mind as causal for choice and executive action, the Divine Will may justly be defined to be the Divine Mind, in the light of perfect knowledge, as causal for whatever God does. It is, thus, that capacity of God by which He chooses and works for ends. As Will, it must involve these four distinct notions: (a) Intelligence. The causality knows why and for what it acts. Will, being a rational power, is inconceivable apart from this. (b) Freedom. There is nothing outside of Him to take away His absolute self-direction. His choices are absolutely in and of Himself. In the highest and perfect sense, He is the Author of them. This, however, must not be supposed to imply anything of what we understand by "arbitrariness"; because in His freedom He is also the supreme and absolute Reason. (c) Power. Choosing is always an exercise of power, an act of self-direction. In the primal Being it must be originative of movement. Absolutely originative power is inconceivable, except as rational free Will. (d) Immanent moral Preference, i.e., God, being eternally holy, always freely chooses the right and good. It is in this that His ethical character holds the life of omnipotence in harmony with righteousness.

The various distinctions usually indicated by theology as marking special modes or relations in the activities of the divine will, must be maintained for the sake of the light they throw upon the divine administration. These are between God's will as, (a) secret and revealed, will not made known and will disclosed; (b) decretive and preceptive, such as pertains to decrees fixing issues of administration, and such as furnishes precepts of duty; (c) efficient and permissive, marking its relation to events as absolutely wrought by God, through forces of His own, and events allowed to take place by and through creature free-agency—the latter illustrated when He permits the evil done by men, the former when He effectively works the good; (d) absolute and conditional: absolute when He wills something unconditionally, as, for instance, the work of creation or the great scheme of redemption; conditional when He subjects certain results to terms to be met by free agents; (e) antecedent and consequent, meaning almost the same as the last, as, for instance, antecedent, in the providing of salvation for the free acceptance of mankind, consequent, in the actual salvation conferred on compliance with the terms of the provision. We can rightly understand the divine government and its administrative dealings with men only as we keep in mind these leading distinctions in the action and bearings of the omnipotent Will.

But it must be viewed also under the conception of power. This expresses an efficiency that is all-mighty. "I am God Almighty" (Gen. 17:1), is the key-note of the teaching of revelation (Job 26:7–14; Matt. 19:26; Rom. 4:17). And the universe of creation, as opened to view through modern astronomy, world on world, system on system, countless and vast, bounding each other in the immensities of space, in every direction of outlook from our globe, extending in distances beyond telescopic penetration, circling in the rhythm of structural harmony and unity, utters everywhere and forever its amen to the Biblical assurance that God is, indeed, omnipotent. The power to create and sustain such a universe as the actual one is found to be, can be nothing short of infinite. For, within the bounds of this universe, wherever these bounds may be imagined to be, there exists such an inconceivable grandeur of established, yet dependent and coordinated forces and efficiency, as to assure us that the Will-power which has originated and sustains all this, could, in freedom and at choice, transcend all present bounds of creative manifestation in infinite fullness of resources.

And yet we must not fail to qualify this predicate of power under real and vital limitations. The paradox of this limiting of omnipotence disappears when we understand that the limitation does not mean a deficiency of energy or might, but expresses only a relation which God's working power bears to the objects of the divine choice, in the light of which the so-called limitations are seen in basal truth to be forms or features of the divine perfection. The attributes of God must not be thought of as if they stood or acted each alone, but as constituting, so to speak, an infinite perfection of being in their unity. Because of the total completeness of the divine nature, in all the attributes existing together, and because of the consequent established nature of things in the universe, some objects are immutably outside of God's choice, and hence cannot be objects of His power. His power cannot effect them because they can never come within its range. It is not derogatory to God to say, as an apostle does, that He "cannot lie" (Tit 1:2), or do anything contrary to His moral excellence. He cannot make right wrong or wrong right, or obliterate their eternal distinctions. He cannot act irrationally or effect things that in themselves are self-contradictory, as that a thing should be and not be at the same time, or make an event already past not to have occurred, or so overthrow the mathematical relations as to have a shorter than straight line between two points, or cause two and two to make five. But the whole limitation thus asserted manifestly means simply that God's power cannot be exercised except in harmony with His perfect nature and self-consistent will. He is unlimited by anything outside of Himself. The limitation comes from the very perfection of His being and His free self-harmony with the expression of Himself in creation. The omnipotence of God, being in free-will power, does not exclude, but implies the power of self-limitation. His freedom gives Him power over the exercise of His power. He is not shut up, either from without or within, to a necessary use of it all. His self-limitation is an exercise of His freedom. It was not an abnegation of omnipotence, but the use of it, when the divine nature humbled itself into the form of human flesh.

8. OMNIPRESENCE—often designated ubiquity or immensity. The Scriptures represent God as being everywhere. (1 Kings 8:27; Ps. 139:7–12; Acts 17:27, 28.) Reason concurs in this view, as the divine working in cosmic creation and preservation implies it. The attribute means His superiority to space limitations as His eternity does to those of time. As He endures forever, without beginning or ending, so He is

present everywhere in the universe. A precise definition of it must cover two aspects of the whole conception, as involved in the distinction between a potential or operative, and an essential or substantive presence. The distinction is legitimate, but both kinds of presence must be embraced in the divine omnipresence. The omnipresence by efficient power or dominion, finitely illustrated in the efficiency of an earthly sovereign with respect to his dominions, God's power extending or acting everywhere in the universe, must enter into a true notion of the divine reality. But we must include also the truth that it is a personal presence, a presence of God in His essential personal being, not at all, indeed, in the way of material expansion or diffusion, or by necessity, as if bound to the universe, but in His freedom and by His will filling all things with Himself. In the reality of His personal essence, He who reveals God says: "Where two or three are gathered in My name, there am I in the midst of them;" "Lo, I am with you always." That this personal omnipresence must stand in the divine freedom, and not in compulsion, is evident from the truth that God may diminish or enlarge the universe to which He gives His presence.

9. OMNISCIENCE, or infinite knowledge. This also, as truly as life and unity, rests in, and coheres with, the divine personality. Knowledge belongs only to a personal existence, and the reality of this attribute stands, in the harmony of Christian theism, in holding God to be the absolute, ever-living personal Spirit. It is well to note, as we mark the attributes, how vital is their union, as well with each other as in the divine Essence.

As rightly defined, omniscience means God's absolute and perfect knowledge of all things which are objects of knowledge, whether past, present, or future. Nothing is beyond His view and full understanding. The mysteries of this reality, while checking the temerity of dogmatism, nevertheless allow, under the teachings of the Scriptures, a large determination of assured theological truth. In few relations is the Scripture revelation more explicit and comprehensive than in this—showing all things, from starry worlds to the secrets of human souls, eternally naked and open before the divine eye. (Ps. 147:4; Matt. 10:29; Ps. 33:13–15; 1 Kings 8:39; Acts 15:8; 1 John 3:20; Heb. 4:13;

Ps. 139:1–6; Matt 6:8; 10:30; Mal. 3:16; Isa. 46:9, 10; Isa. 44:28; Acts 2:23; 1 Sam. 23:12; Matt. 11:21; Acts 15:18; Rom. 11:33.)

We are warranted in marking some characteristics of the divine knowledge. As the human intelligence is an image of the divine, we may understand, in a measure, God's knowing as reflected in the modes of our own minds. Only His is free from all the limitations of ours and infinite in its vision. We are entitled to say that He knows in two ways, viz.: by self-inspection and objective vision. The oft-debated question whether God's cognition embraces the world-existence objective to Him, cognizing it as an external object, which, by its objective existence, becomes knowable, is no longer disputable. The notion that an object-object is inconsistent with the absoluteness of God's cognitive activity, is necessarily abandoned. We may affirm the divine knowing to be (a) Intuitive and immediate. God knows by direct view—unembarrassed by roundabout logical processes of inference and deduction. (b) Simultaneous. It embraces all things at once and always, eternity in all its range and fullness ever-present to His view, not needing to wait on the historical development of the world to know what will be, nor dropping out of knowledge what has been. (c) Full and exact. It is not deficient, is short in nothing, but infinitely inclusive and clear to atomic minuteness. God knows things as they are, the past as past, the present as present, the future as future, the free as free. Hence, (d) Infallible. Its perfection excludes mistake. (e) It is absolute. It is not conditioned on any unknown contingencies. Knowing the futuritions of contingent events, He is dependent for His knowledge neither on any predetermination of events nor on the volition of free agents. What He knows may be conditioned on the free will of men, but not that He knows it. In connection with this last point we will have more to say presently.

In immediate and inseparable relation with these characteristics of the divine knowing action stand the objects of God's knowledge. It is in defining these objects that the mysteries of it impress us. For the most part no perplexities hinder a distinct construing of the Scripture teaching. The difficulties that sometimes embarrass appear only in the more complex relations. This becomes evident when we seek completeness of view. (a) God knows Himself, in all the fullness of His nature, the perfections of His being, and the range of His purposes. There seems to be no propriety in excluding His self-knowledge from place under this attribute, on the basis of a definition which makes omniscience essentially a transitive attribute, as having relation only to the objective universe. God is subject-object to Himself. The infinitude of His personal perfections requires this. He would not be God if he did not comprehend Himself, in His intelligence as well as other attributes. The Christian revelation and Christian theology place Him absolutely apart from the pantheistic god of modern philosophy, in which "the absolute" becomes self-knowing only in human intelligence. God's omniscience reaches, first of all, into the depths and fullness of His own being. Origen thought that since God is "infinite" He cannot be fully known, even by Himself, but he failed to recognize that the "infinite" is not the indefinite, and that the definitely infinite is equaled by the Infinite Himself. God is defined, is contradistinguished from everything which is not Himself, and because He is defined He is also comprehensible by His own thought. (b) He knows all objective reality, reality in the cosmos and history, that either is, has been, or shall be. This, of course, at once involves a knowledge of the future, though that future contains not only the ongoing of the physical universe, but the free conduct of personal life and the course of history. Whatever perplexities may be encountered in effort to explain this, the Scripture statements seem to require recognition of it. It is involved in the facts of prophecy, and in distinct affirmations in connection with prophetic fore-announcements. (Isa. 46:9–11; 44:28; 45:1–5; 53:1–12; Acts 2:23, and elsewhere in almost numberless passages in the Old and New Testaments.) (c) He knows all the relations of things, or all things in their relations—throughout the universe of physical and moral order. In this, manifestly, is based the possibility of his prescient knowledge, and of righteous moral requirements and administration. (d) He knows the essence of things, the very substance of their being, with all their inherent properties. For He is the Creator of all created being, and has formed their constituent existence. (e) He knows the possible, in His own will and power, and in respect to the universe. (f) His knowledge, according to widely accepted interpretation, embraces also conditionate contingencies—or what men would be or do in certain conditions which are never actualized—designated in theological metaphysics as scientia media. It means that the event, the occurrence known, is dependent both on human free-will and on circumstantial conditions which never become actual, and yet God knows what would take place in such supposed conditions. Calvinistic theology has usually declined to accept this representation in the interest of its contention that the divine foreknowledge is based in the divine fore-ordination, leaving no place for such conditionate contingencies. But this scientia media means to preserve genuine freedom for man, and assumes that such future events are open to God's view, not because of any predestination of them, but through God's absolute foreknowledge as capable of foreseeing the truly free acts of men in all possible circumstances, even what would have been had the circumstances and conditions been different. It is a foreseeing of the ideally possible as of certain futurition in the supposed circumstances. Several illustrative incidents appear in the Scriptures in connection with the Keilahites (1 Sam. 23:3–13), and the Tyreans and Sidonians (Matt. 11:21–23). But this problem rests on two others upon which speculative theology has offered different answers, viz.: the oftasserted timeless and successionless consciousness of God, and the divine foresight of the free acts of personal beings. These require consideration.

First, with respect to the alleged timelessness of the divine consciousness, as being void of succession, so as to merge past, present, and future into an eternal now, supposed to be involved in God's "eternity," the affirmation of it stands only as a philosophical notion. The Scriptures, as giving God's self-revelation, represent The Eternal as active in successional creation and providential government, dealing with men and nations according to progressive time relations and changing character. The speculative determination that, in truth, God does not foresee at all, but only "knows" timelessly, that

> "Nothing to Him is future, nothing past,
> But an eternal now doth ever last,"

must be regarded as an unwarranted statement of God's relation to time, and is more and more regarded by modern theology as a mistaken philosopheme in conflict with Biblical representation. For the absoluteness of God's 'eternity' is complete in His being, without beginning or ending, and in His being Himself independent of all the time-limitations which He has established in the world-order. God's knowledge of temporal successions, taking place objectively in world-events, must necessarily belong also to His subjective consciousness, if, indeed, He knows things as they truly are. This subjecting of His consciousness, so to speak, to the knowing of temporal successions is not in derogation of the absoluteness of His knowledge, but the perfection of it. It marks the infiniteness of it, in including the perfect truth and order of the universe of created existence. Instead of the postulate of a simultaneity of knowledge in which time relations and successions do not come, through intelligence, into the divine consciousness, this knowing of things as they really occur in cosmic progress and in human life is required as absolutely essential if we would hold our view in harmony with the representations of the Christian revelation. And it involves all the interests of morality and religion. For every human life is set in time relations and movement, in which, under the eye of God, it is to receive His approval or condemnation, according as it relates itself to the obligations, opportunities, and responsibilities of the passing days and years. If God did not observe the distinctions of time, if to His view the past, present, and future stood before Him eternally alike, the differences between what has already been actualized, what is being done, and what is yet only a possibility of the future, would not appear. The wrongdoer of to-day would not be distinguished in his guilt from the innocent man he was yesterday, nor from the reformed man he may be to-morrow. The moral progress of men and the race would not enter into the divine discernment, and the moral rulership could not ethically correspond to the actual attitude of the moral subject. In like manner, in the sphere of religion, the "eternally similar" view would not mark the transition from the unbelief and condemnation of yesterday to the faith and adoption of to-morrow, in the return of the sinner. In the interests of both morality and religion, we must refuse the suggestion that the divine transcendence of time limitations involves a successionless omniscience. There must be, rather, a perpetual mutation in the divine omniscience, as in the world of history the realities of the present become the realities of the past, and the possibilities of the future become the realities of the living present. But, at the same time, we must remember that "with this change in His knowledge there is no mutation in God Himself given." It is because He is immutable that He knows the changes in what is not Himself. If it should be said that this asserted timeless consciousness of God should be affirmed only—which it is not—of His existence in the solitude of His eternity before His creation of beings other than Himself, in which time and time-measurements are said to begin, we are still in serious doubt whether the affirmation would be fully tenable. The suggestion by Origen, of "eternal creation," creative activity being co-eternal with the very being of God, without any acosmic solitariness before it, though not at all assured to be true, has yet enough in it to justify extreme caution in assuming that there ever was such precosmic divine consciousness. But even if the assumption is conceded, may it not be beyond warrant to declare the consciousness to have been successionless or destitute of distinction of before and after, of the ideas of past, present, and future? For then, as after creation, God was the living God, in the fullness of absolute Personality, embracing perfect intelligence, love, will, or self-determination, a Triunity in life, thought, and fellowship, independent, self-sufficing in resources and happiness—one in essence, but with an infinite fullness of attributes. We cannot contend for the doctrine held by Augustine and Thomas Aquinas,2 reducing the divine unity into a "simplicity," in which the distinctions between substance and attribute, and between the attributes themselves, fall away from the immanent existence of God, all lost in an indefinite motionless identity. For when all these distinctions in God are thus obliterated by being counted as only our own subjective conceptions, the divine Essence proper is left as, in itself, destitute of all determination, intrinsically void of definite perfections of personality and activity, and approaches the immobility and senselessness of the Hindu Brahm, the indeterminate "being," the "no-thing," or "no-thought," of the Hegelian philosophy, rather than the Jehovah of revelation with infinite fullness of positive personal perfections and activity. But if God is thus truly the ever-living personal God, with intelligence, love, and purpose, He, before all worlds, when only Himself existed to be known, must have known His own possibilities of will and power, and must, even from eternity, have thought and purposed the universe-creation before creating it, and, thus, seemingly at least, have included in His consciousness the succession-principle of before and after. The world-idea, with its order of time, was surely in the divine mind and counsel before God created the world, so that time in world-reality is now actual only because the time-idea was real in the divine mind and will before creation. For though His omniscience, from eternity, then already embraced a knowledge of the world, it embraced it, not as eternally actually existing, but as possible and to be; and through what was then present as purpose in God, and its actualization in creation, He certainly appears as holding His own activities to an order of succession. The same result appears when we trace the significance and bearing of the essential divine attributes. If the attributes of knowing and doing (intelligence and will) are really divine attributes, He foreknew the sin of mankind, and, according to His "eternal counsel," or will of love, determined redemption. But the actualizing of its complete provisions waited for "the fullness of time," the omniscience of God thus embracing the sequences of before and after, implying necessarily, if He is truly conscious of His own knowledge, a consciousness also of the time relations which it embraces and covers. Julius Müller well says: If this world, moving itself in time and place, exists as such by the creative Will of God, it is also as such present to God in an objective manner.2 And this, after all, is all that this disputed question has ever legitimately involved. For whether we think of the divine consciousness, either antecedently to creative existence or since the beginning of the world and its unfolding history, the point really in dispute is not whether God in His own being and omniscience is independent of temporal succession, but only whether to that omniscience the past, present, and future are so present as to be only "eternally similar," an "eternal now," so that His consciousness does not embrace the relations of before and after and the temporal mutations as they develop. If God has included in His own counsel or plan from eternity and its accomplishment in time, a relation of sequence—the profoundest reality in the meaning of time—it is certainly unjustifiable to deny that He is conscious of it, or to go on repeating the rash assertion that

> "Nothing to Him is future, nothing past,
> But an eternal now doth ever last."

The second problem has equally vital bearings and naturally has engaged theological thought: the question of the divine prescience of the free acts of creatures. Assured that God knows all things actual in the present and past, and in the future also, so far as their futurition is not left to human free-will or the result of such will-force upon nature, and that, further, He knows these in their order and relations of time; assured, moreover, that He knows all the possibilities of being and occurrence in Himself and the creation, the great remaining question is whether God does, or can, know beforehand what human beings, acting in really free choice, will do, or whether He first knows it when they make their actual decision. The answer involves the reach of the divine foreknowledge on the one side, and on the other the question of human freedom and moral life. While from the early Church down through the scholastic period, and generally also in Protestant theology, the full divine prescience of the acts of human free-will has been maintained, modern thought, both philosophical and theological, has been showing an increasing tendency to question it. The incentive to this is, in part, to escape the paradox of a prescience of the decisions of free-agency before the decision is reached; but much more, to safeguard the principle of moral responsibility from encroachment of determinism. In ancient times Cicero said: "If the acts of man are foreseen, then there is a certain order in them, an order of causation; and if there is an order of causation, then fate is the result." Similarly, Aristotle expressed doubt of the possibility of such foreknowledge.2 And recently various theologians in different branches of the Church, whose prominence and ability add weight to their views, have strongly argued against including the strictly free acts of men in the divine foreknowledge. Martensen, Rothe, Dorner, in Europe, and McCabe and Whedon in America, are types of the modified conceptions which are thought to be required. All of them, except Dr. Dorner, are positive in holding that

God does not embrace contingent acts of human freedom individually in His foreknowledge, while the latter, negatively, hesitates to assert dogmatically their real inclusion. The problem is one of immense importance and embarrassed with varied speculative difficulties. The solution of it, if at all possible, can be reached only through the most careful comprehension of all the elements involved and the elimination of suppositions utterly inadmissible.

We must certainly exclude the supposition of the divine prescience of all human choices and acts on the basis of the divine fore-ordination of whatsoever comes to pass. For such fore-ordination inevitably reduces human freedom to mere semblance, and involves a substitution of divine determination in the place of human self-determination or the liberty of alternative choice. Such fore-ordination is in unqualified contradiction of the very foundation of moral life and responsibility. That human personality includes the normal capacity for the exercise of diverse choice, and that the entire reality of just responsibility arises therefrom, is one of the most indubitably certified realities revealed by God through the psychology of the soul, the constitution of life, and the sacred Scriptures. The whole Christian revelation, from beginning to end, presents and treats man as possessing this personal freedom and as truly amenable for its use. Despite metaphysically alleged difficulties concerning this freedom, all human life and its responsibilities are so organized into it and built upon it, that neither personal nor social life can be lived or achieved in practical repudiation or neglect of it. No solution of foreknowledge, therefore, can be accepted as true which conflicts with the reality of this freedom. But the difficulty with this fore-ordination as a proposed explanation of the divine prescience reaches also to a point beyond its strife with man's freedom. For it involves utterly incredible consequences with respect to God Himself. For if these human volitions are all infallibly known because predestinated, known simply through God's self-consciousness as mirroring the world-life fixed in His decrees, then they all, the evil as well as the good, fall into the category of divine volitions, predetermining and necessitating all human sin. It would trace the authorship of sin back to direct volition of the Holy One. If, therefore, we are to believe that God foreknows the free volitions of men, created with the potency of alternative choice, and all the temporary bends and curves they cause in history, we must have some better reasons for the belief than this evasive theory of absolute predestination, which is thus doubly self-confuting, in menacing at once the fundamental grounds of all human morality and responsibility, and the ethical character and self-consistency of God.

We must also exclude the notion that such prescience is explicable by the theory that the future acts of human freedom are not future to God. The explanation is sought in such a metaphysical conception of the divine 'eternity' and 'immutability' as implies not only that the being of God is without beginning or end, and unchangeably perfect in essence and attributes, but also excludes the reality of divine duration, the basis of the time-idea, which distinguishes the past from the present and the present from the future. It is a remnant of the gratuitous and confusing philosophies of the schoolmen, who, while defining the various attributes of God as human thought must view them, yet, at the same time, strenuously cautioned against supposing that they really belonged to Him as He is in Himself, and made them all stand for one and the same thing, merging all distinctions of essence and attribute, knowledge and will, power and act into an indivisible identity and simultaneity, so that in the divine consciousness there is simply an eternal and immutable "now," a *tota simul*, and God is eternally doing and knowing the same things. It is only a part, a fragment, of this general view, detached from the rest, that this theory uses in the effort to explain this divine foreknowledge—its spurious idea of the relation of God to time. It begins in a false conception of time itself, as time is at all involved in this question. It is hard to follow the kaleidoscopic diversities of meanings in which the word "time" appears among theologians and metaphysicians. Sometimes it approaches the appearance of a concrete entity—a creature of God. Sometimes it is a 'relation' between events, sometimes an 'attribute' of finite existences, sometimes an equivalent for 'duration,' sometimes the reality of 'succession,' or events covered by experience in consciousness. In the easy and rapid shifting of use in these and other different senses, writers inflict upon themselves and others a magic verbal legerdemain in which the truth is lost or an incredibility substituted. So we need to safeguard our thinking from the perversion of these spurious ideas of time. Beyond all question the idea arises in the human mind out of its conscious experiences—not as an immediate gift of experience, but on occasion of experience. Our conscious mental acts and states are known to continue or endure to some degree. This gives us the reality of duration, known in consciousness as belonging to the human personality and its mental states and acts, just as also our sense-experience gives the reality of extension, for material bodies. Still, duration is not "time," as extension is not "space." But consciousness shows one step more in our knowing. After experience gives us knowledge of "duration" and "extension," the mind by an inevitable necessity of mental intuition, discerns the reality of TIME, as required for this empirical reality of duration, as space also is for extension; i. e., both "space" and "time" are directly seen to be the necessary and fundamental conditions or presuppositions for the material world and for personal beings with consciousness of duration, change, events, movement, and progress. Time is, therefore, simply the absolutely necessary presupposition or condition for a continuously existent world with consciously active living beings. It is only a correlate to duration and events in succession. It is not a substance, either matter or spirit; for it has not a single attribute or property of either. It is not an attribute or property; for attributes belong only to substances. It is not simply a relation; for relations can exist only between things that are or occur in space and time. But so far as we can know and define it, it is simply the pre-condition to the possibility of finite, enduring existences and successive events. "Events" are not time, but they require and take place in time. "Succession" is not time, but takes place in it. The moving heavenly bodies, the recurrence of day and night, months and years are not time, but imply it, and form a kind of clock-work by which it may be measured. Even our consciousness of duration, of the relation of before and after, the distinction between then and and now, is not time, but a revealing of time as the prerequisite for the very existence and life of self-conscious, personal beings, with their progressive activities—conditional for this, just as space is conditional for the existence of the material universe. But now, when we recall the conceded truth that before God created finite existence there was nothing but Himself, in His own fullness of life, intelligence, power, and the inner activities of His personal and triune life—only non-entity, nothingness, blank void and vacancy, in which God set the universe—we begin to see what our conception of time should be. If "time" was anything then other than the nothingness in which God placed the moving, advancing order of the world, it must have been the "then" within the self-conscious life, thought, will, and action of God Himself, when "He spake and it was done, commanded and it stood fast." The world-time, in and of which we have our experience and intuition of time, and knowledge of it, must, of course, be due to God's creating and establishing a time-ordered world, with its continued existence, changes, and progress. And in this view, we perceive, too, the truth that for all this world-time, no other creating by God was necessary, nor, so far as we can know, exercised, than that which originated finite existences, material and personal, under the law of beginning, continuance, and change—a world-life, instead of the nothingness that was before; a world-life that in conscious intelligence recognizes its own continuance and advance, and measures the "time" in which the advance takes place. In view of these indubitably evident truths, "time" becomes simply the ideally, yet truly known pre-requisite to the life of intelligent, self-conscious, active beings—the whenness, the beforeness, the presentness, the afterness recognized as real in the duration of such self-conscious, active, intelligent beings. Beyond all doubt, Kant was right when he asserted time to be an "a priori form of thought or knowledge," the absolutely necessary setting in which the mind must recognize all duration or succession, the pre-condition of the possibility and reality of all phenomena. But his error was in his intimation that time might be only a subjective idea, without standing for an objective reality. For as the consciousness of duration, or duration itself, is real, so must be the time which is its pre-condition. But this truth—recognized as truth wholly apart from the peculiar Kantian philosophy—that time is a necessary form of all knowledge in self-conscious intelligence, thought, and purpose, carries us on toward the conclusion, already mentioned, that the divine knowledge, even from eternity, embraced not only "duration," but the idea of "time" as the involved reality. God's 'idea' of the world and His "purpose" to create it, before His actual creation of it, it would seem, must have required this, unless we are ready to admit that He did not know what was going to be so essential and fundamental a feature of the universe He proposed to create. The possibility of all being other than God, lay in the potentialities of God, as able to create. The finite universe, which His power created, instead of the non-existence outside of Himself, shows the eternal time-idea in the mind of God, and that He incorporated it into the finite movements and measurements of the world and humanity; and this warrants a reaffirmation of the view which makes our whole cosmic time only a "portion of eternity." For, as confirmatory of this view, stands the fact that all philosophy is compelled to speak of both space and time, considered in totality, as "infinite"—because the notion of limitation is not applicable, and is as unthinkable as is bringing eternity itself under limitation. Whatever bounds we may set to the reaches of space or time, we must confess to the truth that space and time lie beyond, and no bounds are applicable. God and time, i. e., the possibility of "duration," are, after all, not so far apart as many oft-repeated theological statements have represented.

But on the basis of the exclusion of time from the divine consciousness, the notion that future acts of human freedom are not "future" to God, is made to rest on an untenable conception of God's "eternity," or of His "inhabiting eternity." In connection with the representation that He is without time-consciousness, the reality of His duration is thrown under confusion. It is subsumed and subverted under what would be expressed by an extension of His substance through eternity—rather than His personal living existence and activity, without beginning or end. The perversion of view is connected with the statement that He exists *sub specie eternitatis.* As put recently by Dr. R. S. Foster (italics mine): "He inhabits eternity; not that existing in one time He looks forward through all time, but that He exists in all time. As to the events themselves, there was a time when they did not exist, and in that time He knew them as non-existent, but as to be; but as He was at that very time also existing in all coming time, He knew them in that coming time as existing. If the mode of eternal existence is permanent existence in eternity, and not a passing from one time into another, which we have seen it must be, the position here taken is irresistible.... If we could conceive ourselves to be existing to-day in a day a million years hence as well as to-day, we should then see what now is, for it would be under our present gaze; but we should also to-day see what will be nonexistent for a million of years, for by supposition we are also to-day existing millions of years hence, and are seeing as real and present to us the events of that day.... Things that will be are to Him who now lives in the time they will be.... If at some future time they will exist, and if the infinite Knower has a mode of existence which makes that future time present with Him, then the event now non-existent will be known to Him as then actually existent. Non-existent in itself, it is not non-existent to a knowledge which covers the time when it will be existent. To God it is a knowledge of what is, because His mode of being includes the future.... To Him, as objects of knowledge, because of His eternity, they are real and actual before they exist." This expedient to avoid fore-ordination and yet believe in foreknowledge in the acts of human freedom, in avoiding Scylla runs upon Charybdis:

(a) Because it has recourse to the questionable representation that denies "duration" to God's being and "succession" to His consciousness. It supersedes the Scripture representation that He is each moment wholly Himself as absolute self-centered Personality—with "counsel" for things to be and "remembrance" of things past, the Ever-Enduring One, while generations and worlds pass and cease to be—by the notion that He is God and has His vision of things only by an extension of His essence, fixed and immobile, parallel all at once to all the world-ages. It confounds His "eternal" essence with "eternity" itself, and forms it into a stationary background, in which the cosmic progress reflects itself—"*tota simul*" "an unchangeable now"—contrary to the Biblical idea of a personal Being who lives on forever, and takes note of all change (Gen. 21:33; Deut. 33:27; Ps. 90:1–4; Rom. 1:20; Rev. 1:8), but who only has absolute "immortality" (Rom. 1:23; 1 Tim. 6:16). The representation, if not unthinkable, is so difficult and remote, and so alien to the conception mirrored in the Scriptures, that it looks like a manufactured expedient to make a theological conclusion. We may be told that to take the Scripture language in its humanly linguistic sense is to hold an anthropomorphic image of God. Perhaps so. But as God has given the revelation of Himself, it may reasonably be assumed that it discloses Him as He wishes to be understood, and a worse anthropomorphism may be reached in such human explanations.

(b) It disregards the distinction between the divine essence, or attributes, and the divine acts. The essence is eternal, the attributes are eternal, but the acts are in time.

(c) Because, instead of explaining the possibility of foreknowledge, this theory ends in a denial of it. For the knowledge is resolved into simple vision of the present—despite its use of some phraseology about the futurity of the "events" themselves. The account involves a more exaggerated form of the *tota simul* than even Augustine's now discredited explanation. For that left room for a recognition of a divine glance into futurity by basing the foreknowledge of events on God's fore-ordination of them—that they should so come to pass. Yet Augustine admitted that even his theory left only "*scientia*" instead of pre-*scientia*. But the explanation now offered drops the notion of a divine look into the future, through a fixed predestination, and has nothing left but a present vision—"knowledge" only because the thing "is present." There is no fore-knowledge in the case.

(d) But the fatal feature in the theory is that it involves the absolutely contradictory, in double sense, viz.: that God may, in actual, present vision, see contingent acts really already done when they are not yet to take place for ages to come, and the actors are not yet in existence; and, further, that to His infallible knowledge things may be and not be at the same time. By legerdemain of phrase it is made to seem that centuries before a thing comes to pass God knows it as both something already "existing," and also as something "to be." To His knowledge events are "existent" "and nonexistent" at the same time! From the point of His essence, as present, they are seen as yet non-existent; from the point of His essence, as already living in the future, they are seen as already existent. "To Him they are real and actual before they exist." "To God it is knowledge of what is." This makes God's present Self and His future Self not only the same as enduring through time, but as annihilating all time into a timeless "now." An explanation involving such absolute contradictions—as absolute as that the eternal Truth should lie—cannot be satisfactory.

The failure of these efforts to explain how God can foreknow the doings of human freedom leaves the possibility of such knowledge still in question. The proper answer to it must be sought just where theology rests its whole warrant for religious faith—in the authority and correct interpretation of the Scripture teaching. It is to be conceded, too, that the denial of it among theologians has found place, not from want of respect for the authority of revelation, but from the fact that the doctrine, in its specifically defined particularity, is not seen to be there declared in direct and categorical affirmations. It is not found in fully explicit statement. On the other hand, it is unquestionable that in an immense number of passages and in connection with various fundamental truths it is necessarily suggested and seems to be essentially involved. This is the case in all prophecy, whether it foretells great aggregate futuritions of human condition or the general course of history, or specific contingent events and individual acts. Not only is the Old Testament a distinct foreshowing of the New Testament setting up of a kingdom of heaven, with the manifold human features of its establishment, but is itself thickset with instances of prediction of the acts of nations and person, both good and evil. God foreknew Abraham's continued obedience and commanding of his house (Gen. 18:19), and foretold the bondage of his posterity in Egypt and their return (Gen. 15:13–16). He foretold to Moses the persistent later covenant breaking of the Hebrews (Deut. 31:16). He foretold to Hazael his horrible future crimes (2 Kings 8:10–13). In Isa. 53. He fore-announced in clear specifications the suffering experience of Jesus Christ at the hands of men and the redemptive results. In the New Testament Christ told beforehand of the treatment which the chief priests, elders, and scribes, in their free self-determination, would inflict on Him, specifying the betrayal, mocking, scourging, spitting, surrender to the Romans, and death by crucifixion, as well as His own rising again on the third day (Matt. 16:21; 20:18–19; Luke 18:31–33). He declared in advance the sweeping destruction in which Roman power would overwhelm Jerusalem and blot out forever the Jewish nationality, scattering the chosen people through all lands (Mark. 13:2; Luke 19:43–44). He foresaw Judas' treachery (Matt 26:20–25; Luke 22:21–23). He foretold of the man bearing a pitcher of water, of the disposition in the owner of the colt to be secured for the palm-entry (Luke 22:10; Mark 11:2–4). It was no conjecture when Jesus, in the face of Peter's protesting affection and self-confidence in his unfaltering fidelity, assured him: "Verily I say unto thee, that this night, before the cock crow thou shalt deny me thrice (Matt. 26:34, 75). In connection with the great truth of election to salvation, St. Paul rests the divine action in prescience: "For whom He did foreknow He also did predestinate to be conformed to the image of His Son" (Rom. 8:29), and St. Peter bases it in the same way: "Elect according to foreknowledge" (1 Peter 1:2).

These and similar Scriptures, taken in connection with the general Biblical affirmation of the divine omniscience, manifestly seem to teach a foreknowledge of men's use of their freedom. Nothing short of a clear showing that this conclusion is not necessarily required as the correct interpretation of revelation can justify refusal to accept it. Though the foundation principles of both morals and religion, as unequivocally taught in both Scripture and reason, forbid acceptance of explanations of the mysteries of this prescience by theory of absolute fore-ordination or any device of imagination destructive of the divine self-consistency, yet we would be rash to deny the possibility of it. That we cannot penetrate the mystery of the method is no disproof of the reality. We ought to be easily able to believe—should the belief harmonize with the revealed conception of the perfect divine administration—that God's ways and reaches of knowing are so transcendent to our limited modes and means as to be fully and infallibly competent for such knowledge. And since it is clear that foreknowledge is not in itself causal for its object, but is simply and only prescient of it, it involves no strife with genuine freedom or the foundations of moral responsibility. When the truth is clearly understood that the foresight is not based on fore-ordination or made identical with it—when the notion under which God becomes at once the Author of sin and the Avenger of the sin on its helpless victims is dropped—the doctrine of the divine foreknowledge is relieved of its moral self-contradictoriness, and, indeed, throws a cheering illumination over the order, certainty, safety, righteousness, love, and ultimate triumph of the divine administration. Inevitably, of course, this non-dependence of prescience of free human acts upon fore-ordination as their ground, must hold the divine mode of it to be other than that which belongs to God's knowledge of Himself, i. e., of His own possibilities and purposes, and must belong to His objective view and His perfect understanding of men and the conditions encompassing every human life. The question of its possibility and reality must, therefore, necessarily be narrowed into the possibilities of His outlook through the future life of humanity. Yet, when we remember that God is infinite in His perfections, and His infinite omniscience has resources and modes far beyond our finite possibilities of conception, it would seem to be presumption to declare that His intelligence may not penetrate through the to-us-boundless complexities of the movement of human freedom to an understanding of what men will do in every particular condition.

Some hint of this possibility comes to us in what theology has been wont to term the divine *scientia* media. The term is used to express a knowledge of what would take place, or would have taken place in certain idealized conditions which never are or have been actualized. The idea of it is illustrated in Jehovah's assurance to David at Keilah that the Keilahites would deliver him up to Saul, who was about to descend on the town—whereupon David hastily escaped (1 Sam. 23:5–13); also in our Lord's declaration to Chorazin and Bethsaida, "If the mighty works which were done in you had been done in Tyre and Sidon, they would have repented long ago in sackcloth and ashes" (Matt. 11:21). The divine glance revealed what human freedom would have done in the never actualized conditions.

It must be conceded, at the same time, that while this doctrine of perfect foreknowledge rests on warrant of the most obvious interpretation of the language of revelation (and positive disproof of its correctness has not been shown), nevertheless, the progress of theological discussion has shown that the Scriptural integrity of the doctrine of the divine perfections, and the supremacy and completeness of God's moral and redemptive administration over the world may be consistently and fully maintained, without asserting this particular inclusion of free volitions of men in the divine fore-knowledge. While omniscience is an essential attribute of God, i. e., absolute omniscience of all knowable objects, fore-knowledge in the relation in question may not be an attribute in the same absolute sense. For, since in creation God included an order of rational moral beings, endowed with the lofty powers of free choice and self-direction under responsibility, it was by His own free act, in conferring such endowment, that, if at all, the choices they shall make are placed outside of His foreknowledge. It was by self-relation that the relation obtains—perhaps somewhat after the reality presented when the eternal Son for a while related Himself to the world-history, so that He could say, 'Of that hour the Son does not know.' It was in God's own freedom that He established whatever relation holds in the case. If, then, in the very status so established, truly free human acts are undetermined until the human decision determines them, by very conception they seem to belong only to the possibilities of the future. May we not justly conclude that the divine attribute of omniscience is completely realized in fore-knowing them as possibilities while they are such, and as actual when they become actual? In thus recognizing "knowledge" as indeed an essential attribute of God, and saying that fore-knowledge may not be, we are simply following the admission of the Augustinian theology all through the centuries. For, generally, it has asserted that the foreknowledge in this relation respects things which can be made certain "only by God's decrees." So they are no more contingent on human determination. And even when the foreknowledge has not been conditioned on fore-ordination, but has assumed that the things which are future to us are not future to God, but present, by the device of an eternal now, foreknowledge has really been dissolved into simple knowledge. Augustine wrote: "But what is future to God, who transcends all times? For if God's knowledge contains the things themselves, they are not future to Him, but present, and hence cannot be called foreknowledge (prescientia), but only knowledge (scientia)." In neither representation has prescience of free action been maintained, but obliterated. In the one explanation it is not free; in the other it is not future. Thus, the traditional teaching has largely prepared the way for the modern difficulty about real foreknowledge in this relation, and for the suggestion that it may not be essential to our correct conception of the divine omniscience.

If, then, such prescience may not be a necessary attribute of God, the inquiry arises whether, on the supposition of His creational work having placed free human acts beyond His foreknowledge, it is yet possible to construct a theological view that will be at once consistent with the teaching of revelation and the fundamental requirements for God's sovereignty, and His moral and redemptive administration? Our Lutheran theology has refused to accept the Calvinistic scheme of absolute predestination, but has retained the doctrine of foreknowledge, in basing individual election on divine foresight of faith. This modifies that scheme throughout. God does not draw His foreknowledge from His own self-inspection, in which He knows the future through the all-decisive decrees as to what is to come to pass, but from His view and understanding of men in the use of their given freedom in their life conditions. In recognizing thus, these two kinds of knowledge in God, one unconditional, standing purely in His own absolute causation, the other conditioning itself through the free causalities of endowed human agency, we see that He has related Himself closely, in His providential and redemptive administration, to the time-life of men and of history. He knows the future as future, the past as past, and the present as present; and thus the divine knowledge of what shall become actual out of the possibilities of human self-determination, is the basis of His "election"—according to "foreknowledge." His eternal fore-ordination, that "he that believeth shall have eternal life," finds the ground for realizing itself in His foresight of the individual's submission to the call of the Gospel. The acts of justification and gift of the new life wait on, while seeking, the actual human condition of faith; for the human condition is a time-reality, without which the forgiveness and life cannot really exist—but can only stand to the divine view as something that will be. However, this prescience of the right use men make of the approach of grace expresses the reality of an actual relation between God and the world of free beings, in which the divine aim for human salvation actually weaves its own working into the woof of creature freedom, moving forward with the moving procession of human life.

But may not this representation of theology, which has stood in large measure as the faith of the Church in its earlier period and modern history, be preserved substantially should the divine omniscience be regarded as meeting this "faith" and all the life of human freedom only as the possibilities emerge into the actualities? Already under the accepted doctrine of foreknowledge, since things at first future, and known as such, move into the present, and thence into the past, the contingent possibilities ever passing into actualities, not only must the divine knowledge attend this in its course, but also the divine working in grace and administration. Already there is presupposed, say in connection with the temporal transition from a possible faith into an actual faith, an alteration in the form of the divine cognition, and also in the divine activities of regenerating and saving power. Already God's knowledge and administration are a knowledge and administration conditioned, according to His own plan, by temporal history, intertwining and progressing with it.

But the chief difficulty arises in connection with the larger view of the divine sovereignty and its supremacy for the maintenance of the ordained progress of history and the triumph of the kingdom. The question presses, unless God fully and certainly foreknows all that men, personally and jointly, will do, how can He assure, as He does, the world's redemptive and administrational movement and hold it to its destined goal? How can He know the resultant totality of free action without a knowledge of the almost infinite constituent parts—especially if the truth of predictive prophecy be included, since thousands of contingencies may intervene between the prophecy and its fulfillment, while yet the fulfillment depends on the certainty of every one of them? The real crux appears at this point. The only attempt offered to solve the problem has been through the fullest and strongest emphasis on God's perfect omniscience of all things, except these future free acts alone. With His complete knowledge of all things actual, and especially of all things possible, possible to the freedom of men and possible to His own resources, it is suggested that, matching His own infinite possible resources to the activities of human freedom, He may always hold the Providential course of history to the accomplishment of the essentials of His plan, without annulling that freedom. His relation is conceived of as not that of a mere spectator of unfolding events, but as the supreme ruler in the drama of freedom, carrying it forward in reciprocal conflict and work with human free activities. A statement from Martensen best defines the theoretical view: "If we would preserve this reciprocal relation between God and His creatures, we must not make the whole actual course of the world the subject of His foreknowledge, but only its eternal import, the essential truth it involves. The final goal of this world's development, together with the entire series of its necessary stages, must be regarded as fixed in the eternal counsel of God; but the practical carrying out of this eternal counsel, the entire fullness of actual limitations on the part of this world's progress, in so far as these are conditioned by the freedom, can only be the subject of a conditional foreknowledge, i. e., they can only be foreknown as possibilities, as *futurabilia*, but not as realities, because other possibilities may actually take place. In thus asserting that God does not actually foreknow all that actually occurs, we by no means imply that every event is not the subject of His all-penetrating cognizance. God is not only before His creatures—before the mountains were brought forth, or ever the earth was made—He is also in and with His creatures, in every moment of their development. While God neither foreknows, nor will foreknow, what He leaves undecided, in order to be decided in time, He is no less cognizant of and privy to all that occurs. Every movement of His creatures, even in their secret thoughts, is within the range of His all-embracing knowledge. 'Thou compassest my path and my lying down, and art acquainted with all my ways. Whither shall I go from Thy Spirit, or whither shall I flee from Thy presence? If I ascend up into heaven, Thou art there: if I make my bed in hell, behold, Thou art there' (Ps. 139). His knowledge penetrates the entanglements of this world's progress at every point; the unerring eye of His wisdom discerns in every moment the relation subsisting between free beings and His eternal plan; and His almighty hand, His power, pregnant of great desigus, guides and influences the movements of the world, as His counsels require." Dr. Dorner says: "For the divine Providence the question is of little importance, since it will at all times act most conformably with ethical laws, and since nothing can befall it unexpectedly or unawares, if it still surveys all possibilities eternally."2 An analogy recently offered illustrates how this supreme control and final triumph of Providence may be possible under this view—in the relation of a perfect expert and a novice before a chessboard. The expert is not, indeed, able to forsee exactly what actual moves may be made, but only the possible moves, and yet he knows in advance how to meet them by moves of his own, so as to lead infallibly towards victory. The infinite Creator's plan may supposedly be left contingent as to many of its paths of advance, but with all possibilities marked down and provided for. The contingent ways of men would wait on human determination, but the actualities be safeguarded by the infinite resources of Providence from resulting in defeat of the final triumph of all the possibilities of wisdom and love. The only remaining difficulty that suggests itself at this point is that this overruling guidance seems to involve either an incessant intervention of miraculous correction, or, since the movement lies still in the sphere of human life, such a handling of human wills as would, at least in part, infringe their real freedom. But to remove this difficulty, it is enough to remember that such corrective divine overruling does not mean physical miracles, as in founding Christianity, but only the established action of supernatural grace and power through spiritual forces; and that, without at all involving for a single soul a limitation of its freedom by an absolute predestination of destiny, God may intensify, through His truth and Spirit, the working energies and activities of the obedient subjects of that grace. God may not abridge, but use the freedom of His people to lift up standards against unrighteousness.

This view, however, is not to be preferred to the traditional faith in the divine foreknowledge in the realm of freedom. For the possibility of the traditional view has not been disproved, and, indeed, cannot be. And until the more obvious and natural interpretation of the Scriptures on the subject is shown to be mistaken, there is no occasion for falling back upon the theory of nescience, with its large difficulties of harmonization with the facts of prophecy and the truth of election according to foreknowledge.

10. WISDOM. Though closely allied to knowledge and resting in it, this attribute marks a distinct and special feature of the divine nature. It is more than mere cognition. It is, specifically, that attribute by which God chooses the best ends and perfectly adapts the means for their accomplishment. It expresses the elective quality of God's

intelligence. With His infinite knowledge and omnipotent power, He understands and wills what is best, directing all things to the highest aims under the most perfect adaptations. Human life presents perpetual illustrations of the proper definiteness of the term. The world abounds with men of immense knowledge, but of small or doubtful wisdom. All the attributes of God, so far as revealed to us—real, positive, and distinct—are yet so united in their totality as to act not separately, but together. Power would not mean blessedness without love; knowledge would not suffice without wisdom. But God acts in the fullness of all His perfections. And in His wisdom, all the resources of omniscience, omnipotence, and goodness receive what seems a crowning guaranty of the excellence of His creative work and providential care. "O Lord, how manifold are Thy works! In wisdom hast Thou made them all" (Ps. 104:24). "Oh the depth of the riches both of the wisdom and knowledge of God!" (Rom. 11:33).

MORAL ATTRIBUTES

These express, comprehensively, the ethical character of God. They are His moral perfections, in the chief forms in which they have been revealed to us. Like the natural attributes they belong to the very being of God as the absolute Personality. They describe Him both as to intrinsic character and the form of His activities. It is difficult to define them in clear and sharp lines of distinction, on account of their blending and coming into complete harmony in the divine life. In contemplating any one or all, each is seen as implying the presence and action of the rest. Theology can mark out only the prominent and essential forms of these ethical qualities.

1. HOLINESS, in which the whole character of God coheres, is that attribute by which everything evil, sinful, or impure is eternally excluded from the divine nature and action. It means a positive, self-affirming purity that both is and maintains an immaculate ethical perfection. God is pure in all that He is and in all that He does or can do. (Lev. 11:44; Isa. 6:3; 1 Pet. 1:15–16.) It may be viewed under three aspects: (a) As expressing His interior or immanent character, "I am holy." (b) As transitive, or moving over into an established order in the

moral constitution of the world—this constitution being made after His own nature and organized in relations and laws that are holy and good.

(c) As preceptive, for the free action of moral agents, "Be ye holy." Holiness must be regarded as at once the fundamental and the supreme attribute. More than any other it is that in which the entire moral excellence of God rests, which unites all, and crowns all. It is basal for perfect goodness, it guides and guards justice or righteousness, it conditions love, and reigns in truth. It separates itself from no attribute; it blends its light with all. As theology has rid itself of the false notion of the divine simplicity, in which all the distinctions between substance and attributes were obliterated, it is free to recognize their mutual relations more in accordance with Biblical representation and the redemptory implications. And in these relations the attributes do not appear as merely co-ordinate. Beyond doubt the Old Testament gives fundamental significance to holiness, and the New represents soteriological grace as possible only in a way consistent with its unsullied maintenance. The idea of a mutual relation and harmony of the attributes is revealed from the very heart of the Gospel. And the positive conception of the unity of God does not appear so long as we think of a mere co-ordination of predicates, without a disposing and governing principle which most deeply and in the highest sense expresses the absolute character of Deity. While none of the attributes are contingent in God, yet in their inter-relations the moral attributes appear to have their ethical unity in the eternal holiness. Even that of love, which in the working of grace is so sublimely glorified in the sight of men and angels, achieves its wonders of salvation only in consistence with the infinite purity. It is a mistake to take the New Testament declaration, "God is love," as speaking comparatively. But the emphasis thus put upon love is the fitting and necessary one in the Gospel message. For this message is the voice of invitation to sinners. In the very nature of the case it fastens human view upon the divine goodness and grace as the great appeal to the heart for faith, gratitude, and obedience. But the love that, through the great redemption, seeks to save, is still immutably "holy love," working for holiness through a movement of grace that pays its own homage to the inviolability of holiness. "The Christian mind knows nothing of a love without holiness." With the truth thus reached, accords the moral constitution of man, in which conscience asserts the supremacy of the ethically right and pure over all other elements of character. And the characteristic result with the theologies which abate from this supremacy has ever been a virtual denial of the attribute itself as an essential ethical principle in the divine will, and a consequent discarding of the Scripture teaching concerning the atonement.

The relation of this attribute to the divine Will has already been, in part, noted. We are yet, if possible, to discriminate its relation to the divine freedom of will, and to the ultimate standard of righteousness. Without doubt we must think of God as the Absolute Personality, and so, absolutely and perfectly free. The idea of fate is utterly inapplicable to His being. Fate, as such, is an annullment of all free aims or purposes, and means fixation, irrespective of the claims of worth or excellence. Ethical goodness is inconceivable apart from self-determined preference for right and holiness. The holiness of God is not in contradiction of His freedom. He is holy in and with His freedom. The perfect ideal of the ethically good dwells forever and immutably in the divine intelligence, and the divine freedom eternally determines itself with respect to it. But the question, often raised, whether, since holiness is thus involved in free choice, God might not have chosen other than He has, and so have become unholy, is not pertinent, because it forgets that He is Himself holy, as well as free, and thus immutably wills the good. Because He is holy, He, through the eternal preference or self-consistency of His own nature, chooses the ethically pure and right. The notion of the old Scotist teaching that the absolute will of God might, by mere arbitrary volition, make right, or determine what shall be right, as, for instance, command deceit or theft, instead of truth and justice, can have no place in Christian theism. And in order to bring into view this relation in its fullness between His holiness and His free will, we must maintain, further, that He does not choose the morally good simply as it is in Himself, or because it is in Himself, as a Self-choice, but that He loves and chooses goodness also as such, or goodness as it is in itself. For it would not be an ethical choice that did not determine itself in view of the excellence of its object. The possibility of ethical character in God involves the love and choice of goodness itself as an end. It is only the harmony or self-consistency of the essential holiness of His nature when He thus freely and immutably chooses essential goodness. God is not good simply because He wills goodness, but He is good also in His own eternal nature, and wills in harmony with that nature, forever immutably maintaining holiness in the free choice of that which is holy both in itself and in Himself.

The further relation of the divine Will to the ultimate standard of right comes into view under the light of the truths thus clearly assured. For if holiness is a real and fundamental attribute of the divine nature, and God's omniscience holds immutably a perfect knowledge of what is the ethically good or right, it follows that both His immutable nature and His knowledge preclude the notion that goodness may be a mere effect of changeable divine volition. There is a standard of right in both the absolute nature and absolute knowledge of the absolute Being. It is thus something fixed, to which God's freedom infallibly conforms itself—not something which may be altered by that freedom. The doctrine of an immutable morality thus establishes itself. The logical prius of the divine willing is the divine existence. He must be, in order that He may will. Because He is holy, and, in a perfect knowledge of what holiness or ethical goodness is, eternally loves it as of highest worth, the standard of right exists in His unchanging nature, and its authority is absolute.

In the application of this truth to the question of the ground of right in the constitution of the world and the human consciousness, a few distinctions are properly made. (a) The ground of right may be viewed under two aspects, according to differing relations, viz.: as proximate and ultimate. In respect to the moral constitution of things and the organization of human life, with ethical imperative in the conscience, inasmuch as creation was not a necessary, but free work of God, and the whole world-order a product of that freedom, His Will may be regarded as the immediate or proximate ground of this moral constitution. Yet as His will but expressed His eternal nature, that nature, as holy before it creates, must be regarded the ultimate ground. (b) In like view, in His preceptive administration, the moral law, given to men through revelation, comes in its immediate relation as a direct expression of His will, while ultimately grounded in the divine nature itself. (c) The ethically right or holy can never be thought of as changeable at mere divine volition, or as resting on Will alone. Since with God the right exists in His nature, as the prius of His willing, embodied in the absolute ground of all things, all mutation by God of the standard of the good becomes impossible. To think otherwise would be a denial of the divine holiness itself, for it would not be a holy choice if God did not choose the good as good, and because it is good. In God the ethical order is eternally conceived and eternally realized. (d) There is a sphere or relation, however, in which God can impose or withdraw duty, establish or repeal obligation at or by His will alone—in the sphere of things otherwise morally indifferent. In this sphere the simple command of God makes or changes human duty. It is thus we have positive statutes, ordinances, requirements for local or temporary use, as in the ritual rules and rites of the Old Testament, and Baptism and the Lord's Supper in the New.

2. JUSTICE, or RIGHTEOUSNESS is that attribute by which God, according to His innermost nature, establishes right relations among His creatures and treats them in equity, dealing with them according to their deserts. Though this attribute is grounded in the immanent life of God, it is to be conceived as having specially a creatureward look and administrational activity. In its immanent reality it appears scarcely distinguishable from holiness, and so it is sometimes represented as simply expressing the transitive side of holiness. But because of the fundamental relation of holiness, we are not entitled to view them as identical. If we discriminate, as we may, between "justice" and "righteousness," the latter applies to the divine ordering of right relations and requirements, giving holy laws with proper sanctions; the former to the rewarding of conduct with the recompense or punishment due to it No more than holiness can this attribute be regarded as proceeding in an arbitrary way in either of these ranges of its manifestation. Punitive visitation cannot be in excess of real demerit, and the manifestation of grace or mercy can take place only as the principle of righteousness or justice can be satisfied and preserved. "Shall not the Judge of all the earth do right?" (Gen. 18:25). "All His ways are judgment; a God of truth and without iniquity, just and right is He" (Deut. 32:4). "Who will render to every man according to his

deeds" (Rom. 2:6). "To declare at this time His righteousness; that He might be just and the justifier of him that believeth in Jesus" (Rom. 3:26).

The reason for punitive justice, or why God punishes sin, comes into view in the light of these truths of the divine holiness and righteousness. A correct understanding of it is vital for a true conception of the divine government and the Christian doctrine of the atonement. It is important, too, for a just appreciation of the true relations of human government in the use of penalties. Four leading views have been presented.

One makes the end of punishment to reform the wrongdoer. This means that it is simply an act of benevolence—denying its punitive character altogether. It is only reformatory correction. Doubtless punishment may have this effect. But this, as has been shown, cannot be the whole explanation of it. For (a) it drops out of view the intrinsic ill-desert of sin. If sin is not intrinsically wrong the disciplinary pain inflicted on it would itself be wrong. (b) It is contradicted by the moral convictions of the offender himself, who knows his punishment to be deserved, irrespective of the question of his reformation. (c) If reformation be the end, it fails largely to effect it. Few are reformed. Witness the result of the natural and civic punishments which come on prevalent vices or offenses with which our criminal courts are perpetually occupied. (d) Unless felt to be due for deeper reason, punishment can have no virtue for reformation. The theory is essentially shallow, assuming that nothing else is to be considered but the person who has forfeited his rights.

A second view holds that the end is to deter others. But the deterrent effect is only incidental. For (a) unless the deed in itself deserves the punishment, our whole moral sense would revolt against punishing a man for the sake of others or the good of society. (b) It is only the actual justice of it that ever renders the effect salutary. Therefore, here also, unless there be some deeper reason for punitive action, the effect itself must be nullified.

A third theory makes the object to be the maintenance of the supremacy of law and government. This is closely allied to the second, but is special in that it looks to the law in itself, irrespective of the divine necessity of the law. Grotius represents God's law as simply the product of His Will, that Will in its absolute sovereignty making right or wrong, or determining what shall pass for such. The divine law is made to rest on a contingent action of the divine Will, and punitive action is for the sake of the given law. This is untenable, because (a) It makes the distinction between right and wrong purely arbitrary, whereas, according not only to just moral conceptions, but the necessary Biblical view of the divine holiness as immanent in the divine nature and God's choice of the ethically good as such, this distinction is absolute and independent of all mere volition, human or divine. (b) It removes all absolute necessity for punishment, since, if the law depends only on the divine volition in that sense, the penalty also depends only on it, and can be remitted merely at such will. (c) The thing in exercise in such case would not be essential justice, but simply governmental authority, or, rather, power, which would be tyranny if there were not a deeper reason back of it.

The fourth view—which is unquestionably the true one—is that the eternal holy nature of God immutably determines Him against sin as deserving of penal repression. It is only in this view that the half-truths of the preceding theories get their right place and significance. The explanation has two parts, and both must be kept in mind. The first part is God's own eternal and essential justice, and means (a) That the ethical law is not a product of the divine will, simply as will, but a transcript of the immutable divine nature. All fundamental principles must have changeless ground in God's own being. (b) That the reason for punishing sin arises from the absolute holiness of His nature. As it is said, "He cannot lie," and "cannot deny Himself," so He cannot but hate sin and all unrighteousness. The second part is the intrinsic ill-desert of sin. Evidence of this is found, (a) In the primary affirmations of universal conscience. They assert sin's demerit and desert of punishment. This is so as to our own sins when we awake to the fact of them: "Against Thee, Thee only, have I sinned and done this evil in Thy sight, that Thou mightest be justified when Thou speakest, and be clear when Thou judgest" (Ps. 51:4). Often the sense of ill-desert takes the intensity of remorse. As to the sins of others, the moral sense gives the same judgment—justifying the punishment of wrongdoers, and awakening to indignation when the guilty go free. (b) Revelation sustains this: "It is a righteous thing with God to recompense tribulation to them that trouble you" (2 Thes. 1:6). "Knowing the judgment of God, that they which commit such things are worthy of death" (Rom. 1:32). In the light of this Biblical view, all aspects of allied or cognate truths find their special place and value. When it is seen that the divine holiness is necessarily self-determining against sin as something that deserves repressive penalty, there is clear adaptation to incidental reformatory effect, deterrent service, and the consequent good order of society through the well-maintained sanctity of the law, The law carrying God's own holiness is just and good. It is proper to observe, too, how holiness and love may unite in the use of penalties. Holiness punishes as the necessary vindication of righteousness; goodness requires it for the sake of the welfare and happiness which are possible only through the moral order which holiness maintains.

It is necessary, however, at this point, to safeguard against misapprehension by adding a further discrimination. This absoluteness of the divine holiness as the reason for the use of punishment against sin, might be supposed—but only illogically—to exclude the possibility of divine mercy, or to be inconsistent with the whole redemptory action of grace. But punitive administration has not the same absoluteness that belongs to the divine holiness itself. Punishment is for the sake of holiness—for its vindication and maintenance. Penalty is not a good in itself, its own end, but a means. The final end of the world-system, as involved in both the divine holiness and love, is the ethically good, the supremacy and blessedness of righteousness. Punishment is by no means the end of the system. It may, therefore, be remitted in any case, if, in God's wisdom and resources, the end can be gained in some other way, and, perhaps, in more glorious and triumphant measure. If He can provide an atonement in which at once He can furnish a clear expression of the principle of righteousness and offer to the world conditional forgiveness of sins, and through love win back to holiness millions on millions of the sinful, the means of mercy may be vastly more efficient than that of penalty for the very ends of holiness. The principle of punitive justice is not the supreme or absolute one, but the principle of holiness. To make the former principle first and absolutely governing would leave no room for forgiveness and reconciliation, and form an obstacle to Christian faith.

3. LOVE, or GOODNESS, is that attribute in virtue of which God evermore delights in communicating that which is good and blessed, in harmony with holiness and justice. It expresses His nature as eternally desiring to create and bestow happiness, acting in kindness. It is not the same as holiness, though it can seek its aims only in harmony with holiness. It denotes, distinctively, the divine altruism—the divine self-direction and action for the good of created being. We are, therefore, to see in it the reason of the supreme teleological purpose and plan in the world. Acting in His own immanent love, He acts for ends of love. Since He is holy, and, therefore, chooses holiness as holiness, i. e., the ethically good as the supreme good, this good, as the highest of all, must necessarily be included in all the aims of God's love for His moral creatures. And, thus, that which His love seeks for them through both creation and providence is holy happiness. Evidently, it was to bring into full view and unquestionable clearness this glorious attribute—the attribute that ever expresses the heart of God's teleological order and purpose for man—that He so adjusted His Biblical self-revelation as to make its culminating assurance to the world, "God is love," sustained by the unspeakable fact of redemption for recovery of his self-ruined children to their true life and blessedness. Declarations of His goodness appear, indeed, in increasing measure in that revelation, from the first (Ex. 34:6; 1 Chron. 16:34; Ps. 145:9). The teleology of nature, too, abounds in evidences of benevolent aim. But the full manifestation of this attribute could come only in the gift and work of the divine Savior, in which the glory of the divine love, in its "breadth and length and depth and height," "passing knowledge," may savingly impress and inspire the human soul.

We properly mark distinctions tinder which this attribute may be conceived, according to the different relations to creature existence and conduct. When viewed in the broadest and most universal relation to created being, it takes the generic form of benevolence, a desire for the welfare and happiness of all, and the misery of none. Considered with respect to all that is morally right and good in the spirit, aims, and conduct of men, it assumes the form of moral complacency, approving love, delight in holy character or in all sincere desire or effort toward it by obedient subjects of divine grace. When it is contemplated in relation to the wretchedness of creatures in error and sin, its manifestation becomes compassion, pity, or mercy—love toward the undeserving—widely different in type from moral complacency, yet akin to it in that it is still love, desiring creature well-being. It is patience or long-suffering when it forbears from just retribution, for the sake of rescuing from sin and recovering to righteousness. Because God is holy He hates sin, but because He is love He seeks to win the sinner from it. His goodness, in saving man, is victory for both holiness and love.

It is needful here to guard against the ideas of the old scholastic teaching of the absolute impassibility of God, which, while attempting by misguided representation to explain the divine love, explained it away. In its extreme effort to free the conception of God from all ideas of dependence or change, it carefully eliminated from His love all emotion or mutation of feeling from what creatures do or suffer. It cautioned against supposing that He really feels either pity or affection, or suffers any influence from creature conditions. Love is reduced to pure action of will, without emotion. Though emotion is the very heart of our human idea of love, this element, it was said, must not be included in the divine love. Neither complacency nor compassion was to be imagined, since any experience of such feelings would be inconsistent with God's absolute independence. The existence of a feeling, of either sympathy or delight, in God was supposed to be contrary to His necessary immutability, making Him subject to the changing conditions of human life. But if His necessary independence excludes the possibility or reality of these feelings, from sight of human life, must we not then also hold that the entrance of the ever-changing activity of human freedom into the divine knowledge also destroys God's independence? This notion of the divine impassibility is not only inconsistent with the Scripture portraiture of God and of the way He holds Himself toward men, but, if carried to its logical issues, would forbid all belief in divine concern for human happiness, and the possibility of a divine administration of the world measuring itself to the mutations of moral character and conduct, or adjusting a redemptive provision to a self-corrupted race. If the divine independence means that His love is to be reduced to an unfeeling, immobile will, holding itself utterly apart from all influence from without, or coming from the needs of the creatures made in the divine image, the voice of prayer or praise may as well be hushed. The idea of love is, in fact, obliterated if reduced to mere knowledge and will, acting in a self-determining sovereignty that is irresponsive to and unmoved by the creature needs which creational power has brought under absolute administration. If love in God is only a name for the attributes of "knowledge" and "will," it disappears as a distinct attribute. But as an immanent attribute, it must of necessity involve feeling; and if God is without feeling, impassible to the mutations of His creature's needs and appeals, He is without love. "We must adhere to the truth in its Scriptural form or we lose it altogether." While we ought to guard our conception of God from a spurious anthropomorphism, His self-revelation in the Scriptures is, without doubt, meant to guide us in the conception in which He wishes us to view Him. And the correct method for the actual truth is, not to empty the concept "love" of its distinctive reality, but to purify and elevate it (via eminentiœ) to perfection. Like the attributes of knowledge and wisdom, love is not less, but more real in God than in man. It must be regarded as peculiarly unfortunate that theology has so largely, by a mere dictum, resolved the inspiring reality of sympathy and pitying goodness in God, of which the Scriptures seem specially concerned to assure us, into a cold sovereignty that is without feeling and an absolute independence that never suffers itself to be moved by delight in creature happiness nor compassion toward creature wretchedness—a God whose knowledge and will and power are real, but whose love is only a name, an anthropomorphic attribution of our human imagination. Is it this impassibility that the Scriptures teach when they say, "Like as a father pitieth his children, so Jehovah pitieth them that fear Him" (Ps. 103:13)? Or, "The Lord is very pitiful and of tender mercy "? Or when God exclaims, "How shall I give thee up, Ephraim? How shall I deliver thee, Israel? How shall I make thee as Adma? How shall I set thee as Zeboim? My heart is turned within me, my repentings are kindled together "? Is no affectional emotion implied when Christ says, "God so loved the world that He gave His only begotten Son"? Or when the Holy Spirit led an apostle to declare, "He that loveth not knoweth not God, for God is love. In this was manifested the love of God toward us, because that God sent His only begotten Son into the world, that we might live through Him "? If God's proper 'independence' excludes, as is alleged, both 'complacency' and 'sympathy,' or suffering any impression from without, from human conditions, must it not at the same time exclude divine action in view of the same? But this would shut off the possibility of the whole redemptive divine self-correlation to the need of lapsed humanity and the entire providential and judicial administration, so far as it might be thought to take any account of the moral conduct of men. It would be difficult to frame a dogma more out of harmony with the Scripture portraiture of God and His loving and active interest in the good of His human children, than the oft-repeated, but now discounted, dictum about His absolute impassibility.

Note must here be taken of the difficulties often alleged in connection with the divine goodness. They arise from the phenomena of nature and human life, and appear in two relations:

First, in connection with natural evil, such as physical pain, suffering, and death among men and animals. Modern scientific and philosophical activity has shown a strong tendency to bring these into view. It has given occasion to pessimistic theories of nature. The exacting reign of physical law, the struggle for life, nature "red in tooth and talon," the pains of existence, the "groans of creation," have been used to suggest doubt either of the goodness or of the omnipotence of the Author of the world-system. The facts of pain, suffering, and death must, of course, be admitted. But that these facts are not necessarily inconsistent with the goodness of God becomes apparent from various considerations.

(a) The possibility of pain or suffering seems to be inevitably involved in life-organizations made capable of sentient pleasure. The elevation of creature existence to the grade of sensitivity, capacitating for enjoyment, must, so far as we can see, capacitate also for pain. It opens it to impressions of various kinds and degrees from the environment—a gift adjusted to use and pleasure, but necessarily thus opening also to abnormal contacts and hurt. The possibility of pain is the other half of an organization for sense-enjoyment.

(b) This pain is a necessary and benevolent monitor against what would otherwise injure or destroy the organism. Without this signal, with its warning and guidance, the organization would soon be wrecked. It is the kindly stationing of videttes upon the outposts of the physical system. So far, at least, as the purpose with respect to the organism itself is concerned, everything looks to utility and enjoyment.

(c) These same pains, thus becoming possible as only incidental to organization positively adapted to pleasure, and in their incidental occurrence set to a benevolent office of safeguarding its life, are, further, stimulants to the exertion by which life is elevated. Life remains low and poor where such exercising forces are wanting. The measure of sensitiveness becomes the measure of development and exaltation. In man the discipline becomes a force for training in thoughtfulness, self-control, and moral character. The teleology and fruits of such incidental pain must be fully considered before it can be declared to be in contradiction of divine love. The loftiest heights of noble and blessed manhood have been reached upon the stairways of suffering, where the life of duty and love has become peculiarly invigorating and enriching.

(d) Even death itself, which, with its attendant suffering, carries away every animal life, may not be in direct and necessary contradiction to the divine goodness. The problem here, indeed, is particularly perplexing—especially as the system of nature includes an order of feeding one upon another. But various considerations relieve the view. By absolute necessity every created system must be finite, and every creature good a finite good. It must be limited. The order of death in the system is simply an order of temporary life—an application of the principle of finite existence, giving a natural good, but not in unlimited continuance. That life is made short instead of everlasting, is itself no disproof of goodness. Unquestionably the amount of physical enjoyment far surpasses the pain, if any, in its ending. We probably greatly exaggerate the idea of pain in connection with animal death, by importing into it the extreme sensitiveness which belongs to the human organization, as well as, perhaps, also the fear which makes the fact of human death such a shadow on life. But the lower organizations are mostly far less sensitive, and the animal has no preconception of death. We are not warranted in interpreting the seeming fear and instinctive flight in presence of danger in terms of human intelligence and conscious dread. Within its appointed limit animal life seems filled with positive enjoyment; and death may be an almost painless ending, according to an order which provides for the long succession of individual animals, through new generations, multiplying enormously the numbers that share the pleasures of existence, keeping the world astir and vocal with the joy of fresh life. Even the arrangement by which animals become food for one another falls into this order, under which such multiplication of individuals is incalculably extended. In its perpetual provision of food it is also a provision for life and enjoyment—death itself becoming an order of transfer of nature's energies into the pleasures of ever-new life. Ordinarily, death is, probably, a painless cessation of living functions. And even when, under the system of prey, it is violent, it is an experience of but a moment, and as nothing compared with the whole sensitive enjoyment which it terminates. Most of the colors in recent pessimistic portrayal of the cruelties, tortures, and horrors of nature's system are, to say the least, the painting of an exaggerating imagination and intense verbiage, in disregard of the indubitable fact that the experiences in question are but incidental to a system whose characterizing features look to utility, well-being, and enjoyment Nowhere is there found in nature provision to create or give pain simply for the sake of pain or misery.

But, secondly, in connection with moral evil the question of the divine goodness still offers its mystery. The discussion of the centuries leaves a residuum of it for speculative thought. Sin is such an abnormality that reason is tempted to press the problem to its primal roots, unmindful, probably, of the necessary limitatations of the human understanding. But in the growing light of Christianity the difficulties are approaching the vanishing point. The question must be viewed in two relations: First, as to the suffering, whether physical or mental, which exists as the fruit of sin. Plainly this is not inconsistent with the divine goodness. For such suffering is a direct reflection of the real desert of sin. The highest welfare requires that order and righteousness should be sustained by such penal and corrective consequences upon wrong-doing. Love itself, no less than holiness, manifestly calls for this. Moreover, in a state of probation this may become a means of reformation and a way to highest happiness. And, to such as consent, under grace, to true relation to God, it is a means of constant training into the holiest strength, vitality, and riches of character. It is not inconsistent that true love should guide moral agents through the consequences of conduct. But, secondly, the root difficulty attaches to the existence of sin itself. How could sin come into a world created by a God of perfect wisdom, power, and love? We must pause here to note the main theories that fail to afford the desired solution.

(a) Without counting Manichæism, whose roots were the pagan Parseeism of two eternal principles, one of good and another of evil, a realm of light and a realm of darkness or chaos, from whose comminglings evil arose, the theory that sin is not intrinsically and positively an evil, but only finiteness, limitation, has had large sway. The definition of sin as something negative, the non-existent, τὸ ὀυκ ὄν, as darkness is the absence of light, or sickness the want of health, has had long and large sway. All that exists is declared to be good. Evil has no being. It is only a deficiency in existence. It is an unreality, an appearance. In modern times this negative conception has assumed various forms, under different explanations offered in the name of philosophy and science. It runs through all the theories of cosmic evolutionism, whether of materialistic, pantheistic, or theistic type. It belongs to Leibnitz (Theodicy). Materialism, voiding the universe of spirit, either divine or human, by nullifying freedom, leaves no place for either moral good or evil. Hegel's philosophy of the cosmic evolution, as the Absolute, self-existent Spirit, self-unfolding, and advancing by opposites in an everlasting becoming, carries both antagonism and incompleteness all through nature and life. In man, the infinite appears in finiteness. But the finite consciousness, because of its emergence from the infinite, holds a sense of this incompleteness, which it interprets in terms of evil and fault. Even the current theistic evolutionism of Darwinian science and the Synthetic Philosophy identifies it with the imperfections of development, the yet unrevealed in the excellence of humanity. The advancing evolution, as the gospel of hope, is to bring what yet is not. But this negative conception of sin, as being non-existent, in whatever form it appears, is manifestly inadequate, and simply denies the problem instead of explaining it. For, in invincible fact, sin is something positive—not a mere limitation of being or attainment. It is a most real and woeful refusal to accept the good and right as provided, an active violation of the moral constitution really given, a willful trampling down of conscious duty, persistent, positive wrong-doing, wickedness, defiance of justice, truth, and good order, an assertive, virulent, and destructive badness. The mystery of sin in the world can neither be set aside nor explained by the euphemism of naming it "that which does not exist," and marking it a synonym of human finitude.

(b) The theory that is implicit, if not definitely formulated, in the supralapsarian predestination theology. The type of doctrine which represents the primal eternal decree of God to be the twofold glorification of His love and His justice (or severity), covering the creation of man in innocence and his ordained fall into sin, with an election of some to salvation and a preterition or reprobation of the rest, necessarily fixes the origin of sin in the all-embracing, divine fore-ordination and causation. It comes as something required in the divine decree—constitutive for the world-system. It is unescapable, because predestinated by God. But in this view human freedom, even in primal man, is reduced to a mere semblance, being allowed no choice against the omnipotent decree. This would make God Himself the Author of sin. But, since man's sin, then, was an act of conformity to the divine plan, it could not be sin in him unless it was sin also in the Author of the plan. This connects moral evil with the Divine Will as the determining principle or source, and represents God as invoking sin—bringing it purposely into the world-system as the desired condition for the manifestation of His glorious justice. But how could that be really justice which should punish obedience to the divine plan, an obedience to which there was no human alternative? But, besides thus making God the Author of sin, as decreeing and necessitating it, the theory further confutes itself in the conceded fact that, by very conception, sin is antagonism to the will of God—not a fulfillment of it or submission to it. And still more, since a divine decree is an act of will, the explanation introduces into God a strife of wills—on the one hand to decree sin and on the other to condemn its existence. The only possible avoidance of these contradictions is suggested in the indefensible claim that the distinction of good and evil is not applicable to the divine choices, but is only for created beings as a mere effect of God's absolute will. But this claim would obliterate the ethical from the life or character of God. For the divine choices would not be ethical choices, if God did not choose the good and holy as good and holy. This supralapsarian scheme, which implicitly attaches sin to an infallible divine predestination of it, suggesting, at the same time, that God is so above moral law—instead of being its eternal reality—that He does not sin while working in man the very thing that to man is sin, is abhorrent to the whole Biblical conception of His righteousness, and can never be accepted as the solution of the mystery of sin in the world. That conception forbids us to subordinate His holiness and righteousness to His omnipotence (will-power), and requires us to hold that He evermore uses His omnipotence for the glorious aims of His holiness and love.

(c) Akin to this theory, if not a part of it, is that which suggests that sin was chosen by God as the necessary means of the greatest good. It alleges that the morally good can be conceived and developed only in relation to moral evil, and that the presence of this is the necessary condition for the highest ethical life. The good can best be reached and established through reaction against the evil. Against this it is enough to remind ourselves of the utter groundlessness of the assumption. Moral law lies in the realm of ideal duty, of rational demand and perceived obligations—not simply of experienced and generalized consequences. The realization of the ethical life, in rational free agency, implies and requires only the possibility of sin, not its actual existence. Nothing but frivolous unreason could so reverse the real order of moral conception as to maintain that actual sin is the foundation of holiness or the necessary condition of its perfection. For, thus, God could not be holy—unless by a reaction from existing sin. Moreover, as sin is the greatest evil, God's supposed choice of it as the means of the greatest good involves utter self-contradiction, and violates the fundamental principle of moral life not to "do evil that good may come."

(d) The various forms of theory which ground it in sensuousness, however they may be shaped, are all fatally based in the dualistic notions of the essentially evil nature of matter, and cannot be harmonized with Christian theism or Biblical anthropology. Even that explanation which connects it with the necessary order of development of the human powers, viz.: first, the growth of the physical; secondly, the unfolding of the intellectual; and, lastly, the appearance of the moral capacities and principles, an order putting from the start the moral life under mastery and bondage of the sensuous nature, involves the notion of a malign influence in material existence, and is vitiated and unsatisfactory from this cause.

The explanation of the mystery of sin and its reconciliation with the divine goodness, must be found, if found at all, in connection with the principle of free agency as essential to a moral system. God in His supreme holiness and love created the creature-realm of beings in His own image and likeness. In this the creation was lifted above the grade of impersonal things, into that of personality and moral character, the highest and most blessed life conceivable. This realm of life was established in holiness and for holiness and pure happiness, in fellowship with God Himself. But this freedom of personality, designed for obedience, by the very reality of its freedom involved a possibility of misuse, against God's will. Thus, however, only the possibility of sin belongs to a moral system, not at all the necessity of it. And to exclude all possibility of sin would have required the annullment of the real freedom; for freedom means a power of choice between alternatives. To control inevitably the wills of free, responsible beings can no more be an object of God's power than the working of a contradiction—the contradiction of necessity in free-agency. Though God is omnipotent, He could not prevent the possibility of sin in a moral system without violating and destroying the system itself. This goes far toward a solution—finding, according to the Scriptures, the origin of sin in the abuse of the powers of creature wills, disobedience to God, a thing whose very nature is a contradiction to His will.

The only residuum of mystery thus left is: Why did God, foreseeing the possibility or the reality of this abuse, nevertheless, create a moral world? And with respect to this we are clearly entitled to say: First, that the creation of a moral world, in itself considered, is consistent with goodness, not only as a forming of creature existence with full adaptation to happiness, but as constituting a higher and nobler realm of being, excellence, and happiness than all being and blessedness otherwise possible. God's creative goodness reached the climax of love in forming creatures in the image of His own personal excellence, endowed with the possibilities of life in fellowship with Himself, and sharing the blessedness of such high position. It desired and provided for the supreme happiness of creature existence. Secondly, assuming that God foresaw the abuse of the moral endowment, we may well think that His further "purpose" to add the grace of a redemptive administration for recovery from sin, is no indication that the creational work was lacking in benevolence or goodness. Especially so, since in the redemptory action the goodness rises to the higher grade of kindness to the guilty and ill-deserving, and this, too, through an economy of patience and self-sacrifice. Man's guilty sin is made the occasion for the display of a divine goodness that becomes the crowning proof of God's love. We are justified in believing that God's foresight of creature sin simply did not annul His purpose to crown this earthly creation with its supreme realm of rational life and freedom, and its fellowship in the divine thought and blessedness, and in thinking also that, could we see the whole problem with the eye of omniscience, we should find the divine goodness fully vindicated.

4. TRUTH, or VERACITY. This is the divine attribute by which God's action and communication are always in perfect harmony with His own nature and with things as they are in genuine reality. It is, therefore, that principle in which all the attributes maintain their self-consistency and consummate their perfect import. Truth, correctly conceived, is always that which truly is, either in reality or in conformity of word or life with reality. God's infinite knowledge is a knowledge of what really is, has been, or is possible. His justice and righteousness are true to the perfect standard of His own nature. He is faithful to His words of promise and of threatening. He cannot lie or deny Himself (Num. 23:19; 2 Tim. 2:13; Deut. 32:4; Ps. 100:5; 146:6; Rev. 15:3).

No difficulty need be felt in the exegesis of a few Scripture passages which seem to imply non-fulfillment of some divine threatenings, as Jonah 3:4, 10; Jer. 18:7, 8. It is enough, in all such cases, to remember that the divine threatenings, like the divine promises, are always conditional, the issue being dependent on the question of heeding or disregarding the divine will on the part of man.

CHAPTER III
THE TRINITY

The Scriptures clearly teach that there is One, and only One God, and that this One God is Father, Son, and Holy Spirit. To designate the great truth thus taught, theology, from its earliest days, has appropriated the word Trinity (Greek, Τριάς, Latin, *Trinitas, Triunity*). Our Lutheran Church, in harmony with catholic Christianity, confesses: "The decree of the Nicene Council concerning the unity of the divine essence and of the three persons is true and without doubt to be believed, to wit: that there is one divine essence, that is called and is God, eternal, without body, indivisible, of infinite power, wisdom, goodness, the Creator and Preserver of all things, visible and invisible, and yet that there are three persons of the same essence and power, who also are co-eternal, the Father, the Son, and the Holy Spirit."

The Trinity is a truth, the knowledge of which we owe purely to the revelation of the Holy Scriptures. It is not a discovery of rational theism. Natural theology cannot reach it. It can, and does, indeed, certify the existence of a Supreme Personal First Cause or Creator, and discovers some of His attributes, but evidently cannot reach the mode of His existence. He alone can reveal this. The various so-called trinities of pagan mythologies or philosophies are found to have nothing essentially in common with the Christian Trinity, being so thoroughly different in relation and conception as to show naturalistic thinking a blank as to this truth, outside of the illumination of Biblical teaching. Hence, only what the Scriptures declare or directly imply must determine the content and form of this doctrine. Even as revealed and defined according to the data of revelation, it stands in theology as a mystery—a truth involving inscrutable features and relations—the βάθη τοῦ θεοῦ, of 1 Cor. 2:10. This recognition of it as a mystery by no means consents that it may be declared an absurdity, which is something self-contradictory and incredible. The Trinity merely transcends the reach of human means of full understanding—as is the case with thousands of other realities in the realm of cosmic existence about us. We accept the facts of nature, whose full truth is insoluble. So the Trinity, since divinely revealed and certified, comes within the sphere of a rational faith, with numerous deep and significant harmonies that afford ground for rational vindication.

After all the labors of Biblical scholarship in recent years, much of it under the influence of reconstructive temper, we must still claim that justly interpreted the Old Testament revelation, while not explicitly teaching a Trinity of the Godhead, nevertheless truly foreshadows this divine reality. In its records of the creative work and providential administration, this is reflected through the implications of fact and language. Peculiar forms of thought and expression, here and there surprising the reader's attention, are in such deep and suggestive harmony with the full teaching of the Christian disclosures as strongly to imply that the divine Spirit of inspiration was already speaking out of the center of this great truth. It may be that a plurality in the Godhead may not lurk in the use of the plural term Elohim for God; but it is very significant that both "God" and "the Spirit of God" appear in the very first lines in the statement of the creation, as well as in various passages in the later Scriptures (Gen. 1:1–2; Job 26:13; Ps. 104:30; Neh. 9:20; Isa. 63:10; 48:16). It looks quite like the shaping force of the yet undisclosed mystery, when the narrative phraseology represents plurality, fellowship, and counsel in the Deity (Gen. 1:26; 3:22; 11:7; Isa. 6:8), or gives a threefold benediction in the Aaronic formula (Num. 6:24–26), and the trisagion ascription of Isa. 6:3. Nor can we rightly avoid, if we permit the New Testament revelation to shed back its light upon the preparatory dispensation, recognizing in the numerous Old Testament theophanies actual manifestations of the revealing Son before the incarnation. Equally sure are the foreshadowings of the Trinity in the numerous passages concerning the Messiah which indicate His sonship and divinity, as Ps. 2:7; Isa. 9:6; Micah 5:2, and the gift of the Holy Spirit in Joel 2:28; Isa. 44:3; Ezek. 36:27. While these and other assumptions and adumbrations of the Trinity were insufficient to enable men to read it clearly or certainly, they, nevertheless, formed the underlying basis on which the movement of redemption was unfolding and the result was preparing. Delitzsch well says: "The Trinitarian conception of God ... is a reflex even of the Old Testament facts of revelation. God and the Spirit of God are already distinguished upon the first pages of the Holy Scriptures, and between both, the Angel of God stands as the Mediator of the Covenant, according to Gen. 16, and as Leader of Israel, according to Ex. 14:1–9. The Angel of His presence, according to Isa. 63:9, is the Savior of His people." Yet it must be conceded that these Old Testament passages, taken together, do not necessarily carry the conception beyond that of a threefold manifestation of God, or what is usually designated an "economic Trinity."

But the truth comes into explicit revelation in the New Testament. And here it comes, not so much in the way of formal announcement as in an unqualified assumption of it as the fundamental conception of the real nature or being of God, upon which the great movement of providence and redemption is advancing and consummating its grace. It is openly placed as the basis of the essential facts of mercy and salvation. It is in the activity of God as triune that the divine love reaches down to man, and opens the way of forgiveness of sin and recovery to spiritual and eternal life. The threefold forms of divine grace are directly and formally laid back upon the trinitarian reality in the Godhead. This is not yet the place to give the full Scripture evidence on this point. It is enough here to fix in mind that, whatever advances may appear in Christ's expressions of a conscious identity with God, the fact of such consciousness is certain, if the Gospel accounts are at all reliable, and that the divine claim is recognized and woven-up by the apostles in the very texture of the view they give of the way of salvation and the practical relations men sustain to God. It is this fundamental position and practical bearing that make the doctrine of the Trinity so vital in the theological system. It is not something merely speculative, an abstract, barren metaphysic. It is a centrally constitutive principle of Christianity. It is placed in such living relation to the whole soteriological provision and to the consequent actual life of faith, love, and worship to which it invites and binds men, as to become incorporate in all the distinguishing doctrines of the faith. It not only becomes an essential part of our conception of the Absolute, Self-sufficing Personality of God, with all fullness of blessedness in Himself and power to go forth in creational activity for origination of other being, but through the conjoint offices of Justifier, Redeemer, and Sanctifier enters profoundly into personal Christian experience.

It was inevitable that the theology of the Church, after the Apostles, should seek to realize and fix for itself the true sense and content of the New Testament facts and language. The faith of the Gospel was bound up therewith too vitally, at the points of incarnation, the cross, resurrection, and divine mediation, to permit the Church either to drop the question or to be content with anything short of a definite settlement of the essential verities involved. The theological impulse was quickened by the appearance of different forms of denial of the truth, annulling the integrity and fullness of the faith. So this truth of the Trinity, especially in connection with the question of the person of Christ, became the first great subject for theological settlement.

The beginning of this settlement connected itself with the use of the Baptismal Formula (Matt. 28:19). That formula served not only as itself an expression of the Trinitarian belief of the early Church, but as a convenient basis on which to gather its advancing determinations of the content and definitions of the doctrine. It was thus gradually expanded so as to make distinct affirmations of faith with respect to each "name" of the Three (Triad), with explanatory terms according true divinity to each, until it reached the completed form of the so-called "Apostles' Creed." From the second century on, every phase of speculation that seemed to endanger the traditional and Scripture teaching on the subject was earnestly discussed, and the conclusions reached were carefully formulated in chosen and guarded terms. At the first Œcumenical Council, at Nicæa, A. D. 325, called together especially by the rise of the Arian heresy as to the Person of Christ, the immediate interest was satisfied with an explicit and positive formulation of the Church's Trinitarian faith with respect to the true and full deity of the Son—leaving the generally recognized divinity of the Holy Spirit stand as accredited in the Apostles' Creed—as follows:

"We believe in one God, the Father Almighty, Maker of all things visible and invisible. And in one Lord Jesus Christ, the Son of God, the only begotten of the Father, that is, of the essence of the Father, God of God, Light of Light, very God of very God, begotten, not made, being of one substance (ὁμοούσια) with the Father; by whom all things were made both in heaven and on earth; who for us men, and for our salvation, came down and was incarnate and was made man; He suffered, and the third day He rose again, ascended into heaven; from thence He shall come to judge the quick and the dead.

"And in the Holy Ghost.

"But those who say 'there was a time when He [the Son] was not'; and 'He was not before He was made'; and 'He was made out of nothing'; or 'He is of another substance' or 'essence', or 'The Son of God is created,' or 'changeable' or 'alterable,' such the catholic and apostolic Church condemns."

The second Œcumenical Council, at Constantinople, A. D. 381, carried forward the credal formulation of the Trinitarian faith by adding clauses affirming the true divinity of the Holy Spirit, against the disturbing teaching of the "Macedonians," or "Pneumatomachians."

"We believe in one GOD, THE FATHER ALMIGHTY, Maker of heaven and earth, and of all things visible and invisible.

"And in one LORD JESUS CHRIST, the only begotten Son of God, begotten of the Father before all worlds, Light of Light, very God of very God, begotten not made, being of one substance (ὁμοούσια) with the Father; by whom all things were made; who for us men and for our salvation, came down from heaven, and was incarnate by the Holy Ghost of the Virgin Mary, and was made man; who was crucified for us under Pontius Pilate, suffered and was buried; and the third day He rose again, according to the Scriptures; and ascended into heaven, and sat down on the right hand of the Father; and He shall come again, with glory, to judge both the quick and the dead; whose kingdom shall have no end.

"And we believe in the HOLY GHOST, the Lord and Giver of life; who proceedeth from the Father; who with the Father and the Son together is worshiped and glorified; who spake by the prophets."

With this Nicæno-Constantinopolitan Creed the dogmatic development of the doctrine of the Trinity by the Eastern Church substantially ended. The subsequent insertion of the "filioque" ("and from the Son"), in the clause on the Holy Spirit's procession, by the Western Church, and the elaborate definitions and explanations of the so-called Athanasian Creed, also peculiar to the West, were not meant so much as additions to the content of the Church's doctrine, as explications and safeguards of it as already essentially included in the previous symbols. As the Lutheran and Anglican Churches have formally embodied the Athanasian Creed, as well as the Apostles' and the Nicæno-Constantinopolitan, in their doctrinal standards, its statements on the subject have a proper place here in this glance at the progress of thought through which the Church gave permanent theological setting to its Trinitarian faith:

"The catholic faith is this: that we worship one God in Trinity, and Trinity in Unity, neither confounding the Persons nor dividing the Substance. For there is one Person of the Father; another of the Son; and another of the Holy Ghost. But the Godhead of the Father, of the Son, and of the Holy Ghost, is all one: the glory equal, the majesty co-eternal. Such as the Father is; such is the Son; and such is the Holy Ghost. The Father uncreated; the Son uncreated; the Holy Ghost uncreated. The Father is infinite; the Son is infinite; the Holy Ghost is infinite. The Father is eternal; the Son is eternal; the Holy Ghost is eternal. And yet there are not three eternals; but one eternal. As also there are not three uncreated, nor three infinites; but one uncreated; and one infinite. So likewise the Father is Almighty; the Son is Almighty; and the Holy Ghost is Almighty. And yet there are not three Almighties; but one Almighty. So likewise the Father is God; the Son is God; and the Holy Ghost is God. And yet there are not three Gods; but one God. So likewise the Father is Lord; the Son is Lord; and the Holy Ghost is Lord. And yet there are not three Lords; but one Lord. For as we are compelled in Christian truth to acknowledge each person distinctively to be both God and Lord, so we are forbidden by the catholic religion to say that there are three Gods or three Lords. The Father is made by none, neither created nor begotten. The Son is of the Father alone, not made, nor created, but begotten. The Holy Ghost is of the Father and of the Son; neither made, nor created, nor begotten, but proceeding. So there is one Father, not three Fathers; one Son, not three Sons; one Holy Ghost, not three Holy Ghosts. And in the Trinity none is before or after another, none is greater or less than another; but all three persons are co-eternal and co-equal. So that in in all things, as above said: the Unity in Trinity and the Trinity in Unity is to be worshiped."

It is manifest that these metaphysical affirmations which, together with the assertion of the double procession of the Spirit, completed the confessional development of the Trinitarian view in the Western Church, were meant mainly to fortify the Nicene faith against all Arianism and all forms of teaching that imply an essential subordination of the persons or subsistences of the Godhead.

Our understanding of the Trinity must find its ultimate validity, not in the traditions of the past and formulations of Councils, but from the teachings of the Holy Scriptures. The ecclesiastical formulations are authoritative only as they express, as they essentially do, the doctrine of the word of God. In further considering the subject, some leading facts must here be brought into distinct and guiding view.

1. The Scriptures clearly base the Trinitarian conception of God upon the Divine Unity. In logical relation the Unity is first. Nothing is more fundamental in the Christian Scriptures than that there is only ONE Being that is God. He is ONE AND ALONE. The repudiation of polytheism is absolute. No shadow touches the pure monotheism of Christianity. The fundamental conception of God is Unitarian—in the sense of the absolute Oneness of the Divine Essence or Being. The very proofs of the Trinity find their full conclusive force only when viewed in the light of the Biblical doctrine that polytheistic worship is impiety. The Unity of the God-head is the presupposition for the Trinity. Remove the Unity, and the rendering of homage to Three becomes the thing which the Christian conception of God condemns as flagrant offense. The inviolable oneness of the true God, as alone and unapproachably Eternal Deity, is the starting point in the true Christian thought of the Trinity.

2. The revelation of the truth of the Trinity has been made in the work and history of redemption, and thus comes as a reflection

from these Divine activities. This fact compels us to recognize the theological distinction between the immanent (ontological) Trinity and the economic. A simply economic Trinity, merely a threefold form of manifestation, or outward action (opera ad extra), as in Sabellianism, is, of course, conceivable. But the revelation in the Christian Scriptures, in its distinctly practical character, unmistakably makes the threefold forms of divine working in creation, redemption, and sanctification, stand in a trinal distinction within the Godhead, as Father, Son, and Holy Spirit, the immanent Trinity. The revelatory movement brings to light the inner Trinity (opera ad intra) in and through the threefold form of activity. God's truth in acting externally is also truth within His own Being. The manifested Trinity is made to mirror to us the eternal correspondent reality in the divine Life. In the acting of the One God, there is, from beginning to end of the revelation, the acting of three Personal subsistences, represented as existing and divine, with rights to supreme love and worship, within the full unity and fellowship of the One and only God. Both facts are to be borne in mind—the absolute Unity of the Divine Essence or Being and the tripersonality of the Eternal Life. The revelation of the immanent Trinity reaches us through the manifested or economic Trinity. The detail of the Scripture proofs of this will be given later.

3. To secure clearness in the Scripture doctrine, as properly assured in the faith of the Church, the recognized Trinitarian terminology must be distinctly remembered. In it two classes of words are applied to God—one class when His unity or oneness is referred to; the other when the triune distinctions are expressed. Those applied to His existence as One, are: essence (Latin, *essentia*, Greek, ὀυσία), substance (Latin, *substantia*), nature (Latin, *natura*, Greek, φύσις), being (Greek, ὁ ὢν). That is, in respect to that in which God is one, we use the terms essence, substance, nature, being. Those applied to denote the distinctions, as three, are Person (Latin, persona, Greek, ὑπόστασις), Subsistence (Latin, *subsistentia*). Whenever we speak of that in God in which the Trinitarian distinctions exist we employ one or other or all of these terms.

It needs here to be remarked and fixed in mind that the word Persons, thus used to express the trinal distinctions in the Godhead, is not applied in precisely the same sense as when applied to men. Here arises one of the chief difficulties in the explanation and understanding of this truth—the inadequacy and ambiguity of the term "person." There is a tendency to carry with it from the human connotation some elements of meaning not at all applicable in relation to the divine existence—to adhere too closely to the human analogy. Human personality has an individuality and separateness which will not answer for the conception to be formed of the modes of the subsistences of the Godhead. For instance, the term "person," when used of man, signifies a subject subsisting by itself, with its own separate essence, like the essence of other men, but yet not theirs; but in the Trinity there is only one undivided and indivisible essence or being. There are many men, but not three Gods. Though we say that each man, as a person, partakes of the "one human nature," yet the "human nature," or "humanity," of which we thus speak, is an abstract concept, having no real concrete existence except in individual men. But the "nature or substance" of God is not a mere concept, but actually or concretely exists as the one indivisible essence which is God; and the meaning is that in this one undivided nature there are three differences or distinctions somewhat analogous to the personal characteristics of man. The nature of the whole Godhead is personal, and personality marks it in all the three distinctions or subsistences in which it exists as Father, Son, and Holy Ghost. The natural sense of the word, drawn from individuals who form a class of beings, tends to push thinking in the mould of tritheism—three Gods, the divine class of personalities.

STATEMENT OF THE DOCTRINE

The aim of this is, not to fathom this deep mystery or attempt fully to explain the infinite reality, but simply taking the revealed elements of it, to bring the essential features together in their necessary relations and in a total self-consistent view. It seeks to be true to the data of revelation and so to combine the truths of the divine Unity and Tripersonality as to exclude incongruent or self-contradictory conceptions, and present the whole view in a form open to the unhindered acceptance of a rational faith. In the light of the theological discussion of the past we may rightly formulate the Scripture doctrine of the Trinity in the following propositions and explanations:

I. The fundamental Unity of God: There is one God, numerically one as excluding and denying any other—one God, indivisible in essence, substance, nature, and being. All the Scripture proofs of pure monotheism assure this. This Essence (Substance) in which the Unity stands, it must be remembered, is Spirit-essence.

II. The tripersonality, based on the Unity: This one indivisible Essence or Being, One God, exists eternally as three Subsistences, Hypostases or Persons, three forms of personal Godhead (μορφῆ θεοῦ, Phil. 2:6), Father, Son, and Holy Ghost—all being of the same Essence, but each distinguished by certain incommunicable peculiarities or relations not predicable of the others. These incommunicable properties, by which One is Father, One is Son, and One the Holy Spirit, form, not impersonal distinctions, but determinate personality which employs the pronouns "I," "Thou," and "He." Tripersonality as truly belongs to God as does Unity. This involves no contradiction. For He is One and Three, not in the same respects, but in different respects. In respect of Essence He is One; in respect to His self-conscious Eternal Life He is Three—in total Being triune.

III. The relations between the Persons or Subsistences:

1. The three Persons exist eternally as One Being, or indivisible Essence, that is God. This statement simply holds the tripersonality with the unity of the pure Christian monotheism.

2. Inasmuch as they are one Essence or Being, all the essential attributes belonging to that Essence, belong to each Person. This proposition simply reminds us that the same Essence or Substance must hold throughout all the attributes which mark and identify it as the same. All the essential divine attributes belong to the Father; all the essential divine attributes belong to the Son; all the essential divine attributes belong to the Holy Spirit. The affirmation rests the tripersonality in the unity, and relates the Persons as equal in essence.

3. They subsist in each other. This statement is employed both to guard the truth of the unity, One Essence, and to exclude the idea that the Persons or Subsistences have their divine character independently of each other. It has the aim of repudiating the notion

likely to come from the misleading influence of the word "Person" in human connection, of regarding the three divine Persons as subsisting separately alongside of each other, after the manner of three human persons possessing the same humanity. It excludes also all idea of subordination or inequality, and answers to words of our Lord Himself: "Believe me that I am in the Father and the Father in me" (John 10:38). This feature of the relation has been designated most frequently by the Greek term περιχώρησις, a moving round, or by the Latin *immanentia, immeatio, circumincessio,* or *inexistentia mutua et singularissima,* all expressing the idea that the Tripersonality is wholly within the very life-movement of the divine existence. The specification thus means that the Persons of the Godhead are such, i. e., divine Persons, not by and in themselves, but each with and in the others. They cannot be God—either one or all—separate. They cannot be separated; and if conceived separated, the concept would not be a true concept of God; the result would be tritheism, or three co-equal beings, no one with the fullness of Godhead. The Father is not God or Father without the Son and Holy Spirit; the Son is not God without the Father and the Holy Ghost; the Holy Ghost is not God without the Father and the Son—but each is God in and with the others. Sartorius aptly says: "All that the Father hath is the Son's (John 16:15); and the latter is, not through Himself, but through the Father, His essential equal, the express image of His being (Col. 1:15; Phil. 2:6).... Not as though the Son were, or as though He had, another being beside the infinite Father; for if each had His own to Himself, they would then not have had all in common; they would then have confronted each other in mutual limitation, in a dualistic manner, having, so to speak, infinity, not almighty, but half-mighty, as two half-gods. No, says Christ, I and the Father are one (John 10:30, 38); the Son is not beside the Father as a second God, but in Him, in His bosom (John 1:18), in the one infinite glory of His being, a sharer thereof (ὁμοούσιος) through the infinite unenvious love of the Father (John 17:24), who reserves nothing egotistically to Himself, but imparts all to Him, without thereby losing or alienating anything" (John 3:35).
This subsistence in each other explains the fact, hereafter to be noted, that while the Father, Son, and Spirit are specialized personal subsistences, and manifest themselves in special activities, or opera ad

extra, the distinguishing work of one may be ascribed also to the others. Though the Son is the revealer, the Father may be said to reveal Himself, for He does so in and through the Son (Heb. 1:2; John 5:17, 19; 14:9, 11; 2 Cor. 5:19; John 5:22; compare with Acts 17:31). Whatever the Holy Spirit does Christ may be said to do; for the Holy Spirit is the Spirit of Christ, as well as of the Father. Augustine carefully pointed out how the Three Persons of the Trinity were associated in every divine economic activity, as evidence against the encroaching of tritheism and subordination upon the Divine Unity. This interpenetration, intercommunion, and intercommunication express the oneness of the divine life in all. The Father is not Father or God without the Son. The Son is not Son or God without the Father. One cannot be thought without the other. They are correlates.

4. The incommunicable, or untransferable peculiarities which distinguish the subsistences internally, as made known in the Scriptures, mark the following relations:

(a) As to the first Person, Himself unbegotten, eternally Father—the relation characterized by the terms begetting, γενήσις, generatio, with respect to the Son; and *spiratio* with respect to the Holy Spirit.

(b) As to the second Person, begotten, only begotten, *filiatio*, or *generatio passiva*, with respect to the Father; and, according to the Western Church faith, also *spiratio* with respect to the Holy Spirit

(c) As to the third Person, proceeding, ἐκπορέυσις, processio, with respect to both the Father and the Son. For the source of the term "proceeding," see John 15:26.

We need here, as with regard to the term Person, to guard carefully against understanding the various words employed in marking these relations simply in the sense of the human relations and experiences from which they are drawn. The transcendent realities in the Trinity, in the being of the eternal Spirit, cannot be exactly or adequately named in human speech, as they are beyond all human experiences which mould our words. The point of truth that we are seeking here to designate is, that these intransferable, tripersonal relations, in whatever form they may exist, are not mere aspects of manifestation, but internal in the Godhead, denoting eternal modes of the divine Essence ad intra, or as life-activities in God's very being. They are, so to speak, constitutional and immanent modes of the divine Essence, in which that Essence lives or energizes internally from everlasting to everlasting, and by which it is trinalized in three-form distinctions called Persons. This statement is not made to explain how this can be, but simply to hold together before our view the content of what the Scriptures manifestly speak of as a fact.

It will help our understanding of the use and significance of these terms as marking the Trinitarian personal relations, to keep in mind the following points:

(1) That it is in Spirit-Being that these activities and relations are affirmed to exist. God is not matter. The whole conception of dead material must be put far aside. SPIRIT is in its very nature and essence active. It is life—nothing dead, inert, rigid, immobile in it. Especially must the Absolute and Infinite Spirit be absolute and pure eternal life or movement. "The Father hath life in Himself"—is the "living God." Before all worlds He was active in Himself, all-sufficient in His own being, the eternal *pleroma*, the "fullness," absolute Life, absolute intelligence, love in exercise, omnipotence of will, perfection of blessedness, embracing in Himself the subject and object of knowledge and love. These internal and eternal activities are not dependent for their existence or movement on the existence of other being than God. While, if thought in the forms and limitations of material being, the idea of the Trinitarian tripersonality would constitute blank contradiction, yet such reality in the Infinite and Absolute Spirit, who is eternal life-movement, is surely not beyond a possibility.

(2) These realities of begetting or generation and spiration are not to be thought of as creative activities. They do not originate anything external to God, or other than God. They add nothing to the stun of being, as does the creative working of God in the making of originated cosmic existences. They make no new essence, but express modes in the absolute eternal essence. They denote each a "form of God" (μορφῆ θεοῦ). No originated creature-being can form part of the eternal God—unless pantheism be the true philosophy.

(3) They are eternal, without beginning or end. This is the truth, for the expression of which, as related to the Son, Athanasius

employed the phrase "eternal generation." An eternal Father means an eternal Son. The absoluteness that belongs to the very being of God belongs to every reality in His constitution. These peculiarities are as eternal as is His essence or being. "In this Trinity," says the Athanasian Creed, "there is nothing before or after, nothing greater or less, but all the three persons are co-eternal and co-equal." Accordingly when, in ecclesiastical theology, the Father is called the first Person, the Son the second, and the Holy Ghost the third, no temporal succession or order in time is to be understood—only a timeless relation of the trinal modes. In order to keep out confusing error, emphasis must, at this point, be laid on the attribute of aseity, as belonging to the whole Godhead, to the divine Being as such. And the predicate dare not be surreptitiously explained in terms of positive causation, as self-causation, "self-origination," "self-production, by virtue of which God eternally makes Himself what He is," as is done by Julius Müller, followed by Dr. Dorner.2 For the fundamental Biblical, as well the rational idea of God is that He is the absolutely eternal and immutable Being; and this, surely, excludes the whole notion of origination or creation, whether by another or by Himself, whether wholly or in part. Aseity, no more than self-existence, can legitimately be allowed to stand as an expression as to how God came to be, but only as a term which marks Him as without beginning and absolutely above the category of origination—a predicate affirming, not the way of His becoming, but a feature of what He eternally has been, is, and shall be, without origination or end. It cannot, therefore, be allowable to think of God as originating the Trinality of the Godhead, as though there was a time when He was not Tripersonal in His Being—an assumption that surreptitiously runs through much of the modern speculative effort after an explanation of the Trinity. This would strive violently against the divine immutability, as well as against the proper sense of "self-existence" as exclusive of the notion of begun Being. To keep the Christian doctrine of God self-consistent, the Tripersonality must be held as absolutely grounded in the very being of God. The Christian faith is that both the Unity of Essence and the Tripersonality of God are equally eternal. The true conception and representation must be that God eternally lives His tripersonal life—not that He originates or produces it. And this conception does not need to be reduced to one that holds Him as bound in rigidity or immobility, or as a self-less fate. We have only to bear in mind that as the absolute Essence and Personality He is Spirit, the eternal Life, the eternal "I Am." He lives in holy and full freedom the life of His absolute nature. In Him the seeming contradiction between Absolute Being and freedom is resolved.

(4) Further, these subsistences are necessary, i. e., they so belong to the divine nature that they are not dependent on a special choice or subject to a contrary one. The word necessary, must, however, not be understood as implying something against, or even without God's will. More precisely the reality must be conceived as grounded in the divine nature, which, though eternally free, acts, and, for the very reason of its absolute and infinite perfections, must act consistently with itself. The Tripersonal peculiarities are not a thing of option—to take up or lay aside. They are a feature of the Absolute Existence. Without them God would not be God. In this respect, as well as in respect to being eternal, these opera ad intra differ from the divine activities in creation, redemption, and providence, which are the free acts of the divine love and election.

All these immanent, untransferable properties or activities are, therefore, to be conceived of as eternal modes in the Essence of Godhead, and mean no origination, but unoriginated, eternal, non-contingent movement and relations within the unoriginated and eternal Jehovah.

5. In designating these Subsistences Persons, the Personality which we thus affirm distinctively of the Father, Son, and Holy Ghost is not to be thought of as inconsistent with or exclusive of the Personality which we predicate of God in His Unity. It is not a fourth Personality. The Christian faith holds it fundamental that the One and only God is a personal Being—the absolute and infinite Personality. For in the fundamental oneness of Essence and the reality of a living interpenetration (περιχώρησις), the hypostatical distinctions are not Persons separately—they cannot exist in separation—but in and with each other, i. e., they are grounded in the common personal characteristic which belongs to the undivided essence or Being. We must bear in mind that all the fullness of perfect personality is an

attribute of God as the absolute Essence, the whole Godhead. Personality is not one of the incommunicable peculiarities of one or another of the subsistences, but a common property of the nature that belongs to all. It is modified (from modus) in each Hypostasis according to the special modes expressed, but not defined or described, by the terms "begetting," "begotten," "proceeding." The hypostatical distinctions thus express modes of the life of the Divine Essence (*modi subsistendi*); and the common quality or essential attribute of personality is specialized in the person of the Father, and of the Son, and of the Holy Spirit The distinct or peculiar form (μορφῆ θεοῦ) of the personal consciousness in each divine Person is intransferable; but not the fact of personal consciousness—the fact of personal consciousness being the intrinsic fact of the total Essence, in which each and all participate.

This receives explaining light from the Scriptures, which prove it. Without doubt the Scriptures do show that while generic consciousness, so to speak, belongs to the nature of God in His unity, the specialized forms of it in each Person of the Trinity are so distinct that each possesses a consciousness covering the distinction. The first Person is conscious that He is the Father, and not the Son, when He says: "This is my beloved Son, in whom I am well pleased; hear ye Him" (Matt. 17:5). The second Person is conscious that He is the Son, and not the Father, when He says: "O Father, glorify me with the glory which I had with Thee before the world was" (John 17:5). The third Person is conscious that He is the Spirit, when He receives the things of the Father's love and Christ's work, and "shows them" to men (John 16:14). And manifestly, from equally illuminating points of Scripture, the self-consciousness of God as the one essence, one God, must cover these distinct personal relations in the whole complete divine self-consciousness, viz.: the Paternal, the Filial, and the Spiritual relations, embracing them all and each in a perfect knowledge that includes the whole ineffable reality of Deity (1 Cor. 2:10–11; John 16:7).

It is scarcely permissible to speak, as Dr. Dorner does, of the Absolute Personality as a "result" or "product" of the three "modes "of the Godhead, as if the three Persons, as such, possessed it as a primary reality in such a way as jointly to give the attribute of Absolute

Personality to the Divine Essence. Rather should we think that the Absolute Personality of the one nature or being is in the distinctive Persons, not as a triple repetition of the one and whole God, but in each in a manner corresponding to the mode of life in each. God is personal through and through. Rather, therefore, we must accept other forms of expression used by Dr. Dorner alongside of the representation above, viz., in substance: 'The one absolute Personality is present in each of the divine distinctions in such a way that, though not of themselves and singly personal, they participate in the One Divine Personality, each in its own manner. The one absolute Personality is the unity of the three modes of the divine existence which share therein. Neither is personal without the others. In each, in its own manner, is the whole Godhead.'

6. The relation between the ontological or immanent Trinity and that called the economic or dispensational, as simply forms of divine manifestation or activity (opera ad extra), is that the latter reflects or reveals the former. Thus in the work of creation the Father creates by or through the Son and in the Holy Spirit. In redemption the Father sends the Son, the Son is sent and effects the conditions for reconciliation, and the Holy Spirit becomes our Sanctifier. Neither creation nor redemption is an immanent, absolute, or necessary work of the divine nature, but the transitive, free activity of love and goodness.

The movement of free thought during the last century, though critically aggressive in its hostility, has not dislodged the doctrine of the Trinity from the faith and appreciation of the Church. It seems, indeed, to have awakened doubt in many minds as to the validity of some of the special definitions and speculative determination by the older theology, but, in large part without skepticism as to the great fact of a tri-personal life within the Godhead as an absolute and immutable ground of the threefold manifestation as Father, Son, and Holy Ghost. It may, however, be fairly claimed that to many minds, most thoughtful and acute, the Trinitarian faith has received support and confirmation by the reaches of philosophical thought. Based on suggestions of idealistic philosophy as to the internal cognitive life and movement of the Absolute Spirit, the speculations of various theologians, as Marheineke, Martensen, Sartorius, Liebner, Julius Müller, Dorner, John Caird, Stoudenmaier, have caught glimpses of what has seemed to them a most assuring illumination of the reality of the Trinity. Sometimes, as with Stoudenmaier, it takes the form of simply linking the conceivability of the work of creation, like that of redemption, with the faith of trinitarian theology: "The possibility that there should be a world outside of God lies in the Trinitarian life of the Godhead, and in truth is grounded in it alone. For only through this, that God as the Triune forms for Himself a perfect world (κόσμος τέλειος), can He, without Himself becoming world, posit a creation outside of Himself and stand over this creation, high and exalted, as its Lord, Leader, Conductor, and Source of Blessing. The Divine Love, already satisfied in the interior of the Godhead through the Trinitarian life, proceeds outward, not of necessity, but with absolute freedom." Most generally and most directly, however, is the explanation sought in the analogy furnished by the essential movement of the life of intelligent personal consciousness. In human personality, self-knowledge involves an objectifying of self, a becoming both subject and object, the seer and something seen, and then the recognition of their identity as completing the total movement of consciousness in unity. First, the conscious personality exists; then, in knowing itself, it produces an objectivized self, and, further, through the perception and affirming of the identity, completes the whole course and reality of consciousness. Man's personal consciousness thus holds three forms of life-movement—the living personality per se; the objectivized product of self-knowledge; and then the action that resumes the second again into the conscious unity. It is admitted that in the human personality, because of its finiteness and imperfections, the life of thought and love never fully realizes itself in a perfect image or identical objectivized self, and so, as an illustration, never actualizes the fullness of the triune life as the reality must be conceived in God. It is claimed, nevertheless, that it presents the necessary momenta and order of personal spirit-life generically, without which personality itself is unthinkable. So, it is offered as helpfully mirroring the essential truth of the divine Trinality. As applied to God, whether physically based, as it sometimes is, simply on the divine intelligence, or, also, on the divine love,2 the parallel represents Him, in His eternal and complete knowledge of Himself, as necessarily setting Himself before His own vision as a duplicate of

Himself, of the same essence and in all attributes His co-equal, accompanied with the completing movement that recognizes and maintains the unity of the Divine in the Spirit of love. In thus knowing Himself as subject and object through this image in identical fullness of Being and attributes, He becomes a dual existence, "God with God" (John 1:1); but the personal consciousness not stopping in this direction, by a further movement it unites both again in the oneness of the absolute Being.

The weakness of this illustration, offered as an explanation and certification of the Trinity, is that in human personality self-knowledge does not, in fact, through this process of self-objectifying, establish a second personality. The consciousness in human personality, in self-knowledge, is simply an action of the faculty of intelligence, and the objectivized ideal of self is merely in thought, not in re, a concrete second personal entity. The human personality, the individual man, does not become tripersonal, but remains absolutely unipersonal—failing to present the very reality which the orthodox doctrine of the Trinity seeks to explain and assure. The source whence the offered illustration is drawn does not exhibit tripersonality, but only unipersonality, with a single consciousness, but with powers of idealization. The human analogy, in fact, would illustrate the idea of a unipersonal God. Those who have employed the similitude have, in a measure, felt and acknowledged this shortcoming and inadequacy, and have sought to supplement it in one method by reminding that the divine thought and knowledge have a completeness and take forms that transcend the human. We are told, for instance, in substance, that in man the self-consciousness is never perfect, because, in his limitations, he is never able to set before himself a reproduction fully identical; but that in God the reproduction is the perfect action of a perfect eternal Being, forever thinking forth a perfect thought, or uttering forth from Himself a true and unerring Word, that comprehends and expresses all that His being contains. The perfect Mind, it is said, with a self-consciousness complete and faultless, may be aware of these three aspects of being and know Himself in them. And it is added, these three essentials of self-consciousness may well be real to Him as they are not to men; and when we think of the Perfect Being, it does not seem impossible that to Him each of the three should be a center of conscious life and activity, and that He should live in each a life corresponding to its quality. The assertion that He lives such a life is the assertion of the Divine Triunity. But it will be observed that in this development of the speculative view the merely ideal selfhood, simply the conception of self objectified, is gradually emphasized, and at last surreptitiously transformed and made to assume the character and rank of distinct concrete personality. It disregards the fundamental distinction between thought and a thinker, between knowledge and an intelligent, knowing personality. Even with respect to God this distinction must be counted immutably valid, if we wish to avoid the most confusing mysticism. It is clearly beyond the logic of the premises, i. e., the thought-processes and forms of human personal knowledge of self, to proceed to invest the thought and knowledge, in which God knows Himself, with the attributes of substantive existence and distinct personality. Despite the process in man, man remains only unipersonal; and the use of the analogy shows rather how the self-knowing process of personal consciousness fails to present tripersonality.

The effort of some theologians to supply this inadequacy in the analogy, takes a dogmatic, but illegitimate, form when they undertake to obliterate the distinction between the Being and thought or knowledge of God. Admitting that the analogy has not bridged the difference between ideal and real personality, they invoke the old theologoumenon of the divine "simplicity," which would allow no such distinction, and declare that, with God, to be is the same as to know, and to think is the same as to will; and upon this they assume that the divine thought of self necessarily actualizes another and a third substantive personal self. But we are warned against the use of this expedient by the inexorable logic of the admission of the unwarranted dogma of absolute simplicity, viz.: that it would compel us to concede that all the theological distinctions between the divine Essence and attributes and between the different attributes are only our subjective conceptions, and not at all objectively real in God Himself, although these distinctions are as deeply imbedded in Scripture teaching as are the distinctions of Tripersonality, for whose establishment we would sacrifice them. Moreover, if in God thought and willing and being are one and the same, we must necessarily view creation as eternal and absolute as the divine Existence itself, and also equal in extent or measure with the Divine Thought. To apply that ancient groundless theologoumenon as really true would revolutionize our theology in its fundamental features. We must, therefore, decline to accept it to bridge over the lack in the offered human analogy for the Trinitarian truth.

The effort of theology, however, in framing this offered explanatory illustration is not to be looked upon as without value. For it exhibits a trinal reality of thought-life, which helps us to approach the conception of Triune Being. While it does not exhibit an instance of essential tripersonal Being, and thus form a demonstration of its truth, it nevertheless does offer three thought-centers, upon the basis or in view of which "it does not seem impossible," as Dr. Clarke well expresses it, that in God there should be, in each of them, the further reality of self-conscious personal life and action. It shows the possibility of the Trinitarian truth to be open to the acceptance of faith. The only need, as well as the only problem in the case is not to prove the Trinity, but to show that the Trinal Personality is not necessarily inconsistent with the Personal Unity—tripersonal in one respect and unipersonal in another. It justifies and invigorates faith by showing its credibility.

The utility, in general, of illustrations of this deep mystery, of which there has been a succession in many forms from the days of Augustine, depends upon the care with which they are guarded from claiming to do more than they really do. It is not the accomplished, but the unaccomplished part of the claim that invites criticism and doubt instead of confidence. Up to a certain point they are lawful and helpful. They open the way to see how harmony may take the place of apparent contradiction by viewing the problem from different angles or in the light of genuine analogies. "But the Trinity in Unity, being the mode of the existence of the Eternal, is a thing essentially unique, and is therefore lifted far above the possibility of complete comparison or illustration." It is a justified judgment which Dr. Moule expresses, that the student or teacher does wisely to deal very sparingly in such treatment of the doctrine, and in what he says to bear in mind the transcendence of the problem.

PROOFS OF THE DOCTRINE

Our further view of the Trinity must be in the way of recalling, more specifically, the Scripture proofs of the truths embraced in the foregoing propositions. They will be found in examining what the Scriptures say of the Father, Son, and Holy Spirit, as the manifested Trinity, reflecting and certifying the immanent Trinity. For the proof of the Unity of God there is no need of anything here, as the explanation and evidence of this have been given in the examination of the attributes. Here only the proofs of the trinality are required—that the One God exists as three Subsistences with divine Personality. The proof must take the form of Scripture evidence that each, in the sense defined, is, in and with the others, truly God, with all the attributes of essential Deity.

1. *Of the Father*

There is no dispute as to the true Deity of the Father in the primary conception in which Christian theology assigns Fatherhood to Him, among those who believe in the existence of a God at all. A Fatherhood, through creation, is ascribed to Him. The Fatherhood within the Godhead, not His Deity, is denied. Nor is there any dispute as to His personality, except by pantheists or agnostics. Christian theology, at this point, is not engaged in setting off a divine Trinality against atheism, but against an absolute monadic Deity. Pantheism, by denial of a personal God, becomes equivalent to atheism. But Unitarianism, which denies the divinity of Christ and the personality of the Holy Spirit, concedes the divinity and personality of Him whom the Scriptures call Father.

2. *Of the Son*

That the Son, in and with the Father and the Spirit, is God and a distinct Person, emerges in tracing the affirmations in the Scriptures concerning Him as manifested in Jesus the Christ, with whom He is identified. This identity is the basis of the reasoning and the conclusion. The same passages of Scripture, by speaking of the Christ, are proofs at once of both personality and divinity. The proofs are cumulative:

(a) His pre-existence is categorically affirmed both by Himself and the apostolic explanation. He Himself declares: "Before Abraham was, I am" (John 8:58); "No man hath ascended into heaven, but He that descended out of heaven, even the Son of man" (John 3:13); "For I am come down from heaven, not to do my own will, but the will of Him that sent me" (John 6:38); "What then if ye should behold the Son of man ascending where He was before" (John 6:62)? "And now, O Father, glorify Thou Me with the glory which I had with Thee before the world was" (John 17:5). Equally emphatic statements are made by the apostles, whom we are warranted in regarding as speaking by a wisdom divinely given them for their peculiar service: "Christ Jesus: who, being in the form of God, counted it not a prize to be equal with God, but emptied Himself, taking the form of a servant, being made in the likeness of men" (Phil. 2:6–7); "In the beginning was the Word, and the Word was God. The same was in the beginning with God" (John 1:1–2). Also of like force, Gal. 4:4; Col. 1:17; 2 Cor. 8:9; Heb. 1:2–3. It is to be noted that these passages, with others which might be quoted, carry back this pre-existence of Christ, as the Son of God, so as to declare it not only before His incarnate life, but before all worlds, "before all things," "in the beginning with God." And in that pre-existence He is lifted above all creature being, in "form of God," "the brightness of His glory."

(b) The Divine attributes are ascribed to Him: Self-existence: "Life in Himself," as the Father has (John 5:26). Eternity: "With God" when there was no creation, i. e., in eternity (John 1:1–2), "He is before all things" (Col. 1:17); "The Power of an Endless Life" (Heb. 7:16). Immutability: "The same yesterday, to-day, and forever" (Heb. 13:8). Omnipotence: "Who is and was and is to come, the Almighty" (Rev. 1:8); "Upholding all things by the word of His power" (Heb. 1:3); "Able to subject all things to Himself" (Phil. 3:21); "All authority is given unto Me in heaven and on earth" (Matt 28:18). Omnipresence: "Where two or three are gathered together in my name, there am I in the midst of them" (Matt 18:20); "Go ye, make disciples of all nations, ... I am with you always" (Matt 28:19–20); "The fullness of Him that filleth all in all" (Eph. 1:23). Omniscience: "In whom are all the treasures of wisdom and knowledge hidden" (Col. 2:3); "I am He which searcheth the reins and hearts, and will give unto each one of you according to your works" (Rev. 2:23); "Knowest all things" (John 16:30).

(c) The works of God are ascribed to Him: Creation: "All things were made by Him" (John 1:3, 10); "By Him were all things created that are in heaven and that are in earth, visible and invisible, whether thrones or dominions or principalities or powers" (Col. 1:16). Preservation and Providence: "By Him all things consist" (Col. 1:17); "Upholding all things" (Heb. 1:3); "Lo, I am with yon to the end of the world" (Matt. 28:20). Judgment: "When the Son of man shall come in His glory ... He shall sit upon the throne of His glory, and before Him shall be gathered all nations" (Matt. 25:31–32); also 2 Cor. 5:10; Acts 17:31. These works can be characteristic of God only.

(d) The distinctive titles and names of God are ascribed to the Son: "Thy throne, O God, is for ever and ever"; "Unto the Son He saith, Thy throne is for ever and ever" (Ps. 45:6 and Heb. 1:8); "Take heed to feed the church of God which He hath purchased with His own blood" (Acts 20:28); "Who being in the form of God, thought it not a prize to be equal with God" (Phil. 2:6). Exception is sometimes taken to the argument from the Old Testament use of the term "God," as applied to Christ, that it is also applied to angels, and even to men—beings not divine; for example, Ex. 7:1, "And the Lord said to Moses, See, I have made thee a god (*elohim*) to Pharaoh"; Ps. 82:6, "I have said ye are gods." But the connection shows the modified sense of "God" in these exceptional cases. But the use of it by the apostles was manifestly for the very purpose of being understood as meaning true Deity. And not the designation God (Elohim) alone is so used, but that name of awe, which God appropriated to Himself, Jehovah, "I am," is expressly thus applied, as, e. g., when of Jehovah, high and lifted up, upon a throne, His train filling the temple and the seraphim crying, "Holy, holy, holy is Jehovah," the apostle John (12:41), speaking of Christ, says, "These things said Esaias, when He saw His glory and spake of Him." A similar instance is found when Peter (1 Peter 3:15) employs Isaiah's "Sanctify the Lord (Jehovah) of hosts" (8:13), as the basis of the plea, "Sanctify in your hearts Christ as Lord"; and also in Heb. 1:8–10, where an Old Testament ascription to Jehovah is applied to Christ

(e) He is expressly declared to be God (John 1:1). "The Word"—in verse 14 becoming incarnate—"was God." This is explicit. The form in Greek (Θεὸς ἦν ὁ Λόγος), joining the article with Λόγος, fixes this as the subject and Θεὸς as the predicate, which alone is consistent with the evident fact that St. John was not attempting to define what God is, but who the Logos is. St. Paul (Rom. 9:5) declares: "Of whom [the fathers] as concerning the flesh Christ came, who is over all, God blessed for ever." A legitimate exegetical process can make nothing less of this than an affirmation that, along with His human nature from the chosen people, Christ's higher nature was true God. "For in Him dwelleth all the fullness of the Godhead bodily" (Col. 2:9). 1 John 5:20 is equally explicit: "This is the true God and eternal life." For, as has been well said, "it would be a flat repetition, after the Father had been twice called ὁ ἀληθινὸς, to say now again, 'this is ἀληθινὸς Θεός'." Further, since the "eternal life," which Christians have from God, is always declared to be in His Son (see vs. 11, 12, 13), it is most natural that ἀυτὸς should be referred to ὑιῶ, Son. In this way the grammatical law of nearest antecedent and the self-consistency of meaning are preserved.

(f) Jesus' claim to be "the Son of God," in the face of the fact that this was understood to mean equality and identity with God. This claim was repeated in manifold forms and situations most impressive, being maintained to the last as a truth in testimony to which He was ready to die (Matt. 16:16; Luke 22:70; John 10:33–38; 14:9; 16:15; 17:5, 10, 11, 21; Matt. 26:63–64).

(g) In the baptismal formula Christ unites Himself as the Son in equal divinity with the Father and the Holy Spirit (Matt. 28:19). To be baptized "into the name" of God expresses the establishment of a covenant status in His saving grace; and the form necessarily carries with it the implication of an equal relation of both the Son and the Holy Spirit with the Father to the divine name (ὄνομα) and the one only divine nature. It would be violently incongruous, even a blasphemy, to unite the name of a creature with that of God in such a status. Nothing short of a recognition of the threefold divine causality for salvation and spiritual life can fit and explain the terms of the formula. The formula used as a benediction has the same force.

(h) The true divinity of Christ is witnessed by its harmony with the clearly supernatural and miraculous powers that marked His person. His teaching was a revelation of the thought and plan and heart of God such as the sages of the world never reached, and that fully accords with the claim: "All things that the Father hath are mine" (John 16:15); and His miracles of power and love exhibit activity that finds explanation only in the sphere of divine might and prerogatives. "If I do not the works of My Father, believe Me not. But if I do, though ye believe not Me, believe the works, that ye may know and believe that the Father is in Me and I in Him" (John 10:37–38. See also John 5:36; 5:21). While the characteristics of a true humanity are undeniably evident in His life, they are not more so than are the mind and working of God.

(i) The true and natural sequence of all this is that we find Him claiming and accepting divine worship. "The Father hath committed all judgment to the Son, that all men should honor the Son even as they honor the Father. He that honoreth not the Son honoreth not the Father that hath sent Him" (John 5:22–23). The inspired apostles, in interpreting the person of the Son, exalt him to the position of supreme homage, not only by man, but by all creatures, angels, principalities, and powers (Phil. 2:9–11; Heb. 1:6; Rev. 5:12–13). The strength of this claim, right from the midst of the Christian Scriptures, is rightly appreciated only when viewed in connection with the solemn rigor with which they assert and maintain the principle that worship dare be given only to the one true God (Ex. 20:3–5; Matt. 4:10; Rev. 19:10; 22:8–9). To deny the deity of the Son is to put the Scriptures at war with their fundamental doctrine and make Jesus a teacher of idolatry and the apostles idolaters. But surely no teacher ever lived whose piety was more purely monotheistic, and whose mind carried clearer distinctions between the only true object of worship and any that is not, than were exhibited in Jesus Christ and carried in the intentions and spirit of the apostles. There was no confusion in their minds. This adds full certainty to the conclusion that in this claim and ascription of worship, they directly meant to affirm true Deity of the Son.

This epitome of the chief evidences of the true divinity of the Son is to be taken as only a partial presentation. The full proof appears only when all the Old and New Testament picturing of the promised and given Redeemer are traced in complete outline and in the symmetry of all the elements and features of His unique personality. In these features the rays from the divine have gone so penetratively as to be interwoven in the evangelical narrative almost everywhere, so that thousands of passages bear contributory evidence and give the truth its complete and impressive certitude. The few texts quoted are but summit passages in the Biblical delineation, whose light is reflected everywhere. To eliminate from the New Testament the whole mass of evidence of this truth, in all its shaping presence for the forms of thought and expression, would tear and rend the very warp and woof of the writing into hopeless inconsequence.

It will, without doubt, be seen and acknowledged, so soon as attention is directed to the point, that these same Scripture teachings, thus briefly sketched, requiring recognition of the Son as truly God, are also, at the same time, evidence of His distinct personality. For the personality that is attributed to the Christ as the Son of God incarnate is attributed equally to Him in His pre-existent sonship. Surely, the world has never seen a more distinct, positive, and impressive personality than the Christ of the Scripture history. But when He declared: "Before Abraham was I am," and prayed: "Now, O Father, glorify Thou Me with the glory I had with Thee before the world was," He made His personal selfhood range back into that existence when He had not yet "come into the world."

This immense testimony to the divinity of the Son becomes, if possible, more decisive when compared with the utter weakness of the objections which anti-trinitarians have been wont to allege from the Scriptures against it. The main incentive to deny it is, of course, the incomprehensibility of the Trinity. Confessedly, it is a mystery, a great mystery, as admitted by St. Paul (1 Tim. 3:16). But the mystery is interpreted as a self-contradiction or a contradiction of reason—which it is not. It is psychologically and metaphysically unwarranted, to confound the distinction between what is contradictory of reason and what is simply above it, or beyond the reach of its cognitive resources. An aspect of self-contradiction appears only when attempt is made to image the mystery in the forms of the representative imagination which has no materials but such as are drawn from limited human experience. But the truth in the Trinity is transcendent, a reality in the mode and measure of the absolute and infinite Being. Human experience does not cover all the possibilities of personal life. The reality in God can be known only by His disclosure of it. Its truth rests on His Word. While above proof by reason, it is above legitimate denial by it. For mystery is a characteristic of much in the whole realm of nature where facts abound whose inner modes have proved inscrutable by the human mind. We may justly say that "a God fully known would not be God." But when, under this incentive from the fact of "mystery," effort has been made to adduce from the Scriptures counterevidence to that on which the Church accepts the truth of the divinity of Christ, the result cannot be regarded as successful. The counter-reasoning is drawn from various passages which seem to imply subordination or inferiority of the Son. Some of these refer to work or activity, as, for example, the Father is said to "send" the Son, to have "raised Him from the dead," "given Him work to finish." But it is to be noted that sending, giving work, etc., express activities in the economy of salvation, as opera ad extra; mark relations or activities in the economic, not the immanent Trinity. And while it is said that "God raised Him from the dead," Christ says also: "I have power to lay down my life and I have power to take it again" (John 10:18), and "Destroy this temple and in three days I will build it again" (John 2:19). Some passages refer to worship by Christ. He prays to the Father and submits to His will. But it is to be remembered that this was involved in His becoming true man. Prayer and submission belonged to Him as true man. Moreover, prayer is essentially communion with God, and as such is not inconsistent with the equality of persons in the Godhead. In other passages, Christ speaks of a limitation of His knowledge, for example: as to the time of His second coming and the end of the world (Matt. 24:36; Mark 13:32). But the interpretation of this declared ignorance is found in the economic relations of Christ in the state of voluntary self-emptying in which the Son was "found in fashion as a man." The point is not what the Son knows in the "form of God," but what He knew in the "form of a servant" We must accept it as true that Christ did not know, when He so affirmed. But it was a truth of the limitation under which the divine

Son voluntarily came in His condition of humiliation on earth. To whatever degree Christ exercised the prerogatives of knowledge and power during His ministry, it is in accordance with a just view of His person that He largely "emptied Himself" of the "use" of them, except so far as they were necessary for the accomplishment of His earthly mission of salvation. It is entirely conceivable that, as a declaration of the time, "the day or the hour," when He should come again and the world-dispensation should close, was not an essential part of either His redemptory or teaching mission, the Logos-power of omniscience as to it was not carried down into Christ's consciousness in the state of humiliation. Similar answer must be made with respect to Christ's direct assertion of inferiority: "My Father is greater than I" (John 14:28). The statement applies to the economic relation, in the condition of self-humiliation taken by the Son in the mediatorial work. Over against it, as to essential equality, must be taken His assertion: "I and my Father are one" (John 10:30). It thus becomes evident that the few passages supposed to be counter to Christ's full divinity lack direct pertinency and are insufficient to overthrow the clear, positive, and continued teaching on the subject.

3. *Of the Holy Spirit*

That the Holy Spirit, in and with the Father and the Son, is God and a personal subsistence, is shown in the same way. The appellation, "the Spirit," is, of course, not used to designate His essence, but His distinctive personality. As to substance, He is no more spirit than the Father or the Son. But theology, in this connection, employs it as designative of His distinctive personality, because of the mode of His peculiar relation, i. e., by "spiration," *Spiritus quia spiratus*, just as the Son is called Son because "begotten."

The first part of the twofold affirmation, the Deity of the Spirit, either essentially or modally, is usually conceded. Some denials, however, appeared in the early Church. Both Arius and Eunomius represented Him as a creature, created by the Son, who Himself had been created by the Father. This teaching placed the Spirit as a "creature of a creature," κτίσμα κτίσματος. But the proofs of His divinity run parallel with those of the Son.

(a) The name and titles of God are given Him. In Ex. 17:7, the Jews are said to have "tempted Jehovah," and in Heb. 3:7–11, this tempting is identified as a tempting of the Holy Spirit. In Acts 5:3, 4, the lying of Ananias to the Holy Spirit was lying "to God."

(b) Divine attributes are ascribed to Him, e.g., Omnipresence (Ps. 139:7, 8); Omniscience (1 Cor. 2:10); Eternity (Heb. 9:14).

(c) Divine works are ascribed to Him: Creation (Gen. 1:2; Ps. 104:30); Miracles (1 Cor. 12:9–11); Resurrection of the dead (Rom. 8:11).

(d) Baptism is in His name, equally with the name of the Father and the Son (Matt. 28:19).

The second part of the affirmation, His personality, as over against all notions of conceiving the term as the designation of a simple "energy," "an influence," or a mere mode of divine operation, is equally certain from the whole tenor of the Scripture representation.

(a) The attributes and activities of personality are ascribed to Him. He knows (1 Cor. 2:11); He wills (1 Cor. 12:11); He speaks (Rev. 2:7; Acts 8:29; Matt. 10:20); He teaches (John 14:26); He testifies (John 15:26).

(b) The personal forms of pronoun are applied to Him—as is specially apparent in the Greek Testament, John 14:16, ἄλλον παράκλητον; 14:26, ὁ δὲ παράκλητος; 15:26, ὁ παράκλητος ὅν 16:13, ὁταν δὲ ἔλθη ἐκεῖνος, τὸ πνεῦμα τῆς ἀληθείας. This use of ἐκεῖνος, referring to the neuter πνεῦμα, is strongly significant; John 16:14, ἐκεῖνος ἐμὲ δοξάσει.

(c) Personality, as well as divinity, is implied in the equal relation given Him with the Father and the Son in both the baptismal formula (Matt. 28:19), and in the Pauline benediction (2 Cor. 13:14). Neither a creature nor a mere mode of agency could be thus spoken of. There could be no consistency in uniting in such co-ordinate plane with the Father and the Son a mere mode of energy or influence from them.

(d) The sin of blasphemy against the Holy Spirit also involves His personality (Mark 3:28, 29; Matt. 12:31, 32). For this sin, said to be unpardonable, is put in contradistinction to sin against the other persons of the Godhead. If the Spirit were only a power or influence, blasphemy against God Himself would be made a less sin than against a mere mode of influence from Him.

To the objection made to this teaching, that the Holy Spirit is nevertheless spoken of as "given," "poured out," "sent," and that "He shall not speak of Himself," the proper and sufficient answer is that such expressions, like the similar ones in reference to the Son, refer to economic or official work, express relations in the economy of salvation. "Poured out" is, of course, a figurative expression, referring to the influence and gifts in which He comes to men—as truly so as when believers are said to "put on Christ." That He does not "speak of Himself," means that economically He does not act in private or separate aim, but in the unity and harmony of the plan of salvation, and with respect to the mediatorial activity of the Son, carrying forward and applying the provided redemption.

Thus the second proposition, that the one God exists eternally in the three personal subsistences, each in and with the others truly God, is proved and required by the teachings of the Holy Scriptures. The Church's conception of the relations between the persons of the Godhead, as thus explained, has been determined, not speculatively or by arbitrary dogmatism, but simply in accordance with the fundamental affirmations of the Scriptures, fixing two things, viz.: the truth of the Oneness and the truth of the Trinality of God. The office of reason and logic in the matter has been simply to shape the aggregate conception of God so as to exhibit and maintain these two fundamental postulates.

CHAPTER IV
THE WORKS OF GOD.

These are properly discriminated into three forms—Creation, Preservation, and Providence. Together they form Christian Cosmology. In entering it our order of advance is from the immanent Trinity to what belongs to the economic Trinity, or the Triune God in opera ad extra. The immanent glory of God becomes a declarative or manifested glory, showing His intelligence, wisdom, will, and power in an established cosmos or world order, reflecting the divine character and purpose. His "eternal power and Godhead "are here understood by "the things that are made" (Rom. 1:20).

CREATION

Creation is that action of the Triune God by which He has called the universe of the heavens and the earth into existence. By necessary conception, this is His first work ad extra. The only action that precedes it is the immanent eternal activity of the divine essence or trinitarian life. God is the absolute originating Cause, the Creator of all being, other than Himself. All that is, other than God, is created by God. So the Scriptures clearly teach (Gen. 1:1; Neh. 9:6; Ps. 19:1; Acts 7:50; 14:15; 17:24–28; Rom. 1:19, 20; 11:36; 1 Cor. 8:6; Eph. 3:15; Heb. 1:10; 2:10; 11:3; John 1:3); and the best insight of science and philosophy sustains the truth.

But in accepting this truth, theology seeks, if possible, to vindicate it by reaching some conception as to how God could and did, from the perfection and completeness of His own being in itself, move outward in the origination of other being. The aim is, primarily, not to determine the objective end divinely contemplated and sought in the action originating other existence, but rather to form a conception of the subjective impulse, so to speak, toward ad extra creative production: what in God was the ground of such proceeding outward in originative power. And the inquiry adjusts itself, not to any of the old pagan views of deity, marked by their obsolete emanational cosmogonies, nor to our modern pantheistic views with their blind evolutionisms, but alone to the idea of God as reached in Christian theism. Theology rightly finds the explanation in the truth that while God is absolutely complete and self-sufficient in His intelligence, power, happiness, and holy freedom, He is also the fullness of love. In the very act of knowing Himself in the perfection of His own being, there must be embraced an absolute self-discrimination from every other conceivable or possible object. The idea of otherness is part of the discrimination of self. While intelligence is thus the primary seat of all possibilities, the divine love is essentially communicative, and uses its conscious plenitude of power to actualize its ideals of creature existence and blessedness. It is the nature of holy Love, or loving Will, to look beyond Self, and use its power to create objects upon which it may bestow its kindness and the happiness of which they may be made capable. Love is the reason of creation.

This explanation of the reason applies directly to the creation of the universe of intelligent, holy, personal beings, capacitated for conscious participation in the fellowship of love and blessedness. The aim of Love could not be a mere material, unconscious, non-sentient world, however great or beautiful that might be. For that could have no recipiency for the blessedness whose enjoyment Love means in its divine impulses. Love's aim must look to a creaturely existence made consciously participant in the high life of knowledge, goodness, and happiness. The teleology of the divine creative love means creatures made in the divine "image and likeness"—"children," endowed with kindredship of nature. The realm of inanimate or irrational nature is not the realm in which Love can find its own or establish for others a participation in its excellences and happiness. For our earthly world the aim of creation was Man, the creature "son of God" (Luke 3:38), for fellowship in holiness, love, and immortal blessedness. The physical cosmos was not, and could not be itself, the end, but a means to the end. Physical nature can have only a relative value, as serving God's love in its aims with respect to the welfare of the race endowed with capacities for fellowship in His thought and love, whom He placed in dominion over it (Gen. 1:26, 28; Ps. 8:5–8; Heb. 2:7).

These two truths—that God's love was the motive for His exercising creative power, and that love's aims must seek a world of goodness and blessedness—at once bring into view the necessary answer to the question as to God's objective end in creation. If love must, by very conception of love be altruistic, that end cannot be Himself, or "His own glory," as is often asserted. Since His own being and glory are eternally perfect, above all increase or diminution, He could have no motive to add to them by creation or any work ad extra; no motive to "manifest" or to "declare" His glory, as even that would imply a sense of relative incompleteness. Moreover, were His supreme or ultimate aim to glorify Himself, it would be absolute self-seeking, and the force of the word of revelation, "God is love," would be contradicted with respect to this great work. Without doubt, God does "manifest" His glory through creation, but this truth comes to its full meaning only when that creation is seen to come out of the heart of His love with altruistic aim of love. To say that because God is infinite He cannot act for finite ends, is to make Him absolute Egoism and deny unselfish goodness in Him altogether. And such conception collides with the whole claim of the Gospel. If we accept the redemption as a work of pure love, looking to human welfare, shall we hesitate to believe that the good of the universe of spiritual and moral beings was a great enough end for the work of creation? Further, this source of creation in love, not in self-seeking, is in beautiful harmony with the required supremacy of love in man. For him the whole law of duty is summed up in love (Matt. 22:37–40). He is to be trained into the divine likeness, that the glorious principle of goodness may be established in the life and order of the entire realm of personal existence and activity.
The great truth that God claims ownership of all things, desires to possess all, and hold them subject to His authority and control—the great fact of His self-assertion and sovereignty—is no contradiction of this truth that His holy love thus aims unselfishly, through both creation and redemption, at creature welfare and happiness. For, the maintenance of His sovereignty and rights is the fundamental condition of all creature good. God must desire all things for Himself, for the sake

of His intelligent creatures, in the purposes and activities of His holy love with respect to the universe. It is only as God's rights and sovereignty are recognized that the rational creation attains, or can attain, order and blessedness in the fellowship of this love. But the theology of creation requires further definitions.

1. Creation is a free action of God. It is not of an absolute necessity, or eternal, like the immanent activities of the divine life, but optional in the divine love and choice. The Scriptures clearly attribute it to the will or personal action of God (Gen. 1:3; Ps. 104:30; Col. 1:16). Neither internal nor external necessity can be supposed. No internal, because God, as the perfect personality, is fully self-sufficing in His Trinitarian life and absolute perfections, needing nothing for His self-completeness. There is no necessity for "otherness "or being outside of Himself for the realization of His own personality. The representation that His love "necessitated" Him to create is a misapplication of the idea of necessity. For love is moral, not physical, and by very conception is free. Remove it from the sphere of freedom and it is no longer love. The love out of which creation comes is only the motive for creating. No external necessity is supposable, because nothing external existed. All that is external is the product of the divine creative action. To posit anything outside of God, as necessitating His action of creation, is destructive of the very conception of God as the absolutely self-grounded first Cause of all things. His free-will of love is, therefore, the sole causality of the universe.

2. Creation must be ascribed to God as Triune. It is sometimes attributed to Him in His Unity, or without reference to distinctions of subsistence (Gen. 1:1, 26; Neh. 9:6; Rom. 11:36). But it is sometimes ascribed to the Father (1 Cor. 8:6); sometimes to the Son (John 1:3; Col. 1:16); and to the Holy Spirit (Job 26:13; Ps. 104:30). We are guided, thus, to think of the work of creation not as peculiar to one Person of the Trinity, but as by the whole Godhead, of undivided Will, one counsel, one creative power. Theology, however, is justified in the commonly made distinction, suggestive of realities in the divine working, into the mystery of which we cannot clearly penetrate, when it follows the Scriptures in speaking of the creation as "of God the Father" (ἔξ) (1 Cor. 8:6), "through the Son" (δία) (1 Cor. 8:6; John 1:3), "in the Holy Ghost."

There is in this representation a reflection or echo of the truth of the immanent Trinity. Our theology must recognize the divine Trinality in the work without, however, forgetting to hold the Unity also in clear view. For this the statement of Hollaz is in point: "The three persons of the Godhead are not three associated causes, but one Cause, one Author, one Creator. Although they are three distinct persons, yet they influence the work of creation with one power."

3. The Scripture teaching also requires us to distinguish the creative work as primary and secondary (*creatio prima seu immediata and creatio secunda seu mediata*). The first expresses the original action by which God directly brought into existence, out of nothing (ex nihilo), i. e., without pre-existing material, the elementary substances, with their properties and powers. This may properly be regarded as implied in the chaotic or formless condition referred to in Gen. 1:2. It expresses absolute creation, as wrought without means. The secondary creation is the subsequent action of God by which He originates out of the substances so created, particular distinct forms of existence, especially the different species of living beings with organization, laws, and appointed development, according to His plans. This is illustrated in the successive formations referred to in the Genesis creative week. Thus, while creation of the first order is absolute, i. e., origination out of non-being, that of the secondary order, as it uses the substances originated in the primal action, though still real creation, becomes formative or architectonic.

This truth of the absolute creation of the cosmic material, or world-stuff, from non-existence (ex nihilo), it must be noted, is peculiar to Biblical and Christian cosmology. None of the heathen religions or philosophies have reached or presented this great truth. The Latin phrase, "*ex nihilo nihil fit,*" is a denial of it. Lucretius defends the proposition: "*nullam rem e nihilo gigni divinitus unquam,*" by the consideration that otherwise there would be no need of seed or eggs. Plato and Aristotle postulated an eternal chaotic matter (ὕλη) out of which the world was formed. Plutarch defends Plato's views: "The creation was not out of nothing, but out of matter, wanting in beauty and perfection, like the rude materials of a house, lying first in confused heap. The same view marks the cosmogonies of Egypt, Syria, Babylon, and all non-Jewish Oriental peoples.2 Some claim has recently been set up for a conception of creation from nothing in the Zoroastrian and Vedic teachings and in Egyptian records, but the claim has not been established.

The Scripture evidence of this truth is both direct and indirect. The use of the word bara (כָּדָא) to "create," in contradistinction from asa (עָשָׂה) and yatsar (יָצַר) to form or fashion, in Gen. 1:1 and 2:7, is of force, though not conclusive, in this direction. While it is to be conceded that the first word does not necessarily and always denote production without the use of pre-existing material, it is yet certain that its manner of employment here gives evidence that such is its real and intended meaning. For, since in the context (verse 2) "the earth" is yet chaotic, "formless," and "void," the word bara in verse 1 could not be meant to express any action of fashioning or giving the cosmic forms, but must refer to the calling of the elements into existence. And in the generic Biblical use of the word it is, in the Kal form, found applied only to God, and never to human production, or with an accusative of material. This distinction in its application holds throughout the account of creation. While in ch. 2:7, yatsar is used to express the making of man as a physical being, "of the ground," in ch. 1:27, bara is employed to describe the making of him as a spiritual being, a new existence. In ch. 2:2, 3, both bara and asa are joined in expressing the whole creative action: "Created and made," or "created to make," a phrase that implies at once a distinction between the words and a combination of the two kinds of divine work in the whole outcome of creational power. Beyond doubt the idea of absolute creation was current among the Hebrews. "The later Scriptures show that it had become natural to the Hebrew mind." They show that God was thought of as alone "eternal," "before the earth and the world, from everlasting to everlasting" (Ps. 90:1), "before all things" (Col. 1:17); "of whom" (εξ τοῦ Θεου) are all things (Rom. 11:36). See also John 1:1–3; 1 Cor. 8:6; Col. 1:16. "By faith we understand that the worlds have been framed by the word of God, so that what is seen hath not been made out of things which do appear" (Heb. 11:3), clearly teaches that God did not use visible materials for the visible cosmos. Without classing the apocryphal book of Maccabees with the Biblical Scriptures, we must yet take 7:28 of this book: "God made these things out of nothing" (ἐξ οὐκ ὀύτων ἐποίησαν ἀυτὰ ὁ Θεός), as a positive witness to the Jewish belief of creation without pre-existing material. St. Paul's declaration: "Who quickeneth the dead and calleth the things that are not as though they were," evidently views the divine fiat as calling into being from non-existence.

This feature of the Christian view is sustained from the data of reason and the best light of science. The only rational concept of God, as the absolute and infinite ground of all finite being, disallows the idea of a second eternal, self-existent essence. Beyond all question, the conception of eternal or self-existent being must be admitted. Since something now exists, something must have existed from eternity—as a beginning of existence from nothing without any cause is inconceivable. And that Being must have in itself the potency of causation for the origination. But if the difficult conception of self-existence must be admitted, as it really must, the supposition of self-existent matter duplicates the difficulty, and at the same time introduces an external limitation on the being and work of God. Further, all that science has been able to discover as to the nature of matter, or the physical substance of the universe, in its assumed atoms, reveals a plan or adaptation in their structure, as of "manufactured articles." They bear clearly the marks of subordination to use, or of intentionally prepared materials for world-building. Science does not favor, but discredits, the notion that matter, with its forces, laws, and possibilities, is eternal. Prof. Maxwell, writing of these atoms as the foundation stones of the material universe, says: "They continue this day as they were created, perfect in number and measure and weight; and from the ineffaceable characters impressed upon them, we learn that those aspirations after accuracy in measurement, and justice in action, which we receive among our noblest attributes as men, are ours because they are essential qualities of Him who, in the beginning created not only heaven and earth, but the material of which heaven and earth consist." To make matter with its forces and laws eternal, would place the whole basis of the universe outside of God, and reduce His position or power to that of a mere cunning and skillful Architect. But the orderliness of these laws, their adaptation to the ends of intelligence and purpose is inconsistent with such a theory. The whole

teleological proof for the existence of God, beyond all rational questioning, shows matter with all its powers and laws to be the product of Mind, or intelligent purpose. Kant says finely: "There is a God, because nature, even in chaos, could not proceed otherwise than with regularity and order.... Nature, left to its own general qualities, is rich in fruits which are always fair and perfect. Not merely are they harmonious and excellent themselves, but they are adapted to every order of being, to the use of man, and to the glory of God. It is thus evident that the essential properties of matter must spring from one mind, the Source and Ground of all being; a mind in which they belong to a solidarity of plan. All that is in reciprocal relations of harmony must be brought into unity in a single Being, on whom it all depends. There is, therefore, a Being of all beings, an infinite mind and self-sustaining wisdom, from which nature in the full range of all its forms and features derives its origin, even as regards its very possibility."2 Kant further declares: "The proposition that God as the universal first Cause, is the cause of the existence of substance, can never be given up, without at the same time giving up the notion of God as the Being of all beings, and thereby giving up His all sufficiency on which everything in theology depends." Whatever is that is not God is a creature of God.
If it be alleged that this teaching still leaves us under the necessity of admitting as true the difficult conception of self-existent eternal being, our reply must be that no theory of the universe, as an actual reality, has ever been suggested, or can be suggested, that obviates, or can obviate, this necessity. The recognition of something self-existently eternal is lodged in the necessities of rational thought and knowledge in the presence of existing being, and can be evaded only by ceasing to think. And, therefore, the affirmation of Lotze is sufficient to meet the case: "When we characterize the inner life of the personal God, the current of His thoughts, His feelings, His will, as everlasting and without beginning, having never known rest and having never been roused to movement from some state of quiescence, we call upon imagination to perform a task no other and no greater than that which is required from it by every materialistic or pantheistic view."

4. Even cosmic times and spaces are of God. Neither time nor space, as we have seen, is to be thought of as an 'entity,' as frequent

representations seem to make them. Nor are they mere 'relations,' as is sometimes taught. Nor yet are they mere subjective 'forms of thought,' possibly a fictional and illusory product of the human mind's own action, as in the relativity of Kantian phenomenalism. But they are true and real for the actual objective universe. Yet they belong to the world or universe only as created by God. They appear as limited and measured intervals between or occupied by occurring events and by material bodies. They have in themselves no substance—no ontological existence. Space, in itself, is absolute void, blank emptiness, the precondition or possibility of extended material existences. So, also, Time, in itself, is simply the necessary presupposition of events, change, succession in an order of before and after, or measurably enduring finite existence. Before any creation by God, if we may conceive such 'before,' there was nothing but God. He was the only existence; but then instead of the nothingness or void of other being than Himself, His creational power put finite existences, with material dimensions and successional movement. And so, cosmic space and cosmic time, or, translated into the terms of their equivalents in human experience and consciousness, measured extension and distances, and measured duration, became realities for the universe. Before creation there were only the possibilities—not the realities of these—and their possibilities lay only in the power of God. The potencies were in His Will; and the creation of things, with material extensions and successional movements of change and events, became the birthday of actual cosmic spaces and times.

5. With respect to the secondary creational work, that which, out of the created elements or essences, constructed the cosmic system, with its manifold forms of existence and adjustment, we must look upon it as having been progressive. This conception lies imbedded in the swift sketching of the Genesis account. However interpreted as to cosmagonic details, the work of the six days' creation, on the basis of the chaotic material, moves forward through a series of advances in physical order, through originations of plant life, of animal life, of human life. The creative work is represented as proceeding step by step in ascending grades to that which marked the end or aim of the world-order. With this Science concurs. It is written on the rock-leaves of the

great geological record. But the Scriptures do not allow us to think of this progressive work as a simply self-contained and self-productive evolution of primordial matter or energy. For the advance is connected with succession of distinct creative words of the divine Will and power. "Let there be light," "Let the waters bring forth," etc. The secondary creative work must, therefore, be so viewed as to leave place for the divine freedom to guide and uplift the progress according to its own plan, fulfilling the "increasing purpose" that is unquestionably apparent in historic realization.

Without doubt, this historic and progressive creational work has been marked by the presence and action of 'second causes,' the energies lodged in the nature of the primordial substances, adjusted for the continuance and advance of cosmic conditions. The records of geology, as well as the indubitable facts of present cosmic action and life, are full of testimony to this. It were absurd in face of these facts to deny that either now or in past geologic time, there have been real forces in nature, operating under regular inherent order or law, through which the special existences now filling the world have come to be. God has created, and evermore creates, individual creatures, if not species, by or through second causes acting in the established forces and uniformities of nature. Whatever may be the outcome of the inquiry concerning the 'origin of species,' it is certain that individual plants, animals, and men are thus called into existence. And such work does not cease to be God's, because effected under the action of means or established causal forces. The means are God's, set efficiently to work under His will and through established powers. In Christian theism all power in the universe is ultimately Will Power. As far as it has been creatively lodged in the material or natural forces of the universe it is but the manifestation of the omnipotent energy of the divine Will.

Just as confidently must it be maintained that in His creational work, God did not, after the creation of the world-material with its forces and laws, vacate or abandon all direct creative production. The clear implications of the Genesis sketch exhibit God's direct word of power as the ground of the successive originations from the void and formless condition of the cosmic substances. Let alone, it would seem that the chaos would not have become the actual populated cosmos of the divine purpose. At least it did not become such without specific acts of the divine Will, particularly and directly causal for certain increments in the essential properties, realities, and forms of being. There are such increments, whose appearance is inexplicable from any known or discoverable powers belonging to matter, per se, such as the origin of life, sensation, mind, self-consciousness, and free rational self-determination. Chaos, if left alone, could not have made man. Plant-life, animal life, needed words of creative power for their introduction into the system of world-existence; and for human mind a crowning divine action of specific, direct creation was requisite. And the efforts of human science virtually continue to sustain these Biblical implications, in its confessed inability to deduce either life or mind from the inherent properties of matter—the matter which it generally represents as cooling from the form of fire mists, and as in its early condensed forms for ages azoic. Neither science nor philosophy has been able to translate the mere atomic powers or motions into the terms of life, intelligence, and free-will. No capacity for spontaneous generation of life has been discovered in matter; no way has been shown for the birth of freedom from the realm of material necessity. Theology may well take this impotence of science to explain these originations from the inherent powers of physical nature as a confession of its right to see a divine truth in the Biblical implications, when the record connects these originations with specific fiats for steps of increment to nature's endowment. The primary creation of the material for world-building must be viewed as meaning God's continued presence and potency for whatever working His plan may include for carrying it forward to the high ends of His purpose. And unless science has utterly misread nature's geologic record, cosmic time has witnessed an immense ascent into higher types and forms of existence. This is an impressive evidence of some divine efficiency beyond the simple action of the unchanged sum of nature's inherent forces moving forward. The supernatural is a deeper reality in God's plan than is often supposed. If the cosmic atoms remain forever the same, none added, none lost, none changed, the same in quantum and character, it is difficult, if not impossible, to conceive how, if left absolutely alone, their interactions would take and maintain an ascending movement; and, instead of going on upon a dead level, a simply forward line, a progressus in infinitum, bring ever new and higher beginnings, improved and nobler forms. This lift of nature in its progress shows not only the presence of a preserving power, but of a directive and creational power, a power at work other than natural forces alone.

6. The relation which God established between Himself and the universe, must be theologically determined by these truths of His absolute creatorship, originating and forming it in motives and for ends of love and creature blessedness, and by the general implications as well as specific affirmations of the Scriptures concerning it. The point is one of vast and vital importance to every interest of human life, and the whole question of human destiny. Dark and hopeless is the view offered by materialism, which, wholly denying a personal and purposeful Creator, bids us look on the universe as having nothing but matter whose highest self-evolutions appear in human intelligence and activity, as a mere fate-phenomenon of special organization, necessarily ending with the end of the organization. No less gloomy and paralyzing is the view when human life is pantheistically or monistically represented as only a part of the phenomena of the one absolute spirit-substance, differentially evolving itself into and forming all cosmic existences, and returning—identifying God and Nature, as at present urged by various prominent writers, both philosophical and theological. No more inspiring is the deistic separation of God from the world, in which He is viewed as its Creator indeed, but as having so constituted it that it remains self-working in its own given forces and laws, needing and receiving no immediate divine presence or care—while God lives in some lofty empyrean above the world, without interfering with its established on-going, and without any word of concern or direction for the well-being and issues of life. In this extreme doctrine of the divine transcendence, nature is left a pure mechanism of force and action, with no place for any providential causality, either as revelation, miracle, or answer to prayer. Carlyle's characterization of the relation: "An absentee God, sitting idle ever since the first Sabbath at the outside of the universe and seeing it go," suggests how utter an exclusion from hope and help in God may come with a false conception of His relation to the world.

But when we let the light of His creatorship and His aim of love in it fall upon the question, it is evident that He takes a relation of most real and active goodness to the spiritual beings for whom He forms the world, whom He makes kindred in nature for the blessedness of fellowship. His absolute self-consistency forbids any idea that His continued preservation of the world may mean abandonment of the loving interest in which He created. And unless the entire picture of the divine aim and supernatural providence in the pages of the historical record from Genesis to Revelation is nothing but fictitious sketching, God has been showing an abiding and working presence in the world, adding a redeeming activity in expression of His loving interest in the life and happiness of man. Theology, therefore, as true to its Scripture data, must maintain a twofold reality in the relation of God to the world-universe. First, that He is transcendent to it. As the absolute Cause of it, He is before and above it. This relation is part of the essential truth of the principle of causation. He is "God over all" (Rom. 9:5; Eph. 4:6). "The heaven of heavens cannot contain Him" (2 Chron. 2:6; 6:18; 1 Kings 8:27). Secondly, He is also immanent in the universe. This is a direct implication of His own omnipresence. He fills all things with His presence and energy. "He is not far from every one of us; for in Him we live and move and have our being" (Acts 17:27–28). He is "through all and in all" (Eph. 4:6). The divine efficiency in creation was transitive, and abides as indwelling power in all things. In a true sense, He put Himself into nature—not as an identification of essence with it, but a living Presence. His will-energy, which is lodged as a permanent force in nature, and nature's so-called laws, spoken of as "second causes," expresses the ever-present efficiency of His abiding Will. Neither the cosmic substances nor forces could continue to exist and act in independence of the upholding efficiency of that abiding Will. This power of God fills and permeates all nature, and He is wherever He works. Neither the transcendence nor the immanence, however, is to be conceived of as absolute. An absolute transcendence would mean the deistical separation of God from nature, a constitution of the world as a self-sustaining and self-acting mechanism, and God simply outside of and apart from it. An absolute immanence would signify a transfer of the divine freedom into the established action of nature or identification of God with nature.

This relation of God to the world of nature, as both transcendent and immanent, gives place for both the action of "second causes," or what are termed natural forces, and for special divine action in and among these forces and laws. On the one side, it accounts for all the uniformities of nature, the reign of law or enchainment in relations of cause and effect, of which science speaks; and, on the other, for the reality of Providential ordering of history, the reality of supernatural revelation, miracle, and whatever response the divine Will of goodness in the Infinite Father may make to His children's needs or prayers. It recognizes nature's existence and laws as subservient to the divine plan of love and goodness, and forever susceptible to His use and direction. It recognizes, as experience and science themselves attest, the elastic character of the system, ever open to the use and service of the will-power of human freedom, and even more fully open to the touch of God for the accomplishment of the supreme moral and spiritual aim for which the physical world exists. As God is before nature, above it, under it, in it, and through it, without being a part of it, as its forces and laws are but the modes of His will for its preservation, we must think of Him as, through His omnipresence, abiding forever free for all the special providential causation which His wisdom may choose for the consummation of His purpose of love.

It is no essential part of the theology of creation to explain how its formative steps of advance were effected, or to trace the causal relations between them. Supernatural revelation, because not given to unfold a science of nature, but to afford necessary religious truth, has, in this connection, limited itself to the affirmation of the essential facts that needed to be brought into view for this purpose. Scientific theories which seek simply to explain the method of the creative progression, while recognizing its divine authorship, are not properly subjects of dogmatic notice unless they affect the religious truths for whose disclosure supernatural divine revelation stands. Nevertheless it is interesting and assuring to find in the brief Genesis statement of the creation so many points of agreement with the conclusions of the maturest science in matters apart from religious relations. The extent of the agreement is remarkable, in such large features as (1) The creation of the elements in a remote past; (2) an early state of chaos; (3) a progress through various advances to the earth's present condition; (4) the order of the advance, viz.: First, a condition without life; secondly, vegetable life; thirdly, animal life; fourthly, man. The harmonies on points on which science has come to its conclusions only in the late few decades, are so truly notable and peculiar as to become significant of something supernatural in the Genesis representations, made away back in a period utterly unscientific. For science has only in these last few years read, from geologic pages, the truth of a primal chaos, and azoic period of the earth, the progressive formation of the earth-strata, the beginning of life, the advance in its grades, and the order of advance. But how did Moses know these things? Who taught him? There is reason in the declaration of Dutoit Haller, that what took place in the physical world before the appearance of man must have been revealed to the writer of Genesis; and in the assertion of Biot: "Either Moses had a more profound instruction in science than that afforded by our own century, or he was inspired." But it is in the fundamental position and basal value of the great and determinative religious truths, that the account in Gen. 1–2. exhibits its essential theological importance and shows its divine signature. It is necessary only to note these great truths and recall their bearings in order to see a divine reason of supreme import, why this account has been made to stand at the very beginning of the entire Biblical record of the providential and redemptive self-manifestation of God. For we thus discover that in these, viz.: the existence of God, the creation of all things by Him, the origin of man, his formation after the divine image, his endowment with rational freedom and moral responsibility, his assigned "dominion" over lower nature, his status of holy fellowship with his Maker, and his lapse into sin, there are-presented the great foundation truths that are presupposed and concerned in the entire Bible history of God's dealings with mankind through the revelation of His will and law and grace, from its first pages in Genesis to its last in the Apocalypse. Without the setting forth of these fundamental facts at the beginning, the entire Scripture development of doctrine, worship, commandment, warning, training, and appeals to conscience, hope, and fear, throughout the Old Testament and the New, would lose their intelligibility and meaning. The whole explanation of the consummated revelation stands in the facts or truths made known in the creation record. They never disappear, they are absent from no part, and when the volume closes they have upborne the whole administrational and redemptive movement. It is a fact of immense importance that for the wonderful organism of teaching concerning God and man and eternal life in the completed Scriptures, the great foundation truths are all discovered to have been given on their first pages, and that the theology of creation is heard reverberating through the entire theology of Providence and Salvation to the consummation in "the last things." Surely there must have been some divine direction for the hand that sketched out these foundations.

PRESERVATION

Preservation is that continuous agency of God by which He maintains in existence the world, or universe, which He has created. It is described as an "upholding by the word of His power," and by various equivalent statements (Heb. 1:3; Gen. 8:22; Neh. 9:6; Ps. 36:6; 104:29–30; John 5:17; Acts 17:28; Col. 1:17). It necessarily involves the following points:

1. That the continuance in existence of every created thing necessarily depends upon the power that brought it into being. It has, and can have, no absolute existence. It cannot attain to independence. All creation would fall back into nothing without the divine power in which it has its being. It is no more capable of self-upholding than it could have been of self-origination. We are compelled to think that the divine power could not confer on any part of creation necessary or absolute existence. For this would involve the obliteration of the whole distinction between that which is God and that which is not God, the contradiction of making originated being self-existent or without beginning. Only God can have absolute immortality (1 Tim. 6:16). A creature can have immortality only in the abiding will and power of God, and according to His plan. This plan may give to the creature real objectivity of existence, and lodge in it an endowment of creaturely energies and order, but the continuance must rest in the steady will of

Him who made it, not for instant perishing, but with a view to preservation.

2. Preservation is, therefore, not something merely negative, a doing nothing, a mere refraining from destroying, but a positive exercise of divine power, efficiently sustaining given existence and order. It is, also, something more, and more direct, than a simple self-activity of inherent properties and powers, conceived of as imparted to nature by the act of creation, and able, thenceforth, to operate themselves independently, according to the deistical notion of God's supposed withdrawal and separation from the world, in the otiose relation of merely "seeing it go."

3. This positive divine efficiency of preservation must be conceived, further, as establishing the permanency of existence and the uniformities of action in nature, recognized as "second causes," through which, as means, cosmic processes and advance take place and continuous life-phenomena are presented. We are as little to deny second causes as to think them independent of God. Their actual forces and working which are the subjects of our daily experience and of scientific examination, and which exhibit the "reign of law" in nature, express the abiding will of God both as Author and Sustainer of nature. They are rightly acknowledged as objectively real, and, with their regularities of causation, actually embodied in the system of nature, as the result of God's preservational efficiency upon the products of His creational work. Even the creative act, in itself, must necessarily be viewed as producing something which then has an existence of its own, with its own real, though dependent, forces and properties. Otherwise the Divine cause has really effected nothing. "In the interest of the creation-idea itself, it is important for the divine act of constitution to give rise to something having separate existence, and not remaining inherent in the divine conception and volition. And thus must creative activity itself produce that which is destined to be permanent existence and able to become the object of conservation." Preservation can conserve only what creation brings into existence. God did not create for instant perishing, but with high and unchangeable view to a real world, a real universe, in great aims of love and goodness, whose working out belongs to His eternal will and plan. Hence His

preservational efficiency holds in existence the world-constitution which His power produced. And we rightly regard the permanency and uniformity of this established secondary causation, with its "reign of law," as at the basis of that possibility of human foresight and consequent self-adjustment to conditions of safety and welfare through which the world is made a fitting abode for the training of free personality into self-control and moral character. Forecast of the future, prudence, adjustment to relations, and seizure of opportunities are some of the rich things provided for in these uniformities.

This objective reality of "second causes" in both material and spiritual nature, resting thus on the twofold divine action of creation and conservation, must be made explicit and emphasized. As a result of the double action God has established other being than Himself—being that has its own existence, its given forces and modes. Its actual endowments amount to a conferred relative independence. The closest observation of nature, from its largest forms to its minutest constituents, the most penetrative and exhaustive analysis of its action from masses to molecules, make this impression upon us. But more: When we face the phenomena of human history and scan the consciousness of human personality in its freedom of choice and self-direction, often in conflict with every conception of what must be the divine will, a relative creaturely independence cannot fail to appear as an evidently intended and actually conferred resultant from the twofold divine action. This relative independence is as little to be denied as is the absolute dependence of the whole system upon God. It is just in that part in which the cosmic system comes to its crown, in human freedom, that this truth of a divinely conferred, relatively-independent creaturely selfhood becomes indubitable. And it is a truth that needs perpetual re-affirmation and remembrance in order to guard against the overdrawn theories of the Divine Immanence and Efficiency which attribute every human act or choice, as well as motion of matter, directly to God and annihilate free personality and responsibility.

4. Theology, therefore, cannot accept the oft-repeated representation which substitutes "continuous creation" (*creatio continua*) for preservation, making the continuance of the universe the result of ceaseless instantaneous reproduction. In this the idea of

preservation, as simply upholding an objective existence already given by creative power, disappears in that of a direct divine creational efficiency which, moment by moment, makes nature what it is. But this notion accords as little with the implications of reason as of revelation. Plainly the Scriptures make a clear distinction between preservation and creation, and, indeed, set them over against each other (Neh. 9:6; Heb. 1:2, 3; Col. 1:16, 17). And in the light of reason, whether guided by the principles of natural or revealed truth, difficulties of a very decisive character come into view. To substitute momentary recreation for preservation would seem to imply that God does not, or rather cannot, by a primary creative act, form any creature being, either of matter or mind, with more than momentary existence or constitute it with any measure of enduring energy, but that He must instantly repeat His work in order to give it a form of continuance. The so-called creative action would, in fact, in that case fail to create, i. e., to give and establish real objective existence, endowed with forces or potencies of its own in permanency. And the utter annulling of "second causes" would compel us to refer every event, among minutest atoms, creeping worms, the clothing of continents with myriad trees and flowers and heads of golden corn, and the flashing rays of light in all the skies, each one to a direct and immediate specific fiat of God. The theory would wipe out the whole realm of cosmic and creature causation—nothing being left but immediate divine volitions and their direct effects. Instead of physical forces, with their correlations and transformations, passing from phase to phase and producing their uniform phenomena, we would have to substitute direct divine productions. We should have to drop the idea of the action of one particle of matter on another, of matter on mind, and mind on matter, of ourselves as the authors or directors of our own thoughts or of our own choices. This sweeping obliteration of creature causality, in favor of a supposed direct all-doing of God, implicit in Cartesianism, and developed by Geulinx and Malebranche into the fiction of philosophical Occasionism, would make the created world of nature and life bear a false and deceitful face throughout, and issue in acosmism. Fire would not be the cause of heat, but only the occasion for God's creating a heat. The spring in a watch would not be the cause of the motion that measures time, but only the occasion of divine creation of motion. My will to raise my hand would not stand as cause of the action, but only the occasion of it. This denial of the objective reality of secondary causation, as a reality conferred by creation and permanently maintained by preservation, would necessarily obliterate all free agency, personality and responsibility, and, in making God the only and direct cause of everything that comes to pass, make Him also the immediate author of all sin. The implications of the theory are its sufficient and full condemnation.

And yet there is a great truth covered under the phrase "continuous creation." This creation, however, is a divine action through second causes, not by their nonexistence. They are creatively provided means for the secondarily creative work of bringing into existence ever-advancing originations, perhaps of new species, certainly of ever-successive individuals in crystalline forms, and in vegetable, animal, and human life. The earth of history presents an almost infinite progress of new beginnings, individual creatures that were not but are brought into existence. There has been an inconceivably great creatio continua. But, so far as we know, or have means of discovery, it is of the secondary order (creatio secunda, already defined), and moves upon the basis of the preservation of the substances, properties, and modes given by primary creation. This confirms the Scripture doctrine of conservation, instead of setting it aside.

5. Preservation becomes also the presupposition and basis for the further divine action which we call Providence, which consummates the intention and plan of both the creation and conservation of the world. And when it is viewed especially in connection with the accompanying divine creational activity, new proof of its reality appears. Besides the proofs, already mentioned, from the Scriptures and the dependent character of created beings, a positive divine preserving Presence is strongly evidenced by the progression which nature shows into constantly higher and more advanced stages and forms. If science has indeed found a cosmic truth in the principle or law of the conservation, transformation, and equivalence of the physical forces, no atom added or lost, it is logically inconceivable that the evolution, through motion under simply inherent causality, should

of itself lift the movement and hold it to an ascending or higher order. The fixed quantum of elements, each with its fixed properties and affinities, we must think, could only continue or advance upon a level. But if science has shown us anything decisive, the onward movement has not been on a level, a mere progressus in infinitum, producing evermore mere monotonous replica of earlier things, but has ever been bringing new beginnings, new stages, a progressive ascent. In the rockleaved folio of geology we find, as we have seen, the records of an azoic age, a rise to vegetable life, to animal organization, to the formation of man, the lofty reality of personality with intelligence, reason, and free-self-determination. Science has shown no letter or syllable of suggestion how all these things were, or could be, inherently enclosed in the elements at the start, to be evolved as simply let alone. This elevating progress shows a power at work in conservation with a true efficiency not only for preserving the world but, at the same time, giving direction and increment for holding the movement to the divine plan. There has been a power at work other than the natural forces. Perhaps we should say: the natural forces are filled with God's ever-efficient presence, working through these forces the unfolding counsel of His love and wisdom.

PROVIDENCE

The divine purpose in the work of creation and of conservation is continued and carried forward in that of Providence. This aims to consummate the purpose of both the others. It is properly defined as that efficient forecast and activity through which God's care and power conduct the course of the world onward to the accomplishment of His holy and loving design. In its character, it is distinctively governmental and administrative. It is often designated simply 'government.' Though God is Father as well as Ruler in relation to mankind, His administration, while embracing His fatherly care and favor, is none the less governmental by reason of this feature of it. In God fatherhood and sovereignty are reconciled. With respect to its position and relations in the total divine activities, Providence comes under a threefold view. First, it proceeds upon the presupposition and basis of the real existence of all the material, forces, movements, and possibilities which creation and preservation have given and established as the world-system and order, in both physical and spiritual realms. Secondly, it uses all these creature powers and endowments, especially in and through the intelligence and free activities of mankind, for the regulation and direction of the advance to the realization of the divine plan. Thirdly, in its teleological character, it means the active supremacy of the divine wisdom and love, to the exclusion alike of all notions of chance or fate or deistical withdrawal from interest in the world. It thus affords sure ground for the faith that commits itself to the guidance of the divine truth and grace, as it conducts the world history on to the triumph of the kingdom of God.

It is plain that the theoretic view of Providence must be based on that understanding of God's relation to the world which recognizes both His transcendence and immanence. In His transcendence, as God over all, His supreme dominion moves in absolute independence for the aims of His goodness and will. It excludes all ideas of the compromise of His perfect freedom by a pantheistic confusion of the divine essence with the world itself. In His immanence, as "in all," His real and ever-living presence keeps His will and power in adequate contact with the possibilities of all the second causes that operate in the world. The counter-theories of God's relation, namely, that of absolute transcendence and that of absolute immanence, are both contradictory of the whole conception of Providence. The former, connected mostly with the materialistic and mechanical view of nature, as a machine constructed, wound up, and thence self-acting, besides being both un-biblical and irrational, removes God from all present agency in the world and surrenders it wholly to the action of second causes. The latter, whether the outcome of pantheistic ideas, or of some other form of denial of second cause, and making God the immediate author of every event, annihilates human freedom and the whole principle of responsibility.

Providence is properly distinguished as ordinary and extraordinary. It is ordinary when carried on by the ordinary means, i. e., through the regular, established forces and laws of nature, in matter and mind, or through the regular, instituted redemptory and supernatural means or agencies of grace. It is extraordinary when God works either without means, or beyond or above the reach of means, apart from, or transcendent to, the established order of natural forces and laws, as in miracles.

1. Of ordinary providential government we must discriminate clearly between two kinds, viz.: that which is directly causal, and that which is permissive merely. This distinction must be held as deeply real and profoundly important, in view of its relations to the questions of freedom and responsibility. It distinguishes between what God Himself does, and that which He allows human freedom to choose and to do. It marks the difference between that of which God is alone or immediately the cause, and that of which He permits the will of man, enfranchised with the attribute of freedom, to become the determining and effective cause. While providence embraces the realm of both lower nature and that in man, and its superintendence connects itself with both the sphere of physical existence and that of human self-determination, it is necessary to believe that it deals with each according to the constitution divinely given and preserved to it. In His providential causality God respects the lofty endowment of free personality in which man's life is to be lived.

In this causal order four forms are clearly distinguishable: (a) Absolute causality—that is to say, in the ranges of movement of the simply physical or mechanical forces of nature, in which changes or events take place under purely natural laws, as chemical interactions, crystalizations, atmospheric and electric changes, clouds and rain, gravitation, flow of tides, falling of bodies, etc. The causation in these spheres is of God's own absolute establishment and conservation, and the effects are of His working. (b) Hindering causality—the action of His presence and will, especially in relation to the contingent activity of man or lower orders of creation, through influences or means held subservient to His employment, that shall hinder what would otherwise take place. It is limiting action. Human will even is competent to prevent foreseen contingencies in the order of events. And God, in His omniscience and omnipotence, may, without infringing liberty, touch the springs of human thought, or intervene in complex conditions, for the prevention of evil. We are told of His restraint of the "remainder" of "man's wrath" (Ps. 76:10). (c) Directive causality—also especially in the range of human free action. He may, and does, touch the minds of men and masses with directive influences, so as to guide the movements of life and history to the ends of His will (Matt. 2:12–13; Acts 4:28). The Old and the New Testaments are gemmed with illustrations of His providential ordering. Christ's kingdom of grace and power, working on through the truth, the Church, the Holy Spirit, and all the spiritual forces of redemption, historically expresses and illustrates this great fact of God's directive moral administration on the earth. He works in men both to will and to do of His good pleasure. (d) Overruling causality—bringing good out of evil, bending the lines of consequences so as to make them prove corrective, and cooperative with the order of the divine preference and love. The history of Joseph illustrates this (Gen. 1:20). What his brothers meant for evil against him placed him in high power for happy service—a beautiful overruling, suggestive of providential possibilities. The crucifixion of Christ (Acts 3:13), including the crime of Judas, the iniquity of the Sanhedrim and the wrong of Pilate, overruled to bear a part in bringing about Jesus' redemptory self-offering on the cross and opening the way of eternal salvation to a world of sinners, stands as the historical triumph of this divine strategy of providential love. By wheels within wheels God reverses the natural consequences of men's wickedness, bringing good out of evil in victories of conquering grace.

The permissive form of providence relates to the abuse of human freedom in purposes and acts of sin. It implies the reality of this freedom as a fundamental endowment of man, conferred in creation and continued in conservation, an endowment in which human personality is established as an actual and imperishable factor in the determinations of conduct and the movements of life. This abides in the world-plan as a system of moral possibilities, obligations, and responsibilities. To the activities of free-will, so far as they work wrong and evil, God relates Himself only permissively, as simply allowing to men the use and exercise of their own essential attributes of personality. The old representation of a divine concursus, not simply in conservation, but also in active, governing providence, as an efficient factor in all human self-determinations cannot be accepted because of its logically making God a direct and active sharer in the sinful and guilty volitions of men. In essential constitution and by very conception, free personality can operate itself on the basis of simple existence or preservation, and needs no help of concursus for sinful choices. Creation itself constituted the human will autonomous. And by absolute moral necessity, sin being, per se, something against God's will, He cannot and dare not be conceived as directly concurring in making the choice of it. Moral wrong is possible as an abuse of freedom, a choice for which man is creationally made capable and responsible, but for which the Divine Will can have no power of concurrent choice. We are fully justified in saying that the human will can and does of itself antagonize God's will. God's attitude toward sin is not that of co-operation, but that which says, "Oh, do not this abominable thing that I hate" (Jer. 44:4). By nothing in the entire Biblical representation in connection with creation, preservation, or providence can it be shown to be His aim or desire to have men sin, do wrong, or violate their moral relations, or that He co-operates in making the choice of sin. The whole work of redemption is just an expression of desire to save men from it, a movement of the divine endeavor to recover men from this abuse of their free powers. Though for preservation of the existence of free personality, to which has been given a relative moral independence, there belongs a direct concursus, yet in providence, as an active, directive efficiency, there, manifestly, cannot be a real concurrence when men, in contradiction of God's holiness, use their conserved personal endowments in forms of disobedience. The unquestionable truth, "God cannot be tempted with evil, neither tempteth He any man" (Jas. 1:13), surely forbids any idea that He pre-curs in the way of pre-direction or influence for human sinful choices. Just as certainly does it imply that He does not and cannot co-operate in making them. With respect to choices of what is good and right, providential concurrence, and also pre-currence, must be emphasized; for God "works in men both to will and to do of His good pleasure" (Phil. 2:13). All the provisions of His redemptory grace are proof of this precurring and co-operating efficacy for human working in righteousness. And just in the degree in which it is certain that God does concur, for righteousness, with the endowed or enabled possibilities of human choice, by that degree it is certain also that He does not concur in choices of sin. Theology must represent God as consistent with Himself, and His providential activities as consistent with His attributes of holiness and goodness. This is the import of the effort of some Lutheran dogmaticians, who carry the doctrine of the divine concursus into the sphere of providence. In order to avoid implicating God with sin, they introduce strained distinctions between the volitional "effect" and "defect," or between the volitional "material" and "form," through which an appearance at least is secured of repudiating divine concurrence with the sinful quality of the choice, while concurring for the choice. The ungodly choices and deeds of men need no invoking of an immediate co-action of God for their explanation. The attribution of it is entirely superfluous. The human will is competent for them, left purely to itself.2 The Scriptures teach, and our theology rightly maintains, that though, by reason of corruption in their affectional nature, men are unable without grace effectually to will spiritual good, they nevertheless have ability of will in evil, to resist divine grace, and to continue in sin. The form of Concord theologians made this explicit for our Lutheran theology when they distinctly explained why many who hear the word of God are not converted but perish in sin, finding the explanation in the fact that men, though without natural ability to exercise faith, are, nevertheless, abundantly able to resist, remain in unbelief and perish.

The term "permissive," in defining providence in relation to moral evil, must, therefore, not be conceived as involving any approval of it, even the least. It can imply no softening or relaxing of the antagonism of the divine holiness to it—no co-operative action of God's will with the human will in determining a preference for it. The few passages of Scripture which have sometimes been explained as meaning divine co-action or even propulsion in this relation (as Ex. 4:21; Rom. 9:17; 1 Sam. 18:10; Prov. 16:4) are capable of far more legitimate interpretation, and will receive it when exegesis is freed from the dogmatic prepossessions of supralapsarian predestinationism and its dogma that all things, the fall included—"whatever comes to pass"—have been immutably chosen and fore-ordained in God's free will.

2. Ordinary providence is properly distinguished also as general and particular. The Scriptures give clear basis for this distinction.

General providence rests in the truth that the divine administration is grounded in one great aim as the goal of the world's purpose, viz.: "the kingdom of God," and it expresses the generic broad superintendence of the course of earthly affairs for this. God "works all things after the counsel of His will" (Eph. 1:11), His 'kingdom ruling over all' (Ps. 103:19), with helm set to the consummation. Special providence is that which takes account of all the minute details for specific and immediate effects in connection with personal individual welfare and particular needs. It is that without which the sparrow does not fall, and by which the hairs of our heads are all numbered (Matt. 10:29–30; Luke 12:6–7). Some men who have been ready to believe in a general providence have refused faith in a special providence. They have consented to recognize a great cosmic order in the earth and planetary systems, and some exercise of divine power in the support and directive care of it all as a whole—possibly also in determining the course of empire and the destiny of nations. But they have deemed it derogatory to God, to conceive of Him as condescending to the minor matters of individual life and interests. Their attitude comes from the deistic notion of God's transcendence, as implying that He has at least so withdrawn from the world as to "limit His activity to the maintenance of general laws." But in truth a general and special providence imply each other. They are two aspects of one and the same divine superintendence which covers all things. The particular providence becomes tributary to the general. The general is made up of the particular, and is impossible without it. The universality of the particular means reach and supremacy for the total. The smallest things often send their effects through the lives of men and the course of empire. Indeed, it is little beginnings that history finds at the root of movements which become world-wide and dominant phenomena. God must care for the least as the order of care for the greatest.

It is through the combination of these two aspects of providence that we reach the view of the divine administration which is most inspiring and richest for Christian faith. Without doubt, since the accomplishment of "the kingdom of God," in its increasing reality in the earth and for its consummation in heaven, is the goal to which the generic movement is directed, great emphasis must be laid upon the general providence that holds to the development. The realization of this all-embracing aim has a supreme importance as expressing, in the aggregate, the issue which redemption was designed to bring for the good of man and the glory of God's love. The keynote of this was given in the Old Testament promises of the Messiah's dominion. The New Testament is resonant with proclamation and parable of the founding and progressive establishment of this kingdom—in process during its earthly advance, in completion in its heavenly reality. Than that God should consummate this ultimate inclusive goal, there can be no greater aim for Him. He will bend the world's lines of history to this. But this emphasis upon the great goal and the Scripture assurance that God lives and reigns for its realization, means no diminution of importance and guaranty of the interests involved in particular providence. It might seem that it would signify relative withdrawal from care of individuals and the minutiae of their interests or welfare. But, in truth, it is just in the emphasis and certainty with which God holds the grand generic purpose in hand, that we have love's guaranty for each believer's completest care. For, not simply is perfection in that which is least the only way to insure the great goal, but the consummated kingdom is for the sake of the individuals it embraces. The kingdom is not a mere abstraction, but an issue sought for the sake of God's children. It is for them that He, in Jesus Christ, is conducting the historic movement into triumph, and, in the divinity of His concern, numbering the hairs of their heads. His kingdom is great and precious to Him because it gathers them into its holiness and immortal blessedness. And it does not trouble Him to condescend to minutiæ. He who, while sweeping rolling worlds and systems through space, in the music of the spheres, paints with its own beauty the delicate flower or enamels a beetle's wing, is the God of providential care and love.

It is well here, from this view of the different forms of ordinary providence, to recall the three distinct ranges or grades in which the divine action moves. There are differences in the kind of action according to the place or elevation of the natural or established spheres through which the divine efficiency works. First, the lowest range, in and through the regular laws of cause and effect in material and physical nature. God has care of this entire realm, with its forces and properties. He preserves it for the moral drama and issues of human life. Its place is basal and instrumental. It is a means for the great spiritual purpose. He has ordered and keeps its energies and forces plastic to the touch and use of human will and life, and thus closely related to the opportunities and possibilities of moral progress. "He causeth the grass to grow for the cattle and service of man" (Ps. 104:14). "Fire and hail, snow and vapors, stormy winds fulfilling His word" (Ps. 148:8). "He maketh His sun to rise on the evil and the good, and sendeth rain on the just and the unjust" (Matt. 5:45). Indeed, it is easy to conceive of the physical conditions of life, to which mankind are very sensitive and by which they are affected every day, as being divinely employed as providential means of human stimulation, guidance, or limitation. Secondly, a higher range in the realm of mind, through its ever-open susceptibilities of thought, desire, and will, under which life takes direction and character. Without doubt, God, who is immanent in nature, may operate through mere human reason, affection, or conscience, to help righteousness, check wrong, and bend lines of earthly life and history to His purposes. We may adopt Bishop Berkley's statement: "The universe is God's ceaseless conversation with His creatures," and its multitudinous voices to the ear of human souls may well be conceived of as something for providential direction. Thirdly, the highest range, in and through the specially constituted means and powers of redemption and grace. This range, distinctively, is that of the regularly established system of supernatural truth, agencies, powers, and means of spiritual recovery from sin and the restoration of men to God and eternal life. It expresses not something that belongs to the "natural" world, as nature was constituted by creational action, but an order of divine administration, made needful by sin, and superadded to the merely natural system as the redemptory and soteriological economy. It includes the supernatural provision for human reconciliation, and all the divine truth, agencies, and forces for its application to individuals and society. It embraces the divine institution of the Church and the means of grace for the regeneration of personal life and the evangelization of the world. Altogether it forms a supernatural economy for the overthrow of the intrusion and work of sin, and to gather mankind into the kingdom of God. This is the great range of movement through which God is working on His providential administration toward its great consummation. It is through these instrumentalities of the Gospel and the Church that He is entering into the minds and hearts and lives of millions and millions of men, from early childhood to old age, for direction of human thought, will, and energy. Through these things He secures control of the order and movement of, family life, of communities, of states and nations. It is thus He creates civilizations and uses them in tributary relation to His will. He makes the wonders of science and invention, from Christendom's enfranchised intellect, serve the ever-enlarging reach of Christian light into the dark places of the earth. He employs the consecrated activities and means of His people for the overthrow of wrong and the victories of righteousness. Even when, through ambition and crime, states and nations sweep the desolations of war through defenseless tribes, He shows His overruling power for reversal of issues, by moving the ready powers of Christian love and enterprise upon the scene for fresh triumphs in truth and goodness. And thus it is through this high range of the supernatural and redemptory economy, that God's providential action is most peculiarly and effectually reaching on toward the goal of His purpose.

3. Extraordinary Providential action is properly defined as that employed by God in rare and exceptional events designated miraculous, i. e., without means, or apart from the ordinary relations of cause and effect through which He commonly works in nature and grace. In contradistinction to the regular administration through fixed order of means to ends, in natural, moral, or spiritual life, this is distinctly exceptional, and without any linkage of ordinary cause and consequence that we may know, previse, and employ. It is by an immediate action of God, and incalculable—the true "miracle." It is not only supernatural, as all the redemptive working through established means of grace is, but it is by special direct causation. It is the kind of divine action belonging to the giving of a revelation and its authentication in "signs," "wonders," and "powers." The Old and New Testaments abound with illustrations. The incarnation, the mighty deeds of Christ, His resurrection, etc., are examples. The initiation and establishment of the redemptory economy, the setting up and

verification of it for mankind, was necessarily by this direct and extraordinary manifestation. But theology properly teaches that this is no longer a part of the providential activity in the world, inasmuch as all the provisions of redemption have been wrought out, and the adequate economy of application to human life regularly provided through an established and divinely authenticated order of means of grace. The abiding presence of the "supernatural" in the system of divine means for spiritual ends, supersedes the need of "miracles," which formed a necessary feature in the earlier history of redemption. The "supernatural" or redemptive economy now has its own laws or order of uniformities, in spiritual powers that have been organized for man's spiritual and eternal life. Through the word of the Gospel, with its ever-present Spirit of light and power, God comes into the human soul through its intelligence, conscience, and capacity of consent. And the law of faith is that of acceptance of this divine order and conformity to its working. Its very heart-principle is that of harmonization with the divine plan and provision as essentially made known to us. There is no call to look for "miracles" to effect or show us something more than that which has been provided to reach us through established means. The blessings of grace and the realization of redemption appear according to the measure of submission and conformity to a spiritual order. Everywhere personal salvation comes to men through the instituted means, and advances according to the use of means. Everywhere the kingdom of Christ extends according to the rule of the commission: "Go ye, make disciples of all nations." It is not upon the "miracle," God's working without means, that our faith is now to turn, with respect to personal salvation or the world's conversion.

It is not, however, to be said that extraordinary providence, in the sense of transcendence of uniform means, has no permanent place in the divine administration. It certainly belongs to the closing events of the world's history. Even always, in His supreme invisible omnipresence, we must regard God as touching, with more or less efficiency of directive or interventional powers, upon the ongoings of human life and history, for the care of men and the interests of His kingdom. The reality of special providence and answer to prayer imply as much as this. Though God's plan has obligated men to the order and use of means, He has not bound or limited Himself to them. The instruments of His ordinary providence, as already shown, embrace the whole universe of the physical, mental, and redemptory economies. But these do not exhaust His powers. In His immanence in the universe He is still more than it, and the infinitude of His possibilities is at the service of His holiness, wisdom, and love. He has not said in vain: "Ask, and ye shall receive; seek, and ye shall find."

> "That from us aught should ascend to heaven
> So prevalent as to concern the mind
> Of God high-blest, or to incline His will,
> Hard to believe may seem, yet this will prayer."—Milton.

"Prayer moves the hand that moves the world."—J. A. Wallace.

"All things work together for good to them that love God."

DIVISION II
THE DOCTRINE CONCERNING MAN
(Anthropology.)

The doctrine concerning Man follows naturally the doctrine concerning God and creation. It stands between these and the doctrine of redemption. Linked on the one side to the truth of creation, it is joined on the other to the whole scheme and work of salvation. We shall rightly understand man as the subject of redemption only as we understand his place in the world-system and the essentials of the constitution, endowments, and relations creationally given him.

We recognize the fact of a scientific anthropology. Our directness of access opens man to an examination and study closer and more thorough than any other subject of knowledge. And the various forms of scientific investigation, physiological, psychological, ethnological, and historical, have accumulated a large aggregate of well and firmly assured anthropological truth. What manner of being man is, in his physical, mental, and moral constitution, has thus, to a great extent, been made indubitably known. He is even shown to be a religious being, with instinctive and almost ineradicable aptitudes to recognize a relation of amenability to some divine Power or powers above him. It is needful, however, to bear in mind the limitations of scientific anthropology. In no case does science alone explain beginnings. It investigates the facts and processes of existence as established and seen in operation. It can tell us little or nothing about origins, because they lie back of its reach of observation and investigation. To such things as the origin of life, of sensation, of self-consciousness, it cannot extend its sight. For this reason the origin of man is extra-scientific, as something beyond our range of observation and analysis. But theological anthropology views him specially in his spiritual endowments and relations to God and a future life. Not less scientific in its methods than the secular sciences, and accepting all that philosophic anthropology can establish, this carries the view up to the human attributes in which the religious instincts are rooted and through which man is designed and adapted for fellowship with his Maker. It takes man, indeed, in all his nature, faculties, and condition as scientific examination shows him to be. The spiritual investigation always assumes and acknowledges the realities that are natural. But the whole view of man is secured only when, in addition to all that rational science can show of him, he is viewed also in the light of revelation—the revelation given for human duty and life by Him who knows what is in man. Our full anthropology must be theological. It is 'in God's light that we see light' as to what men are and are meant to be.

It is to be observed, however, that theological anthropology restricts its consideration of man to his constitution, endowment, and condition as nature presents him, and as he becomes a subject of divine care and providence. It omits those special characteristics which distinguish his life as regenerate and sanctified, since these things belong peculiarly to the action of a restorative supernatural redemption and are described under that division of theology. The subject embraces: I. His State of Integrity; II. His State of Sin; and III. Specific Truths Common to Both States.

Milton Valentine

CHAPTER I
MAN'S PRIMITIVE STATE

This designates his original condition, as created by God. With the full consent of science, Christian theology holds man as presenting the highest creational reach in the grade of being in this world. In him the process came to its summit and crown. The world was built and prepared for his habitation; and the whole work, in the long ages of its advance, was justified only when he appeared, as a being lofty enough in endowments to be given possession of and dominion over it. As basal for correct understanding of this state, we must remind ourselves of the chief facts which the Scripture revelation gives concerning his creation. The account of man's creation is given in Gen. 1:26–27, 2:7, and reflected in many passages throughout the Old and New Testament Scriptures: "And God said, let us create man in our image, after our likeness, and let them have dominion over the fish of the sea, and over the fowl of the air, and over the cattle and over all the earth, and over every creeping thing that creepeth upon the earth. So God created man after His image, in the image of God created He him; male and female created He them." "And the Lord God formed man of the dust of the ground, and breathed into his nostrils the breath of life, and man became a living soul." Echoes of this account reverberate through the whole volume of revelation. It clearly covers the following points: First, that man is not a mere product of simply natural, i. e., precedently established, earthly forces. His existence is referred to a cause directly moving from outside of nature, a uniquely distinct creative act of God. The creative act is not, as in precedent creations, an appeal to the inanimate world: "Let the waters bring forth," "Let the earth bring forth," but is special and peculiar in divine counsel and plan: "Let us make man." Secondly, that while constituted in individuality, man was created also a race. The whole organization of man includes a structural continuity of the species. The term "Adam" is primarily generic, for the racially, or bisexually organized creature designated by that term, and of whom it is added: "Male and female created He them." Manifestly the truth here involved is that, in exalting the earthly creation into the lofty grade of personality, God organized personal individuality into social life. Thirdly, that man, by creation, is a compound being. He is made of the "dust of the ground" and a life created by the 'breathing' of God. He is composed in part of material from the physical earth, and in the higher and distinguishing reality which makes him Man, i. e., a rational "soul," of an immaterial part given by the divine spiration or direct action of creative power. We do not take the phraseology "breathing into him the breath of life" literally, but as a symbolism of expression for a direct and positive gift of spirit-life. Fourthly, that he exists in a single race or species. The Scriptures place this single pair at the beginning of the entire race descent (Gen. 1:28; 3:20; 9:19; Acts 17:26). This fact underlies the doctrine of original sin, and the adaptation and applicability of the provision of salvation for all men (Rom. 5:12–19; 1 Cor. 15:21–22; Heb. 2:16). The truth of the unity of the race is supported in manifold forms of natural evidence. For example: (a) Physiology exhibits the human organization as always and everywhere having specific sameness. (b) The propagation of fertile offspring by crossings between all varieties of the human race, in contrast with the law of infertility of hybrids of different animal species. (c) Psychology shows the identity of the mental faculties and laws throughout the entire race. (d) The historic pointings, as they are read in the earliest and remotest records and monuments, imply a common starting-point for the migrations of mankind, and (e) Philology, in the root forms of human language, suggests a common origin of all the most important tongues of the world.

But this reminder of preliminary facts in man's creation opens the way to a proper understanding of the characteristic endowments and position given him, as expressed in the declaration that he was made "in the image of God" and "after His likeness." Despite frequent effort to distinguish between these two terms, "image "and "likeness," we must regard them as essentially synonymous. The duplication of terms has, rather, intensive force, making the idea emphatic. Quenstedt defines: "The image of God is a natural perfection, consisting of an entire conformity with the wisdom, justice, immortality, and majesty of God, which was divinely created in the first man, in order that he might truly know, love, and glorify God his Creator."

1. Beyond doubt, the fundamental characteristic of man's being, made in the image and likeness of God, consisted in his personality, i. e., his endowment with the powers of intelligence, sensibility, and self-determination. He is made a rational, free, moral being, to know, to choose, and to direct his own way in his given relations. This was an endowment wanting in all the other grades of created existence on the earth. In it man is placed not only immeasurably above, but in strongest contrast with nature about him. He stands apart from it, in that which constitutes his distinctive being, by the whole difference which separates persons from mere things. This personality has often been designated a "natural likeness," in contradistinction from "moral," since the designation is meant to denote simply faculties creationally given, and not their ethical state. As faculties, however, these endowments are manifestly already the essential constituents of a moral nature, absolutely conditional for moral or spiritual action or character. In these lofty attributes of personality, faculties of knowledge, love, and freedom, God formed a being after His own type of existence, of kindred capacities, establishing a linkage of communion of life, thought, and blessedness with the earth. It is to be distinctly observed, also, that since God's personality is that of "Spirit" (John 4:24), this human personality, made in His image, necessarily means spirit-essence for the rational selfhood of man. His thinking self is that of a spirit. Materialism is excluded. This Scripture view is in accordance with all that we can know of man. For the elements of personality, intelligence, sensibility, and rational freedom have never been found scientifically explicable in terms of matter.

The Biblical affirmation of man's formation in the image of God in this respect is at the same time one of the most direct deductions of reason and most assured realities of experience. It is a truth that underlies all scientific research, and is confirmed by its results. For nature is intelligible to man. God's thoughts, all through creation, are legible and impressive to the human mind. The human apprehension answers to the divine expression, to the divine working. A certain community of natures unquestionably exists—as certainly as between man and his fellow-man. At the very basis of the translation from one human language into another is the likeness of human mind to human mind. Man is "in the image" of man everywhere. Thought answers to thought and recognizes its own. In the same way the legibility of the meanings of nature, the purposes, adaptations, and aims of cosmic order and movement, the ideas, principles, and laws, everywhere luminous to the human mind, must rest upon a community of rational intelligence between man and the Author of all things. The great scientific and, at the same time, most practical truth of our lives, that we are able to "read God's thoughts after Him" in nature, is a synonym for the declaration that we have been created "in the image of God." And it is well to fix in mind how deep and far-reaching is this form of witness. For example, the human mind, in its purely subjective and idealistic action, creates the mathematical sciences, i. e., of pure thought, determining what can be real and true in the possibilities of space and time. The whole system of geometrical truth as well as arithmetical, is thus a creation of the human mind under its own laws. But it is startlingly significant of the likeness of the human mind to that of God when these truths of pure thought, if applied to nature, are found to tally with the actual facts and structures of the universe. The mental order which, in us, fixes the mathematical formulae, mirrors exactly the arrangement which the Creative Intelligence has thought and wrought into the actuality of nature around us and in the movements of far-off worlds. There is an exact adaptation between the laws of mind and the realities of the objective constitution of things. We can take these creations of our pure thought and go out into the universe, and find that the same order and system have been there before us, rhythmic in the forces, motions, distances, and correlations of the great astronomical realm. The mind's products, as adjusted by its laws, are found to be reflex of the realities of the universe as molded under the 'ideas' of the Creator of all. In man God has lifted the earthly creation up into the lofty position of fellowship with His own thought, and possible communion with His love and blessedness. It is only in this truth that we get a conception of the measureless value of man in

His Creator's sight, or of the grounds of his destination to an immortal life—as, indeed, a "child of God" (Luke 3:38).

2. The divine image in primitive man consisted also and especially in being created holy. As made by God, the nature given him was absolutely pure, free from moral evil, and adjusted in positive conformity to the law of righteousness. "God made man upright" (Eccl. 7:29). The regeneration which redemption is to effect is to be a 'renewal' into righteousness and true holiness (Eph. 4:24). This is distinctively a spiritual and moral likeness, which is, indeed, the supreme thing in man's original excellence. It is to be clearly distinguished from the first feature in this, that while the first refers to man's essential faculties or capacities, this denotes the state of those faculties, as in positive harmony with righteousness. That state was not simply negative, as an absence of evil, but positive, as in actual accord with holiness. It is not enough to say that man was created in "innocence." He was truly "good," "very good" (Gen. 1:31). This feature of the divine image was specially accentuated by the early Latin Christianity; and rightly so, for holiness is the fundamental and supreme attribute of man's Creator.

There is, therefore, no room for the dogma of the donum superadditum, framed by Roman Catholicism in the middle ages, asserting the righteousness of the first man to have been, not a concreated excellence, a quality or state of his nature as originally constituted, but a gift of grace afterward supernaturally added. The notion that human nature, as divinely given, was without real harmonization with righteousness, ethically non-adjusted, or mal-adjusted, is not only against the plain implications of the Scriptures throughout (Gen. 1:31; Eccl. 7:29; Eph. 4:24; Col. 3:10), but involves a charge of moral indifference or want of goodness on the part of the Creator. For it implies that His creative work left man without a right moral disposition, or a true setting of his conscience and affections with respect to right and duty. We must view the original holiness as so truly and thoroughly natural that, but for the fall, it would have been a permanent feature of the race through propagation, as depravity or sin now is through hereditary descent.

3. As a further and dependent fact in the "image and likeness," was dominion over impersonal world-nature (Gen. 1:26–28; Ps. 8:5–8). This dominion rests back upon man's endowment of personality, in intelligent, rational self-direction and control. By inherent constitution he was exalted into a position of free-will and responsibility, made capable of receiving commission to enter into possession and right charge of the provision and possibilities given in lower physical nature. As the cosmic nature looked to man and was designed for him, he was placed in dominion over it. It had been created in forces and movement, under laws intelligible to the human mind and plastic to human will and handling. With man's self-rulership of freedom in holiness was thus connected this further deputative and representative rulership over nature, manifestly intended to extend and establish the dominion of reason and holiness in the order and life of the earth (Heb. 2:7–10). Thus man was given a truly princely nature and position in the world-order.

4. Still further, we must connect with this reality of likeness to God in spiritual and ethical personality and economic activity a bodily organism adapted to immortal life, free from disease, and corrupted by no fleshly passion. Though this in itself can be regarded as no part of the "image and likeness," since God is pure Spirit, yet the spirit-essence, the center of the personality of man, created by the spiration of God, being designed to "live forever" (Gen. 3:22), manifestly requires us to view the material side of His being also as constituted for permanent vital existence. We know not how this permanency was to be maintained—whether by the force of the internal pneumatic or psychic life, or by the appropriation of resources from without, or by the conjoined action of both. Before any hint of the fall into sin, the Mosaic sketch represents the fullness of the earth's foods as given him "for meat" (Gen. 1:29–30), and immediately after the lapse points to a "tree of life" that had been made accessible for 'living forever' (3:22). But whatever natural external provision had been made, there seems to be much force in the suggestion offered concerning the potency of an unfallen, true spiritual life itself for the conservation of its physical organ and instrument. The suggestion bases itself on the twofold constitution of man. In his physical organism and life he is a natural

being. As a material organization he belongs to Nature. But in that part which constitutes his rational, personal self, he is a created spirit, with attributes, capacities, and activities in which he is an intelligent ethical being, linked in kindredship with God and competent for dominion over Nature, which was ordered in subservience to his higher life and destiny. In this reality of his being he stands above all the essences and forces that produce and maintain physical organizations. It is to be conceded, indeed, as asserted by common experience and empirical science, that all physical organisms, after their growth to maturity, exhibit a tendency to wear out and decay, a tendency so actual and sure that the use of no externally provided nourishment can prevent their dissolution. So far as man is a natural being, a vitalized physical organization, belonging to Nature, Nature may enforce its own law of temporalness and demand the body of man back to itself. But in man God created a being whose constitution and position were exceptional and transcendent, a being whose personality and life belonged to spirit-essence, and to whose destiny and blessedness all inferior Nature was meant to be tributary. And there is unquestionably reason in the suggestion that it belonged to the very life of the human spirit, as designed to be maintained in the pure vigor of its holy powers, to preserve thereby to itself its bodily organ and instrument, and immortalize it in its given relation of service in the divine teleology for man. Human experience is full of testimony to the susceptibleness of the body to the influence of spirit. The corporeal organism may be inspired and sustained to a most wonderful measure by the energy of mind and will. It is no unreasonable supposition, therefore, that in connection with the distinct provisions made for the sustentation of the human body from without, the unbroken inner spiritual life of man, if lived in its true fellowship with God and in the given energies for its appointed holy "dominion," would have sufficed to hold that body above the reach of the dissolution which marks all other types of animated Nature. But whatever may have been the force and way through which the physical side of man was to have been preserved in the composite structure of his being, we may be sure that he, the "son of God" (Luke 3:38), the one spiritual personality, for whose high position and welfare the entire earth-nature was created, "was not made to die," under the law of physical death which belongs to impersonal nature. The Biblical view requires us to recognize for him a unique position and an immortal destiny; and without doubt the balance between the spiritual and material in him was divinely adjusted for a victorious life of the composite personality—not, indeed, in necessity, but in freedom.

5. The holiness of this first estate, together with the full reality of dominion, was nevertheless dependent for continuance and confirmation on man himself. Being a moral trait, committed to a free agent, it was amissible, and needed to be made secure and permanent by habits of righteousness. Natural tendencies or adaptations acquire steadiness and momentum through activities in which life exercises and establishes itself. The law of habit is cumulative of facility and certainty. The primitive goodness may be conceived of as comparatively unconscious goodness, spontaneously active in and out of the inner constitutional adjustment to holiness rather than as goodness which has established itself in conscious conflict with evil. The concreated rectitude furnished the true initiation to the life of holiness, to be maintained, confirmed, and made victorious. It is the law of virtue or righteousness to grow strong and forever triumphant through its own action in the midst of moral conditions.

6. The Pelagian view, whether of ancient or modern type, representing the primitive man as created a moral agent or with faculties of moral agency, but in a state of moral indifference, must be condemned as at once without Biblical or rational warrant. It makes the image of God consist in mere personality. The grounds alleged for it are, primarily, that man could have been free only if no bias had been put into his nature, one way or the other; and, further, that personal character is reached only through the exercise of free powers—not at all in the possession of the faculties or any state of them, except as self-determined. But, in truth, freedom does not stand in indifference or an equipoise between good and evil, but in power or faculty of will, despite either internal adjustment or external motives, to choose between them. The assertion that character was a thing wholly left to be yet formed out of a characterless state by man himself, is altogether without proof and against proof. For God, infinitely holy and good, could not create a

personal being indifferent to holiness, any more than He could create a sinful or wicked being. Moral indifferency in a moral being is of itself of the nature of sin. Character, being the sum of attributes or qualities of a personal being, may consist in the state or attitude of the faculties toward righteousness as well as in the exercise of these faculties. To maintain the contrary is to maintain that man's own acts and help are necessary to complete the Creator's work and make it good, or that God could not give a holy set to the creature's faculties. Moreover, unless we claim that God Himself is marked by moral indifference in the very attitude of His essential nature, the fundamental affirmation of man's creation, "in the image and likeness of God," forbids this negative theory. Man's original holiness must be viewed as positive (Eccl. 7:29; Jas. 3:9; Eph. 4:24; 1 Cor. 15:45).

7. The theory of man's primitive savagery, whether proclaimed by the Positive Philosophy or held as a conclusion of Evolutionist Science, stands strongly in conflict with the Scripture representations and implications concerning the origin and original status of man. The wide acceptance of the evolutionist theory among professional scientists and certain types of theologians requires some review of the facts, to enable us to reach a conclusion according to truth. The question, as it concerns theology, is not whether or not there may be in nature an evolutionary principle that, by self-contained forces and reactions, has produced the varieties and species of life-organizations inferior to man, but whether the origin of the human race is to be so explained. We are concerned here only with the formation of Man. And in considering the question, it is immaterial whether the evolutionist theory be based on atheism or on a theistic view of the world and a divine creation, ex nihilo, of the world-matter. And yet with this limitation of the question to the origin of man, it will be necessary to take into consideration some of the difficulties and weaknesses of the evolutionist theory in its offered explanation as to the lower orders of animate nature and its lack of absolute conclusiveness even there. The effort will be, not to disprove the general evolutionist view, but to call attention to the fact that the theory is "not proved." It is not "science" (*scientia*), actual knowledge, but a speculative or tentative hypothesis.

The theory is wont to be based back upon the nebular hypothesis of an immense mass or mist of glowing vapor filling the spaces of the universe, as the starting-point of world-structure. Thence, under the principle of gravitation, through a conjoined action of motion and cooling, worlds and systems are formed. Our world, as one of the planets, cooling and condensing, takes form, first in the earliest geological period, moving then successively through its later eras, marked by gradual advances in its conditions and forms of life and organisms. But for our present purpose we need go back no further than the beginnings of life on the earth, and start with Darwin's somewhat hesitating admission of a Creator and a direct creation of life: "I imagine that probably all organic beings that ever lived on this earth descended from some primitive form, which was first called into being by the Creator."

The most representative form of the theory is that shaped by Darwin, known as that of natural selection and survival of the fittest. It assumes and depends on the conjoint action of two leading principles—the principle of heredity as inherent and active within the living organism, and the principle of environment, as modifying the action of heredity—the latter, i. e., environment, acting in two ways, viz.: as stimulating and improving, and as eliminating and destroying. And thus, it is alleged, under the continuous propagation of living organisms with accidental variations, amid different environments, all the so-called species of living beings, including man, have been produced. It involves the essential bestiality of primal man, as Darwin expressly tells us that he sees no distinction in "kind," but only one in "degree" between man's highest intellectual faculties and the feelings of a brute.

The competence of this evolutionist hypothesis for the proof of man's origin is rendered doubtful not only by the weakness and difficulties that appear in it at the point of transition from brute to human state, but also by all the mere assumptions, unfilled gaps, and varied difficulties in the offered account of the movement up to that point. These show it to be an unproved explanation. The following points deserve to be noted.

(a) At the very beginning the ambiguous phrase, "natural selection," is adopted to denote the explaining cause of the evolutionary advance. The word "selection" expresses mental choice, something confessedly not present in the case. It is "selection that does not select, except metaphorically." Its use tends to an impression that it acts positively as a direct efficient cause, whereas the outcome of the explanation exhibits it mainly, if not entirely, in the form of a negative result, viz.: that in the struggle for existence the weaker organisms fail to survive and cease to exist. "Natural selection works not constructively, but destructively." For the positive progress in the evolution, this showing that some weak organisms do not "survive," is not, as has been often pointed out, equivalent to an explanation how higher forms "arrive." The ambiguous phrase, with its simply surreptitious active sense, is plainly and peculiarly weak when used, as it is, to show positively the way these higher and better forms appear.

(b) To accomplish this task particularly, however, another working principle is invoked—"accidental variations" through natural descent. But this is, if possible, even less reliable and satisfactory than the other, to account for the rise of nature from its lowest organisms up to the human grade. For the "accidental variations" depended on, as between improvements and destructions, are too many-sided, uncertain, and shifting, to warrant rational faith that they will all, or a controlling majority of them, unite in the formation of Man out of the primordial life, or even from an ape—that is, that the "accidental," in the modifications in all the organs, senses, and complex adjustments will, in their particularities and combinations, move on to one point, the evolution of a human being. That all the needful modifications should take place by chance variations and chance destructions and chance preservations, and hold their own gains and carry them on through millions of years, is utterly incredible—as any calculation of chances will show. St. George Mivart justly styles the process: "The haphazard action of the destructive forces of nature on minute haphazard variations in all directions." It simply relegates the life-forms of the earth to chance-work. Yet this is Darwinian evolution.

(c) The addition of the affirmation of the "survival of the fittest," is not sufficient to carry the offered proof to its conclusion. The import of this phrase must be analyzed before we can see whether that which it stands for is assuring for the result. It is a correlate designation to the failure and perishing of the weaker organisms in the struggle for existence in environment. The theory requires—for reaching the goal of the evolution—that those surviving be the more highly, finely, and effectively organized—a progress in excellence. But are these "the fittest," i. e., the ablest to survive? In the struggle of existence, the strongest live and the rest go under. Are not the higher and advancing forms of organization the more complex and susceptible to injury and destruction? Do not the conditions which kill off the feeblest harm the rest? Are severe conditions the best for the development of high organizations? Are not those that survive rather an injured class, with less fineness of structure and rank? When summer's drought destroys half of the vegetable organisms, the remaining half are not likely to be an improvement on the ordinary standard. Or if the improvements should be credited to the specially helpful environments, as these are also "accidental" in the variations of actual life, how shall their gains be continuously preserved and guided on the upward line? The strongest are not always "the fittest" for this elevating and spiritualizing process by which the complex and highly organized human race is to come from molluscs or amœbæ.

(d) It is to be borne in mind that no new species has been discovered to have been actually produced by it. This is an impressive fact. Though the theory teaches us to think of "species" as an illusion, it yet admits the reality of present grades, lower and higher, in the forms of life. If these specific types are viewed, not as fixed, but each as in constant progress, the advance over the differentia between the so-called "species" becomes what has been meant by "transmutation of species." But no scientist has discovered an instance of such an advance. Only varieties within the species have been produced—even by artificial crossings and culture. So with Darwin's pigeons. Fossil geology gives indubitable evidence of new species appearing one after another, with no proof whatever of lineal descent or the evolution of one out of the other. Prof. J. P. Cooke, of Harvard, though accepting the hypothesis, confesses: "It seems strange that with all the attention which has been directed to the point during the last twenty-five years the fact of a transition between two well-marked species has not yet been established conclusively.... We can in no case point unhesitatingly to other species in lower strata from which they descended, on the evidence of an unbroken series in the intermediate forms between the two. Take the case in which we are the most interested, that of our own race. Assume all that is claimed in regard to the antiquity of man. Still there is a definite horizon of the tertiary epoch below which man is not, but above which his remains are found in ever-increasing abundance, with all the features of man and his works as strongly marked as they are to-day. Skeletons of these primeval men, and their belongings, are to be seen in our ethnological museums; and there are no greater differences of structure between them and ourselves than between the different races which inhabit the earth at the present day. But if man be descended from 'an anthropoid animal of arboreal habits,' it is passing strange that, so far as any direct evidence goes, he should have appeared on the earth thus suddenly, and that we can find no traces of his progenitors of the first, second, third, or any other generation." This is a far-reaching confession by an evolutionist.

(e) We must add to it the further fact, that the asserted law of evolution has not been found effectual, within the world's historical period, for any such modifications as promise transmutation of species. There is not an instance within these thousands on thousands of years, of animal forms having developed new organs or improved the old. The ancient sculptures and pictures exhibit them as they are now. All this time the forms have been essentially stationary, except in modifications under domestication, from which they tend to return under the law of atavism. A process so slow as to have done nothing perceptible in forty or fifty centuries cannot be justly credited with having created all the earth's life forms, except upon the clearest and most positive evidence. This view of the question is fortified by the well-established fact that species are held in fixed lines of descent, with specific identity permanently continued, by a law of sterility of offspring, where offspring have been obtained by enforced crossings between different species. Varieties, or races within the species, have been secured, but no new species. The possibility of the last is barred by the scientifically certain fact that hybrids, the product of crossing between "species," are either utterly sterile, or so nearly so as to bring the descent to a quick and certain end. Hybridity makes a new line of continuous evolution an impossibility. This is very significant of the breadth of differentia between species and the persistence of their essential types—that each abides self-identical or perishes. Surely it does not suggest that the animal organizations are but the onward flow or evolution of a common bioplasm, differing simply by being in different stages of development. In such case it ought rather to show the supposed identity of life by uniting, blending, and continuous fertility at any and every point where crossings can be made to take place. The infertility of hybrids points to impassible specific differences and discredits the hypothesis of a simple, common and universal bioplasm.

(f) Force is added to this difficulty by the theory, having best scientific support, that all animal organizations, including that of man, are psychogenetic, i. e., that an immaterial psyche (ψυχή), life) is the cause or explanation for each living individual, and a species of psyche (life) for each species. The matter of the body does not form or create the soul; that would be materialism. But the psyche (life) is organific for the body as its instrument. The psyche determines the organization—never passing into another, or failing to secure its own organism unless by injury or death. That the organism is an effect of some psychic reality that we name life, whatever the mysterious reality may be—a series of activities resulting from a union of this reality with matter—is the idea almost everywhere dominant in human thought and in accord with scientific, especially with psychological, research. St. George Mivart says: "Just as an individual animal, in its process of development, generates by its internal force its own body, so specific changes must be above all due to the action of an organism's innermost life; that is to say, it must be a result of a process of psychogenesis." But this runs into a further point, viz.:

(g) The utter inconclusiveness of the argument, especially relied on by Darwinists, based on embryonic morphology. The claim that the human embryo, in passing, prenatally, through semblance of the lower animals, fish, reptile, bird, mammal, etc., presents "a sketch of the past history of the race," an epitome of the evolutionary advance to man, needs only to be carefully examined to see its worthlessness. Even admitting the embryonic "appearances," there is no logic for the conclusion. The "appearances" are illusive; the conclusion built upon them is factitious. Though the human embyronic form looks successively like lower animal organizations, it is not any of them, and never mistakes its goal or loses its pure human self-identity. The principle or law of psychogenesis holds complete sway. The life in the human embryo is not that of reptile, quadruped, or monkey, but is human life, the organizing life and action of a human psyche, a fixed species, unconvertible into another. To build a bridge on these evanescent physiological and material "appearances" to carry back the life of human beings into life-identity with that which was evolving along the lineage of countless animal progenitors, is pushing the interpretation of appearances too recklessly.

The invalidity of this argument from morphology is seen when it is reduced to the form of syllogism, viz.:

Whatever passing appearances are exhibited in the growth of the human embyro, present the genetic evolution of the race. The embyro exhibits successively the appearances of fish, reptile, bird, quadruped, man. Therefore, the race was genetically evolved from fish, etc.

Of this argument these facts are to be noted:

(1) It begs the whole question by assuming the conclusion in its first premise. It just says so at the start, and when it comes to the conclusion, just repeats the say-so.

(2) Whatever force it has rests on analogy, i, e., the likenesses of appearances between embryonic growth and the different orders of animal organizations. The question arises, then, Is this assumed analogical basis sufficiently real and clear to assure the conclusion? That it is not, is easily made apparent.

First. The supposed analogy is worthless in this case, because the conditions of the progress are utterly unlike. Between the conditions of the embryo in the womb, advancing by the inner life-force in the same environment all the time, and the conditions of changing environment through which in immense geologic ages the animals had to progress in the struggle for life, as a "survival of the fittest," there is no similarity or equality. As the value of analogy rests on the principle of like causes producing like results in equal conditions, the whole bottom for the conclusion drops out from the supposed analogy of these appearances. The embryological "appearances "stand utterly dirempt from the logical principle that gives validity to analogical reasoning. Supposing these morphological resemblances really appear, the conditions of their occurrence preclude explanation in that way. It is simply gratuitous and unproved assertion that they are a record of the chief steps in an evolutionary advance from initial life-forms up to the human. Can any man even conceive of a way that would connect these ephemeral appearances, as the effects of movements and stages of movement superseded and lost millions of years ago, with the goal to which human bioplasm in the embryo is evolving? Is there anything reminiscent in the human life-germ, acting as a cause for such temporary diversion from the straight line, to make record of the forms it once had? In testing the offered theory, we must squarely face the difficulties involved. The embryo life in question is human life from the start, by human propagation. Are we to conceive of this human life, at the very beginning of its embryonic state dropping back from the human grade into the fish or reptile life of ages on ages ago, thus becoming causal for the successive embryo "appearances," and, at last, before birth, attaining again the human type—either blindly or reminiscently repeating its old evolutionary accomplishment? Or are we to conceive of it, at the start of the embryonic development, as true and actual human life, with the causal forces of the human rank, nevertheless beginning to build its embryonic structures after the forms due to the causal laws of the different ancient animal stages of bioplasm? How can we think of human life, instead of working according to its attained constitution or reality, as working according to a reality and state that no longer exist? The argument from morphology asks us in fact to set aside the law of causality. The teaching that alleges these morphological semblances as at once a result and a proof of the evolutionary emergence of Man from the earliest forms of earthly bioplasm is not science, but a dreamy fancy.

Secondly. The argument confounds two very different things—ontogeny, growth in an individual organism by which the organism is perfected, with phylogeny, the genesis of species, or the supposed development of species, in the course of geological or earth-time. But these two are not identical or necessarily parallel. Growth is open to observation and scientifically understood. Its function is distinct and definite—to complete the individual being, after its kind. Phylogenesis, assumed to have taken place in prehistoric ages, is not open to observation, and if proved to be real, must find its proof in causes discovered in some way to have been operative in those ages. Its movement is altogether different from that of growth, and looks to an altogether different result. While growth finishes its work in completing the specific organism after its type, phylogenesis seeks for possible and effective causes for the origin of new and higher types or species. It is evident from the mere statement of the case that the development of the individual animal is not the same as, or equivalent to, the origin of a species through long geological ages. But this argument quietly and against right assumes them to be equivalent, and that the working of embryonic growth is still reflecting, in its successive physiological semblances, the phylogenetic movement which created the succession of species. A more illegitimate inference could hardly be conceived.

(h) Against the notion of evolution as an improving or creative process stands the geological fact admitted by Le Conte: "Although species, so far as individual numbers are concerned, come in gradually on the margin of their natural region, reach their greatest abundance in the middle portion, and again gradually die out on the other margin, yet in specific characters we see usually no such transition. In specific character they seem to come in suddenly, to remain substantially unchanged throughout their range, and pass out suddenly on the other margin.... The apparent fixity of animal species within certain narrow limits of variation is even more striking than in the case of plants." This is directly in conflict with the hypothesis of a gradual evolution of species from one into another. The force and largeness of this fact is seen in Barrande's tabulated exhibit of his discoveries in the Silurian of Bohemia. After an accurate study of its 640 species of brachiapods in their geographical and geological range, with respect to the question of evolutionary relation to each other, he gives his finding as follows:

1. Species continued unchanged,.... 28 per cent.
2. Species migrated from abroad, ... 7 per cent.

3. Species continued with modification,. 0 per cent.
4. New species without known ancestors,. 65 per cent.

Such absence of transitional forms in the supposed linkage leaves the evolutional account by successive modifications simply an hypothesis, even as to the animal world.

(i) Evolution is incompetent to account for instinct. So long as this immense and wonderful phenomenon is left without solution, the theory cannot be held as proved. Every attempt evolution has made to explain instinct, especially in its higher forms, has broken down in contradiction and absurdity. As an unreasoning impulse that operates for ends which it knows nothing of, it certainly looks like "lapsed intelligence," as Darwin and others have viewed it. The only account offered is that it is the fruit of intelligence, a habit formed by rational, purposive action, at earlier stage, the product of a process minus the process. But this explanation as "lapsed intelligence" is in direct contradiction of the fundamental law of evolution, a progress from the lower to the higher, from the simpler to the more complex, attaining at last to the lofty and aspiring rational faculties of humanity. And where are the traces, in all the past, of the intelligent ancestors of the bee or the sphex, or like types of instinct? Both Darwin and Romanes acknowledge that "many instincts are too low in the zoölogical scale to admit of our supposing that they can ever have been due to ancestral intelligence.3 In so far as their origin and special forms have been credited to "accidental variations" and "natural selections"—or rather destructions—the case is no better. For how could it be possible for such variations and selections, in the realm of non-intelligence, in and of themselves, to construct organisms or the instincts of organisms to do the work of intelligence?

(j) Evolution fails to account for language. The essential presupposition to language, as a characteristic of man, is the ability to think in concepts, abstract idealizations, expressed by general or class terms. It is a far other and higher reality than the cries by which physiological or instinctive action serves as a directive means among animal orders. There is no evidence of "language" in any creature of earth but man. It is said, indeed, that when the evolutional advance reached the ability to think in concepts and the human stage was attained—the transition made from the mechanical action of physiology and instinct into free rational thought and idealization—then emergent man began to build up registering vocabularies and languages. But there is no assuring evidence either that any non-speaking animal, even at the highest point of reach, has ever crossed that line, or that there is a psychical possibility of doing so. Inasmuch as "no traces of man's progenitors, either of the first, second, third, or any other generation, have been found," there is an utter break, physiologically, of the linkage by which an actual physical descent with transition into capacities of thought and speech might be proved. But the difficulty becomes still more perplexing when, of the only asserted line of the supposed descent, some "simian of arboreal habits," the confession has to be made that none of the simians yet discovered, whether fossil or living, are found with the requisite preconditions for the transition. When Mr. Romanes says that "anthropoid apes are the most intelligent and would, under training, probably show greater aptitude in sign-making than any other kind of brute," but yet confesses that "the species (or genus) which did give origin to it must have differed in important respects from any of its existing allies," in being "more social" in habits and "more vociferous" than any existing species, all of which "appear to be on the high road to extinction," there is no wonder that Prof. Max Müller declares: "Against such argument the gods would fight in vain. We are told that man is descended from some kind of anthropoid ape. We answer that all anthropoid apes known to us are neither social nor vociferous. And we are told in that case man must be derived from an extinct ape who differed from all known apes, and was both social and vociferous. Surely, if this is a scientific argument, scientific arguments would in future rank very low indeed. I know of no book which has proved more clearly that language forms an impassable barrier between man and beast than the book lately published by Mr. Romanes on the "Origin of the Human 'Faculty,' though his object was the very reverse."2

(k) Evolution has also failed to explain Conscience or the Moral Power. This is too phenomenal a characteristic of man to be ignored in any view of his origin. It is to be fully admitted that the reality and authority of the conscience do not depend upon the mode of God's creative action in incorporating it as constituent of man's endowment, but upon the fact of it. But in claiming evolution as the mode, the hypothesis is logically required to show evidence of it, or at least the possibility of it. Here is the point of failure. The incompetence of the only offered explanation in a positive way—the theory asserting conscience to be the "result of accumulated experiences of utility, gradually organized and inherited"—leaves no pending theory of it. That account misses the explanation of the moral faculty by the whole breadth of the essential difference between "utility" and "right" or ethical obligation. The formidable difficulty of making credible even the possibility of such derivative origin is still pressing. Keeping in view the fact that the very center of the conscience function appears in the regulation, and often denial, of inherited feelings and habits, the difficulty of attributing its creation to hereditary action is palpably apparent. It has been well pointed out that the injunctions of the conscience do not run with the stream of our hereditary tendencies, but against them.2 That a law of the work and victory of hereditary forces should issue in organizing an endowment for control and repression of hereditary tendencies seems too much of a contradiction to be accepted. Even in the theistic form of the theory, in which evolution offers itself as presenting not the cause but only the mode of creation, it is hard to conceive of the adaptation of such a process for the production of such a result—a result standing apart from the means by such a total difference in both their nature and direction. Even Prof. Huxley, in one of his latest utterances, felt constrained to say: "The practice of what is ethically best, what we call goodness or virtue, involves a course of conduct which, in all respects, is opposed to that which leads to success in the cosmic struggle for existence. In place of ruthless self-assertion, it demands self-restraint; in place of thrusting aside or treading down all competitors, it requires that the individual shall not merely respect, but help his fellows; its influence is directed, not so much to the survival of the fittest, as to the fitting as many as possible to survive." The millions of years of the battle of might with feebleness, nature "red in tooth and talon," is not the creator of the law of love, kindness, and generous helpfulness.

(l) Nor can it account for freedom in man, out of unfree causation. That the advance of physical life from protozoa, through ages, under reign of the law of cause and effect, in a chain of variations and survivals, all the links being locked up in necessary antecedence and consequence, should issue at length in the production of the opposite principle of freedom, and set man forth a free self-determining being acting in liberty, seems to require us to believe that "the effect" shall not be as the cause, but the reverse. How shall necessity give birth to freedom? How shall that which has no freewill confer it? How can the reign of fixed law, dominating every change or advance from protoplasm through the animal series, be conceived of as even the carrier of freedom up to the point of its human manifestation? Yet in accepting the hypothesis we should have to accept this contradiction—that causes acting in necessity establish the higher and contrary reality of free choice. For it is to be borne in mind that the hypothesis is, from beginning to end, a protest against admission of supernatural intervention or direct creation—except with such advocates of it as exclude the origin of Man from it save, perhaps, as to his physical organism, and confidently postulate a direct or supernatural divine act for the increment that appears in his endowment of rational soul and personal freedom. This exception, with its postulate, becomes in fact an abandonment of the evolutionary creation of man.

These few considerations are recalled in evidence that the current theory of evolution is yet an unproved hypothesis—by no means established. We are not, however, to maintain that there is not a deep, far-reaching principle of evolution divinely embodied in nature and its movement. All geology, in its rocks and fossils, is a history of it. The Christian theologian finds a progressive movement, whatever it may have been, reflected from the Biblical creational progress and ascent from chaos up to material order, into forms of plant life and animal life. It is a question of true or misleading interpretation. It is to be observed, too, that the Bible simply ascribes creation to God without defining the mode of it. And should science ever be able really to show it to have been by a process of evolutionary action, the essential truth would still abide—that God created man, gave him his nature and position, his high endowments of moral personality and responsibility, supplying, by direct creative power, the increment of rational soul at the point of transition, as making Man in His image for fellowship with Him and dominion over the earth. Christianity would not be proved false by a scientific demonstration of any Theistic form of evolution. But because of the rush of the foes of Christianity to shape and use the hypothesis for unbelief, and the uncalled-for precipitancy of many theologians in falsifying and destructive modifications of it, it is needful that the unproved status of the theory should be borne in mind. Within the animal kingdom there is no evidence whatever of an evolution across the wide differences that separate the families or the genera from one another. Whether across the smaller intervals between different species, is yet very doubtful. For the inclusion of man in the genetic evolution, there is positively no proof. And this is manifestly the reason of the fact that so many of the most eminent, sober-minded, and careful scientists, while admitting and asserting a real evolutionary principle in nature, see its limits, and refuse its application to the origin of man—as A. R. Wallace, St. George Mivart, Principal J. W. Dawson, Quatrefages, the Duke of Argyll, Prof. James D. Dana, and others. We are not without warrant in taking it as good scientific thinking when we find Sir William Thompson writing: "That man could be evolved out of inferior animals is the wildest dream of materialism, a pure assumption which offends me alike by its folly and by its arrogance;" or when we read from Prof. James Dwight Dana: "The present teaching of geology very strongly confirms the belief that Man is not of Nature's making. Independently of such evidence, Man's high reason, his unsatisfied aspirations, his free-will, all afford the fullest assurance that he owes his existence to the special act of the Infinite Being whose image he bears."

A further consideration of force in closing this sketch of the problem of evolution, is the unseemly, incongruous relation in which even theistic evolutionism necessarily places all primal creation in respect to God as Creator. It puts the widest conceivable chasm between the Creator as the Absolute Personal Reason and the initial form or rank of all created beings. It teaches that God, the Absolute Personality, the supreme perfection of Being, creates the universe only through the method of unfolding from the initial or homogeneous form to the heterogeneous, from the lowest and crudest beginnings of things to the final completion in the highest and best. Life, at the start, is only indeterminate, undifferentiated bioplasm, and is thence evolved through countless ages into all the successive actualized forms up to man. Immense periods of working were required to reach the creation of any lofty or noble type of being. "The lower order of being exists only in the process of evolution into the higher. It exists only in transitu, and its individuality is fleeting." "When the animal progresses beyond recollection and fancy to generalization, he becomes immortal as an individual." But see in what relation all this puts all initial forms or orders of living beings with respect to God. For long æons nothing intrinsically great or lofty appears—nothing suggestive of His "image or likeness." An infinite chasm yawns between Creator and creation. Things are only started with a view—if there was a view—to a realization of a justifying cosmos after millenniums of ages. How utterly incongruous, that in the creation that starts closest to God, the most immediate to the productive impact of the Absolute Intelligent Personality, there should be found only what is most unlike Him; what is, indeed, the utmost antithesis to that which created it; what is able to reach "personality" only after untold æons of evolutionary working. This might fit Brahminism, in which Brahma, or the Divine, is only abstract unity, void of form or predicates. In it the idea of the prime existence is the negation of all intelligent personality and freedom. But it will not fit the Christian conception of God as the absolute and free Personality.

And it is a significant phenomenon that under the tendencies and affinities of the acceptance of the evolutionist origin of man, we are having numerous writers, both philosophical and theological, who are abandoning Christian theism and urging monistic conceptions of the universe as being the necessary forms and parts in the evolution of the Absolute. The Divine and the human, God and nature, are one, and Christian theism is being confused and lost behind an ideal pantheism.

CHAPTER II
MAN'S STATE OF SIN

This will require distinct consideration of the Fact of the Fall, its Moral and Penal Consequences, particularly what is usually called Original Sin, and Actual Sin.

THE DOCTRINE OF THE FALL

The possibility of a lapse from righteousness has already been adverted to. It lay in the lofty reality of man's creature being and position, gifted with rational freedom and capacities for the higher blessedness of holy fellowship with His Creator and of dominion over lower nature. It is worthy of note that the possibility of sin was found in the endowments that were the supreme excellences and elevation of man's nature, lifting him into divine similitude. It was not from any stint in the rank of his being or its privileges. In his free, holy personality God placed man alongside of Himself, a creature capable of the loftiest divine reality—holy character. But the possibility of free conformity to the divine holiness is the correlate to the possibility of non-conformity; and this gift of personality was perversely misused in violation of righteousness. Even reason itself sees that the moral evil that marks man is possible only to a nature of lofty endowments.

1. The fall must be viewed as a historical fact. It is so represented in the Biblical account (Gen. 3:1–19). Whatever symbolism interpreters may find, or think they find, in the narrative, the account is manifestly meant to affirm a historic event of immense moral and spiritual import in the conduct and experience of the newly-created human race. We see no necessity for resolving it into a simple allegory or empty legend, nor propriety in doing so. Though, after the oriental manner, symbolic or figurative forms of representation appear, yet the account moves on with evident air of historic purpose, to certify, in its essential reality, an actual transgression of divine commandment, a

perversion of the human will from its true principle of holy obedience to God. And the genuine historicity of the account is implied and guaranteed by its clear linkage with the precedent record of the nature and status creationally given to man, and with the onward narration, sketching various consequences wrought by the moral lapse which had thus "brought sin into the world," and opening into the whole providential dispensation of divine forbearance, corrective discipline, and redemptory grace and provision, whose record fills the Old Testament and consummates itself in the New. The New Testament distinctly treats the fall as a historical event (Rom. 5:14; 1 Cor. 15:22; 1 Tim. 2:14).

2. Man fell through an external solicitation (Gen. 3:1–7; Rev. 12:9; 20:2). He was not wholly self-moved. The fall was not purely and absolutely from within. It did not originate by the inner forces of man's nature, by constitutional set of his powers to the deed. These forces, in their direct adaptations and initial action, were in themselves either morally good or morally indifferent, i. e., some of them were positive and specific adjustments to righteousness, others per se only to physical functions; e.g., natural appetite for attractive food was not in itself wrong. It was good and holy in its place. The natural desire for knowledge, appealed to, was a noble feeling given for man's exaltation in holy intelligence. And the distinctively moral forces of his constitution, such as the affirmations of his reason and conscience, were positively conformed to righteousness. So had no temptation and deception come from without, it seems credible that the actual conditions of transgression might not have been realized. The external Satanic assailment, to which the Biblical representation attributes it, worked toward its issue, (a) by awakening doubt as to the fact of God's prohibitory law and responsibility for its violation; (b) by stimulating the desire for knowledge in unethical way; and (c) exciting ambitious pride, aspiring to rank as divine. To this fact of the external source of the temptation and deception must be added the further fact of the first man's privative condition, as utterly without experience. No long use of the powers of freedom had, through the law of habit, established a habitude of obedience. The concreated harmony of his nature with holiness was yet without the teaching and supporting power which

comes from experience in moral life. These facts do not annul the guilt of the transgression. But they throw explaining light on the way of its occurrence.

3. The effects of the apostasy could not but be unspeakably serious. (a) Necessarily the sin brought actual guilt and condemnation. In the truest reality, the offenders were guilty, and amenable to the penal consequences which the guilty act might work in their nature and relations. Their sin, by the very necessity of its own essence, placed them not only outside of God's approval, but under bond to retributive consequences. Viewed in connection with the infinite claims of God and the eternal ethical principles which the apostasy set at nought, its guilt must have been exceedingly great. (b) It brought spiritual death, a dissolution of the true spiritual union and fellowship of the human life with God. Made in the divine image, a child of God, man's divinely-meant life and blessedness could be realized only in God. But by this disruption of the given spiritual relation, the true life was lost. This is indeed the deepest reality in the woeful consequences of that primal sin—a nature that by its free, but false, action had disordered itself, withdrawn itself from harmony with God and righteousness, and thus "died" to the holiness and blessedness for which it was created. Man had perverted, corrupted, and depraved his own nature by turning away from God. By inevitable law of moral reaction the will is enslaved by the power to which it allies or surrenders itself: Whosoever committeth sin is the servant of sin" (John 8:34). "In trespasses and sin" man is 'dead' with respect to his true life. It is in this we are to find the meaning of the Edenic warning: "In the day thou eatest thereof thou shalt surely die." (c) This depravity became the heritage of Adam' s posterity.The law of descent, each nature after its kind, made the fallen nature the nature of the race. Before the fall, holiness was natural to man; after the fall depravity became inherent and transmissible as a sinful condition. Sin is not indeed the "essence" or "substance" of man, but a state of moral disorder self-introduced by man—corrupt tendencies in the soul's life powers. There can be no doubt that, by a natural law, evil does propagate and intensify itself. But such propagation and intensifying imply the corrupting power of the individual lapses from righteousness. From what we thus know of this

law of propagation, it is only a consistent conclusion when we accept the Biblical teaching that the primal Adamic disobedience and self-perversion left, for hereditary descent, a human nature already wounded and despoiled of competent spiritual power for the true holy life. (d) It brought to man eternal death, if not recovered by Divine grace. By this we mean—assuming his Divine destination to immortality of existence—an endless continuance of his alienation from God and corruption of his nature, if left to himself. 'Eternal death' expresses the prolongation of the self-wrought condition of 'spiritual death' beyond the redemptory opportunities and grace of the earthly life into eternity. (e) Bodily or temporal death, for man, is Biblically made in some way consequent on his lapse into sin. It seems to have been included in the warning: "Thou shalt surely die" (Gen. 2:17), and the exclusion from the "tree of life." This connection of temporal death with the lapse into sin is plainly implied in the great fact that the work of redemption brings resurrection of the dead, restoring what sin took away (Rom. 8:23).

THE DOCTRINE OF ORIGINAL SIN

Among the consequences of the fall has been noted the corruption or depravity introduced into man's nature and made continuous for the race through hereditary relation. This claims further consideration. It is, confessedly, a subject of great difficulty, presenting some of the profoundest questions in anthropology and religion. It has formed one of the chief battle-fields between orthodox Scriptural theology and almost every form of variant and misleading error. Prom the days of Pelagius down to modern Socinianism and Unitarianism the church has been obliged to face denials of the fact of "original sin" or false views of it, and to vindicate the Biblical doctrine concerning it.

The designation itself, "original sin," is, indeed, not Biblical but ecclesiastical. It is a coinage of theology to name a truth of Scripture teaching. The term "original" is not employed as referring to any evil belonging to man by virtue of his own origin, but to two facts: (a) the origin of human sin in the sin of the first or original man; (b) the fact that it is the fountain or source from which comes the "actual" sin in our personal lives.

The teaching of the Scriptures, in its essential truths, as understood by our Church, is stated in the Augsburg Confession: "Our churches likewise teach, that since the fall of Adam all men who are naturally engendered are born with sin, that is, without the fear of God or confidence toward Him, and with sinful propensities; and that this disease or original sin is truly sin, and still condemns and causes eternal death to those who are not born again by baptism and the Holy Spirit." The Form of Concord re-asserts the substance of this Article, guarding the truth from both Pelagian and Manichæan error.2 With this the Ninth Article of the Church of England is in substantial agreement, as are the chief Confessions of the large historical churches of Protestantism.

A representative definition or two may well be quoted. From Quenstedt: "Original sin is a want of original righteousness, derived from the sin of Adam and propagated to all men who are begotten in the ordinary mode of generation, including the dreadful corruption and depravity of human nature and all its powers, excluding all from the favor of God and eternal life, and subjecting them to temporal and eternal punishments, unless they are born again of water and the Spirit, or obtain the remission of their sins through Christ." From Hollaz: "Original sin is a want of original righteousness, connected with a depraved inclination, corrupting in the most inward parts the whole human nature, which was derived from the fall of our first parents, and is propagated to all men by natural generation, rendering them indisposed to spiritual good, but inclined to evil, and making them the objects of divine wrath and eternal condemnation."2 Analyzing any or all of these statements, which may be taken as correct, we find they include the following distinct points: (1) Original sin arises from Adam's sin and fall. (2) It belongs to all men, without exception, born according to the order of nature. (3) It is propagated by hereditary descent. (4) It consists of two things, first, a want, a privation of original righteousness, a state of soul indisposed to good; secondly, a positive inclination to evil, a real corruption or depravity, an active and strong tendency contrary to the law of holiness. Even this kind of sin is no mere negation—an absence simply of what is good, the μη ὄν of some speculative teaching. (5) It is really sin. (6) It involves guilt, draws divine condemnation. (7) Unless forgiven and overcome by grace, it brings eternal death.

These various points will be more fully understood as the essential features of the doctrine are recalled and considered in order.

1. The fact of original sin is, of course, basal for the whole consideration of the subject. In Christian theology the first and ruling authority for this is drawn from the Scriptures. Beyond doubt the Scriptures teach it. It is involved not only in the account of the fall, but fundamentally underlies the whole conception of the divine administration described as dealing with a race alienated from God, love, and righteousness, and deeply corrupt. Startling expressions of it are continuously given in word and event. "God saw that the wickedness of man was great in the earth, and that every imagination of the thoughts of his heart was only evil continually." "I will destroy man from the face of the earth" (Gen. 6:5–7; Ps. 14:2–3; 51:5). It underlies the entire order of the legal, sacrificial, and prophetic dispensations of the Old Testament. It is directly taught in Rom 3:9–23; 5:12–21; 1 Cor. 2:14; Eph. 2:2–10; John 3:5–6. Just as decisively is it involved in all the Scriptures which teach the necessity of regeneration or renewal in order to holiness and heaven (John 3:3; Eph. 4:21–24; 2 Cor. 5:17). The "new creature," "new man," is correlate to "the natural man" as despoiled of the innocence and holiness in primal man. Every word in the Bible assertive of the necessity of regeneration or renovation of man for his true life and destiny is a reaffirmation of the truth of this depravity. And so is every statement that connects man's universal bodily death with sin, and opens to view a resurrection from the dead as an outcome of redemption (Rom. 5:12–21; 8:19–23; 2 Cor. 5:4; 1 Cor. 15:20–26; John 11:25). All die because all are in sin. If the attempt be made to discredit this relation of sin to death by scientific evidence that death was in the world, reigning over animal life, and that it still reigns, though they have not sinned, the answer is that their dying is nowhere made to rest on this cause. They were never included in the covenant or scope of immortality. Their case is not the same as that of man. Animal death is a problem by itself. The divine revelation was not given to throw light upon it, but upon man's condition and way of recovery to his true life and immortality. And the whole form of

Christian doctrine is found deeply structured to the needs involved in this sinfulness of the race.

The prevalence of sin as a fact in the world is strongly confirmatory of the Scripture teaching. Wherever man is found, sin is found. It is manifestly congenital. No one can look on human life as it is in fact, as exhibited in the condition, character, deeds, and spirit of the earth's population in all nations and history—the everlasting sway of ambition and wrong, the interminable horrors of war and carnage, the selfishness, hate, and violence torturing every community, the omnipresent evils that disfigure and desolate family and personal life wherever the eye is turned—no one can look on it all and count our nature a holy and unfallen thing, as made by a God of love and righteousness. The bias to sin shows itself in the first dawnings of self-conscious individual life, universally. A universal effect must have a universal cause. This doctrine of native sinfulness is not due simply to our Biblical training. Pagan writers have asserted it strongly. Plato represents some evil in every one as a corruption from his parents. Aristotle finds, along with the reason which inclines every man upward, another inborn principle which fights and strains against the reason.2 Ovid confesses: "I see the better and approve it, yet I follow the worse." Seneca says: "It was the complaint of our ancestors, it is our own, it will be that of posterity, that morals are subverted, that corruption reigns."4 From all over the vast Orient has been coming for ages the ache and shadow of inborn sin which theory there counts as brought by transmigration from a pre-existent state. The various attempts to account for this prevalence of actual sin without admitting the corrupted condition of human nature through the Adamic fall, have not been successful, either singly or together. For example:

(a) The Pelagian teaching, holding moral indifference, absence of all native "bias, whether good or bad," to be essential to the liberty of free-agency and responsibility, has alleged such "original sin" to be contradicted by the fact of responsibility. But this effort to explain every man's acting as he does as an ultimate fact of his free agency, each one falling for himself, breaks on the illogical assumption that the universal fact of sin can be fairly explained by any indifferent cause. If the will or nature is without bias, how is it that it makes sinners of all men?

(b) It is explained as due to the influence of example. But the inadequacy of this remains evident till it is shown how evil example could have obtained universal supremacy except through a disordered condition of the nature itself. Moreover, the tendency to sin shows itself in the face of the holiest and purest example.

(c) It is asserted that hereditary sin is simply the result of the necessary order of the development of man's powers, i. e., first, the animal; second, the intellectual; third, the moral. By the time the moral faculties come into play, the physical and merely mental have attained strong and misleading sway. But this would make sin of physical origin and a material quality, whereas matter possesses no freedom for responsible choice or action. Moreover, this account, while refusing the Biblical doctrine of a fall, concedes a real enslavement of the spirit to the flesh and makes God the actual author of the condition.

(d) Of similar import is the evolutionist theory representing sin as but the remaining force and manifestation of the animal nature in man. Prof. John Fiske says human progress "means throwing off the brute inheritance." And he prophesies that in the gospel of Darwinism salvation will come: "The ape and the tiger in human nature will become extinct." To this it is enough to say: first, that this suggested origin of man from brute ancestry is far from being proved—is, in fact, confuted by what are yet insuperable scientific difficulties; secondly, that it confesses the bad brutishness which, in fact, blots the nature of the race; thirdly, it discredits its anthropology by its failure to explain the genesis of the human conscience except as mere inherited judgments of utility; fourthly, in pointing the hope of salvation to the slow movement of evolutionary extinguishment of the race brutishness, it is voiceless as to divine help for the millions on millions of the individuals of the generations till that tardy natural relief may come. For evolutionism rejects the idea of supernatural revelation and leaves man to himself and the laws of nature.

2. This "original sin," as a race inheritance, is intrinsically a moral fault. That is, it is not a mere physical corruption or evil, dwelling simply in the flesh, but belongs to the soul, as a sinful

condition of the psychical nature, of the personal, self-determining ego that acts in intelligence and choice. The old Manichæistic identification of the principle of evil with matter still reappears in various phases. But in whatever shape it comes, both Biblical teaching and sound reason require its emphatic rejection. That sin is lodged in the mind, or exists as forms of mental action or state, is evident from various points of view. Biblically, the sin in which the fall took place was an act of the human will in deciding to follow a temptation rather than a known divine direction. The appeal to physical appetite or other appetencies, morally indifferent in themselves, was the tempter's persuasion addressed to the will. The initial sin was an act of the choice. Moreover, from the very nature of sin as something for which there is responsibility, it must have its seat in the voluntary power. Mere physical ailment or disease is not voluntary, and, therefore, not essentially sin or guilt. The physical human organism, with its appetencies, belongs to man for the sake of his higher personal life in the image of God. It is part of that range over which the "dominion" of mind, ethical reason, and righteousness was to hold. The moral sovereignty of conscience and freedom is set in obligation to rule the sensuous nature while using it, and its not doing so lodges the responsibility on itself. It is distinctly confirmatory of this view of the origin and seat of evil, that many of the most heinous sins, when analyzed, are found wholly destitute of any sensuous element, as pride, anger, malice, enmity to God. Sin is not "bred in the bone," but created in the choices, states, and activities of free-agents. But the decisive evidence in the question is the incarnation. That the Divine Son should take human "flesh" into fellowship in His own person for His earthly life-time, and have no sin in Him, shows that there is no inherent evil in matter itself. Sin consists in the action or attitude of the will.

3. The degree of corruption belonging to this "sin." Since the days of Augustine and the Pelagian controversy, extreme views have been in strife. From the Pelagian denial of "original sin," its reality has been confessed by theology generally in different types of positiveness, culminating in wide acceptance of Augustine's teaching that the depravity is "total," leaving man "one mass of perdition." "The first man made himself a total damnable mass." Protestant theology has largely

accepted the Augustinian anthropology—explanatory and modifying statements, however, accompanying the acceptance. The term "total" involves a point requiring such explanation.

Negatively stated: (a) This original sin is not total in the sense that man is so depraved that he cannot be or grow worse. In fact, beyond all doubt, the birth-degree of depravity attains larger and stronger force as unimpeded sway is allowed to its tendencies, and no limit can be fixed beyond which it may not advance. (b) Nor is it total in the sense that it does not leave in man any better elements or capacities, such as conscience, perception of right, and sense of obligation. He has such powers, though obscured and impaired, on which God's grace may take hold and operate. Else there would be no capacities left in him through which spiritual truth and moral powers could enter and move him to repentance. (c) Nor yet is it total in the sense that he is incapable of many natural and moral virtues, as love of kindred, admiration of excellence, kindness, friendship, disinterested, self-sacrificing affection and action. As a matter of fact, unregenerate men show these virtues—often in impressive beauty and true heroism. And these virtues are not sins. Augustine and many others since have been wont to class them as "splendid sins." Theologians and preachers have often foolishly spoken of all natural virtues in this way as sins all the more condemnable by reason of their being virtues. But this is to blot out the very distinction between right and wrong, in which the guilt of sin rests. These virtues in the unregenerate, by being without the true and high motive of love to God are, indeed, imperfect, partial, and insufficient as ground of desert before God. But to claim that they are "sins," is both false to fundamental ethical principles and uncalled for by any fair interpretation of the word of God. The justice, honesty, truthfulness of men, in their natural state, are not sins so far as they are justice, honesty, truthfulness, etc. We must preserve fundamental distinctions and not confound the question of what is right with the question of what is perfect (infinite) or justifying before God. The Biblical doctrine of original sin can never be rightly understood through obliteration of the prime ethical distinctions.

Positively stated, this depravity may justly be held as total, (a) in the sense that all man's powers, intellect, sensibility, and will have been directly or indirectly injured or corrupted by the disordering power of sin in the soul's nature. No faculty is unaffected by it. (b) And in the sense that the whole is depraved in and by the depravity or alienation from God and holiness of the governing disposition. That which the Scriptures call "the heart," the affectional nature, being perverted, without true and ruling love of God and righteousness, and dominating the will, the whole man is held enslaved in bondage to evil. His personality is as the governing quality of his nature. (c) And in this, too, that the total nature is thus helplessly subservient to this ruling evil—the present degree of sin, growing by ascendency, moving toward the complete depravity of which the present is the potency and prophecy. Self-salvation is not man's opportunity. Divine redemptive grace is the economy of the Adamic world.

4. But there are some further affirmations which theology has felt constrained to add in explaining the Scripture doctrine of original sin. Their aim is to express the elemental conceptions or ingredients which must be included in a true and full view. Two of them, often represented as involving serious metaphysical difficulties, and, in fact, forming the crux of long, earnest, acute, and still continued controversy, must be briefly considered here.

(a) The truth that this corruption or inborn evil is "truly sin." This, as already said, is the affirmation of the Confession of our Church. It is the prevalent faith of Christendom. Is it Scriptural and true? Or is this depravity a state without moral quality, simply a condition of injury or disadvantage, a calamity, void of sinfulness? From the days of Pelagius there have been those who have said that "sin" is predicable only of personal or voluntary acts—that the moral nature back of these is simply capacity-endowment for personal choices and action to which alone moral quality or character belongs. They assert that as moral character is something for which man is held responsible, there can be no predication of sin as fact or feature of the individual human life back of the exercise of personal choices and behavior. Each human life attains character for itself only by and in these. But this criticism of the doctrine is far more specious than sound. Beyond all question, the Scriptures speak of this innate disposition to evil as sin. When the apostle (Rom. 6:12) says: "Let not sin, therefore, reign in your mortal body, that ye should obey it in the lusts thereof," he so characterizes it; for he specifically designates the "lusts" or depravities existing prior to the acts of free choice, which men may "obey" or resist, as "sins." The same conception is seen in "Sin shall not have dominion over you" (verse 14), and "Whereas ye were servants of sin, ye became obedient from the heart to that form of teaching whereunto ye were delivered, and being made free from sin, ye became servants of righteousness" (verses 17–18). In fact, the apostle's entire discussion in this connection seems meant to give prolonged emphasis to the sinfulness of the corrupt state of human nature, as well as to the necessity of the grace of salvation from it through the new life of faith. In verse 6 he speaks of "our old man," i. e., the old ego or self, the personality in its entire sinful condition before regeneration, as so alive with impious and immoral tendencies that the bad ego must be "crucified" with Christ if the bondage is to be overcome in a true liberty of manhood. (Compare Eph. 4:22–24; Col. 3:9.) St. John's definition of sin fully embraces the innate moral disorder: "Sin is lawlessness" (ἀνομία), non-conformity to law, which may mark a state or disposition of the soul, as settled aversions or affinities, as well as outward acts or separate choices. (See also 1 John 5:17.) The same view is clearly embedded in Jesus' statement: "Out of the heart proceed evil thoughts, murders, adulteries, fornications, thefts, false witness, railings" (Matt. 15:19), for the states and impellings in the inner depravity are the fountain sources of the acts of will and conduct. They give the character that is seen in action. The critics of the truth in question will need to revise their restrictive definition of sin if they are to reach harmony with the Biblical teaching in its more comprehensive and profound representation of it We must say "more profound," because it is based in the deeper and necessary principle that moral good and evil are such by virtue of what they are in their very nature, and not by virtue of their cause or source, and that the grounds of the moral distinction are immutable.

This conclusion is sustained when we penetrate and mark the essence of sin. From the time of Augustine Christian thought has prevailingly conceived the central essence as selfishness—self-seeking as over against duty to God and fellow-men. It takes on innumerable forms, whether it violates the obligations on the divine or the human side. But whatever form it assumes in either relation, sin is the placing of self-will or selfishness above the claims of right and love. It is the adoption of a false and discordant principle. It is so in sins of omission and commission. In the mirror of the very first human sin, a disobedient assertion of self-will is seen as the all-embracing beginning of humanity's infinite forms of sin and sinfulness. It is plain that the sway of this spirit must alienate from God and fellow-men, and throw all the vital relations of life into unspeakable disorder and moral wrong. And if a person sins in an act of free choice, he thus, eo ipso, places his nature in a sinful and guilty attitude toward duty and righteousness. He has dropped his nature out of its true harmonies and adaptations to God and his fellow-men, broken and disordered its normal working and life-forces away from the supreme law of love. And if, as was the case with Adam, beyond this personal actual sin and guilt, and the state of moral disorder into which his powers are thus reduced, there is the further principle of hereditary transmission of constitutional nature, pure or corrupted, to which human experience has ever given impressive witness, this corruption becomes part of the intrinsic character of descendants as a sinful state.

It is evident, thus, that sin is predicable of both acts and states of personality. It may belong to deeds, or to the character of the manhood existing back of the deeds. They are different forms of sin, but in each it is sin. It is a plain mistake to affirm sin of acts and deny it of depravity—to refuse to recognize it in the condition or attitude of the soul itself, in its settled alienation from God, its aversion to the duties of love and holy obedience. If a single act of disobedience is sin, something in its essential quality wrong, which the moral sense asserts "ought not" to be, what shall be said of the deep, abiding temper of lawlessness, whose wrong affinities of evil are lodged in the very life-forces which lie behind and cause the evil acts or choice? The badness is not merely superficial or a mere appearance, or harmless prior to an act of will, but a breach with the principle of duty in the very life of the soul, a bad fountain polluting its streams. Surely this per se evil, evil in the ethical sense, a moral "onght not," "sin." The error that denies this is grounded in one of two mistakes or in both, viz.: a more restrictive definition of sin than that of Bible usage, or in a superficial estimate of the import of this inborn antagonism to righteousness.

There is one fact, however, that must be noted at this point, and remembered for consideration in another relation, the fact that theology makes, as it must, the clear distinction between this "original sin" and "actual sins." Our view of the whole subject, and of the problems it involves, must bear this distinction constantly in mind, if we are to reach precise and just conclusions as to the import of this form of sin, and especially concerning the responsibility which it involves.

(b) But there is a further and more complex question—the question most perplexing in the long discussion of the problem of original sin—whether this depravity, thus truly sin, also includes guilt. The Augsburg Confession says of it, that it "condemns and causes eternal death." After the prolonged controversy, how are we to hold on this point? We must clearly distinguish between sin and guilt. Sin, as we have seen, is the wrong act or state of the soul, diverging from the law of duty or righteousness; guilt may be defined as the consequent ill-desert or demerit involved in the sin, its desert of punishment (*reatus pœnæ*). Doing right, or being right, is intrinsically that which ethically "ought to be," and deserves favor and happiness. Correspondently to this good desert of righteousness, is the bad desert of sin. It merits ill, it calls for punitive repression. Because it is sin it involves guilt, and involves the one because it is the other. The two things are inseparable. But here objection is made. It is conceded that such guilt is affirmed in conscience in connection with our sins as committed in our free agency, but in the case under consideration we are involved in the sin by no act of our own, but from a point back of our own agency. It has come upon us and has a place in us by the sin or actual disobedience of the first human being. It came by his guilty self-determination, corrupting the powers and bent of his nature, and allying them with evil. And this depravation sustains the relation of a penal consequence of his sin upon the moral constitution of humanity and is expressive of the ill-desert of the alienating transaction. So, it is argued, we not being the authors of the bad condition or inborn evil—not having created this "sin of origin," whatever it may be—its "guilt" can in no just sense be ours. This guilt, it is thought, can be regarded as predicable only of Adam's own act of sin and the depravity which he established in his own moral life. It is claimed, especially by those who deny the term "sin" to everything but voluntary acts, that to assert "guilt" of the human infant in its unconscious incapacity for rational and moral action, confuses and overthrows the very foundation ideas and principles of moral responsibility. This reasoning has won wide acceptance in rationalizing theology.

But it is not conclusive. Rather, a better reasoning and closer logic may, and indeed must, assert guilt as well as sin for this immoral attitude or state of the soul. For as, according to the Scriptures and reason, "sin" is predicable of it, on the principle that right and wrong have their character by virtue of their nature, and not by their cause, so "guilt" belongs to sin, not by reason of the contingency of the authorship, but by the real existence or quality of sin itself. The demerit exists in the sin. The ill-desert, per se and primarily, is due to the evil as something wrong and condemnable. Wherever sin is, there is that which is condemnable and intrinsically ill-deserving. So it "condemns" in its language to the conscience and before God. The wrongdoer, indeed, falls under the responsibility for his relation to the thing of bad merit, but because the thing calls for condemnation. In this case, too, as in that of applying the term sin to tempers of soul back of acts, the definition must be made broad enough to cover the twofold or double application of the term guilt to either the voluntary acts of moral agents or to the sinful state of human nature. Of course, as theology universally makes a distinction between original sin and actual sin, between sins of voluntary act and the sin of an evil nature, so, too, it must distinguish between the guilt or types of guilt in the two cases. The guilt of original sin is not the same as of actual sin. And the further affirmation of the sin: 'It works eternal death to those who are not recovered through Christ,' is consequent upon the nature of the sin. For in its essence it is incipient "death," a state of actual spiritual deadness to the true life in God, love, and holiness.

The question whether it was right in God to permit the race to come into this state through the solidarity of our humanity and the law of hereditary transmission, is altogether a different question from the intrinsic guiltiness of the state itself. On this question of the divine justice or goodness in the system of a race propagating a continuously depraved nature, we must acknowledge that we are not competent to sit in judgment. The problem is too large. Nothing short of omniscient intelligence, in survey of the infinite bearings of moral forces and the possibilities of the divine administration, is adequate to give the answer. God must be trusted in the order which His wisdom and love have established, assured as we are that His ways will be eternally justified.

But the entire doctrine on this subject will be best understood by a reminder of the speculative theories that have been offered of the "imputation" of Adam's sin to all the race. A widespread effort has been made, through the use of this designation, to explain the mode or philosophy of all the race being, in each individual, held as guilty by reason of Adam's transgression. In the earlier period of the Church, and down to the reformation times, theology was satisfied with accepting the general truth of original sin, as that truth has been already marked out, without forming a philosophy of the way in which men are involved in its consequences. It was maintained, in general, that through an actual unity or solidarity of the race, as starting in Adam, human nature fell in him and, through the vitiation thereby of generic humanity, every individual, by the law of hereditary transmission, is involved in the consequences and corruption of the fall. This general view was adopted and set forth by the reformers. Nothing beyond this is found in the Augsburg Confession or any of the reformation symbols of the sixteenth century. But in the seventeenth century the doctrine of the imputation of Adam's sin to each and all of his descendants was elaborated and pressed forward as necessary to the orthodox truth. "The doctrine of the imputation of the guilt and punishment of our first parents was fully developed only by the later theologians, from about the time of Calovius" (1612–1688).

This doctrine of imputation is presented in two leading forms: (a) Immediate Imputation.—The word imputation is used as equivalent to הָשַׁב, or λογίζεσθαι, to reckon or put something to the account of any one, crediting him with and holding him to responsibility for it. Immediate imputation reckons Adam's transgression or sin directly to every individual of his posterity as his sin and guilt, regarding each one responsible as fully as if he had personally committed it. The meaning of the word "immediate" is that Adam's sin is imputed, not through or by reason of any depravity consequent in human nature and existing as sin in each man personally, but directly and antecedently to any question of inherited corruption. It means that the imputation is not because of the fact of this corruption, but irrespective of it, and in the order of sequence prior to it. This immediate imputation is explained upon two different bases. (a) Some give it a realistic basis, taking the suggestion of Augustine's statement on Rom. 5:12: "Omnes enim fuimus in illo uno, quando omnes ille unus." This asserts that all humanity was really and actively in Adam. As a generic spiritual substance it corrupted itself by its own apostatizing act. Every man was a guilty co-agent. Quenstedt explains "Not only our first parents were the subjects" (i. e., grammatical subjects, doers) "of the first sin, but all their posterity to be propagated by natural generation. For Adam and Eve were in the place of the whole human race." All sin, viz., in Adam. Baier says, "All sinned in one."2 Dr. Shedd, who adopts this view, explains: "The first sin was a common, not an individual sin." "All men were in Adam when he disobeyed." "The psychophysical human nature existing in Adam and Eve" is represented as not yet distributed and individualized—the "human nature as it was in Adam, prior to any division and individualization of it." This explanation is grounded specially on Rom. 5:12, where ἐφ' ᾧ is translated in the Vulgate "*in quo omnes peccaverunt*," and not as in our English version, "because that all have sinned." "The first man," it is asserted, "had the wills of all his posterity gathered up, as it were, in his will, whence freely for himself and all his posterity he declared his will and that of posterity against the law that had been given. As far as the Lutheran dogmaticians adhered to immediate imputation, they adopted this realistic explanation. But (b) another explanation has been offered—the Federal Theory, developed by Cocceius, of Leyden (1603–1669), and fully elaborated by Turretin (1623–1687). According to this, Adam was constituted by God's sovereign appointment the legal representative of all mankind, God entering into a covenant of works with him, that he should stand a moral probation for himself and all his descendants, and that his obedience or disobedience, with all its consequences, should be held as theirs. The idea is grounded in the principle of covenant obligation and responsibility. This theory of Federal Headship, in legalistic way, has largely characterized the Calvinistic, or Reformed theology as over against the Lutheran. Under both the realistic and the federal explanations the doctrine of immediate imputation has often been carried into very extreme representations. How far it has been pressed is seen, for instance, in Quenstedt's declaration: "As we are made righteous by the imputation of the righteousness of Christ, so we are made unrighteous by the disobedience of Adam." Which, since we are made righteous by the imputation of Christ's righteousness without being really personally righteous, must mean that we are treated as personally un righteous without being really so; i. e., by simply, and contrary to the truth or fact, putting unrighteousness to our account and holding us, though innocent, as guilty.

Concerning this doctrine of immediate imputation on these different bases, our reply must be: (a) As to its basis in a legal covenant headship of Adam. First, such covenant is something in clear excess of Scripture teaching. There is no mention of any such thing in connection with Adam's probation. Secondly, the explanation really contradicts Scripture, in making the first result of Adam's sin to be God's regarding and treating the race as sinners, whereas the Scriptures distinctly declare that Adam's offense constituted men sinners (Rom. 5:19). We are not sinners because God, on the basis of a covenant, merely arranges to treat us as such, but we are treated as sinners because we are sinners (Rom. 5:12). (b) As to the realistic basis: First, the exegesis of Rom. 5:12, as "in whom all sinned," used as Scripture support for it, is quite untenable. Jerome's translation was a mistake and misleading. Secondly, the assumed actual existence in Adam of all the subsequent human personalities, in such a sense as to make them veritable personal participants in his choice and co-agents in his act, presents an abstraction, a mental fiction, confounding the conceptual existence of the race with the real existence of its personalities. Only the possibility of other men after Adam and Eve was "in him," not their actuality. In the Biblical order the creation of two personal individual human beings was the prius to the creation of any others of their rank through the mode of race propagation. We must not juggle with the abstract term "humanity" at this point. Thirdly, to make Adam not an individual personal being, but the aggregate "unindividualized" humanity, destroys his character as real and true man and his capacity to act as a really personal agent and representative. Dr. C.A. Stork has well said: "If he was a collective being he was not a man at all." Of human personality without individuality we know nothing, and if Adam was not a true individual human being, how could he be the natural progenitor of the real personalities of the race? The offered explanation is an illusion.

(b) Mediate imputation, as a theoretic explanation, was first advanced by Placaeus (1606–1655), professor of theology at Saumur, France. It teaches that the sin and guilt of Adam's transgression are imputed, not directly, but only through and on account of the actual corruption or sinfulness resulting to all men from his sin. Quenstedt puts this: "For no one is considered a sinner by God, to no one is the first act imputed, except to him who descends, contaminated with original sin, from that same Adam."

The distinction between these two views of imputation becomes clearer, if we note that immediate imputation is often called "antecedent"—making all men responsible for Adam's sin as participants in actu or by representative, condemning independently of and prior to natural depravity, hereditary guilt preceding, in logical order, hereditary sin. Mediate imputation is termed consequent, as following upon the inherited corruption and its condemning guiltiness. The sin of the apostasy is ours, not because God imputes it to us, but it is truly and properly ours, and, therefore, God imputes it to us.

This theory of mediate imputation accords with the language and general spirit of the Holy Scriptures, and violates, per se, no principle of reason. In it the word imputation means simply "to hold responsible for," viz.: to place the guilt and penalties to men's account because the sin or sinfulness is really theirs. They are "condemned," and under "death" spiritual, because they are corrupted and polluted with sin. This view resolves itself substantially into the doctrine confessed by the Church before the rise of these theories. "Calvin and all the first reformers and creeds were principally concerned in emphasizing the fact that original sin inherent, as distinguished from original sin imputed, is intrinsically and justly, as moral corruption, worthy of God's wrath and curse."

On the other hand, this theory fails to solve what the theory of immediate imputation was invented to explain, viz.: on what ground and order of racial propagation of moral depravity from parent to children was there incorporated in the system of human life, or on what basis is the whole race punished with, this corruption of nature? For, original sin seems to come as a penalty on Adam's actual sin, the penalty covering not only the actual offenders, but all their posterity. And the question at bottom is, by what right is this inflicted on all the race? The extremest defenders of immediate imputation admit that all the other elements of evil than inherited sin itself, such as disease, suffering, temporal and eternal death, come on us because of this inherent sin and our actual sins. But why is inherent sin itself ours? Mediate imputation is the sufficient explanation of all but the descent of depravity to Adam's posterity. We are entitled to take this theory as far as it reaches with its explanation, viz.: the truth that original sin is sin and is under condemnation. This remaining problem, which seeks the ground on which God has constituted human life with the principle of hereditary descent as carrying a self-induced corruption, must be explained, if explained at all, on some other theory. The theory of immediate imputation, invoked to solve it, is worse than a simple failure. It brings in more difficulties than it clears away—in an alleged arbitrary covenant arrangement without warrant of Scripture or reason, or in taking the abstract term "humanity" realistically, as identical with the concrete personal being Adam, and viewing him as the undivided, undistributed, unindividualized human substance, thus destroying his real personality and substituting an undifferentiated mass of potential, but yet impersonal, human nature.

Without doubt, the right thing for us to do is to recognize original sin, as taught in the Scriptures, in its form of fact in the natural and revealed constitution of the world, accepting, as we are warranted in doing, the theory of mediate imputation, as in its measure explanatory of truth. Thus, taking Adam as an individual, the first man and natural head and root of the race, both physically and spiritually, we recognize, as the Christian revelation affirms and the actual state of the world has always shown, that his offspring have inherited his fallen and corrupt nature. We can afford to leave the explanation of it with the rest of the aggregate mystery of which it forms a part—the mystery of sin in the world. In this way we accept all that revelation and the Church's confessions declare, and avoid making explanations which do not explain, and to which we can find no response in conscience or reason. There are three points on which we may be sure, and with which we may well feel satisfied: First, that God is not the author of sin. Its very essence is antagonism to His will. It has come from abuse of creature free-agency, and continues in its abuse. Secondly, that the relation of the human race to its head in Adam, by which his sinful condition descends to his posterity, could we see and fully understand it all, would be found to involve nothing in violation of either God's goodness or justice. Thirdly, that God takes no pleasure in the corruption and misery which sin brings, as is clear from the perpetual assurances of His word and the provision and appeal of the redemptive administration He has established in the Gospel.

(c) There is, however, a still further point in the doctrine of original sin which here claims careful consideration, if we wish to understand it under the fullest light of the Gospel teaching. This light fully justifies the Church's confessions in holding this natural depravity as "truly sin" and as involving "guilt" and drawing "condemnation." No concessions can be made to denials of inborn sinfulness or the ill-desert of its innate alienation or aversion from God and righteousness. Nevertheless, the orthodox theology of the Church has always and everywhere recognized a distinction and real difference between this so-called "original sin" and "actual sin." The difference is clear and important. The sinner stands in a different relation to the sin in the two cases. In actual sin, he is the doer. It is of his personal free choice, his own act. In original sin it is an inheritance—in him back of all personal activity or consent. Thus in actual sin, the sin is one's own in a sense in which it is not in original sin. The relation of responsibility with respect to it is modified by the difference. In actual sin one is responsible for the origination or existence of the sin; in original sin there can be no responsibility for this. In view of this deep and inerasable distinction and difference between original sin and actual sin, the different relations in which men stand to each, and the consequent modification of responsibility, the question arises whether theology has always and fully developed a view of the bearings of redemptive grace on the possibilities and terms of forgiveness and salvation, consistent with the clearly recognized distinction? From the beginning, child-membership in the Church, inherited from the Old Testament covenant, rested in recognition of the grace of forgiveness of sin and of regeneration as reaching the condition of those who were in original sin alone. This covered the question of responsibility for original sin so far as it concerned infants within the organism of the Church. But there was a vast infant-world outside of the reach of this order. Gradually, from misapplying to infancy the condition of salvation through faith addressed in the Scriptures only to adults, theology settled into denial of salvation to infants dying without baptism. They were regarded as lost through original sin and its demerits alone. This view held sway through the Eastern and Western Churches. It is the teaching of the Roman Catholic and Greek Churches to-day. Protestantism inherited it. The problem of God's holding infants dying before actual sin responsible, has been upon it from the Reformation. The discussion of it has been constant and immense. The great Protestant confessions and general dogmatics were loyal to the Scriptures in affirming the innate depravity to be sin, and, in its very essence, ill-deserving. Nevertheless, theology could not rest at this point, without theoretic search into the full truth of the bearing of God's redemptive provision and administration with respect to the question of His penal exaction of the demerit of original sin. Luther broke with the prevalent view, in believing that God does not hold responsible for it the unbaptized children of believing parentage: "He will think kindly of them." Lutheran and all Protestant theology has, in the main, followed him. It has, largely, gone further. Searching more and more thoroughly into the significance of the redemptive economy through forgiveness and spiritual recovery, and interpreting its scope of inclusion as adequately reached both in the Church's charter covenant, embracing unconscious infancy as well as believing parentage, and in the Redeemer's assurances of the Heavenly Father's care for little children, it has gradually reached general belief that under this order of divine grace, forgiveness of original sin, as distinguished from actual, is no more hindered with respect to the whole world of infancy than to the child of the believer, by the want of baptism or personal knowledge of Christ. This belief is regarded as warranted by the necessary implications of the great fundamental fact, that Christ, as representing universal humanity, made Himself, in His work and sufferings, a propitiation for the sins of the whole world and "tasted death for every man," and that thus the whole human race, in all its individuals, is under altered relations and conditions of responsibility with respect to sin. Whether held to it, or released from it through forgiveness, depends, for those who have and know the Gospel, upon their acceptance or rejection of the revealed Saviour and salvation. The standard and measure of responsibility for the heathen, among whom the Gospel, with its message of redemptive love, light, and opportunity is unknown, has not been distinctly revealed. An apostle implies that they are judged according to the light they have. And with respect to infants among them, dying before commission of actual sin, and without 'rejection' of the Gospel, it is difficult to see how, under the economy of a gracious salvation, they should be regarded as held to responsibility for original sin, while in Christian lands such children, at least those of believers, dying unbaptized, are regarded as not so held. Those, no more than these, have sinned or can sin, against the Gospel light and have not personally refused faith in the Savior.

The majority of our Lutheran dogmaticians, while agreeing as to the salvation of the unbaptized children of believers, have, nevertheless, hesitated with respect to the children of non-Christians, though hoping the best for them. Some, however, have confidently denied their damnation. So Dannhauer, Balthasar Mentzer, Musaeus, Scherzer, and Cotta in his notes on Gerhard. They reason from the generic import of the Gospel teaching and conclude that "the analogy of faith makes certain that no one is condemned absolutely (absolute, i. e., irrespective of some conditions), and that only actual resistance of the means of faith, unbelief alone, condemns." They agree in asserting that "original sin alone is not adequate cause of damnation." All the grace God has to give He gives without condition to those who are absolutely incapable of complying with any conditions. An echo of this conclusion is heard when Dr. C. P. Krauth, interpreting the Augsburg Confession in the light of its fundamental principles and essential theology, says: "It is not the teaching of the Confessions that there ever has been or ever will be a single soul lost by original sin alone."

This principle of the divine administration that, through a full propitiation for sin in the suffering love and righteousness of Christ, God holds all infant human life, which has no guilt save that of original sin, under the grace of forgiveness instead of the disfavor or displeasure due to moral evil—a stay of judgment by an active reign of love for sin's overthrow and the rescue of its subjects—opens to our view the real sense and limitations in which all men are held in actual responsibility with respect to sin. To faith in the Lord Jesus Christ and its self-surrender to the love of God in Him, all sin is cancelled in forgiveness and is in process of vanquishment through regeneration. To childhood, before the age of moral discernment and knowledge, there is no requital of original sin, but a gracious acceptance and divine love. With respect to this condition of sinful nature, those to whom belong the care, nurture, and molding of the child-period into Christian knowledge and obedience, sustain a tremendous responsibility with respect to the continued existence and issues of this evil, the overthrow of whose working is demanded by all the high interests of the life and destiny for which man has been created. On emergence from childhood into the moral personality of youth and manhood there is the pressure of an unspeakably solemn responsibility upon every man for whatever sway he, in his freedom, gives to the inborn depravity in face of the behests of conscience and the known will of God—especially in despite of the redemptory grace that provides pardon of guilt and recovery of the soul to the sinless holiness divinely meant for its life and blessedness. Men are thus accountable through free adoption of inherited sin as the life of their lives, making it their own choice, and carrying it on into actual sinning, which still further debases the subjective constitution.

ACTUAL SIN

As distinguished from sin inherited, actual sin means sin in conduct, and presents no problems of speculative difficulty. Though it flows from the fountain of evil in a corrupted nature, its defining characteristic is that it consists in personal violations of moral obligation or the law of righteousness. It stands in personal abuse of free-agency in relation to God and fellow-men. Of it the world has always been full, in every conceivable form of evil, wrong, vice, violence, and crime. It is the wreckage of character, personal welfare and happiness, social order and peace. It is the self-ruin of individuals, the overthrow of families, the blight and destruction of nations. Its misdeeds make the atmosphere of the world vibrate with horrors.

The traditional classification suffices to mark proper distinctions:

1. Internal and external, as sins of thought, feeling, purpose, etc., in the inner activities of the soul, whether revealed or not; and as sins of word or deed in the outward life.

2. Voluntary and involuntary, such as free or deliberate violation of known duty; and wrong-doing through ignorance or infirmity (Acts 15:39; Gal. 2:12–13; Rom. 7:15).

3. Sins of commission and of omission, viz.: on the one hand, such as transgress in positive action; and on the other, leave required duty undone or given privileges unused. Among sincere Christians positive transgression of the divine commandments is probably far less than neglect of known duty and nonuse of opportunities of good which leave Christian life negative and poor. We should say: "Forgive us our debts"—what we owe both as penalties for evil done and for unmet duties—rather than "forgive us our trespasses," this term failing to include our numerous sins of omission.

4. Venial and mortal. By venial sin is meant sins of such kind and import as do not break the believer's relation of acceptance with God in Christ, but are forgiven at once under the graciousness of that state in which he abides. As this state exists through faith in Christ, sin can be venial only as it does not annul true faith or prove a professed faith to be dead (Jas. 2:17–20). Mortal sin is either the unbelief that refuses acceptance of Christ, or, after faith, relapses into it and breaks the saving relation. The distinction of sin as venial and mortal does not arise from the desert of sin, as of small or great sins—for the greatest sins may be forgiven—but from the fact that unbelief per se rejects the provided and offered pardon. Romanism, however, has made such

dangerous and misleading use of the distinction that it has not been much favored by Protestant theology.

5. Pardonable and unpardonable. All sin is pardonable under the redemptory economy except the one pointed out as "unpardonable" in the words of Christ (Matt. 12:31–32; Mark 3:28–29; Luke 12:10, and apparently referred to in 1 John 5:16; Heb. 6:4–6). After all the long discussion of the subject, the unpardonable sin, as a sin to which men are still liable, may best be defined as that of so resisting and refusing obedience to the Holy Spirit in God's message of truth and grace through the Gospel as to become irrecoverably hardened and settled in an invincible habit of disobedience and unbelief. It may be reached through the indurating force of long-continued resistance of the truth and the Holy Spirit, or by willful apostasy, sinning against the increased responsibility of having been graciously "enlightened," given "taste of the heavenly gift," made actual "partaker of the Holy Spirit," and yet, despite all, returning into full self-subjection to the principle of sin. Reached in either way, its characterizing fact is callous impenitence that cannot be turned into repentance and faith by all the powers which God has lodged in the truth and the Holy Spirit's work of enlightenment and persuasion through it. For the order of salvation does not proceed by compulsion or the overthrow of the moral or free constitution of men. "It is impossible to bring them to repentance"—the essential condition for faith's appropriation of pardon and spiritual enjoyment of the holy life. Thus, the reason of its unpardonableness is not that God's goodness and Christ's atonement have not made adequate provision for forgiveness, or that the divine love is unwilling, but that by the reflex action of the sinner's sin on his moral constitution he has become obdurate beyond the possibility of effective reach of moral truth and spiritual suasion. The sin is necessarily fatal, moreover, because, rejecting Christ, the only Saviour, it also at the same time quenches and makes ineffectual the work of the Holy Spirit, the final divine agency of love for the recovery of sinners.

CHAPTER III
SPECIAL ANTHROPOLOGICAL TRUTHS

The topics to be looked at under this head are the questions of the Origin of Souls since the first human pair, of Dichotomy or Trichotomy, the Freedom of the Will, and Human Ability. They present problems that have not only a speculative interest, but a close relation to man's position and constitution as a subject of redemption and grace. Theology has busied itself with them from its earliest periods. It will be enough to sum up its best established conclusions.

THE ORIGIN OF SOULS SINCE THE CREATION OF ADAM AND EVE

This has close connection with the questions of original sin, the organic unity of the race and of the individual, and the relation of the humanity of Christ to the universal humanity of man. Three theories have divided speculative view, Pre-existentism, Creationism, and Traducianism.

The theory of pre-existence arose from Platonism, and represents human souls as having been created before or at the beginning of the world, and from a pre-existent state passing over into the human life. It was adopted by Philo, the eminent Jewish writer of Alexandria, and by a number of the Church Fathers, as Justin Martyr, Origen, Synesius, and others. Some have held that these pre-existent souls, one by one, pass freely into the actual human state; others that they are brought into the body as a punishment for sin, and with the benevolent design, at the same time, of giving an opportunity of recovery through redemption. The theory was condemned by the Council of Constantinople, A. D. 540. It has had but little following, and this little mainly among "mystics." It was favored by Duns Scotus and Henry More. In recent times Dr. Julius Müller, the eminent author of "The Doctrine of Sin," and Dr. Edward Beecher, in his "Conflict of Ages," have used it in an effort to explain the problem of hereditary guilt, by referring it back to sin in pre-existent state. It has no Scripture basis, and is rationally inadmissible because contradictory both of the real humanity of the individual and of the natural homogeneity of the race. Each human body would house an alien unrelated soul, and the race reality and continuance would consist only in the physical organization perpetuated.

Creationism is traced to Aristotle, who made a distinction between the animal soul (ψυχή) and the rational principle (νοῦς), and derived the former (soul or life), with the body from generation, and the latter (reason), from above as part of the reason of God, or a direct creation by Him. According to this theory the generation of the body is the occasion to God, according to the theological principle of concursus, for direct creation of the soul. The intervening of the direct divine act leaves physical propagation simply the occasion of the soul's existence. The majority of Roman Catholic and Reformed theologians have been creationists. Dr. Charles Hodge gives as arguments for it: (a) It seems to correspond best with the Scriptures which represent the soul as coming from God. (b) It is most consistent with the nature of the soul as indivisible. (c) It explains the freedom of Christ's soul from sin, although He was conceived and born of a woman. But against it must be urged: (a) It is hard to reconcile it with the fact of universal depravity, i. e., to think of God as either creating souls sinful, or creating pure souls and imprisoning them in bodies of sin and death. (b) It would destroy the organic unity of the race; for there would be no descent or continuity of soul-life, the deepest reality that identifies each individual as human, and forms full interrelationship of the race. The only race unity left would be a corporeal unity, and this would have no part in the transmission of soul-life. (c) It tends to destroy also the personal oneness of the individual man; for body and soul would have alien origins, the one by the action of secondary or natural causation, the other by an immediate creation ex nihilo. It disrupts the basal unity of the personal human constitution. (d) It thus fails, further, to explain the fact of the conveyance of mental or psychical traits, as well as moral, from parents to children.

From the inadequacy of these two theories, theology has turned to the principle of linkage naturally suggested by the analogy of all organic race-life, that the whole constitution is transmitted in and by the mystery of propagation. It is called Traducianism. It was propounded by Tertullian, but his advocacy, because of his connecting with it some materialistic conceptions, failed to break the ascendancy of creationism through the early and middle ages. Since the reformation it has been maintained in the Lutheran Church generally, and by most of the New England theologians since Dr. Hopkins. It is supported by such passages as Gen. 5:3; Ps. 51:5; John 3:6; Rom. 5:12, etc. These imply that propagation by natural descent carries all the parts of the human being together. Arguments in proof of it are: (a) The slow development of the psychical faculties with that of the body seems most in harmony with this theory. (b) The mental and even moral peculiarities of parents are found descending to their children. (c) The truth of original sin is best stated and explained in the light of this view. On the whole, this theory accords best with the known order of divine procedure in nature, and has the fewest difficulties. It must be understood, however, that traducianism does not deny, but implies a certain reality of creationism. But it is the creative reality that is ever going on through 'second causes.' It signifies, not creatio prima, but secunda, the divine power fixed in means, which makes the result just as truly and really God's work. It is not immediate, but through the power that He has established in active force in the law of propagation. Souls are potential, therefore, in the life-force adjusted by God for evermore creating fresh personalities. Prof. J. T. Beck says: "In the beginning of new life, a divine creative use of means must be conceived of as going on together and mutually implying each other. Consequently even the continual beginning of human souls is neither the result of absolute creation (creationism), nor of an absolute reproduction (traducianism). But that abiding, effectual Power of God, which conditions all life, acts immanently in generation.

DICHOTOMY OR TRICHOTOMY

This question concerns the number of constituent elements in the human constitution. Trichotomy divides man into three parts or different essences, body, soul, and spirit; Dichotomy into two, body and soul, or spirit. While interesting as a scientific problem, this subject is of some importance theologically in the interpretation of various passages of Scripture.

The Scriptures were not meant to teach a scientific psychology. Their language is to be understood according to the modes of expression of truth in the times when they were written. Yet it is reasonable to believe that, if interpreted correctly, their popular forms of expression will not mislead from the real truth, as it lay in the thinking back of their phraseology. The difficulty here is in the fact that some passages speak dichotomously, others trichotomously. Two trichotomous forms are: 1 Thess. 5:23, "The very God of peace sanctify you wholly, and I pray God your whole spirit and soul and body be preserved blameless," etc.; Heb. 4:12: "The word of God is quick and powerful, ... piercing even to the dividing asunder of soul and spirit," etc.—in which a distinction is apparently made between 'soul' and 'spirit.' Dichotomous forms are: 1 Cor. 6:20, "For ye are bought with a price; therefore, glorify God in your body and in your spirit, which are God's"; Jas. 2:26, "For as the body without the spirit is dead, so faith without works is dead." The precise question is: Is man composed of two essences, the matter forming the body and a spiritual essence called also "soul," which, as the life-principle, organizes the bodily structure; or is there besides the matter of the body and the rational πνεῦμα (spirit), also a ψυχή or "soul" as the life-principle of the bodily organism and the source of the lower passions and instincts?

In answer, the following facts as to trichotomous teaching are to be noted. (1) Many languages have words expressive of a threefold distinction. In Hebrew: basar, nephesh, and ruach or neschama, the last two being synonymous. In Greek: σῶμα, ψυχή and πνεῦμα. In Latin: corpus, anima, and animus or mens. In German: Leib, seele, and geist. In English: body, soul, and spirit. (2) Forms of trichotomy appear among the earliest attempts at a philosophic view of man. Plato had a threefold division, a soul as desire or affection (τὸ ἐπιθυμήτικον), as passion or courage (τὸ θυμοέιδες), and reason (τὸ λογιστίκον). The last was thought to be immortal. Aristotle included, in addition to the body (σῶμα) and soul (ψυχή), the mind (νοῦς), the principle of rational intelligence as existing before the body and entering it as something divine and immortal. The σῶμα and ψυχή were regarded as common to brutes and men; the rational principle as the unique and lofty endowment of man. Plotinus, the great neo-Platonist, developed a full trichotomy. The reason (νõυς) comes from the supreme Being. This produces the soul as its image, and both precedes and survives the body. Apollinaris probably got from this neo-Platonism his view upon which he denied to Christ the possession of a rational soul, the divine Logos taking its place.

In the church, during the early centuries, the teaching was largely trichotomistic, especially among writers of the Alexandrian school. Justin Martyr, Irenæus, Origen, Clement of Alexandria, teach a triad of essence in man. Gnosticism so taught. In a later period trichotomy declined, superseded by the simpler division into body and soul. Occam, however, of the fourteenth century, was a trichotomist, distinguishing between the thinking mind (anima intellectiva) and the feeling soul (anima sensitiva) and making the intellective soul another substance than sensitive soul, and capable of existence apart from the body. Franz Delitzsch presents what he calls the true trichotomy of man. He starts with the idea that in creation God made Adam at first only a physical organism, unvitalized. Then He breathed into him the Spirit or breath of life. This created in man the human spirit. This spirit then quickened the body or produced the animal soul. "The soul is related to the spirit as life to the principle of life, and as effect to that which produces it." "The spirit, as spiritus spiratus, endows the body with soul as spiritus spirans." This view of Delitzsch, though termed "the true trichotomy," in the end really abandons trichotomy and gives us dichotomous humanity. For the "quickening" of the physical body is attributed to the "spirit" created by the divine Spirit, and the life or "soul" becomes the "effect" merely of this created spirit. The soul, in this explanation, is not an essence other than the spirit, but the given life or animate condition of the organism.

How thoroughly the trichotomistic teaching has failed to hold the homage of recent psychology is seen in the fact that in Flemming's "Vocabulary of Philosophy," from thirty-seven different modern philosophers who have attempted to define the soul, only one presents a really trichotomistic view, viz., Rothe. He says: "The spirit is something higher than the soul. In the spirit is the unity of our being, our true ego. The soul is but an element in its service. At death the soul passes away; the spirit ripens to a new existence."

The Scripture evidence seems to be against any positive trichotomy. (a) The Biblical statement as to creation (Gen. 2:7) implies that man was not endowed with an animating soul before or apart from the inbreathing of the Spirit (b) That the terms nephesh, and ψυχή, soul, are used as in some degree equivalents of ruach, πνεῦμα, spirit, is implied in frequent passages in which they designate the self-conscious thinking ego, e. g., Jer. 4:19: "Thou hast heard, O my soul (nephesh which corresponds to ψυχή), the sound of the trumpet," etc In 1 Sam. 20:4, Lam. 3:24, Ps. 139:14, the soul is spoken of as desiring, speaking, and knowing. In Deut. 4:9, memory is attributed to it. These are functions, not of a mere animal soul, but of the intelligent, rational, permanently self-identifying personal spirit of man. This attributing of them to the "soul" implies the use of this term as but another name for the same thing. (c) James 2:26 writes: "The body without the spirit is dead." How could this be said if the bodily life were due to a principle of vitality other than the spiritual essence? (d) "Glorify God in your body and in your spirit" sums up our whole man in two parts, and plainly uses spirit (πνεῦμα) as an equivalent term for (ψυχή). (e) In Matt 6:25, Jesus epitomizes care for ourselves as care for the body (σῶμα) and the soul (ψυχή). In Matt. 10:28, He admonishes: "Fear not them which kill the body, but are not able to kill the soul." Can "soul" here mean the merely animal "life" which, in the trichotomistic view, is extinguished at death? In Mark 8:36, He asks, "What shall it profit a man, if he shall gain the whole world and lose his own soul? "Can this be justly interpreted into a simple teaching of the self-evident truth that no worldly acquisitions can be profitable at the cost of the physical life? (f) Deceased persons are sometimes called "souls" and sometimes "spirits," used as equivalent terms, Ps. 16:10 and Acts 2:27, "Thou wilt not leave my soul (nephesh, ψυχήν) in hell;" Rev. 6:9, "I saw under the altar the souls (ψυχὰς) of them that were slain;" Heb. 12:23, "to the spirits (πνεὺμασι) of just men made perfect"

But if we reject trichotomy, how are we to understand the passages that seem so directly to imply it? The following points will sufficiently explain.

(1) The term soul, while expressing all man's spiritual essence acting in his higher faculties, and used interchangeably for this with the term spirit, is, rather than the latter, particularly employed to designate the sum total of the bodily activities and tendencies as the natural "life." Thus, the whole life of the body, though due to the quickening of the spirit, is specially designated by "soul." As it is thus employed in this particular application to the physical life—which the word spirit is not—it becomes the natural term to express the carnal or fleshly appetites, desires, passions, and depravities.

(2) The rupture in human nature by the fall and sin, dissolving the right control of the spirit, in its higher rational and moral powers, over the body, is peculiarly shown in the unregulated action and ascendency of the physical appetites and corrupt inclinations. Like the word nephesh in the Old Testament, in the New Testament soul (ψυχή) is specially used when the action of the sensuous nature is involved, the action which turns the σῶμα (body) into σάρξ (flesh). This accounts for the fact that the adjective ψυχίκος (psychical or sensual) in New Testament usage denotes a man who is governed by the "sensual" principle or animal life (Jude 19; 1 Cor. 15:44; 2:14; Jas. 3:15). In like manner the adjective πνεματίκος (spiritual) denotes a man who is governed by the higher reason, the 'soul' acting as νοῦς or πνεῦμα, enlightened and strengthened by the Spirit of God.

(3) When St. Paul prays for the sanctification of "body, soul, and spirit" he is not making a scientific enumeration of the constituent parts of man, but praying that grace may pervade and keep not only the higher powers of intellect and will, but all the lower life-impulses, inclinations, and passions by which the man is in danger of being carnalized. When he writes of the word of God as sharper than a two-edged sword, dividing "soul and spirit," he simply assigns to the divine word a dividing efficacy which extends to the entire moral life of men, the language not being literal and scientific, but a highly figurative statement of the proper pervasiveness of the word's needed action.

FREE WILL

Mention has already been made of man's creation "in the image and likeness" of God as his endowment with the sublime attributes of self-conscious rational intelligence, sensibility, and self-determination—gifts opening to him at once the inexpressibly lofty realities of fellowship with God's thoughts and will, and the blessedness of ethical excellence or holy character in such fellowship. The abuse of the free agency given by God, though it brought sin into man's nature, did not destroy the faculties that make up his essential being. And as the redemptive recovery through grace must, therefore, be through moral forces, dealing with moral agents for a moral change, a full analysis of man's psychological constitution might seem to be a prerequisite to the theological view of salvation. For, to effect such recovery, God necessarily comes into the souls or lives of men through their natural faculties of intelligence, conscience, and will. But since the capacity to know and feel are clear and undoubted, it seems sufficient here to deal only with the psychology of the will or the principle of freedom, and consequent personal responsibility.

This subject is one of great importance, deeply integrated in Christian theology and analyzed through long and acute discussion. But as it is not necessary to rehearse the weary metaphysical strife over some of its mysteries, but simply to exhibit the essential features of the actual truth, the discussion need not detain us long.

1. The Will, as the designation of a psychical faculty, is the soul's power of causality for choices. In it the ego, or personal self, acts as a self-determining, free agent. This means that the soul itself, in its powers of personality chooses—makes or causes its own choices—in the presence of different possibilities in self-regulation. This direct causal relation of the soul to its own activities is essential in all its characteristic personal faculties. In the intellect the soul, as the personal ego, is causal for thought or knowing. The soul knows. In the sensibility, the soul is causal for feeling. It feels. So in the will, the soul is causal for choices or volitions. The soul wills. Each soul can say: 'I choose, make my choices,' in the presence of alternatives. This self-determination, of which every man is directly conscious, is not an illusion. The claim that it is an illusion must include denial of the reality of consciousness itself. For consciousness, the immediate and fundamental form of knowing, covers not only the actual choice, but the power to make it as the soul's own elective act. To allege that this

self-determination, of which every one is directly conscious, is an illusion would dissolve all human knowing and feeling, as well as willing, into unreality, phantasmagoria, and fraud. The further suggestion that not the person, but the "motives" playing upon him determine the choice, utterly misinterprets the actual relation between personality and motives. In sober sense every person knows that motives neither choose nor compel choice, but are only considerations or reasons in view of which he chooses or makes his choice.

2. This personal power of self-determination in the presence of multiform motives is not reducible to what is often named "voluntariness," a mere spontaneity or passiveness, a movement due to some invisible, unfelt necessity, to external causation in fixed and inviolable enchainment of sequences, or as shut in by an eternal predestination of whatever is to come to pass, but is a capacity in freedom for alternative choice. It is not the freedom of the star to move in its orbit, nor of the stream to flow in its channel, but the high prerogative of self-direction in the free possibilities of life and conduct. If free-will is not at its innermost core such a faculty of actual election between open alternatives, to choose to do or not to do, to choose this or that or another thing, the whole conception of free-agency is but a dream, and the holding of any one responsible for anything is the basal injustice of human life. Bishop Butler's reminder that whatever speculative theories necessitarianism might put forth, the actual life and affairs of the world have to be conducted on the principle of freedom and responsibility, remains of valid force in evidence that this principle is basal in the constitution of humanity.

3. Man's original freedom, possessed before the fall, was that of this alternative choice. In this and his other endowments in which he was created in the image of God, his nature gave him the sublime gift of ethical personality, with riches of blessed life, under its inseparable duties and responsibilities. Because of his freedom he was capable of the lofty reality of holy character and of maintaining it. His life came under the law of obligation and the principle of free obedience. Original man was not only constructively free, as having real personality with faculty of diversifiable choice, but, further, was endowed with real and

adequate strength of moral constitution for its use in harmony with the will and law of God.

4. But the question arises, whether this attribute of free-will still belongs to man in his fallen and corrupted nature. The point is one of exceeding importance in view of his personal responsibility in respect to the opportunity of recovery through the redemptive provision of grace. To determine it, we must carefully distinguish between "formal" (or "normal," "psychological") freedom, and "real" or "actual" freedom. This distinction will enable us to see in what sense man may be declared still free and in what sense not.

(a) Formal freedom is the freedom which is the essential constituent of personality, the endowment with faculty of self-determining, self-variable choice. It is the attribute in which personality exists. To lose this formal freedom would be to lose personality altogether and cease to be a man. Without it one would not be a human being. The characterizing attribute, the constitutive element of the human being, would be wanting, and he would sink to the rank of a mere animal or a thing. No human persons would exist, to be saved. There is no ground, in either revelation or reason, to think that man's personality was destroyed by his lapse into sin, or his free-will, in this prime sense of human faculty, lost from his essential constitution. Only its use is turned into misuse. The power of election, or real choice, of actually making choices, is a fact of consciousness—known truth, if anything is known. This formal freedom is fundamental to the manhood of man, indestructible save by the annihilation of manhood itself. It lies at the basis of the universal sense of responsibility under which each sane man embraces himself and others—at the root of the necessary judgments of approval or condemnation which men pronounce on their own and others' actions. The administration of justice, the judicature of the world, rests on it. God does not save men by ignoring their free-will, but through it, reaching it by the light and power of the truth of the Gospel and the enabling help of the Holy Spirit for the choice or consent of faith and obedience. Salvation has been made conditional upon its acceptance. Men can refuse, despite call, enlightenment, and divine persuasion. Disregard of the constitution of man is not in the system. That constitution is God's own work, and He does not overthrow it in saving. The poet is here the true metaphysician and theologian:

> "For He that worketh high and wise,
>   Nor pauses in His plan,
> Will take the sun out of the skies,
>   Ere freedom out of man."

(b) Real or actual freedom, as related to the unabridged fact of formal freedom, represents the measure of man's ability to use his personal free-agency in harmony with reason and righteousness. The question of this freedom is a question of the moral strength of the personal ego, corrupted by depravity, for the task of exercising the power of choice aright in the midst of the moral or spiritual duties and responsibilities of life. While real freedom, i. e., strength for right and holy choices, as well as formal freedom, belonged to man in his primitive integrity, the teaching of the Scriptures, sustained by observation and experience, is that he has lost actual ability for the due exercise of his formal and personal liberty in true holiness, i. e., according to reason, truth, righteousness, in right love to man and in fellowship with God. There is in him an evil bias, an alienation from God and goodness, a depravity of disposition, a sinfulness of inclination or of the affectional nature, from which it comes to pass that though he still exercises his power of choice, he does so in accordance with his inherent depravities and impulses, and consequently in what is fairly called "bondage" to his own corruption. Man has not lost the faculty of Will, but the health and order of it. Its energy for right willing in spiritual things has been lost, or so weakened under the sinful sway of inborn selfishness and godless propensities, as to be incompetent for effective choice of God's will of holiness and return to it. The loss of freedom is, therefore, not to be understood as though man has lost the human attribute and function of free-will, or the use of formal freedom, but that, while he is exercising it every day and hour, he is, if unregenerate, exercising it and making his choices in subserviency to the inherent evil of his fallen nature. His real and actual free-will has become false to God and the law of holiness. Only in things morally and spiritually indifferent, destitute of moral quality, is his Will in unbiased freedom.

This want of real freedom for its true office or function in religious and spiritual obligations, in connection with the continued possession of the psychological faculty of free-will, leads to the last topic in anthropology.

NATURAL ABILITY

Specifically, the inquiry here seeks to understand how much, if any, power man has in himself, left in his fallen state, to live the holy life of faith and obedience toward God, and love and duty to men, for which he was made; and, especially, how far, if at all, his free-will may be able to concur or co-operate with redemptive grace in his recovery and salvation. In respect to the first half of the question, the answer has already been indicated in the thraldom of the will to the dominating depravity in man's affectional nature. The true aptitudes and affinities of his heart for God and holy life have been broken and disabled by inherent sinfulness. In the loss of the order of holiness from his faculties, and of the right ethical co-ordination of his powers and affections, his life necessarily fails to realize his divinely meant standard of character, whether viewed in relation to God or his fellow-men. Without divine help, the selfhood of his personality is incompetent for the moral and spiritual task. "Without the Holy Spirit the human will cannot produce the spiritual affections which God requires." This is the uniform teaching of the Scriptures (John 3:6; 15:5; 1 Cor. 3:5; Rom. 5:10; 7:14, 23, 24; 8:7; Eph. 2:1–5). This sad truth of Scripture teaching—the utter inability of fallen and corrupt man, of himself and apart from supernatural redemptive provision, to live the true life of holy obedience to God and duty to men—stands in thorough repudiation of the current rationalistic claim that salvation from sin is simply the human work of ethical self-culture under guidance of the moral teachings of Jesus.

With this truth, the conception of prevenient grace comes into view. Human inability underlies this prevenience in the method of grace. And it means that, necessarily, God's grace precedes man's moving or working in the matter of salvation. God has not only gone before in making provision for salvation through redemptive atonement, but in the application of it. He comes to men through the truth and invitation of the Gospel, with its enlightening and persuasive power, in and through which the Holy Spirit convinces of sin and enables faith. "How shall they believe in Him of whom they have not heard?" It is in this prevenient working of grace that God brings men to the point of possibility of meeting the condition: "He that believeth shall be saved." God comes to us all before we come to Him, and His coming enables ours.

The second half of the question of ability is closely connected with these truths. 'How far, if at all, may man's free-will co-operate with divine grace in his conversion and salvation?' This is the long-discussed question of synergism and monergism. It is whether man in any degree concurs and thus co-operates in his own conversion. Melanchthon taught a synergism of men with God in this great change, and this conception marked the representation of some of the leading Lutheran theologians till the writing of the Form of Concord. In this formula synergism was rejected, and the dogmatic theology of the Church, as a rule, has maintained the monergistic emphasis of Luther. The reason of this repudiation of synergism and vigorous maintenance of monergism was, and continues to be this, that the very willingness in which the human will "assents" to the call and intent of the Gospel and complies through faith with the condition of salvation is possible only under the prevenient working and grace of God, and is not to be credited to man's account, but to God. It is, indeed, true that man acts in the "consent" of will in the act of faith, but not from himself alone; for God is working in him to will and do. In faith man "believes," not God for him, but the act is enabled by grace and so is to be credited to grace. It is sufficient to settle the practical bearings of the question of inability to see and accept this fact that, without such prevenient and enabling gracious action, men will not and cannot come to God in true repentance and the exercise of saving faith in Christ. To make possible the very act that meets the condition of salvation by those who hear the Gospel, God must, through the truth and Holy Spirit, give the ability. This makes salvation wholly of grace, excludes self-dependence, and allows no claim of merit. It does not, however, fully determine and exhibit the question of synergism. The latter traces and finds the monergistic movement until the assent of the human free-will needs to be given to the effectual working of God's grace. All parties agree that, after regeneration, the human subject of grace co-operates in continued exercise and obedience of faith. But the question, in speculative view is whether, at the very meeting point of the divine and human action—the initial assent of faith—this assent itself can be regarded as a human concurrence, 'co-operative' with God's working of grace, or is it purely a product of it? It is a product of it—in the very positive sense that without and apart from that divine working it would not and could not take place. This justifies the monergenistic attribution. But it may be viewed from another angle—from which there is recognition of the equal truth that "faith" is man's act, while it is a resultant of the divine working. If so, there may be recognized a truth in each contention. And that this may justly be maintained becomes clear by a closer discrimination of the meeting point in the two factors. While the work of salvation is from the beginning to completion possible only through the communicative grace of God, it is to be observed that the requisite to this possibility involves, not a divine act of "assent," but the Holy Spirit's work, by which, step by step, He enables the human will to act in its constitutional function of free-belief. The point to which the prevenient grace carries is that at which the natural necessity of resistance of grace is superseded by the possibility of accepting it. It means, thus, that the freedom of decision is restored (*liberum arbitrium liberatum*), the possibility of either faith or continued resistance. And as faith, "assent," "yielding," is man's act, it meets or fulfills the Gospel condition of salvation, and becomes per se co-operative with the plan and working of God. On the one side it is the outcome of prevenient grace; on the other it becomes human concurrent action in the divine work. And as this faith, thus secured and becoming actual, is essential for conversion and salvation, the exact truth seems to justify Melanchthon's counting of "three causes," the Holy Spirit, the Word, and the human will, in the great transitional change from the one state to the other. This does not imply that the causes are equal, or of the same order. God and His word express productive causality, while that in the free-will is rather mediatory, i. e., the free assent is an essential "mean" to the passing of grace into newness of life. Yet this mean is supplied in the believer's free act. Because it is an 'enabled' freedom that acts in assent, the credit is monergistically ascribed to God; but because the "assent" is at the same time a human act, it actually fulfills the required "condition" for salvation, and becomes a concurring element in the great change. And when it is remembered that our Lutheran theology, including the "Form of Concord," asserts synergism after prevenient grace has quickened the soul into regenerate life, it is easy to see that the synergistic element may be included also in the moment or act of human belief—especially as this faith is, by the teaching of Christ and the Apostles, made the essential human condition for the realization of the divinely provided regeneration and salvation; and is, moreover, the only way of escape from the absolute predestinarianism that holds election and renewal as irrespective of foreview of faith, a predestinarianism which our theology rejects. When the movement of the divine application of grace is conceived of under the fundamental doctrine of justification and salvation by faith, its normal progress is, not regeneration before faith, while the sinner is still stiff-neckedly resisting the Holy Spirit, but beginning in a prevenient grace empowering the will to cease opposition and to "assent" and believe, it reaches "regeneration and renewal" through the faith that accepts or yields to the regenerating word and work. While the *ordo salutis* of absolute predestinarianism may place regeneration before faith, as it is wont to, such an order would be utterly abnormal to a theology that recognizes the universality of the atonement, the sincerity of the Gospel call, and the determining principle of justification through faith alone in the application of redemption. The assertion, sometimes made, that this faith, or the soul in it, is merely "passive," is a contradiction in terms, since faith, even in its lowest form of "assent" is a human act.

The extreme representations of the Form of Concord on this subject have not been received by all Lutheran theologians without some qualification. In making qualifications they have evidently not felt themselves at variance with Luther himself. For Luther not only allowed but approved Melanchthon's view as the latter incorporated it in the "Variata" of the Augsburg Confession, and as stated in his "Loci," which Luther endorsed in the highest terms. And he himself expresses the essence of it when, in his "*De Servo Arbitrio*," he says: "If God does not will death, it must be imputed to our will that we perish. Rightly, I say, if you speak of the proclaimed God, for He wills that all men be saved, inasmuch as by the word of salvation He comes to all, and it is the fault of the will, which does not admit Him.... Therefore, the Incarnate God says, 'How often would I have gathered thy children, but ye would not.' " Moreover, Melanchthon's view was distinctly held by the prominent theologians, Brentz, Selnecker, Chemnitz, and Andreæ, and the activity of the will in faith or conversion was widely recognized in the old Lutheran teaching. And some of the later and modern dogmaticians have shown a sense of need of modifying the rigor of the Form of Concord's statements. Thus Musæus, Quenstedt, and Hollaz explain it as meaning only that the excitation of the Holy Spirit through the call of the Gospel brings the possibility of faith along with the possibility of unbelief, restoring thus freedom of decision, which manifestly contains the substance of Melanchthon's teaching. Among our recent leading theologians, it is sufficient to note that Thomasius, Sartorius, Kahnis, and Luthardt present essentially the same view, setting forth conversion as a divine work of grace in which the human liberated will becomes an active factor.

One thing is certain. The monergism of the Form of Concord, being thus manifestly introduced in order to exalt the divine grace and exclude human merit, giving all the glory of salvation to God, is not the absolute monergism normal to Calvinistic predestinarianism. It is radically and necessarily modified from that. However easily its phraseology may suggest it, it is not that, and was not intended to be so viewed. For the Formula, at its very heart, carries the all-determining truth of justification by faith, through a provision of salvation for all men, a sincere call through the same Gospel and the same Holy Spirit who, as God, truly "would have all men to be saved" (1 Tim. 2:4). Its fundamental postulate wholly excludes the Calvinistic doctrine of an absolute eternal predestination of men to life or eternal death, irrespective of anything in them, or of any faculty of assent or dissent or possibilities in its use, as a reason for the difference. In that system the monergism is "absolute," as simply the "absolute" working out or effecting of the eternal and unchangeable decrees. No such monergism can have place in the Lutheran system. It is fundamentally and organically excluded. It can be connected with it only illogically and destructively. For it is a primary, integral, and ruling principle in this system to bring into clear recognition, not only that salvation is wholly and purely "of grace," but that responsibility of its failure in any to whom the offer and the prevenient grace of it have come is, nevertheless, due to the factor of a graciously enabled "will" in which "faith" has thus been made possible along with a remaining possibility of rejection or neglect (Heb. 2:3). It is not, therefore, the absolute monergism of unconditional predestination, but simply a relative monergism that has respect to empowering prevenient grace whose issue is yet dependent on the assent or faith, which is the human personality's laying hold of the provided salvation. For the Scriptures are clear in their representation that the "conversion" or "regeneration" involved is conditioned on this faith—not a means to it. This relation will become fully evident when, in connection with the application of salvation, the scriptural order of the divine process shall be, in its essential features, fully traced.

www.ingramcontent.com/pod-product-compliance
Lightning Source LLC
Chambersburg PA
CBHW051814090426
42736CB00011B/1466
* 9 7 8 0 6 9 2 2 4 8 2 5 6 *